POWER AND CHANGE IN THE UNITED STATES:
EMPIRICAL FINDINGS AND THEIR IMPLICATIONS

POWER AND CHANGE IN THE UNITED STATES

EMPIRICAL FINDINGS AND THEIR IMPLICATIONS

KENNETH M. DOLBEARE

The University of Wisconsin

JOHN WILEY & SONS, INC.

NEW YORK · LONDON · SYDNEY · TORONTO

Preface

THIS collection of articles and excerpts began as part of an effort to merge empirical findings about the "is" of power and change in American politics with understanding of the evolution of political ideas and ideology, and to use the product to critically evaluate contemporary prescriptions for change. I was—and am—convinced that empirical studies, properly employed, can be a vital building block toward rational judgment and action in politics. Students of political thought, and perhaps others who would seek improvement in the policies and practices of the American political system, badly need the sobering knowledge that research can provide. At the same time, understanding of the implications of this body of research could be greatly enhanced by approaching it with the concerns and questions of political theory.

This mutual-aid possibility was central to the design of the combined text and reader (*Directions in American Political Thought*) of which this collection was originally an integral part. Preceding these materials was my analysis of the evolution of political ideas and ideology in the United States, and selections from the work of fourteen major writers. Following them was my analysis of some of the contemporary difficulties of American ideas, and selections from the work of several major contemporary writers. The decision to publish this intervening collection as a separate supplement was made partly in response to the sheer bulk of the combined materials, but also to make it available for a larger variety of courses involving American political ideas and ideology.

The organizing framework reflects my concern for defining the locus of power, the relative roles of elites and masses, and the nature of political values and ideology in the United States. These seem to me to be prerequisites to the later attempt to explore some of the conditions that permit, promote, or prohibit political change. The still-open nature of many of these questions, the ambiguity of some of the research findings, and the special needs of students of political thought, have obliged me to contribute some fairly extensive essays. I do not think it is possible to sort out the implications of even this modest body of research with any degree of care in fewer pages—though I freely concede that others might perform this task in very different ways. My essays are in effect a personal interpretation, to which teachers and students may react much as they do to the original articles themselves.

I am grateful to many people for help in putting together this somewhat unorthodox collection. Gerald Papke, College Editor of John Wiley & Sons, Inc., not only first saw promise in the attempt to merge empirical "reality" with prescriptions for improvement but also patiently and flexibly steered the project to completion. The authors · represented here (and their publishers) generously granted permission to reprint their work. Lane Davis, Robert Pranger, and Robert P. Boynton read the first drafts of my essays and made many helpful suggestions. My colleagues Judith Stiehm, Booth Fowler, and Stuart Scheingold helped immeasurably, not only reading my chapters but also serving as sounding boards for assorted revisions and second thoughts. Joel Brenner, formerly editor of the Wisconsin *Daily Cardinal,* provided me with vital substantive and stylistic criticism. Three graduate students in political science at the University of Wisconsin, Henry Lufler, Jon Lampman, and Michael Kirn, also contributed significantly to the selection of materials and the character of my essays. Mrs. Jeanene Alery was a very competent and tolerant typist.

My most demanding critic has been my wife Pat, whose suggestions from the perspective of sociology have saved me from many of the parochial pitfalls of political science. Both she and several of the others who have tried to help me overcome my idiosyncratic interpretations, however, still find much to disagree with—and no doubt others will, too.

The book is dedicated, as is the text-reader to which it is a supplement, to my students at the University of Wisconsin. Their determined confrontation with political ideas, power distribution, and political change processes in the United States is, for their teachers, both a constant challenge and a continuing satisfaction. I hope this book reflects some of their wide-ranging and skeptical interests from which I have drawn so much intellectual stimulation.

KENNETH M. DOLBEARE

Contents

POWER AND CHANGE IN THE UNITED STATES: EMPIRICAL FINDINGS AND THEIR IMPLICATIONS

CHAPTER 1

Empirical Studies of Politics: Their Evaluative Implications

AT the close of the 1960's, the United States is a country resounding with calls for change—in leadership, in policies, in political practices, and in the priorities that are assigned to such political values as equality, security, justice, property, and order. Change is inevitable, but its form and substance are not. We must ask, what kind of change, and how might it be achieved? The answers to such questions call for a sophisticated knowledge of the present structure of politics. Without a sense of where power is now located, how it is used, what values and interests are dominant—and how change may come about in those respects— there is neither a rational basis for judgment between competing prescriptions nor any idea of how to bring them about in the real world.

If we knew the answers to some of these factual questions, we would be ready to make the value judgments necessary to action in politics. Value judgments— and value conflicts—are the prime movers of politics. But a sound description of the "is" provides a base for evaluation, judgment, and action. Assumptions are no substitute for evidence, and enough evidence can narrow the value choices that lie before us so that we can see them clearly and deal with them honestly. The task of this book is to draw upon empirical evidence to build a framework for critical evaluation of prescriptions for change in American politics.

In recent years, political scientists have reported some findings from their empirical studies which, if valid, shed important light on some recurring problems of politics and political thought. At the same time, some of their work has been severely criticized as biased, inaccurate, or (worse yet) irrelevant. To make use of such findings and establish the "reality" of the contemporary political context, we must first be assured, insofar as possible, that we are indeed dealing with "facts." To some extent, this involves methodological issues—the representativeness of a survey sample, or the propriety of the wording of a questionnaire—which we cannot expect to resolve here, but on which we can secure expert advice. But the crucial issue is whether the researcher has consciously or unconsciously injected biases of omission or commission into his study.

We are all, including the most rigidly "scientific" researchers, children of our culture and captives of our ideology. We operate with assumptions generated out of our heritage and our personal experience and the findings of our most recent research. Some of us escape relatively well into objective or "value-free" realms, and some never try. But it seems safe to say that none of us is ever entirely successful in this effort, and that what appears to one to be objective may seem quite the opposite to others who do not accept the same factors as givens, or who operate with a wider frame of reference or different definitions. The difference is really no more than one of degree of "value-freeness" or objectivity, and there may be highly value-laden and biased elements, perhaps unrecognized, in the thinking and research-designing of the most objective person. The most likely kinds of values to find in the works of empiricists (or behavioralists, as political scientists who concentrate on empirical studies of the actions of men in politics are known) are the same ones that are visible in other Americans. In some respects at least, we can look at empiricists as characteristic American thinkers, fully in the evolved American tradition, who are distinguished by the fact that they use a somewhat different and less direct medium—data, tables, charts, and statistical techniques—to say much the same kinds of things that other American political thinkers have said. In particular, we should be alert to their definitions of "democracy," for this is the concept most susceptible to unrecognized assumptions, either from the American liberal past or the experience of the American present. We shall deal with this in detail later.

There is much to be gained by making use of the evidence about the "is" that has been developed, but there is also considerable risk that we may simply be trading our own assumptions for the researcher's—thereafter to be controlled by whatever controlled him. We must develop and apply criteria of selection—if possible—which allow us to distinguish reliable and generally valid findings and interpretations. This is a large task, requiring considerable sophistication, but we can at least sketch the outlines of some of these criteria and approaches.

I think that the best beginning is to quite self-consciously construct a set of critical questions, the answers to which will reveal vital aspects of a person's political thinking. We can learn what questions should be asked by trying to specify what needs to be known about politics and political ideas in order to understand the present and prescribe for the future. In short, we must try to understand the essence of politics as a facet of human thought and action. Classical political theory merges with systematic observation and practical applications to yield—for those who work at this task—a sense of what politics is all about. Then we shall be better able to articulate the right questions, and apply them to the empiricists as well as to others who write about politics. What are the researcher's unstated assumptions? Why did he decide to ask the kinds of questions he did, structure his research the way he did, make particular inferences and linkages between findings and conclusions? Are there unasked questions that would give rise to explanations of the relationships found that are different from the ones offered by the researcher? Knowing the essence of politics, we know what needs to be known, and we know how to challenge authors and researchers. We recognize the trivial, and dismiss it; we become aware that the researchers have addressed themselves to only half the problem, and we guide our use of their findings accordingly. The key in all cases is the sense of politics and the political that we have in our minds and can employ to make demands upon authors and researchers.

One of the first and most difficult goals of this chapter is the development of just this sense of the nature of politics. It is a task that is never fully accomplished, of course, and everything read and observed about politics now and throughout one's life will make further contributions toward completion of the job. The length and difficulty of the task is no reason not to begin it; indeed, the only alternative to beginning it for oneself is to frankly concede willingness to accept whatever others choose to do with the world. Subsequently, we shall look at the perspectives employed by empirically oriented political scientists, at what one can hope to extract from this body of knowledge for purposes of political evaluation, and at how to go about this task.

POLITICS: THE CRUCIAL NATURE OF A DEFINITION

In seeking to understand the present as comprehensively and as accurately as possible, our first problem is to conceptualize our intellectual needs. What do we need to know about the "is" in order to understand it and prescribe for its appropriate improvement? What type of information should we seek about what aspects of man's environment and behavior? We can hardly be expected to assemble evidence concerning all facets of every phase of man's individual and social activity or the context in which they occur, yet neither can we afford to omit matters of importance to our evaluative and prescriptive intentions. This can be a cruel dilemma: our time and resources for obtaining knowledge are limited, but we must judge and act in timely fashion; there is little in the way of knowledge about man's behavior and environment that is not relevant in some fashion to our needs, but we must exclude the vast bulk of that knowledge in order to be able to cope with some of it. Clearly, we need some severe criteria of relevance that will order the body of knowledge in terms of its importance to our task.

A first step in this process of selecting those aspects of social life and environmental circumstances that are of greatest importance for our purposes occurs when we define the field of "politics" with some precision. This is an arbitrary act, of course, but one which is absolutely fundamental to everything that follows: it creates a set of cutoffs which, however artificial, will henceforth prevent us from seeing some matters as even involved in the problems we are considering— although they may be causes of the effects we are examining, or explanations superior to the ones we are able to see. Establishing these parameters of our concern without due regard for their scope or inclusiveness, or for the possible range of explanations that they may permit, may have the effect of preordaining the conclusions we reach about the nature of "reality." As an obvious and homely illustration, suppose our definition of politics encompassed matters pertaining to education but somehow downgraded or eliminated social and cultural factors. Then suppose we find from data analysis that college education correlates with Republican Party voting. Would we not be tempted to conclude that better educated people vote Republican *because* they are better educated, or perhaps, if we really get carried away, because it makes more sense on the merits to vote Republican and the better educated people are more likely to recognize this? College graduates *do* vote Republican by a substantial margin, and in much greater proportion than other educational levels. But the explanation lies in the social and cultural levels of people who *go* to college, and in their economic status both before and after college—not in the fact of education by itself. Thus, our explanation would have been false and misleading if our definition had somehow excluded consideration of social, economic, and cultural factors. Of course, we would not make such a mistake. But the factors that a definition of politics may omit from consideration, or the effects of assuming certain relationships to be fully established beyond all doubt, may create results that are just as great a distortion of reality as the conclusion that better understanding of the world causes people to vote Republican. (It may, of course, but those tests have not yet been made.)

Thus it is that the definition of politics that a researcher or a political theorist adopts determines the universe that he will consider and may structure the conclusions he can reach. In part, this is a problem inherent in the fact that social activity is integrated and can only be separated for analysis by an essentially arbitrary act of definition. Man does not behave politically one day and economically the next; his behavior is integrated, with simultaneous economic and political ramifications, and the social scientist who would analyze such behavior, whether he be political scientist, economist, sociologist, anthropologist, or social psychologist, must deal with an abstracted dimension of that multifaceted activity. But also in part, the adoption of a particular definition of politics is almost inevitably related to one's values and assumptions, forming an element of the intellectual infrastructure of interpretations and incipient prescriptions. This may not be recognized by some theorists or researchers, and they may sincerely argue about the factual validity of their findings and interpretations without realizing that their differences proceed from different premises as to the relevant factors to be considered or to what has been sufficiently established to be accepted as truth. In short, a researcher's definition of politics may not tell us as much about politics as it does about the researcher.

Because so much is at stake for each individual in his formulation of the definition of politics that he will employ, I am reluctant to do more than spotlight the problem. But neither am I content to leave the impression that I consider all definitions equally useful. I think that, to avoid structuring conclusions or perpetuating culture-boundness, a definition of politics must involve the widest possible frame of reference; it must admit possibilities that most Americans would automatically reject; and it must make no assumptions whatsoever about the inevitability or desirability of any political system, particularly including that of the United States. Only if we get outside of the standard body of assumptions and ideological beliefs about the American political system can we expect to see it accurately. Despite some misgivings about the precision with which it can be measured, I believe power offers a neutral focus from which to construct a definition. For me, "Politics" is composed of those uses of power that have to do with whether and how government shall act in a given subject area.

I use the concept of "power" in the broad sense of being the possession of resources (talent, money, fame, social prestige, institutional position) which brings about behavior on the part of others that they would not otherwise have engaged in if they were wholly autonomous individuals. Under this definition, one may have "power" even if others "voluntarily" conform to what they perceive to be the preferences of the holder of one or more of these resources. There is no attempt to mark off boundaries between power and mere influence, and no requirement that power-holders (who may be persons, groups, corporations, etc.) consciously exercise coercion. Of course, we cannot know with certainty what men would do if they were truly autonomous individuals, for they never are; instead they are caught up in a web of continuing power relationships with many others. But some are dominant, affecting more than they are affected. Some guide their behavior more consistently by the perceived standards and preferences of others whom they use as referents. It should be possible to identify those with the greater possessions in the way of resources, explore their locations within the system, their attitudes and activities, and then to ascertain whether and when others condition their behavior accordingly.

The merit I see in this approach to definition is that it includes analysis of activity outside of government, and outside of the established processes of elections and lobbying as well. It includes the teaching of values in the schools, for example, or the interpretations of the media that structure understanding of an issue as a political one. It also includes uses of power that result in either private or governmental decisions *not* to act. It suffers from overbreadth, but I correct for this by cutting back my own analyses to those points close to the threshold of government action, where there is at least a chance for efficient description of what has happened and how power has been employed.

In seeking to define the nature of the distribution and usage of power in the present context, we shall be asking questions derived from the central concerns of political theory. Who rules? How many persons or other units of power hold what preponderance of the resources of power? What are their values and attitudes, and how do they compare with those of others? What do they do, and how are their actions perceived by others? What factors condition the behavior of power-holders? of the relatively powerless?

When the distinguishing features and characteristic processes of present power distribution and usage have been identified, we may then seek to assess the prospects of change. What shifts are occurring in either distribution or usage of power? Why? What environmental pressures militate toward changes in these respects? How firmly held are the relevant ideas, values, and ideology that contribute to the present pattern of distribution and usage of power? How and under what circumstances has change occurred in the past? By asking such questions, we shall begin to amass the evidence necessary to an understanding of key features of the contemporary political landscape. From such landmarks, we may proceed to an evaluation of the prescriptions of others and to our own independent judgments.

I stress the importance of deciding what it is one wishes to know (and about what types of questions) at this early stage because it is crucial to independent and critical use of the work of the empirical researchers. Unless one has a clear sense of his own purposes, he may be captured by the unconscious assumptions and definitions of whatever author (empirical *or* prescriptive) he happens to be reading. Let us look briefly at the kinds of assumptions and definitions that are characteristic of contemporary researchers.

EMPIRICISTS' APPROACHES TO THE STUDY OF POLITICS

In describing the approaches to the study of politics that are characteristic of various empiricists, let me make clear that I am only marginally criticizing their efforts. An approach that looks at what men in politics actually *do,* rather than at what the Constitution or the rules *say,* is an immense advance over some other possible approaches to analysis. It is the only way to reach toward the realities of description and explanation. It is a vast improvement over the approaches of thirty or forty years ago when analysts were satisfied to study the texts of the opinions of the Supreme Court (as if these would provide full disclosure about how men in government would act) or the powers of the Congress (as if they would tell comprehensively what Congressmen did or what effect their actions had on others). But acceptance of the view that the critical datum for analysis is actual behavior, rather than norms or powers or exhortations, does not mean that one must accept any particular researcher's choice of behavior and determinants as ever-controlling on one's conclusions. Let us turn to some representative approaches to the study of politics and see the diversity of assumptions and definitions that are involved.

1. Input or Process Foci in the Study of Politics

Empirically oriented social scientists began to collect evidence concerning political behavior (rather than merely describing rules and powers) in the early 1930's, but their approach came into its own only after World War II. Their principal concerns, understandably enough, were the same ones that had animated other students of politics in that period: What were the characteristic processes of a stable government, and what were the dangers to it? How was democracy sustained in the modern world? How did popular desires become manifested within the halls of government? These are orthodox democratic concerns, heightened by the events of the immediate pre-War and post-War years. The innovation of survey research techniques in the mid-1930's, and the inspiration of much evidence-collecting during the War, led to the feeling that many of these much-controverted issues could be put to rest in ways that would contribute to a better understanding of "democracy," which was often innocently defined as the form and processes of government in the United States.

Given these assumptions and interests, the major concerns of these social scientists were with the linkage between the people and the decision-making of governmental institutions. One of the earliest discoveries was that members of the society were not equally active in the political process, and that there existed a number of "pressure groups" or "interest groups"—voluntary associations of relatively small numbers of like-minded people who shared a particular goal and sought to attain it through government action. A whole school of political scientists developed around the insight that many such groups existed in the United States, and their frequently demonstrable effect upon government action was expanded into a complete theory of politics: all interests and claims upon government were conceptualized as being expressable by a group, and the whole process of conflict-resolution through government was interpreted as the product of group interactions. David Truman articulated this total view in his *The Governmental Process* [1] in 1951, and it was applied by others to analyses of the Congress, the Presidency, and the courts.

A vital sense of the dynamics of politics was conveyed by this school of analysis, particularly as regards the Congress and the decision making of administrative agencies. Drawing on earlier analyses of the propensity of Americans to form voluntary associations, it was possible to extend this analysis into an explanation of stability. The argument was that the formation of a group to press claims upon government frequently led to the subsequent formation of a countervailing group that would balance the first group. In this way there would develop not only an additional means of representation and a basis for negotiating compromises between conflicting interests, but also a kind of democratic laboratory, in which many citizens would gain experience in presenting their claims and eventually acquire norms of tolerance and acceptance of the demands of others. As if in confirmation, survey evidence showed that officers of such groups did in fact display higher levels of "tolerance," defined as recognition and rhetorical endorsement of civil liberties values, than did members of the general public. [2]

At about the same time, survey techniques were turned increasingly to the study of another highly visible political act—that of voting. [3] Both panel studies (reinterviews of the same persons) and broader-gauge national sample surveys were employed to ascertain the bases of voting behavior of the mass public. The results were anything but encouraging to the simplistic democrat, for popular knowledge about government actions, issues, and candidates was found to be very low, and heavy reliance seemed to be placed on the personal qualities of candidates and long-term identification with political parties. Voting frequently followed a pattern established by experiences of the distant past, such as the Civil War or the Great Depression of 1930, transmitted in some cases for generations through the family's socializing effects. The potentially discouraging implications of these studies for the traditional Town-Meeting style democrat were moderated by the researchers' authoritative interpretations to the effect that the whole system nevertheless operated well, either through a kind of division of

---

[1] David B. Truman, *The Governmental Process* (New York: Alfred A. Knopf, 1951).

[2] Perhaps the major landmark of this research is Samuel Stouffer's study of public attitudes during the so-called McCarthy era of the early 1950's. See Samuel Stouffer, *Communism, Conformity and Civil Liberties* (Garden City, N.Y.: Doubleday, 1955).

[3] For an incisive summary of the approaches and findings of this literature, see Peter Rossi, "Four Landmarks in Voting Research" in E. Burdick and A. Brodbeck (eds.), *American Voting Behavior* (Glencoe, Ill.: The Free Press, 1959).

labor in which segments of the public performed different vital roles, or through *noblesse oblige* behavior on the part of elites.

These two forms of analysis, though not the only approaches taken by political scientists in this period, were dominant influences upon assumptions about the nature of the "reality" of the political process. They were linked and merged by other empiricists who sought more comprehensive interpretations of the characteristics of stable democracy (the United States) and whose principal concern was the people-government nexus. Building upon studies of a city's decisional processes and voting behavior, Robert Dahl articulated a major theory of politics in the United States which is called "pluralistic democracy."[4] The key postulates of this theory are that major interests are represented by groups whose leaders seek to serve the group's goals in a context of agreed rules that assure fair hearings to all; disagreements between groups are mediated by the office-holding representatives of the interested public, except for those occasions on which severe disagreements force the issue into the broad public forum where it can be decided by the electorate; the structure of government is envisioned as facilitating this process through its multitude of available pressure points and veto opportunities; those interests not represented in an ongoing process can, by forming into a group, make known their claims and cause the decisions of office-holders to be modified in their direction; and the net result of all these interactions is flexibility, goal attainment, and stability and democracy for all.

Parallel and nearly simultaneous interpretations of survey and other data by a political sociologist illustrates a body of work amounting to an updating of de Tocqueville's famous *Democracy in America*. In *The Politics of Mass Society*,[5] William Kornhauser developed a theory which held that alienated masses threatened stability unless elites were protected by the intervening structure of voluntary associations, and that masses were threatened with totalitarian manipulation unless protected from elites by the same group involvement. Much influenced by the demise of Weimar Germany and communist successes immediately after World War II, Kornhauser and many others saw alienation and authoritarianism on the part of the lower classes as the primary threat to stability, and sought to moderate the prospect by an emphasis on the supposed democracy-teaching qualities of voluntary associations.

All of these approaches concentrate exclusively on the linkage between people and government, defined in traditional democratic terms. In other words, the only things these researchers looked at were the relationships that they had been led to anticipate by their American and "democratic" heritage. They engaged in

---

[4] Robert A. Dahl, *Who Governs* (New Haven: Yale University Press, 1961) and, for the national analogy, *Pluralist Democracy in the United States*, (Chicago: Rand McNally and Co., 1967).

[5] William Kornhauser, *The Politics of Mass Society* (Glencoe, Ill: The Free Press, 1959).

some debunking of certain supersimplistic traditional assumptions, but unfailingly reassured any anxious readers that other characteristics of the political system performed vital functions sufficient to make for overall performance in accord with the established expectations. In effect, they began with democratic assumptions (people affecting government policy through elections and pressure tactics) and, therefore, researched only particular processes; although they did not find exactly what the democratic mythology said existed, they knew from extra-empirical conviction that the United States was a democracy and they were concerned about stability in a world of great instability of governments; they, therefore, innocently redefined "democracy" to fit the admittedly stable system that they found, and proceeded to celebrate its "achievements."

This is a harsh indictment, but it is essentially what these "pluralists" were charged with in a still-enduring controversy that erupted at the close of the 1950's. The attack on the dominant and benevolent pluralist interpretation of American politics took two basic forms. One drew upon empirical problems, unasked questions, and unstated assumptions to challenge the validity of their conclusions. For example, it was asked whether significance should not be attached to the fact that group involvement was a principally middle-class phenomenon, and that the vast majority of Americans were represented by no active group.[6] Skeptics pointed out that there was a self-validating aspect to the pluralists' conclusions that all significant interests were represented by groups: they had defined interests as those claims that groups pressed! Was it not possible that many interests felt by many people were *not* expressed in group terms? And that the full range of popular goals was therefore unexpressed by the present plurality of active interests and groups? Or that there was an unrepresented public interest which transcended *all* groups? This line of criticism led to the question of whether pluralism might better be described as a friendly division of labor among elites, with little contact or base among the general public at all. With the public effectively excluded, could it legitimately be called democracy?

Some of this criticism was also based on methodological concerns. The pluralists had frequently analyzed patterns of political activity for the reason that they occurred in connection with the actual decisions of government, and their challengers raised the question of whether there might not be important (and revealing) findings to be realized from looking also at occasions when government did *not* act.[7] They charged the pluralists in effect with looking only at the

---

[6] The argument of this and the immediately following sentences is best represented by Robert Paul Wolff, "Beyond Tolerance" in Wolff, Moore, Marcuse, *The Critique of Pure Tolerance* (Boston: Beacon Press, 1965). See also Henry Kariel, *The Decline of American Pluralism* (Palo Alto; Stanford University Press, 1961).

[7] For the most cogent statement of this phase of the argument, see Peter Bachrach and Morton Baratz, "Decisions and Nondecisions: An Analytical Framework," *American Political Science Review,* Vol. 57, pp. 632-642 (1963).

open and visible aspects of the political process and ignoring possible covert or merely unrecognized uses of power to prevent government from acting. What can become a political issue in this system? Who decides whether or not a question will rise to the status of being a publicly recognized political issue? Public awareness and involvement is, at least in part, the product of elite action, and it is likely that the absence of a desire to raise an issue to public attention on the part of some segment of elites could mean that the question would go unrecognized.[8] Under such circumstances, it becomes an important question whether elites concur with each other on most major issues, or whether they include substantial disagreements. For the most part, however, these are unasked questions.

The second major form that the attack on pluralist interpretations took was that of offering a complete substitute theory, by now well known under the title of the "power elite." This theory, emanating from the 1956 publication of C. Wright Mills' book of the same name,[9] holds that essentially self-perpetuating elites have such independence and such a preponderance of power within the American system that they are for practical purposes the sole determinants of government policy. In Mills' eyes, the relevant elites included wealthy, politically involved families, corporate managers, and high military officers. Much of the evidential base for this alternative theory lay in the social and economic background characteristics of members of the "elite," and the pluralists quickly responded by denying the validity of an analysis that failed to take into account the question of whether dispositive power was actually wielded by such elites and, if so, in ways that were at odds with popular desires.

The debate still goes on, with each side charging the other with being affected by ideological preferences and assumptions. Some of the disagreement is rooted in the difference between social and political approaches. The social background analysis tends to assume that behavior will be in accord with differences of outlook and interest that are inferable from the backgrounds of political actors, and it also frequently posits a likelihood of action by elites inimical to the interests of the many. The political approach tends to focus narrowly on the demonstrable behavior of men in government, to the point where it fails to consider larger questions of the relationship between popular preferences and government action. Much of the disagreement, however, lies in the differing importance attached to specific empirical findings, because of differing definitions of "politics" and "democracy." But with all their interpretive differences and their variant definitions of what to look at, these two schools of thought on the nature of American politics still share a similar focus: they are both concentrating on the process by

---

[8] This point is well presented by E.E. Schattschneider in *The Semi-Sovereign People* (New York: Holt, Rinehart & Co., 1960).

[9] C. Wright Mills, *The Power Elite* (New York: Oxford University Press, 1956).

which the claims and demands of people are made known to decision makers in government and translated into action. This is a focus that reflects democratic assumptions, because it starts with people and traces their demands up through the actions of government, and it looks at government action chiefly as a response to thrusts of one kind or another emanating from some segment of the society.

And yet, while this is the most familiar perspective from which we are likely to look at politics, there are other quite distinctive approaches that do not necessarily have the concerns or make the assumptions (or lead to the same value-based disagreements) which originate from this version of the democratic heritage. Two of them may be described briefly by way of contrast.

2. Output or Distributive Foci in the Study of Politics

The last set of approaches studied what went *in* to government, and how peoples' wants were translated into government action. It is possible to reverse this perspective, and look at what comes *out* of government and what effect this output has on people or problems. In other words, what are the consequences of government action, taking that action as a given for this purpose? Who won, and who lost, because of this action? What changes in behavior, attitudes, and political demands of citizens occurred because of this government action? How did the action bear upon the public problem it was designed to cope with: did it achieve intended goals, exacerbate the existing difficulties, create side-effects, leave the problem untouched?

The concentration of researchers and theorists has been so disproportionate with the inputs and processes of politics in this country, perhaps because of American liberalism's fascination with methods and procedures, that there is very little consideration of the consequences of government action except in impressionistic and frequently contradictory terms. Shortly before World War II, Harold Lasswell articulated a wide-ranging view of politics under the title *Politics: Who Gets What, When, How*.[10] Perhaps because of the concentration of scholars on the problems and preservation of democracy in the three subsequent decades, this work has not always been seen as more than a somewhat different way of looking at the process of politics. But it contains much of the essence of an output approach: Lasswell would view politics from the perspective of an attempt to understand the nature and consequences of the distributions accomplished by government. In so doing, he would fit together analytic constructs not limited to people, their wants, or their activities. For example, he would define power, identify the resources that contribute to the possession of power, and then explore its uses within a political system; this would enable him

---

[10] Harold Lasswell, *Politics: Who Gets What When How* (New York: McGraw-Hill 1936).

to identify relationships that other inquiries might miss, and place factors explanatory of government output in a different perspective.

This is an approach that is more likely to lead to different types of evaluations, at least, and quite possibly to more frequent opportunities to evaluate, than the process approach. When researchers produce (almost for the first time) evidence concerning the tangible consequences of government action, it is a ready step to compare such findings with the stated intentions of policymakers, or with the preferences of the general public. Instead of evaluations of the quality of the system based on the nature of public participation, evaluations are based on whether government action succeeds in attaining goals which are considered desirable by some or by the many. It is not necessarily a change away from democratic evaluations so much as it is to a different dimension of "democracy." The procedural focus of process orientations, in other words, is replaced by a substantive focus: did government produce results (not just symbolic expressions) which the people sought, or which were responsive to a public problem? Consistent with Lasswell's intentions, this approach is a tool that can be used for more deliberate goal-attainment, as well as for understanding the origins of public demands and orientations toward government. It suffers, however, from the difficulty of defining the extent of secondary and tertiary consequences, the uncertainties in tracing causal relationships back to specific governmental acts, and from the problem of ascertaining consequences of an intangible nature.

3. All-inclusive Systems Approaches to the Study of Politics

Having contrasted the input or process approach with the output or distributive view, it may be anticipated that the systems approach is to be understood as a combination of the two. In a way it is, but it has its own special concern: explanation of the ways in which the "system" adapts to pressures and maintains itself. A systems view of politics posits a comprehensive and highly interrelated web of activities and responses by other actors, such that a continuous stream of actions and reactions may be envisioned, the net result of which is the continued adaptation of the system to changes in its environment. In the context of this continued interaction, demands arise and are presented to governments, are acted upon, creating consequences that give rise to new demands, and so on. The process is continuous, with no beginning and no end.

The principal articulator of such a view in political science is David Easton, whose *Systems Analysis of Political Life*[11] and other works have structured the thinking of many empirical researchers. Acting under systems theory premises and interests, researchers are likely to steer clear of democratic assumptions and

---

[11] David Easton, *A Systems Analysis of Political Life* (New York: John Wiley, 1966).

instead seek out indications of the many unconscious processes by which support for the system itself is maintained. Evaluation is unlikely to be provoked by this approach, because an aura of inevitability surrounds the workings by which governments sustain themselves and respond to goals within their societies, and interest is focused instead on the continuity of the whole system. On the other hand, this very assumption about adaptability and continuity may lead researchers into belief that stability and equilibrium are always the natural condition of mens' relationships, with the result that they may look for the wrong things, or interpret their findings incorrectly.

Related to systems approaches is the structural-functional view of politics, which holds that institutions and processes perform functions within a political system.[12] This assumes that the preservation of the polity requires the performance of certain definable tasks somewhere within it, and researchers look not only at the behaviors of men and the workings of institutions, but also at the implications of such findings for the discharge of the defined tasks. One problem arising is the still-unanswered question of whether every political system *must* have the same tasks to perform, or whether such functions may not be time-, culture-, and developmental stage-specific. Clearly, it would seem that the United States' and Ugandan political systems would not be performing exactly the same tasks, and the expectation that they should leads either to applications of culture-bound demands, or to such generalized interpretations that meaning is lost. Furthermore, there is a potential conservative bias to interpretations that assume that the natural thing is for institutions and processes to foster stability and inhibit change, and perceive those activities which do not as dysfunctional. For any particular polity at any specific time, change could be highly functional— if "function" were given a definition other than inhibiting change.

These three broad categories of empiricists' approaches to the study of politics emphasize the point made earlier about diversity of assumptions and orientations. As I have sought to point out, each approach has certain strengths and weaknesses; none is necessarily better or worse, until one can specify particular purposes for which it is to be employed. The critical realization for us now is that we must examine the premises and assumptions—and particularly the perspective toward "politics"—of each researcher just as one would examine the underlying values and goals of prescriptive writers. But having done so, there is no reason why we cannot make use of the evidence that they produce, cleansed of any errors or faulty assumptions or interpretations, to build our own set of landmarks of descriptive convictions. That is, provided that we have a clear sense of our

---

[12] Perhaps the best known example of this approach is to be found in Gabriel Almond and James S. Coleman, *The Politics of the Developing Areas* (Princeton: Princeton University Press, 1960.)

own purposes that will serve as a basis for our independent and critically selective use of the empiricists' findings. Each of us needs badly to develop a set of factual landmarks, both for the purpose of testing the prescriptions that are thrust upon us and for the purpose of beginning to generate our own prescriptions. Once again, we cannot know all, but we must know something: let us try to assure that among the few things that we can know are some of the things that we should know.

WHAT DO WE NEED TO KNOW?

What should we seek to extract from the empiricists' work? Among all the possible directions for investigation, I have suggested that we may proceed efficiently and productively by (1) defining the character of the distribution and usage of decisive political power in the contemporary United States, and (2) specifying the requisite conditions and characteristic processes for change in either the distribution, nature, or usage of that power. We can only begin these tasks under present limitations of time and data, of course, but I think that even this truncated effort will serve to test my conviction that empirical research can substantially improve individual judgmental capacity. These two central foci for investigation are neither comprehensive nor even necessarily the best that might be devised; I choose them because they seem to me central to the problem of judgment and action in politics.

The next question is, where shall we start? At what bodies of data can we most profitably direct our questions? Needless to say, the requisite evidence is not all available and awaiting our perusal. Not even the most sophisticated mining of the empiricists' contributions would establish conclusive and sufficient knowledge for our needs. The state of knowledge is neither certain enough nor comprehensive enough to permit it. But I think we can proceed on a partial and illustrative basis, extracting some useful findings in four critical problem areas. These are not the four *most* important areas, but they *are* important. I probably could not convince readers that my nominations of the most important areas were correct, even if I had the time, space, and inclination; all I seek to suggest is that, among other areas, these are some of the important objects for inquiry. My choices, to be frank, are shaped in part by the availability of empirical studies: I suggest that we consider data and interpretations in the areas of elites, values and ideology, mass-elite linkages, and political change processes. Let me simultaneously defend these choices as being important for our purposes and specify what sorts of questions we might derive most profit from asking.

1. Elites: Their Composition, Selection, Attitudes, and Behavior

"Elites" are people who hold more of the resources of power than others. Men in public office are clearly among those high in such resources and, therefore, must be included by definition. Because a modern political system inevitably has relatively few men in positions of official authority, inequality of political power necessarily ensues. It seems to me that this is a completely neutral and unexceptional usage of the concept of elite, and that it offers no evaluative implications. There is, in my view, no way in which 200,000,000 people can live in close proximity to each other and engage in some coherent joint ventures without a division of labor in which some men hold more of this kind of power than others. By contrast, the uses of the concept of elite that give rise to evaluative implications derive from two somewhat different dimensions. The first has to do with who elites are, and the second with what they do with their power.

In the first of these, we may ask what sorts of people acquire official positions. If they are a special group, distinguishable by some social, economic, educational, or other special characteristic, we have a basis for a limited form of value judgment. Some analysts will probably be outraged at the discovery of an "aristocracy" operating behind the scenes, others will breathe easier at the thought that leadership is in the hands of men perhaps more competent than the average, and some will shrug at the inevitabilities of life. In each case, the evaluative implication arises out of the mere fact of *who* is holding the official positions of power and not (except as evaluators may themselves supply inferences) from what they do with their power. It is, therefore, distinguishable from the second, and I think much more important, evaluative dimension. In the latter, we should raise the key questions, such as whether men in official positions think and act according to their own preferences, those of other power-holders, or those of some segment of the general public. What constraints actually shape their actions, what priorities do they follow, what interests do they serve? Again, evaluations may differ, depending upon the observer's own preferences; whether elites are found to operate for their own private benefit or exclusively as the public would prefer, some will approve and some will object. Because there are so many more possibilities and so many more areas to investigate in this second dimension, most of the specific questions for inquiry that I shall suggest are aimed in this direction.

The composition of elites is a subject for which both breadth and depth of inquiry is essential. By breadth, I mean that inquiry must extend well beyond the official holders of political power to reach all those outside of government who hold resources that give rise to such power. Money, skills, fame, social prestige, institutional positions such as executive status in a corporation, university, foundation or mass communication medium—any of these may give rise to the potential of power. In some cases, no effort will be made to develop these resources for political purposes. But regardless of the intentions of the perhaps reluctant possessor of the resources, others may perceive their existence and act as they understand the possessor to prefer. In other words, a process of role-taking occurs in which some imagine how others (whom they rightly or wrongly perceive to hold the resources of power) might like them to behave and act accordingly. In this anticipatory and, in one sense, voluntary process, power exists and conditions political actions even where such results are not sought. In many instances, of course, holders of the resources of power deliberately wield their power in order to influence as much of the behavior of others as possible, and in some cases those who seek goals in politics consciously seek to develop the resources of power in order to be able to wield influence over others.

By depth of inquiry, I mean two additional refinements. There should be some time dimension to the analysis, so that we are not presented with only a snapshot of elite composition at a single moment in time. Established and recurring patterns suggest wholly different and more meaningful conclusions than perhaps coincidental or casual convergences of particular characteristics, possibly attributable to special circumstances. We must also, and necessarily arbitrarily, envision some cutoffs that can be used to distinguish those whose possessions of the resources of power mark them as "elite." We shall find that empirical researchers have employed different definitions of elite (some based on holdings of power resources, some on offices held) as well as different cutoff points to distinguish them from nonelites. Given the state of the available data, it seems to me appropriate to limit the use of the term elite to those who hold visible institutional (governmental and extragovernmental) power resources and those who can be shown to hold highly disproportionate amounts of the other power resources.

An important corollary to the issue of who holds power is the process by which it was acquired. Did it accrue by birth, by training, by election, by self-selection, or by some combination of these or other factors? To what extent did established power-holders structure the recruitment and selection of their colleagues or successors? In other words, what are the criteria and processes by which one attains elite status? Once again, more than superficial inquiry is required. It is not enough to examine the standards of appointment to office or even the early stages of the nomination and election process. We must also seek to learn how early and how fully the office seeker has shaped his behavior in the image of what he understands power-holders to expect, and how much deliberate co-optation by power-holders is involved. Are there some who rarely or never rise to elite status? If so, selection processes of some kind must be at work. I suggest that the question of the standards of selection may be more revealing of the true nature of the system than the background characteristics of those who hold power, if only because it is possible to find and co-opt "right-thinking" individuals with all kinds of social and economic background characteristics.

When the composition and selection bases of elites have been established, further questions still remain. These questions cut to the heart of the pluralist-power elite debate. They center around the issue of the criteria on which power is actually wielded: elites may be utterly self-serving, justifying their actions with democratic rhetoric and repressing opposition in the name of law and order. But it is possible that elites who are socially or economically representative of only a small fraction of the total population might nevertheless hold internally divergent and conflicting attitudes, much like those found in the general public. Or, if the public was of one mind on an issue, elites might be quite similar to the rest of the society. Even if their attitudes were very different from those of a unified public opinion, their behavior might nevertheless acknowledge many restraints that would bring it into conformity with popular preferences or the "public interest." We must, therefore, seek to compare the values and attitudes of elites with various segments of the general population to ascertain in whose image government is conducted. Elites may disagree among themselves, of course, as the pluralist argument contends. If so, we should seek to understand the level at which that disagreement occurs: is it merely over such relatively inconsequential matters as who shall receive how much of some governmental product, or is it over more fundamental questions of general purposes and goals of government? If elites disagree only about details, no matter how sharply, then the pluralist effort to place a democratic gloss on the demonstrably disproportionate distribution of power in the United States is somewhat blunted.

Thus, when we understand the nature of elite attitudes, we must seek to relate them to the attitudinal structure within the general public on similar questions. We may find that elites are indeed representative attitudinally even if they are not representative socially. Even where they differ, judgment depends on questions of direction, substance, and the observer's preference: it is possible, of course, for one to conclude that the political system functions "better" just *because* elites hold attitudes on certain issues that diverge in a particular way from those of the general public.

The final and perhaps most critical issue is the question of elite behavior. Government action is, after all, the ultimate payoff by which the quality of a system is best measured. By whose values, on what standards and for whose benefit, does the American government operate? What (if any) constraints do elites abide by: Internal, self-imposed limits arising out of a sense of *noblesse oblige?* Perceived legal limitations, perhaps supported by a highly developed sense of tradition? Prospective or expressed opposition from other elites, perhaps leading to mediation of the dispute by some segment of the electorate? Or popular preferences, ascertained in one of several possible ways? Those who wish to explore the democratic qualities of the system might concentrate on defining the extent and manner of broad popular structuring of elite behavior: How are such preferences made known to elites, and what effect does it have on their behavior?

2. *Values and Ideology*

Ideology consists of the operative myths held by numbers of people concerning how their government works, should work, and why. We may view ideology as having two levels: the more fundamental level of commitments to such political values as limited government, property rights, individual freedoms, etc., and a second tier of political applications of those values, such as separation of powers, campaigning and voting, or specific rules of procedure. This use of the concept of ideology may be supplemented by the addition of "values"—those culturally transmitted commitments and assumptions that structure individual and social life in the most basic ways. To an extent, these values (such as religion, self-reliance, materialism, etc.) may overlap with the more fundamental level of ideology. I add this item in this connection only because such values are not always included within the concept of ideology, and their political relevance may, therefore, be overlooked.

The first questions that should be asked in this area pertain to the substance and distribution of values and ideology. What are the underlying beliefs that give rise to political thought and action in the United States? Are there differences in values or ideology between classes of people, or between those who take part in politics and those who do not? What are the determinants of such diferences: is it life style, or cultural heritage, or the day-to-day payoffs of the political system, that shape patterns of values and ideology within the society? If we knew how fully shared some key values are, we would gain useful perspective on the findings of elite analysis. If nearly all Americans hold to the same basic values, for example, it may be less significant evaluatively that power seems to be held by a relatively small and stable fraction of the population. In any event, inquiry into the substance and distribution of values and ideology would enable us to construct an image of the base that supports the present system, and to know how firmly it is rooted. Within this context, further inquiry might be directed at the extent to which particular values, such as racism or property, affect or are linked into the overall belief system.

Perhaps the greatest payoffs from inquiry in this area are to be anticipated as emerging from analysis of how values and ideology are acquired and how they evolve or are changed over time. If, as now seems evident, socialization processes carried on through the public school system and the mass media have important effects in structuring childrens' values and ideology, we should examine the content and effects of what is being communicated. There is at least some evidence to suggest that children of different class levels are taught different sets of values and expectations about politics, for example,[13] and analysis of these processes might lead to useful insights as to the system's self-perpetuating capacities. If values change over time, why? How much of the change results from conscious agents of socialization, and how much from events and the environment? Could the conscious agents of socialization be deliberately employed for the purpose of changing the underlying values and ideology of the society? (The question of whether they *should* be, even if they could be so employed, is of course the nonempirical parallel issue.) Inquiry of this kind might well contribute to enhance understanding of the prospects and problems of change in American political ideas and practices.

Both of these directions for inquiry should be seen in a context of a continuing question as to when, how, and in what respects values and ideology affect political behavior. It is possible, though I think unlikely, that other determinants would be more responsible for structuring the behavior of men in politics. Written constitutions or economic necessities might force political actors to proceed in ways which they perceived to violate their values and/or ideology, thus rendering the latter relatively insignificant. The chances are that such occasions would not be numerous, however, if only because there would probably be modifications of values and ideology to fit practice; perhaps more likely is the prospect that political actors would fail to perceive contradictions between ideology and actions. Although we can all point to such occasions, they are also probably relatively few in number compared to the occasions of congruence between values and ideology and political behavior. The closest and most revealing questions are likely to be found when a particular issue raises conflicts between two or more values, or between different aspects of ideology. From analysis of such occasions, we might gain a sense of the relative priorities attached to particular values, and the relative strength of particular values as against other factors in shaping political behavior. Many studies, for example, consider whether political party identification is relevant to particular issues; sometimes an issue appears to be highly party-related and sometimes positions seem to be rooted in other determinants. The point is that these are empirical questions to which we might aspire to find answers. Greater certainty in knowledge of the role of values and ideology would permit more sophisticated analysis of the bases of present ideas and practices as well as of the prospects of change.

---

[13] See Edgar Litt, "Civic Education, Community Norms, and Political Indoctrination," *American Sociological Review,* Vol. 28, pp. 69-75 (1963).

3. Mass-elite Linkages

In any political system, rulers and ruled exist in a symbiotic relationship. Their interactions are many, varied, reciprocal, and recurring. Elites seek to generate and maintain support for the actions they consider essential. To do so, they must be attentive to both present preference and prospective response on the part of other elites and relevant members of the general public. Every action by government stimulates some form of response on the part of the governed, or some of them. The context in which that stimulus is received, and the process which it sets in motion, lead to changes in mass behavior and in demands upon government, which then become factors in the next stage of the elites' decision-making processes. Elites respond with self-justification, modification of their policies, and/or coercion of compliance with their policies, at various times. In political systems with a substantial degree of popular involvement, the nature of this interactive process provides important evaluative opportunities: although the ultimate judgment will depend in critical ways on the definition of democracy that an observer employs, it is specification of the nature of popular impact on governmental decision making that opens the question of whether or not the system is a democracy.

There are many forms of linkage between masses (nonelites) and elites, ranging from pressure groups and elections to public opinion polls and riots to personal interchanges during a taxi ride. Essentially, what we seek to ascertain is how nonelites' preferences and attitudes are made known to elites, and to what extent elites' behavior is affected by them. In pursuing this inquiry, we must promptly make some refinements in our conceptual approach: we should recognize that in regard to specific policy issues, we are actually talking about the attitudes and preferences of some segment of existing nonelites, because it is clear that not all members of the society have views on each issue. Furthermore, there will probably be a diversity of views among those who hold opinions, with several rather than merely two or three sets of preferences obtaining. This leads to problems of weighting the various viewpoints, particularly since the number of proponents of each may differ sharply, the intensity of their respective preferences may vary widely, and the priority that various proponents assign to their preferences may also be different. These are only some of the problems that confront elites even if they do seek to conform their policymaking to "majority will," and which regularly bedevil professional students of "public opinion."

For our present purposes, we might limit ourselves to some of the more basic issues of mass-elite relationships. For example, we might ask to what extent large-scale popular participation in policymaking depends on focusing of the issues by leaders. Can the people formulate their preferences and decide where they stand before government has acted, or before a candidate has come forward with a clear position? Evidence seems to indicate that the act of leaders helps to create visibility for an issue and to develop and polarize reactions so that broad-based decisions can be made by the electorate. This suggests that self-generated preferences on the part of masses are infrequent, and that initiative by elites is a prerequisite to popular participation in policymaking—which itself may more often take the form of after-the-fact ratification or rejection than a priori instruction. But how much did elites seek to manipulate popular suport for *their* programs, how much did they genuinely reflect at least inchoate *popular* preferences, and how much did they simply assert their policies against popular wishes? These are difficult questions, but they contain some of the answers to the question of democracy. In a sense, these questions are the other half of the issue of the nature of the constraints observed by elites, which I raised in that subsection. When and how *do* popular views constrain the behavior of elites? If we can even begin to answer that, we are on the way to judgments about the relative presence or absence of democracy.

We should also ask about the extent of knowledge of the issues and rationality in the choice-making between them displayed by masses. Indeed, the full range of determinants of the outcome of elections, and their general meaningfulness under the circumstances, are before us in this area. If the general public is unaware or uninvolved or irrational, or otherwise incompetent at political decision making, we shall have grounds both for testing the assumptions and prescriptions of others and for evaluative judgments of our own. If we can define the "maps" of the political world which people actually carry in their minds, we shall be better able to speculate on the probability that they will respond to particular proposals for change. Although still far from complete, the empirical research in this subject area is probably more extensive than in any of the other three areas.

4. Political Change Processes

Every political system contains stabilizing and conservatizing features that operate to channel new demands and thrusts toward change into forms that can be dealt with without fundamental modification of the basic structure of authority. Those pressures that it cannot convert into such forms, or to which it is unable to adapt, may simply be repressed or deflected in some way. The issue then becomes whether enough pressures build up over time to destroy the system itself. The point is that all political systems exist in a context of internal and external pressures toward change—creating a kind of equation between stability and change—and they may be conceived of as evolving through time, though at varying rates of speed and with frequent discontinuities as entire governmental structures are overthrown. In the case of the United States, it seems clear that stability has triumphed, at least over the past 180 years or so. We may well ask how and why this has occurred, in contrast with repeated revolutionary changes around the world.

In preparing for this inquiry, some conceptual clarification may be helpful. By "political change" I mean differences over (a specified unit of) time in the characteristics of either (a) the distribution of dispositive power within the system ("the structure of authority"), and/or (b) the tangible consequences of government action (policy impact) in particular subject areas. Thus, either change in *who rules* or in *who is benefited or burdened* by the action of government would constitute political change for our purposes. Obviously, we must devise some measures of degree to complement these basic definitions: we must specify how *much* change must take place in what length of time to qualify for our label of "change." We may anticipate that these limits should vary according to the particular subject area in question, but that in all cases what seems modest or incremental to some will appear drastic or fundamental to others. The value preference component of the act of judgment in this matter suggests that for the moment we confine ourselves to what can be learned from empirical research prior to interpretive conclusions.

We can reasonably seek empirically to identify the conditions that permit, promote, or prevent political change in some form in the United States. If we know something about why the system works the way it does now, we can point to areas or points at which change would have to take place in order for things to come out differently; we might then examine the extent to which those features are permanently rooted, and speculate as to what would be required for them to be revised into some new state. Or we might proceed from occasions of change, empirically identified from the recent past, and seek to identify the forces that caused it and the manner in which they interacted. In both approaches we would be seeking to construct an image of the processes by which change takes place in the American political system, and the forces which succeed in bringing it about. For example, can change occur only in times of great and widely perceived emergency? What does it take to mobilize forces sufficient to counter the natural inertia and status quo orientations of both institutions and people? Must elites, or some of them, take the lead—and if so, when and why does this happen? Perhaps most important, what is the range of change that the present system's conservatizing features will permit, and which goals can be realized only by going outside its rules and processes?

In a sense, the study of political change processes is a way of summarizing and incorporating the areas of inquiry previously marked out. One of the important payoffs of developing understanding in each of the three previous areas is to be able to evaluate the prospects of change in the United States, and to employ such constructs to critically analyze the prescriptions of today's theorists.

In each area, perhaps naturally, the questions posed far outstrip the availability of empirical evidence. This does not result from the empirical researchers having been idle, but from the scope of the problems that they have sought to answer. When we have examined their work we may be better able to assess the extent to which they have advanced us.

Appendix

On Reading Reports of Empirical Research

Most students of political science encounter empirical studies at an early stage, but for those who have not, a word or two of explanation may be useful. We have already considered the care with which a reader must examine the researcher's (sometimes unstated or unrecognized but nevertheless structuring) assumptions, premises, and habituation to democratic interpretation. Three other areas in which care may enhance understanding deserve mention also.

DATA

Most of the data reported in the articles that follow were obtained by means of questionnaires administered to respondents by mail or in interviews. This method of ascertaining opinions and attitudes is based on the assumptions that the actual respondents are representative of the population whose attitudes are sought to be measured, and that the responses are accurate indicators of attitudes. The problem of representativeness is one for which generally agreed standards are available. If the relevant population is national nominating convention delegates, for example, respondents' background characteristics would be carefully checked in order to reduce the possibility that the people who happened to send back their questionnaires also just happened to hold atypical attitudes. In the case of a survey that sought to measure attitudes of the general public of the United States, random sampling would probably be used—a technique that could make a smaller number of people "representative" of the national public than would be satisfactory as "representative" of national convention delegates.

Random sampling is a technique that relies on mathematical probabilities: it is based on the principle that if every person in the United States had an equal chance of being selected for an interview, then the people actually chosen will be representative of all. The trick is to randomize so carefully and methodically that one can demonstrate that every person had an equal chance to be interviewed. If there were lists of all Americans, names could be drawn from a giant hat to do the job; but because there are no such lists (the telephone book will not do because some people—usually lower income people, but sometimes those who wish to be exclusive—are not included), geographical locating systems are frequently employed. All communities, and all parts of all communities, have equal chances to be chosen. The researcher systematically and randomly selects the particular streets. When the interviewer reaches the assigned spot, he may alternate between men and women and skip every other house in order to preserve representativeness. There are many other ways of randomizing, but this illustration will suffice to indicate that representativeness is a soluble problem. Accuracy of measurement is more difficult to assure, because it depends heavily on the wording of questions, the perceptions of the respondent, the interview situation, and the interpretation of the analyst. Questions may be worded in such a way as to elicit particular responses, as when "loaded" words such as Constitution, democracy, President, or communism, criminal, etc., are used to describe something in a question. We are all familiar with the kind of question that assumes a preexisting state of facts ("When did you stop beating your wife?") or that poses two perhaps equally unpalatable alternatives ("Do you favor escalation of the war in Vietnam or unilateral withdrawal?") "Polls" conducted by Congressmen among their constituents are frequently transparent attempts to *form* rather than to measure opinion, and are celebrated for these sorts of questions. Most researchers are aware of this problem, but sometimes not even an experienced opinion researcher realizes in advance what his respondents are going to see in a question or how it structures responses in particular directions. Furthermore, upper class respondents may understand the question in totally different ways from lower class respondents, in which case their answers would be quite incomparable and the question would have to be rejected. The interview situation too may affect the accuracy of measurement, because circumstances may be sufficiently disruptive to prevent serious consideration of answers, or the respondent may be inclined to tell the interviewer what he thinks the interviewer wants to hear; the latter possibility has led in recent years to the nearly exclusive use of Negro interviewers in Negro areas.

Thus the data presented are no better than the questions and the circumstances of the interview that elicited them. The researcher has coded the responses into categories, either preestablished by the nature of the alternatives to the questions, or grouped according to actual answers in the case of "open-ended" questions, and probably used punched cards and a computer to tabulate the totals. The resulting numbers frequently seem impressive when they are shown crisply laid out in tables and percentages, but it is well to recall that their validity as portrayals of what people believe rests on the assumption that all of the foregoing and many other possible problems have effectively been circumvented. Even when a survey is technically perfect, of course, intervening events may occur (riots, elections, international tensions) which make an opinion study out of date before it can even be completed. Nevertheless, responsibly executed research with carefully constructed questions, repeated over time and with different groups of respondents, can produce evidence about patterns of belief and levels of attitudes toward various issues, which can be taken as indicative of opinion characteristics.

PRESENTATION

The researcher has many formats available in which to present the reports of his research. The most familiar one is a simple table, in which different groups of respondents (Democrats and Republicans, or men and women) are compared as to their responses to particular questions, usually by means of percentages. Experienced students of empirical reports are likely to spend more time with the tables than with the author's description of what the tables mean, because the author himself may not have seen all the implications of his data, or he may have misread the relationships that are there. Small differences in percentages between groups of respondents are not very important, because errors in the sample alone or mistakes in the recording of answers could account for differences of three or four percentage points. Large portions of "don't know" or "undecided" answers indicate an uncertain or fluid opinion situation and lead analysts to exercise great care in attributing meaning to the results.

Other means of presentation may on occasion succeed in dramatizing a point that the researcher believes is a valid finding, but they carry commensurate risks for the reader. Graphs, for example, may focus on a limited time period that emphasizes the interpretation favored by the author. Textual presentation of salient percentages only may conceal the fact that nearly as many respondents answered the question differently. All in all, the reader is well advised to seek a full report on all categories of response to a question, and to examine the wording of the question as he studies the breakdown of responses; then he should compare answers to that question with response patterns to similar or related questions, to see whether one or the other is an isolated or idiosyncratic response or whether an interpretation is sought to be rested on a single possibly inaccurate question.

Finally, the reader should be cautious of concluding that because there is a correlation between two variables, one is the cause of the other. They may both be caused by still a third, or it may be coincidence. (Recall the previous illustration: college education correlates with Republican voting, but apparently both are caused by the precollege economic status of the respondent.) This fact would be demonstrated by comparing respondents from high economic levels with those from low economic levels while holding education constant, which means comparing college graduates with college graduates, and high school graduates with other high school graduates. (If the differences in voting are associated with the economic levels rather than with the level of education, the point is proved.)

INTERPRETATION

The researcher, having presented his data in a manner he believes is fair and responsible, normally then proceeds to indicate his own interpretation of their meaning. We may acknowledge the validity of a finding, but totally depart from the interpretation he puts on it because we see faulty weighing of the evidence, or illogical or unsupported leaps from finding to interpretation, or because the author has injected his own value preferences or assumptions into his conclusions. One way to guard against becoming captive of an author's interpretation is to try to imagine all the possible conclusions that might follow from the data and findings that are deemed acceptable: How many of these are refuted by other evidence in this or other studies? How tight an evidential and logical case has the author made for his preferred interpretation, and what unstated assumptions lie behind his choice? How far does he carry the implications of his findings: does he assume, for example, that behavior automatically follows from the existence of particular attitudes, or is he alert to the possible gap or even inconsistency between attitudes and behavior? A conclusion may be drawn out of a piece of research if it is supported by the evidence presented, but all beyond that which is actually supported by the data should be recognized as a more or less plausible implication or a frank speculation and thereafter employed as such.

These guidelines may seem to portray the use of empirical studies as a dangerous enterprise. They are not so intended, of course, and they are no more than careful empiricists employ in making use of each other's work. Nor should the reader be intimidated by collections of numbers, graphs, charts, and statistical manipulations. Common sense and patience are the only necessary tools for comprehension of these findings, and a little experience soon renders them valuable sources of insight into the characteristics of contemporary politics.

CHAPTER 2

Elites

THE three selections in this chapter are efforts to specify what sorts of people become government officials and holders of power in other forms, how their attitudes compare with members of the general public, and in what ways their behavior is constrained by popular preferences. Vital as these questions are, research has only begun to provide data that bear on them.

Professor Hacker's article is one of the very few studies that examine backgrounds of members of national elites and compare groupings within them. He is a political theorist teaching at Cornell University; his books include *Political Theory: Philosophy, Ideology, Science* (1961) and *The Study of Politics* (1963).

Professor McCloskey's article is a major landmark of comparative attitudinal research. There are few studies of elite attitudes, and only a handful have sought to compare the preferences of elites and the general public. He is a political scientist specializing in survey research techniques and teaches at the University of California at Berkeley.

The late Professor V. O. Key, Jr. was one of the leading figures in the political science profession for many years. The chapter reprinted here is the concluding chapter of *Public Opinion and American Democracy* (1961), a major work in which Professor Key reexamined a vast body of survey data and articulated a sophisticated speculation about the nature of elite behavior. His other books include *Southern Politics* (1949) and *Politics, Parties and Pressure Groups* (five editions, 1942-1964).

A selected bibliography of other studies follows Chapter 5.

The Elected and the Anointed:
Two American Elites

ANDREW HACKER

In all advanced societies there is a distinct tendency for political and economic power to be held and exercised by different kinds of individuals. Even in modern totalitarian states it has been possible to observe quite distinguishable groups playing the leading roles in political and economic life. The aptitudes that go to make a successful political leader and those that produce an effective economic manager are analytically separable. And if the men who comprise the political and economic elites in a single society are markedly different in character and social background, then certain tensions are bound to arise in the areas where their power and authority interact. These tensions may develop even if the two sets of people profess to sharing a common ideology and even if they are ostensibly committed to working toward common objectives. For the kinds of men who enter political and economic vocations are prone to view social reality from different vantage points, and consequently they will interpret their shared ideology in the light of different experience. What will follow, then, is a comparative study of two elite groups in contemporary American society. The purpose of this study, quite simply, is to ascertain what the members of these elites have in common and what they do not.

Once this knowledge is in hand it will then be possible to speculate on the connection between the disparate backgrounds of the political and economic reality held by the members of the two groups. If it is granted that a legislator's or an executive's view of society is shaped

by a wide variety of forces, it will also be acknowledged that the true weight of only a few of these factors can be evaluated in a systematic way. To infer that selected aspects of a man's environment determine his perceptions of the world around him is bound to be a risky affair. Only if these admonitions are kept in mind can the generalizations ventured at the close of this paper be read in a proper light. As conclusions they will perforce be both limited and tentative. For the sake of clarity of presentation, however, some emphases will be highlighted and certain contrasts will be underlined. While appearances may occasionally be to the contrary, the writer has not been carried away by the simplicity of his theme. And neither will the well-advised reader be so stampeded.

The 200 men (in fact, 199 men and Mrs. Margaret Chase Smith) to be considered here constitute the totality of the two elites in question: 100 United States senators and the presidents of America's 100 largest industrial corporations. But the study is, in another sense, based on a sample. The 100 senators are those who happened to be the incumbents in mid-October, 1959. The 100 corporations are those which happened to be tops in sales during 1958, and their presidents are the men who happened to be the incumbents in mid-October, 1959. At this time the Senate was rather heavily weighted on the Democratic side. Prior to the 1958 election there were 49 Democrats and 47 Republicans in the Senate; after that election there were 65 Democrats and 35 Republicans. But this line-up was not changed appreciably by the 1960 election.

As for the corporations, in the five years from 1955 through 1959 a total of 119 companies have been listed among

SOURCE. Reprinted from *The American Political Science Review*, Vol. 55 (1961) by permission of the author and publisher. Copyright 1961, The American Political Science Association.

the top 100 at one time or another. In other words, during the five years ending with 1959, nineteen companies fell below the top 100 and nineteen new ones came in to take their places. It should be pointed out, however, that of the nineteen which took this fall, thirteen were still in 1959 among the top 120. Only six really lost significant ground in the half-decade.

While the Senate in 1959 was overweighted with newcomers, the median tenure of office was still approximately seven years. The median tenure of the presidents was somewhat over four years. On the whole it is true that the corporation executives do not stay in office as long as their legislative counterparts. Indeed, one of the noteworthy features of the modern corporation is the fairly rapid rotation of top personnel. At all events a necessary limitation of this study was its being based on a single point in time. Information on the senators and presidents was obtained from standard reference works and additional data were secured by means of personal correspondence.[1]

Much of our folklore, academic and otherwise, manages to convey stereotyped images of the men who fill our legislative and corporate offices. James M. Burns, for example prefaces his *Congress on Trial* with a vignette entitled "The Congressman and His World." This portrait (of a representative, but clearly intended by Burns to apply to the senators as well) is meant to be characteristic of the men who make our nation's laws. Burns writes:

Above all else the Congressman believes in Boone Center and the rest of the Ninth District. An unashamed booster of the district, he is an expert on its products, its history, and its importance to the nation. . . . The Congressman's world then, is largely confined within the boundaries of the Ninth District and is shaped by the business spirit and way of life of Boone Center. It is a world where old ideas and myths still survive, blurring the alignments that economic and political forces inevitably produce. As the champion of his world, the Congressman defends it against its real and imaginary adversaries outside. As the product of his world, he puts its imprint on Congressional action.[2]

If the congressman is commonly seen as the product of provincial America, the corporation executive is most usually invested with what may be called a metropolitan background. The really important group in C. Wright Mills' trinitarian power elite consists of the top business leaders, and he refers largely to these when he describes America's men of power:

They derive in substantial proportions from the upper classes, both new and old, of local society and the metropolitan 400. . . . Their fathers were at least of professional and business strata, and very frequently higher than that. They are native-born American of native parents, primarily from urban areas, and . . . overwhelmingly from the East. They are mainly Protestants, especially Episcopalians or Presbyterians. In general, the higher the position the greater the proportion of men within it who have derived from and who maintain connections with the upper classes. The generally similar origins of the members of the power elite are underlined and carried further by the fact of their increasingly common educational routine. Overwhelmingly college graduates, substantial pro-

---

[1] The one hundred corporations were taken from the "The *Fortune* Directory" of the 500 largest industrial corporations; the "Directory" was published in August 1959 and covers the 1958 calendar year. Information on the senators and presidents was secured from 1959 editions of *Who's Who in America, Who's Who in Commerce and Industry,* and the *Congressional Directory.* The remainder of the data were obtained by personal letters sent out to the 200 presidents and senators by the students in my undergraduate course in "Political Behavior." Their hours of toil over their typewriters and their uncomplaining—and unreimbursed—expenditures on postage stamps have my heartfelt appreciation.

[2] James M. Burns, *Congress on Trial* (New York, 1949), pp. 5, 17. For more systematic analysis of Senatorial backgrounds, see the cumulative studies of Donald R. Matthews: "United States Senators and the Class Structure," *Public Opinion Quarterly,* Vol. 18 (1954), pp. 5-22; *The Social Backgrounds of Political Decision-Makers* (New York, 1954); *United States Senators and Their World* (Chapel Hill, 1960).

portions have attended Ivy League colleges.[8]

It is easy enough to point out that both Burns' and Mills' portraits are caricatures, and there is every reason to think that both authors know that this is so. But— if these are caricatures—it remains to ask just where the reality lies. How far is it possible to generalize about the men who make up America's legislative and industrial leadership? There are important elements of truth in both the provincial and metropolitan stereotypes. But they can also be misleading insofar as they obscure some interesting and subtle differences which are important features of the composite elite picture.

EARLY ENVIRONMENT

Seventy-eight of the senators were raised in the states they currently represent. This means that, in geographic terms at least, the legislators constitute a fairly representative cross-section of the country. What is more surprising is that the executives are similarly diversified. Table 1 gives the regional breakdown of the two elite groups, based on the towns where they went to high school. Quite clearly the South is over-represented in the Senate, and the corporations draw slightly more heavily on the East and the Midwest. However it is important to note that almost as many executives hail from the Midwest as do from the East. In this respect what Mills has to say falls rather wide of the mark: the corporate elite may once have been an Eastern preserve but the current generation has been recruited from all sections of the country. Both

[8] C. Wright Mills, *The Power Elite* (New York, 1956), p. 279. There are four full-length studies of business executives: Mabel Newcomer, *The Big Business Executive* (New York, 1955); W. Lloyd Warner and James C. Abegglen, *Big Business Leaders in America* (New York, 1955); Warner and Abegglen, *Occupational Mobility in American Business and Industry* (Minneapolis, 1955); The Editors of *Fortune, The Executive Life* (New York, 1956).

TABLE 1. EARLY ENVIRONMENT: SECTION OF COUNTY

	Senators ($N = 97$) (%)	Presidents ($N = 95$) (%)
East	30	36
Midwest	27	35
South	27	13
West	16	15

Mills and Burns are largely correct, however, when the character of the hometowns of the two elites is examined. Table 2 shows the kind of city in which the legislators and executives received their secondary education. It should be pointed out that the three categories were construed very liberally: a "metropolitan center" is any city with a population of over 100,000 and includes the suburban fringe; a "medium-sized city" ranges from 25,000 to 100,000. From these figures it is plain that the senators are preponderantly provincial in origin. While, again, the number of small-town executives is surprisingly large—not a few hail from such hamlets as Red Lodge, Montana, Crystal, North Dakota, or Sour Lake, Texas—the far larger group were raised in cities like New York or Chicago or their immediate suburbs. An individual's hometown is generally selected for him by his parents, and his real choice of environment (if he gets any) comes after he completes his higher education. Nevertheless, to the extent that the milieu of one's early upbringing instills in a person a certain social outlook, it may be said

TABLE 2. EARLY ENVIRONMENT: HOMETOWN

School	Senators ($N = 100$) (%)	Presidents ($N = 95$) (%)
Metropolitan center	19	52
Medium-sized city	17	17
Rural or small town	64	29

that the legislators begin life with an exposure to its provincial manner whereas the executives tend to start in a metropolitan environment. And as an individual's decision to make a break with his hometown surroundings is an important fact in his biography, this information on early environment can be regarded as a point of departure for further analysis.

EDUCATION

In the United States, as in most other countries, a man's education tells us a good deal about his overall social background. The two elites show a basic similarity in that the overwhelming majority in both groups attended college. But significant variations appear when we look into the type of school they attended prior to college and the kind of college in which they enrolled. Table 3 breaks down their schools and colleges into the conventional categories. Such a classification in no way presupposes the educational superiority of one type of institution as compared with another. It can be said, however, that at the time the members of

TABLE 3. EDUCATION: SECONDARY
SCHOOL AND COLLEGE

School	Senators (N = 94) (%)	Presidents (N = 90) (%)
Private school	15	28
Public school	85	72
College[a]	(N = 100)	(N = 95)
Ivy League college	15	29
Other private college	36	27
State university	40	31
No college	9	13

[a] By "Ivy League" colleges are meant Harvard, Yale, Princeton, Columbia, Dartmouth, Brown, Pennsylvania, Cornell, and also Amherst and Williams. Included with "State universities" are the U.S. Naval Academy and the City College of New York.

the elite groups were receiving their education, attendance at a private school or an Ivy League college was evidence of coming from a fairly well-to-do family. About twice as many executives had private school and Ivy League educations as legislators. For the senators, the roughly equal apportionment between non-Ivy private colleges and public universities probably reflects the middle to upper-middle class backgrounds of these men. More than half of the senators who did go to private schools did not attend the fashionable Eastern seaboard preparatory schools but rather went to local institutions in or relatively close to their hometowns.

The corporate elite, on the other hand, departs markedly from the stereotype. Over two-thirds of them went to public high schools and the same proportion attended non-Ivy private colleges or state universities. And of the minority of executives who did go to Ivy league colleges, by no means all of them preceded this with private school training. Of the 28 such corporation presidents, eighteen were prep school graduates and ten were not. In other words, only 20 per cent of the corporate elite had the educational background usually associated with privilege in this country.[4] The remaining 80 per cent of the executives diverge from this pattern in important particulars, and Table 4 shows that one of the most significant of these is an engineering training. While the engineers do not constitute a majority of the corporate elite—but neither, for that matter, do the liberal arts graduates—they are nevertheless a large

[4] Two thoughts occur here: The corporate elite might have displayed a more privileged background had the heads of large banks, investment houses, and insurance companies been included in the study. Industrial corporations may be less concerned about a man's origins than financial institutions seem to be. At the same time, had the ten (or fifty) men in each company immediately below the president been studied, a greater prep school and Ivy League proportion might have been noted. When the final promotion to the summit is made it may well be that questions of background are given less stress than they are for subordinate executive positions in the company.

TABLE 4. EDUCATION: FIELD OF STUDY
(PRESIDENTS)

	Ivy League (N = 28) (%)	Private (N = 23) (%)	State (N = 23) (%)
Liberal arts	78	15	30
Engineering	11	70	40
Other	11	15	30

enough group to command attention. What emerges is that the executives, once more contrary to Mills' analysis, do not form a homogeneous group. There are, to be sure, those from privileged backgrounds and with training in the useless arts. But they are easily outnumbered by those with humbler beginnings and educations geared to the practical. The Ivy League executives, it ought to be said, seem to possess certain advantages. The members of this group ascended to their presidencies at a median age of 47 years, whereas the non-Ivy presidents had to wait until they were 52 or 53, on the average, for this promotion. It would appear, furthermore, that engineers "waste" several years while working on the technical side, and transfer over to management slightly later in their careers. But once such a shift is made they seem to stand an equal chance of getting to the top.

NATIONAL ORIGINS AND RELIGION

As the years move on it is increasingly difficult to analyze social backgrounds and basic attitudes in terms of national origins. Of course it is still true that a second-generation American of southern or eastern European parentage is going to begin life with a lower social status and greater career handicaps. On the other hand third-generation Americans of northern European stock are less and less frequently regarded as other than full-fledged citizens. This is certainly the case

with Germans and Scandinavians, and it is increasingly so for Irish-Americans. The outlook is bound to change for Italians, Poles, and Jews as the second generation makes way for the third. At the same time America is filled with tens of millions of "poor whites" of venerable Anglo-Saxon stock. For the offspring of these less successful Mayflower families, the road to career advancement can be virtually as difficult as that for a third-generation American of Polish background. So long as caveats such as these are kept in mind it is possible to proceed with an examination of the national origins of the two elites.

Table 5 gives the birthplaces of the grandparents of the legislators and executives. A grandparent of one of these men would have been born at about 1840, and if he was born in the United States this would be sufficiently early to be termed "old American" stock. However, for purposes of this study only those with four native-born grandparents were put in the "old American" class. Those with three, two, one, or none who were born in the United States were classified as coming from immigrant backgrounds. In the vast majority of cases, it should be said, either all grandparents were born in this country or all were born elsewhere. While only a total of 128 members of the two elites supplied information in this area, the pattern for them, at least, is quite straight-forward. There is a basic similarity between the two elites, and both are largely the preserve of grandsons of "old American" families. While it is conventional to sup-

TABLE 5. NATIONAL ORIGINS:
GRANDPARENTS' NATIVITY

	Senators (N = 69) (%)	Presidents (N = 59) (%)
Old American	70	60
Northern Europe	21	34
Southern or eastern Europe	9	6

pose that political careers are one of the first roads of advancement opened to recent immigrant groups, this rule has as yet to be applied in the Senate. It should be noted, moreover, that in the case of both elites the grandparents who are designated as coming from "Northern Europe" tend to hail from England and Scotland rather than Germany or Ireland. Ours is probably the last generation in this country's history in which an analysis of national origins will be of much value. For in thirty years' time an inquiry into the nativity of an individual's grandparents will shed very little light on his own character or social opportunities. By the year 1990 virtually all white Americans will be thoroughly assimilated, and national antecedents will be little more than interesting curiosities.

Religion, like education, has been traditionally employed as a social index. The religious affiliations of the senators are a matter of record, and a high proportion of the presidents were willing to give this information. It has never been easy to classify the various denominations. But most members of the two elites are Protestants, and the "high-status"-"low-status" breakdown is a fairly useful one. In this classification, Episcopalians, Presbyterians, Congregationalists, and Unitarians are termed "high-status" and Baptists, Methodists, Lutherans, and others "low-status."[5] Table 6 gives the church memberships of the two elites. Any such attempt at general analysis is bound to be plagued by regional variations. In the state of Utah, for example, a large part of the population belongs to the Church of Latter Day Saints. And in the South membership in Baptist and Methodist churches can be every bit as "high-status" as Episcopal or Congrega-

tionalist membership elsewhere. Indeed, of the twenty-two Southern senators, only five belong to what in national terms might be called "high-status" churches and seventeen are "low-status" affiliates. If the Southerners are left out of consideration, the "high-status"-"low-status" ratio among the non-Southern legislators is 54 to 46 per cent—compared with 75 to 25 per cent among the executives. In other words, while the majority of non-Southern Protestant senators belong to "high-status" churches, the proportion is appreciably greater among the presidents. One further point can only be raised as a matter of speculation. The church memberships reported here are the current ones attested to by the men in the two elite groups. It would be of some interest to know how many of the legislators and executives ˙ have continued with the religious affiliations in which they were originally raised. There is a suspicion, raised by correlating current church membership with data on the early environment, that at least some of the presidents now professing "high-status" religions affiliated with these churches later in adult life. Hardly any similar evidence exists for the senators. If this is in any way so, then the implication is that the legislators are content to retain the religious identification of the provincial middle-class into which they were born, whereas the executives prefer to associate themselves with the churches of the metropolitan upper-middle class.

[5] This classification of religions according to status is employed by Matthews in his *The Social Background of Political Decision-Makers,* op. cit., p. 26. It was devised by Wesley and Beverly Allinsmith, "Religious Affiliation and Politico-Economic Attitude," *Public Opinion Quarterly,* Vol. 12 (1948), pp. 377-89. The church memberships of the senators are given in *The Congressional Quarterly,* January 8, 1961, p. 61.

TABLE 6. CHURCH AFFILIATION

	Senators (N = 100) (%)	Presidents (N = 72) (%)
"High-status" Protestant	36	60
"Low-status" Protestant	45	20
Unspecified Protestant	4	8
Roman Catholic	12	9
Jewish	3	3

THE NEXT GENERATION

If the last observation is only a matter of speculation, it may be strengthened by examining the aspirations of the members of the two elites for their children. Contrary to the popular literature, not all Americans are embroiled in the game of status-seeking—although some are more than others. It may be presumed that the goals which an individual sets for his children reflect in some way his own sense of values. Table 7 shows the colleges to which the senators and presidents sent their sons or daughters.[6] Out of the 200, some 142 replied to this question; but this number 45 had either no children or children who were too young for college. It is no surprise to learn that the presidents tend to send their children to Ivy

TABLE 7. COLLEGE OF CHILDREN

	Senators (N = 44) (%)	Presidents (N = 53) (%)
Ivy League college	27	70
Other private college	34	17
State university	39	14

League colleges even if most of them did not attend such institutions themselves. The typical executive would not yet have been the president of his corporation when his offspring started college; however, he was clearly close to the top by that time and well exposed to the metropolitan life. The information on the senators is more revealing. Our legislators are not so poorly paid or without outside sources of income that the expense of an Ivy League education is beyond their

[6] By "Ivy League" colleges are meant the ten cited in the note accompanying Table 3, plus Smith, Vassar, Wellesley, Bryn Mawr, Radcliffe, Barnard, and Mount Holyoke. If a senator or president had sent more than one child to college, and if different children went to different types of institutions, then "Ivy League" was recorded in preference to Non-Ivy, and private colleges were recorded in preference to public institutions.

means. And it is plain that an Ivy League college would be as happy to have a senator's child on its rolls as it would a president's. The thought arises in consequence that most senators simply do not have metropolitan aspirations for their sons and daughters any more than they do for themselves. They prefer, on the whole, to have their offspring identify with more familiar surroundings and they elect to send their sons and daughters to non-Ivy private colleges and state universities closer to home. Indeed, it is the very definition of what constitutes one's "home" that comes closest to differentiating the two elite groups.

GEOGRAPHIC MOBILITY

It has already been noted that senators tend to begin life in provincial surroundings while presidents are more apt to have metropolitan boyhoods. The first opportunity for a break with the home environment usually comes with the decision of where to go to college. Table 8 indicates the distances traveled by the members of the two elites from their hometowns to college. If it is asked whether it was the youthful legislators or executives who were more venturesome in this sphere, the answer is ambiguous. On the one hand, the median distance travelled by the college-bound future senators is higher; on the other, twice as many presidents-to-be went over 500 miles in order to attend college. It is clear, however, that the future executives

TABLE 8. MOBILITY: HOMETOWN TO COLLEGE

	Senators N = 84) (%)	Presidents (N = 79) (%)
Same town	15	18
Under 100 miles	38	30
100 to 500 miles	34	27
Over 500 miles	13	25
Median distance	101 miles	90 miles

did not hitch-hike across the country to get their educations. Only a quarter of them travelled a great distance, and it is doubtful if they had to journey by means of upraised thumb. Furthermore almost half of the legislators went to colleges over 100 miles from home. These figures—especially if 100 miles is taken as the dividing point—are strikingly similar.

The current location of the two elites is quite another matter. Table 9 shows the distance between the hometown and the current residence for the senators and the presidents. Here the typical executive will be seen to have travelled over fifteen times as far in pursuit of his career. If 100 miles is again taken as the dividing point, approximately 70 per cent of the legislators now live within 100 miles of their hometown whereas 70 per cent of the executives have set up residence over 100 miles from where they started. It is well known that the corporate life is a nomadic one and that the road to advancement in large companies is paved with a series of transfers throughout the country.[7] The presidents, of course, are now residing in or near the cities where the company headquarters are located. These centers are not in point of fact, as "metropolitan" as might first be thought. Only thirty-seven of the corporations are based in New York; nine are in Chicago, and six each are in Detroit and Pittsburgh.[8] After that the spread is wide, including such towns as Moline, Greensboro, and Bartlesville. What is important, however, is that all of these corporations

TABLE 9. MOBILITY: HOMETOWN TO CURRENT RESIDENCE

	Senators (N = 92) (%)	Presidents (N = 91) (%)
Same town	41	12
Under 100 miles	30	18
100 to 500 miles	11	34
Over 500 miles	18	36
Median distance	22 miles	342 miles

are national in their operations. Their presidents spend a great deal of time travelling throughout the country, and their constituency—for so it may be called—consists of suppliers and customers and employees and shareholders from coast to coast. It is truly nationwide in its proportions. This metropolitan world was entered at the moment the executives decided they would not return to the hometowns in which they were raised. And, for most of them, this was the first decision they made upon leaving college and embarking upon their corporate careers.

If what distinguishes the senators is their decision to return to their hometowns, there is good evidence that they ventured beyond familiar territory during their formative years. A simple way to measure such mobility is to set up four "compass points." These are: (1) the town in which a senator or a president was raised (in most cases this is the town where he went to high school). (2) The town where he went to college (if he did). (3) The town where he went to graduate school (if he did). (4) The town where he currently resides. By plotting a "map" for each senator and president, four general patterns of mobility begin to emerge. They are: (1) the "non-leavers," whose hometown, college and graduate school (if attended), and current residence are all within the same state; (2) the "temporary leavers," whose hometown and current residence are within the same state, but who travelled to another state for college or graduate school; (3) the

[7] See Robert Sheehan, "We've Been Transferred," *Fortune*, July, 1957, pp. 116-118, 198-200.

[8] For those who like to keep in touch with the world of affairs, the following intelligence may be of interest: of the 37 corporations with head offices in the New York area, eleven are located around Wall Street, eight are in Rockefeller Center, and seventeen are on the Upper East Side—chiefly Park Avenue. (One is in suburban White Plains.) Tourists to the Soviet Union who wish to set straight the dialecticians of Red Square may point out that "Wall Street" is a thing of the past and "Park Avenue" is the new center of industrial capitalism.

"late leavers," who went to college or graduate school in their home state, but whose current residence is in a different state; and (4) the "early leavers," whose hometown, college and graduate school (if attended), and current residence are all in different states. Table 10 applies these four patterns, based on the four "compass points," to the senators and presidents. Those with the first two patterns are called "returners"; those displaying the second two are called "nonreturners." What is perhaps most interesting is that while most of the legislators return to their home state, so large a proportion of them leave temporarily for purposes of furthering their education. Significantly, also, this movement on the part of the senators was more typically for graduate school than for undergraduate studies. Of the 65 legislators who attended graduate school (and this was usually law school), as many as 41 took their advanced work in another state. The general pattern, then, was to go to college in one's home state, to attend graduate school in a different state, and then to return home with a law degree. The senators may be characterized, in sum, by their early decision to follow their careers in the surroundings in which they were raised. The majority of the presidents made a quite different choice: on completing their education they decided

TABLE 10. MOBILITY:
DURATION OF ABSENCE

	Senators (N = 100) (%)	Presidents (N = 97) (%)
Returners		
Non-leavers	21	5
Temporary leavers	57	24
	—	—
	78	29
Non-Returners		
Late leavers	14	39
Early leavers	8	32
	—	—
	22	71

to make the nationwide business community their new home.

In summary it may be said that the members of the two elites are similar in several important respects. In terms of regional origins, of level of education, of national origins, and of pre-career mobility the pictures are pretty much the same. The respects in which they differ are, on the whole, more significant. These have to do with the size of the hometown, the character of education, current religion, education of children, and career mobility. On this basis it may be said that the provincial characterization of the legislative elite is not an inaccurate assessment. Even though the senators travelled away from home for their education, their early decision to return suggests their choice to identify with the section of the country in which they grew up. That such an identification continues to persist is suggested by the findings on their children's education. There are, to be sure, exceptions to these generalizations. But the major patterns hold. On the other hand, the metropolitan attributes of the executives are as much acquired as they are the product of early environment. Almost half of the presidents, it will be recalled, were raised in medium-sized cities or small towns or rural surroundings. There are, furthermore, two quite distinct groups among the executives: the "Ivy League-liberal arts" contingent on the one side, and the "State University-engineers" on the other. The latter group, in terms of origins and education, has much in common with the senators. But the law students who were to become legislators returned home, whereas the engineers who were to become executives did not.

Furthermore, of the executives who studied liberal arts subjects and who attended Ivy League colleges, only a part came from the higher strata of society. Indeed, having attended a private school is in most of their cases evidence of an upper-middle class rather than an upper-class background. Of the 37 presidents who currently live in or around New York City, only four are listed in the *New*

York Social Register.[9] Most of them clearly lack the family connections which entitle an individual to membership in the established citadel of metropolitan society—or, more properly, Society. Yet these men of real power and not inconsiderable wealth, and those who had provincial backgrounds have long since put these behind them. The chief reason why the corporate elite does not gain entry into the world of the *Social Register* is that they hold their positions as top executives for too short a time to establish themselves as individual personalities. Nor does it follow that their children will enter this world. For a corporation president may give his sons and daughters a good education and a modest inheritance, but there is small likelihood that he can pass on to the sons top jobs in the company.[10] At this point we do not know what careers are followed by the children of the executives, nor is it clear how large are the fortunes which are left to them. But it must not be thought that most of the presidents end up as more than modest millionaires, if that; the amount of money which will descend to the second generation is not going to be particularly impressive.

The corporate elite, then, is a group whose membership is always in the process of circulation. The men who comprise it at any given time have not been at the top for long, and for this reason they have not been able to acquire substantial wealth or traditional social connections. It is an elite based on talent rather than on birth, and its overlap with the upper class of the *Social Register* is negligible. If it is metropolitan, therefore, it is because it lives in an exercises power over a nationwide economy. And it is this experience of life in a national constituency which gives it its image of American society.

It ought not to be necessary to allude to the structural differences in the organization of the political and economic elites. The senators meet regularly and they make their legislative decisions jointly. While they are ever mindful of the interests of their constituencies, the actions they ultimately take concern the formation of national policy. The presidents belong to no common organization and their interactions with each other are irregular and informal.[11] And most of their decisions concern the operations of their companies rather than the business community as a whole. Nor is either group the exclusive elite in its province. The senators share power with the representatives, the President, and the Administration. The presidents, within their own corporations, share power with the directors, the chairmen of the boards, and frequently the large lending and underwriting institutions. All of these facts are quite obvious, and if analogies are being suggested between the two elites these must not be strained. It is clear, however, that both senators and presidents are men of substanial power. As an in-

---

[9] *Social Register New York 1959* (New York, 1960). The idea of examining the overlap between "elite" and "upper class" in a metropolitan area comes from E. Digby Baltzell, *Philadelphia Gentlemen* (Glencoe, 1958).

[10] The facts of limited tenure of office and corporate bureaucracy raise important questions which can only be broached here. John Kenneth Galbraith, for example, minimizes the role of individual executives: "Organization replaces individual authority; no individual is powerful enough to do much damage. Were it otherwise, the stock market would pay close attention to retirements, deaths, and replacements in the executive ranks of large corporations. In fact, it ignores such details in tacit recognition that the organization is independent of any individual." *The Affluent Society* (Boston 1958), p. 102.

[11] This process is discussed by Floyd Hunter, *Top Leadership U.S.A.* (Chapel Hill, 1959). Even more illuminating is Hobart Rowen's brief discussion of the Business Advisory Council. *Harpers,* September 1960, pp. 79-84. The sixty members of this group, almost all of them corporation leaders, meet periodically for several days to discuss national policies. Despite its recent dissociation from the Department of Commerce the B.A.C. has made clear its intention to continue meeting as a corporate entity. Another gathering point is the National Industrial Conference Board, which assumes importance because the National Association of Manufacturers' membership rolls are dominated by smaller businesses.

dividual, each legislator and executive has a substantial jurisdiction in which he can act on his own discretion; and as collectivities, each elite group constitutes a major force in American society. The senators, for example, participate in presiding over a governmental establishment with approximately 2.5 million employees and they enact a budget which disposes of over $80 billion in taxes. The presidents, for their part, head companies with over five million employees and they produce goods which bring in almost $120 billion in sales. In our time power lies with major political and economic institutions more than ever before, and one is frequently tempted to conclude that these organizations dictate the conduct of the men who work in and for them. Yet it is also true that the behavior of institutions, of legislatures and corporations, will reflect the character of the men who staff them.

The hypothesis to be advanced here is that serious tensions exist between our major political and economic institutions. And this state of affairs stems in no small measure from the fact that different kinds of individuals fill the legislative and executive roles in American society. There is, at base, a real lack of understanding and a failure of communication between the two elites. This hiatus, and the consequent tensions, stem largely from the disparate images of society held by the respective groups. And the void is most especially pronounced in the areas where politics and economics come into contact with one another.[12]

This hypothesis is, of course, tentative. No one has conducted a systematic survey of the attitudes and outlooks of senators and presidents; and while there are good studies of both groups, they overlap neither in method nor in substance. At this juncture, therefore, the suggestion that there is a mutual misperception of needs and goals must be regarded as a starting point rather than as a conclusion. If this initial impression has been gained from rudimentary observation of the two elites, it is subject to correction and revision. I have not undertaken to match individual views and individual backgrounds against group misperceptions. There are, furthermore, dangers in generalizing about a legislative elite, for in such bodies not all members are equally powerful. Nevertheless, in the case of the Senate there is ground for believing that the more powerful members are also more heavily provincial in background. At the same time there is the anomaly that the more metropolitan senators may, in spite of the characteristics they share with the businessmen, be those most feared by the economic elite. Thus Prep School-Ivy League Democrats like Joseph Clark of Pennsylvania and William Proxmire of Wisconsin are regarded by corporation managers with no small hostility. (But it should also be noted that Prep School-Ivy League presidents such as Thomas Watson, Jr. of I.B.M. and Henry Ford II of Ford are surprisingly liberal in their politics and not nearly so worried as their colleagues about welfare legislation or high government expenditures.) But the real problem under consideration has to do with the handful of vocal anti-business senators, many of whom are admittedly metropolitan in background. Rather it centers on the broad legislative majority; the large group of lawmakers from provincial environments who harbor no

---

[12] It might be mentioned as a gratuitous note that this study was largely impelled by two personal experiences of the author. In August of 1959 he was asked to testify before the McClellan Committee on the political activities of corporations. He was unable to persuade the legislators that a national corporation was something more than an expanded version of a locally owned and managed enterprise. "Investigation of Improper Activities in the Labor or Management Field," 86th Congress, 1st sess., Part 57, pp. 19900-19908. In November of the same year he was asked to speak at a meeting of the National Industrial Conference Board on corporation activities in politics. He was unable to persuade the executives

that the Congress was something more than a Washington Branch Office which was not up with the times. "Executives Eager to Get in Politics," *New York Herald Tribune*, November 25, 1959. But then this may be only a commentary on the persuasive powers of the author.

overt antagonism to the business community.[13]

Most of the legislators are sympathetic
to the needs of business and they sincerely
desire to maintain our economic system—
as they understand it. Problems arise,
however, because the legislative image of
the business world is cast largely in
provincial terms. Most of the senators
have had little direct experience of metropolitan institutions and almost none have
worked with the national corporations.
At most, they are familiar with branch
plants which may happen to be in their
constituencies; but they have little appreciation of the national outlook of the
large firms. The world of business they
have been exposed to is the realm of
small, locally owned enterprise. And it
is their ignorance of the metropolitan
economy which leads to some of the most
pronounced ambiguities in legislative behavior. On the one hand, legislators seek
to protect and encourage small and local
businesses, for to their minds these are
the rightful foundations of the economy.
Consequently there is much rhetoric
about "aid to small business" and peren-
nial calls for "vigorous anti-trust action"
directed against the large corporations.
On the other hand, they are faced with the
very real fact that our nationwide firms
must be given access and listened to with
respectful attention. Corporation lobbyists are never denied entry in our capitols,
and their power is such that more often
than not they secure the legislation they
want. Indeed, a provincial assembly of
lawmakers seems again and again willing
to accommodate itself to the wishes of
these metropolitan institutions. The problem is that the legislators are faced with
a power they do not really understand and
with demands about whose legitimacy
they are uneasy. If they acquiesce, it is
frequently with no small qualm of conscience. At the very same time, they are
unable to protect the small, local enterprises to which they are ideologically
committed. Small business loans and

anti-trust legislation are ineffective instruments, yet these are the major weapons in
a paper arsenal. While the lawmakers
believe strongly in the institution of
private property, their image of the
economy is such that they are incapable
of seeing the real conflicts between small
and large businesses. Contracts which go
to the one cannot be available to the
other; tax laws which benefit the one will
work hardships on the other. And the
rise in market and distribution power of
the nationwide corporations tends, if not
to drive small firms out of business, to
deprive their owners of prestige and independence by reducing suppliers and
retailers to a state of vassalage. Yet because legislators have been brought up to
view the business world as a seamless web,
they are able to face up to these problems in a serious way. They never launch
a serious attack on the activities of large
corporations, even though their hearts are
with the welfare of small enterprise. Indeed, it is hard for them to be "anti-
business" in even the most selective of
ways.

A further consequence is that even
though the Congress will oftentimes
make sincere efforts to accommodate the
desires of large corporations, the result
is that the economic elite remains dissatisfied with their handiwork. Thus we
saw the ironic spectacle of an essentially
conservative Congress enacting a labor
law which placed further restrictions on
unions, and for this act it got not thanks
but renewed criticism. The program
sponsored by large corporations to "get
businessmen into politics" arose in 1958
while a Republican was in the White
House and the Congress was controlled by
a coalition of Republicans and Southern
Democrats.[14] That very Congress was
seen by executives as dominated by labor
unions and bent on destroying the founda-

---

[13] I am grateful to Robert E. Lane for helping
me to think through some of the problems
raised in this paragraph.

[14] The literature exhorting businessmen to
get into politics is voluminous. The author
has in his files well over one hundred speeches
by executives and statements by companies
on this subject. A typical call to action is
Horace E. Sheldon's "Businessmen Must Get
Into Politics," *Harvard Business Review*,
Vol. 37 (1959), pp. 37-47.

tions of a free economy. While the "businessmen in politics" movement ended up with more talk than action, it was also deeply symptomatic of the economic elite's dissatisfaction with the overall record and outlook of our lawmakers.

It may be argued, and with some justice, that corporation executives are lacking in political sophistication and they will never really be happy until taxes cease to exist and regulatory agencies padlock their doors.[15] Yet the very fact that the economic elite does not feel that its needs are understood by the men who make the nation's laws is a fact having broad ramifications. In American society the level of employment, the rate of industrial growth, and the success of our involvement with other nations—all of these and more depend on the prosperity of our large corporations. At the heart of the executive plaint is the feeling that our legislators cannot bring themselves to acknowledge that corporations are here to stay and that they are national in character. It is wrong, they would argue, to treat a major corporation as simply another "pressure group" bent on getting a larger share of the spoils. There is, in the corporate world, no small anxiety about the politics of democracy as they are expressed in legislation. This is not because the politics are democratic, but rather because they are focussed through a provincial lens rather than a metropolitan compass.

These tensions would not arise in such graphic form if the men who comprise the nation's political and economic elites were more similar in background and experience. While in no society can there be real homogeneity between these two groups, in a country like Great Britain political and economic leaders are far more similar in character. For this reason, legislation affecting the British economy can secure political ends with a high degree of effectiveness and at the same time gain the approval of the corporate institutions which are directly affected.[16] The American pattern, because it is more democratic, has been far less smooth in its operations. The provincial outlook which is represented in the Congress will, in the final analysis, have to bow to the power which inheres in our metropolitan institutions. Again and again, the lawmakers have been forced to admit—although not necessarily to understand—that there is nothing they can do to prevent the rise of corporations or to preserve in any meaningful way the provincial life. The debate will, of course, be conducted in muted tones; but the conflict is real. The elected elite will vainly try to devise ways and means of meeting the challenge of the men anointed with corporate power. As matters now stand they are incapable of licking them and unwilling to join them. If the legislators are to make any headway at all they will have to recast their image of economic reality from local to national terms. If they are unable to make such a revision they will be increasingly plagued with the sensations of frustration and bewilderment.

---

[15] Very little is known about the political attitudes of executives. For a sampling, see the "Report from 75 Presidents" published by Elmo Roper and Associates in their *The Public Pulse,* September, 1958, pp. 2-3.

[16] See Arnold A. Rogow, The Labor Government and British Industry (Ithaca, 1955). For a study of the relations between the business community and the nationalized industries in Great Britain, see Clive Jenkins, *Power at the Top* (London, 1959).

Issue Conflict and Consensus Among Party Leaders and Followers[1]

HERBERT MC CLOSKY, PAUL J. HOFFMAN, AND ROSEMARY O'HARA

American political parties are often regarded as "brokerage" organizations, weak in principle, devoid of ideology, and inclined to differ chiefly over unimportant questions. In contrast to the "ideological" parties of Europe—which supposedly appeal to their followers through sharply defined, coherent, and logically related doctrines—the American parties are thought to fit their convictions to the changing demands of the political contest.[2] According to this view, each set of American party leaders is satisfied to play Tweedledee to the other's Tweedledum.

I. PRESSURES TOWARD UNIFORMITY AND CLEAVAGE

Although these "conclusions" are mainly derived from *a priori* analysis or from casual observations of "anecdotal" data (little systematic effort having been

made so far to verify or refute them), they are often taken as confirmed—largely, one imagines, because they are compatible with certain conspicuous features is the entrenchment of a two-party system which, by affording both parties a genuine opportunity to win elections, tempts them to appeal to as many diverse elements in the electorate as are needed to put together a majority.[3] Since both parties want to attract support from the centrist and moderate segments of the electorate, their views on basic issues will, it is thought, tend to converge. Like giant business enterprises competing for the same market, they will be led to offer commodities that are in many respects identical.[4] It is one thing for a small party in a multi-party system to preserve its ideological purity, quite another for a mass party in a two-party system to do so. The one has little hope of becoming a majority, and can most easily survive by remaining identified with the narrow audience from which it draws its chief supporters; the other can succeed only by accommodating the conflicting claims of many diverse groups—only, in short, by blunting ideological distinctions.[5]

SOURCE. Reprinted from *The American Political Science Review*, Vol. 54, 1960, by permission of the author and publisher. Copyright 1960, The American Political Science Association.

---

[1] This article is the first of a series reporting the findings of a national field study of political belief and affiliation among American party leaders and followers. The study was carried out through the Laboratory for Research in Social Relations at the University of Minnesota under grants made to the senior author by the Committee on political Behavior of the Social Science Research Council, and supplementary grants from the Graduate School Research Fund. The manuscript was prepared at the Survey Research Center, University of California, Berkeley, under a Fellowship in Legal and Political Philosophy awarded to the senior author by the Rockefeller Foundation.

[2] Maurice Duverger, *Political Parties, their Organization and Activity in the Modern State* (New York, 1955), p. 102.

---

[3] The analysis of these and related tendencies associated with the American party system is ably set forth in Pendleton Herring, *The Politics of Democracy* (New York, 1940), p. 102 and *passim*. Also, James M. Burns, *Congress on Trial: The Legislative Process and the Administrative State* (New York, 1949), p. 34.

[4] See especially E. E. Schattschneider, *Party Government* (New York, 1942), p. 92 and *passim;* and V. O. Key, *Politics, Parties and Pressure Groups*, 4th ed. (New York, 1958), ch. 8; Howard R. Penniman, *Sait's American Parties and Elections*, 5th ed. (New York, 1952), p. 162.

[5] William Goodman, *The Two-Party System in the United States* (New Jersey, 1956), p. 43.

Constraints against enlarging intellectual differences also spring from the loosely confederated nature of the American party system, and from each national party's need to adjust its policies to the competing interests of the locality, the state, and the nation.[6] Many party units are more concerned with local than with national elections, and prefer not to be handicapped by clear-cut national programs. Every ambitious politician, moreover, hopes to achieve a *modus vivendi* tailored to the particular and often idiosyncratic complex of forces prevailing in his constituency, an objective rarely compatible with doctrinal purity.[7] Often, too, local politics are largely non-partisan or are partisan in ways that scarcely affect the great national issues around which ideologies might be expected to form.[8] The development and enforcement of a sharply delineated ideology is also hindered by the absence in either party of a firmly established, authoritative, and continuing organizational center empowered to decide questions of doctrine and discipline.[9] Party affiliation is loosely defined, responsibility is weak or nonexistent, and organs for indoctrinating or communicating with party members are at best rudimentary.

Cultural and historical differences may also contribute to the weaker ideological emphasis among American, as compared with European, parties. Many of the great historical cleavages that have divided European nations for centuries—monarchism vs. republicanism; clericalism vs. anti-clericalism; democracy vs. autocracy, etc.—have never taken root in this country. Apart from the slavery (and subsequently the race) issue, the United States has not experienced the intense class or caste conflict often found abroad,

and contests of the capitalism vs. socialism variety have never achieved an important role in American politics. In addition, never having known a titled nobility, we have largely been freed from the conflicts found elsewhere between the classes of inherited and acquired privilege.

Consider, too, the progress made in the United States toward neutralizing the forces which ordinarily lead to sharp social, and hence intellectual and political, differentiation. The class and status structure of American society has attained a rate of mobility equalling or exceeding that of any other long established society. Popular education, and other facilities for the creation of common attitudes, have been developed on a scale unequalled elsewhere. Improvements in transportation and communication, and rapid shifts in population and industry have weakened even sectionalism as a source of political cleavage. Rural-urban differences continue to exist, of course, but they too have been diminishing in force and have become less salient for American politics than the differences prevailing, for example, between a French peasant proprietor and a parisian *boulevardier*.[10] In short, a great many Americans have been subjected in their public lives to identical stimuli—a condition unlikely to generate strong, competing ideologies.

The research reported here was designed not to refute these observations but to test the accuracy of the claim that they are sufficient to prevent differences in outlook from taking root in the American party system. We believed that the homogenizing tendencies referred to are strongly offset by contrary influences, and that voters are preponderantly led to support the party whose opinions they share. We further thought that the competition for office, though giving rise to similarities between the parties, also impels them to diverge from each other in order to sharpen their respective appeals. For this and other reasons, we expected to find

---

[6] Duverger, op. cit., pp. 187, 418.
[7] Pendleton Herring, op. cit., p. 133.
[8] *American State Legislatures,* ed. Belle Zeller (New York, 1954); but see also Malcolm E. Jewell, "Party Voting in American State Legislatures," this *Review,* Vol. 49 (Sept. 1955), pp. 773-791.
[9] Report of the Committee on Political Parties, American Political Science Association, *Toward a More Responsible Two-Party System* (New York, 1960), *passim.*

[10] Data bearing on these generalizations will be presented in companion articles which especially deal with sectional and rural-urban influences on issue outlook.

that the leaders of the two parties, instead of ignoring differences alleged to exist within the electorate, would differ on issues more sharply than their followers would. We believed further that even in a brokerage system the parties would serve as independent reference groups, developing norms, values, and self-images to which their supporters could readily respond.[11] Their influence, we felt, would frequently exceed that of ethnic, occupational, residential and other reference groups. In sum, we proceeded on the belief that the parties are not simply spokesmen for other interest groups but are in their own right agencies for formulating, transmitting, and anchoring political opinions, that they attract adherents who in general share those opinions, and that through a feedback process of mutual reinforcement between the organization and its typical supporters, the parties develop integrated and stable political tendencies. Other hypotheses will be specified as we present and analyze our findings.

II. PROCEDURES

The questions considered in this paper were part of a large field study made in 1957-58 on the nature, sources, and correlates of political affiliation, activity, and belief in the American Party system (hereafter referred to as the PAB study). Pilot studies on Minnesota samples had led us to suspect that many "settled" notions about party affiliation and belief in America would not stand up under careful empirical scrutiny; further, we felt that little progress would be made in the exploration of this subject until a comprehensive portrait of party membership in America had been drawn. Ac-

cordingly, a nationwide study was launched to acquire a detailed description of party leaders and supporters, gathering data on their backgrounds, political experiences, personality characteristics, values, motivations, social and political attitudes, outlooks on key issues, and related matters.

For our samples of party "leaders" we turned to the Democratic and Republican national conventions, largely because they are the leading and most representative of the party organs, their delegates coming from every part of the United States and from every level of party and government activity. Our samples ranged from governors, senators, and national committeemen at the one end to precinct workers and local officials at the other. In the absence of comprehensive information about the characteristics of the party elites in America, no one can say how closely the convention delegates mirror the total party leadership. We felt it fair to assume, nevertheless, that the delegates represented as faithful a cross section of American party leadership as could be had without an extraordinary expenditure of money and labor. Using convention delegates as our universe of leaders also held some obvious advantages for research, since the composition of this universe (by name, address, party, state, sex, place of residence, and party or public office) can usually be ascertained from the convention calls. Of the 6,848 delegates and alternates available to be samples, 3,193 actually participated; 3,020 (1,788 Democrats and 1,232 Republicans) completed and returned questionnaires that were usable in all respects.[12] The proportion of returns was roughly equivalent for both sets of party leaders.

---

[11] Cf. James W. Prothro, Ernest Q. Campbell, and Charles M. Grigg, "Two Party Voting in the South: Class vs. Party Identification," this *Review*, Vol. 52 (March, 1958), pp. 131-139. Also, Peter H. Odegard and E. Allen Helms, *American Politics: A Study in Political Dynamics* (New York, 1947 ed.), pp. 809-821.

[12] This gratifying large number of returns of so lengthy and detailed a questionnaire was attained through a number of follow-up mailings and special letters. These and other procedures designed to check the adequacy of the sample will be fully described in the volume containing the report of the overall study. The difference in the number of returns from the two parties was largely a result of the greater number of Democratic delegates to begin with.

The rank and file sample, which we wanted both for its intrinsic value and for its utility as a control group, was obtained by special arrangement with the American Institute of Public Opinion. In January 1958, Gallup interviewers personally distributed our questionnaire to 2,917 adult voters in two successive national cross-section surveys. Some 1,610 questionnaires were filled out and returned, of which 1,484 were completely usable. This sample closely matched the national population on such characteristics as sex, gae, region, size of city, and party affiliation, and though it somewhat oversampled the upper educational levels, we considered it sufficiently large and representative for most of our purposes. Of the 1,484 respondents, 821 were Democratic supporters (629 "pure" Democrats, plus 192 whom we classified as "independent" Democrats) and 623 were Republican supporters (479 "pure" Republicans, plus 144 "independent" Republicans). Forty respondents could not be identified as adherents of either party.

The lengthy questionnaire developed for the study was designed to be self-administered. It contained, in addition to questions on the respondents' personal backgrounds, a number of queries on their political history and experience, their attitudes toward the party system and toward such related matters as party organization, discipline and responsibility, their self-images with regard to social class and liberalism-conservatism, their reference group identifications, and their views on party leadership and ideology. The largest part of the questionnaire consisted of 390 scale items, randomly arranged, which when sorted and scored fell into 47 scales for measuring the personality, attitude, and value characteristics of each of the respondents. We had validated and used all but three of these scales in earlier studies.

The questions most relevant for the present article were those which asked each respondent to express his attitudes toward twenty-four important national issues, and to state whether he believed support for each issue should be "in-creased," "decreased," or "remain as is." The list of issues and the responses of each sample will be found in Tables 2a through 2e, where for convenience of analysis, the issues have been grouped under five broad headings: Public Ownership, Government Regulation of the Economy, Equalitarianism and Human Welfare, Tax Policy and Foreign Policy.

In tabulating the results, we first scored each individual on each issue and then computed aggregate scores for all members of a given sample. To begin with, percentages were used to show the proportion who favored increasing, decreasing, or retaining the existing level of support on each issue. But as it was clumsy to hand three figures for each issue, we constructed a single index or "ratio of support" which would simultaneously take account of all three scores. The index was built by assigning a weight of 1.0 to each "increase" response in the sample, of 0 to each "decrease" response, and of .50 to each "remain as is" (or "same") response. Thus the ratio-of-support score shown for any given sample is in effect a mean score with a possible range of 0 to 1.0, in which support for an issue increases as the scores approach 1.0 and decreases as they approach 0. In general, the scores can be taken to approximate the following over-all positions: .0 to .25—strongly wish to reduce support; .26 to .45—wish to reduce support; .46 to .55—satisfied with the *status quo;* .56 to .75—wish to increase support; and .76 to 1.00—strongly wish to increase support. Note that the differences in degree suggested by these categories refer not to the *strength of feeling* exhibited by individuals toward an issue but rather to the *numbers of people* in a sample who hold points of view favoring or opposing that issue.

Because they include "same" and "no code" as well as "increase" and "decrease" responses, or ratios of support sometimes flatten the differences between groups. Had we employed only the percentage scores for the "increase" or "decrease" responses, the differences between samples would in many instances have seemed larger. Nevertheless, the ratio of support offers so many advantages that we have employed it as our principal measure. For one thing, as the equivalent of a mean score, it takes into account all scores, omitting no respondent from the tabulation. For the same reason it enables us to assess the amount of dispersion or homogeneity exhibited by any sample and makes it easy to calculate significances of difference.[13] Reliance upon a single, uniform statistic also allows us to make ready comparisons not only *between* but *within* samples, and to determine quickly how large the differences actually are. By observing whether a ratio of support is above or below .50 we can see at once whether a particular group predominantly favors or opposes the issue in question, and how strongly it does so. The use of ratio scores also makes it possible to compare issues as well as groups, e.g., to see whether one issue is more preferred than another.

For further information on the meaning of the issue responses, we also compared samples on a number of related scales and items. Tabulating and statistical operations were carried out to control for demographic influences like education, occupation, age, and sectionalism; to ascertain homogeneity of opinion within the several samples; to rank the issues according to the magnitude of the differences between samples; to compare members' positions on issues against official platform statements; and to determine whether leaders and followers are able to name the issues which actually

divide the parties. Some of the findings yielded by these operations will be considered here, while others, for reasons of space, will have to be reserved for future publications.

A word of caution before we turn to the findings. The respondents were offered only the twenty-four issues that impressed us in February, 1957, as most significant and enduring. However, they may not all be a salient today as they seemed at that time. Nor, within the limitations of a single questionnaire, could we explore every issue that informed observers might have considered important. Some presumably vital issues such as states rights, political centralization, and expansion of government functions could not be stated explicitly enough within our format to be tested properly. These are issues that are so generalized as to encompass many other specific issues, and so highly charged as to awaken a profusion of symbolic and emotive associations.

The *form* of our issue questions may also be open to criticism, for space limitations prevented our subjects from indicating how strongly they felt and how much they knew about each of the issues. This deficiency, however, may be less important than it appears, since for the groups we most wanted to compare (e.g., Democratic vs. Republican leaders), the degree of political knowledge and intensity is likely to be rather similar. The difficulty is greater when comparing leaders with followers, but is somewhat offset by controlling for education and socio-economic status. Although some subtleties of interpretation are bound to be lost because these variables have been omitted, we are satisfied that our issue questions in their present form furnish a useful measure for assessing *group* (as distinguished from *individual*) opinion. [See Table 1.]

Finally, one may wonder about the value of opinions stated on a questionnaire compared with the worth of views formally expressed by an organization or implicit in the actions of its leaders. Advantages can be cited on both sides. The

[13] The measure of dispersion used for this purpose was the standard deviation, which was computed by using the scores of 0, .50 and 1.00 as intervals in the calculations. To avoid having to calculate separate significances of difference for each of the comparisons we wanted to observe, we simply made the assumption— erring on the side of caution—that the maximum variance of .50 had occurred in each instance. The magnitude of the significance of difference is, in other words, often greater than we have reported. The significance test used in this procedure was the critical ratio. Unless otherwise indicated, all the differences reported are statistically significant at or beyond the .01 level.

TABLE 1. AVERAGE DIFFERENCES IN THE RATIO-OF-SUPPORT SCORES AMONG
PARTY LEADERS AND FOLLOWERS FOR FIVE CATEGORIES OF ISSUES

Category of Issues	Democratic Leaders vs. Republican Leaders	Democratic Followers vs. Republican Followers	Democratic Leaders vs. Democratic Followers	Republican Leaders vs. Republican Followers	Democratic Leaders vs. Republican Followers	Republican Leaders vs. Democratic Followers
a. Public ownership of resources	.28	.04	.06	.18	.10	.22
b. Government regulation of the economy	.22	.06	.08	.10	.12	.16
c. Equalitarianism, human welfare	.22	.05	.08	.21	.06	.25
d. Tax policy	.20	.06	.06	.20	.04	.26
e. Foreign policy	.15	.02	.05	.08	.07	.10
Average differences in ratio scores for all categories	.21	.04	.07	.15	.08	.20

Sample sizes: Democratic leaders, 1,788; Republican leaders, 1,232; Democratic followers, 821; Republican followers, 623.

beliefs expressed in official party statements, or in legislative roll calls, it might be claimed, represent the *operating* beliefs of the organization by virtue of having been tested in the marketplace or in the competition of legislative struggle. Positions taken on issues on which a party stakes its future may be more valid evidence of what the party truly believes than are the opinions expressed by individual members under conditions of maximum safety. On the other hand, the responses to the issue and attitude questions in the PAB study represent the anonymous, private opinions of party leaders and followers, uncomplicated by any need to make political capital to proselytize, to conciliate critics, or to find grounds for embarrassing the opposition at the next election. Hence they may for some purposes represent the most accurate possible reflection of the "actual" state of party opinion. The controversy over the value of the two approaches is to some extent spurious, however, for they offered different perspectives on the same thing. In addition, considerable correspondence exists between the party positions evident in congressional roll calls and the privately expressed opinions of the party in our study.[14]

III. FINDINGS: COMPARISONS BETWEEN LEADERS

No more conclusive findings emerge from our study of party issues than those growing out of the comparisons between the two sets of party leaders. Despite the brokerage tendency of the American parties, their active members are obvi-

[14] See, for example, the congressional roll-call results reported by Julius Turner, *Party and Constituency: Pressures on Congress*, The Johns Hopkins University Studies in Historical and Political Science Series, LXIX, #1 (1951). The complexities affecting the determination of party votes in Congress are thoroughly explored in David B. Truman, *The Congressional Party: A Case Study* (New York, 1959).

ously separated by large and important differences. The differences, moreover, conform with the popular image in which the Democratic party is seen as the more "progressive" or "radical," the Republican as the more "moderate" or "conservative" of the two.[15] In addition, the disagreements are remarkably consistent, a function not of chance but of systematic points of view, whereby the responses to any one of the issues could reasonably have been predicted from knowledge of the responses to the other issues.

Examination of Tables 2a-e and 3 shows that the leaders differ significantly on 23 of the 24 issues listed and that they are separated on 15 of these issues by .18 or more ratio points—in short, by differences that are in absolute magnitude very large. The two samples are furthest

[15] Conservatism is here used not in the classical but in the more popular sense, in which it refers to negative attitudes toward government ownership, intervention, and regulation of the economy; resistance to measures for promoting equalitarianism and social welfare through government action; identification with property, wealth, and business enterprise; etc.

apart in their attitudes toward public ownership and are especially divided on the question of government ownership of natural resources, the Democrats strongly favoring it, the Republicans just as strongly wanted it cut back. The difference of .39 in the ratio scores is the largest for any of the issues tested. In percentages, the differences are 58 per cent (D) vs. 13 per cent (R) in favor of increasing support, and 19 per cent (D) vs. 52 per cent (R) in favor of decreasing support. Both parties preponderantly support public control and development of atomic energy, but the Democrats do so more uniformly.

V. O. Key, among others, has observed that the Republican party is especially responsive to the "financial and manufacturing community,"[16] reflecting the view that the government should intervene as little as possible to burden or restrain prevailing business interests. The validity of this observation is evident throughout all our data, and is most clearly seen in the responses to the issues listed under Government Regulation of the Economy,

[16] Key, op. cit., p. 239.

TABLE 2a. COMPARISON OF PARTY LEADERS AND FOLLOWERS ON "PUBLIC OWNERSHIP" ISSUES, BY PERCENTAGES AND RATIOS OF SUPPORT

	Leaders		Followers	
Issues	Dem. (N-1788)	Repub. (N-1,232)	Dem. (N-821)	Repub. (N-623)
	(%s down)			
Public ownership of natural resources				
% favoring: Increase	57.5	12.9	35.3	31.1
Decrease	18.6	51.9	15.0	19.9
Same, n.c.[a]	23.8	35.2	49.7	49.0
Support ratio	.69	.30	.60	.56
Public control of atomic energy				
% favoring: Increase	73.2	45.0	64.2	59.4
Decrease	7.2	15.3	7.1	10.0
Same, n.c.	19.6	39.7	28.7	30.6
Support ratio	.83	.65	.79	.75
Mean support ratios for the public ownership category	.76	.48	.70	.66

[a] n.c.-no code.

TABLE 2b. COMPARISON OF PARTY LEADERS AND FOLLOWERS ON "GOVERNMENT
REGULATION OF THE ECONOMY" ISSUES, BY PERCENTAGES AND RATIOS OF SUPPORT

	Leaders		Followers	
Issues	Dem. (N-1788)	Repub. (N-1232)	Dem. (N-821)	Repub. (N-623)
		(%s down)		
Level of farm price supports				
% favoring: Increase	43.4	6.7	39.0	23.0
Decrease	28.1	67.4	27.6	40.3
Same, n.c.	28.5	25.8	33.4	36.7
Support ratio	.58	.20	.56	.41
Government regulation of business				
% favoring: Increase	20.2	0.6	18.6	7.4
Decrease	38.5	84.1	33.4	46.2
Same, n.c.	41.3	15.3	48.0	46.4
Support ratio	.41	.08	.43	.31
Regulation of public utilities				
% favoring: Increase	59.0	17.9	39.3	26.0
Decrease	6.4	17.6	11.1	12.0
Same, n.c.	34.6	64.5	49.6	62.0
Support ratio	.76	.50	.64	.57
Enforcement of anti-monopoly laws				
% favoring: Increase	78.0	44.9	53.2	51.0
Decrease	2.9	9.0	7.9	6.6
Same, n.c.	19.1	46.1	38.9	42.4
Support ratio	.88	.68	.73	.72
Regulation of trade unions				
% favoring: Increase	59.3	86.4	46.6	57.8
Decrease	12.4	4.5	8.9	10.6
Same, n.c.	28.3	9.2	44.5	31.6
Support ratio	.73	.91	.69	.74
Level of tariffs				
% favoring: Increase	13.0	19.2	16.6	15.2
Decrease	43.0	26.3	25.3	21.3
Same, n.c.	43.9	54.5	58.1	63.4
Support ratio	.35	.46	.46	.47
Restrictions on credit				
% favoring: Increase	24.8	20.6	26.1	25.7
Decrease	39.3	20.6	22.2	23.8
Same, n.c.	35.9	58.8	51.8	50.5
Support ratio	.43	.50	.52	.51
Mean support ratios for "Government Regulation of the Economy" category	.59	.48	.58	.53

TABLE 2c. COMPARISON OF PARTY LEADERS AND FOLLOWERS ON "EQUALITARIAN AND HUMAN WELFARE" ISSUES, BY PERCENTAGES AND RATIOS OF SUPPORT

	Leaders		Followers	
Issues	Dem. (N-1788)	Repub. (N-1232)	Dem. (N-821)	Repub. (N-623)
		(%s down)		
Federal aid to education				
% favoring: Increase	66.2	22.3	74.9	64.8
Decrease	13.4	43.2	5.6	8.3
Same, n.c.	20.4	34.5	19.5	26.8
Support ratio	.76	.40	.85	.78
Slum clearance and public housing				
% favoring: Increase	78.4	40.1	79.5	72.5
Decrease	5.6	21.6	5.8	7.9
Same, n.c.	16.0	38.3	14.6	19.6
Support ratio	.86	.59	.87	.82
Social security benefits				
% favoring: Increase	60.0	22.5	69.4	57.0
Decrease	3.9	13.1	3.0	3.8
Same, n.c.	36.1	64.4	27.5	39.2
Support ratio	.78	.55	.83	.77
Minimum wages				
% favoring: Increase	50.0	15.5	59.0	43.5
Decrease	4.7	12.5	2.9	5.0
Same, n.c.	45.2	72.0	38.1	51.5
Support ratio	.73	.52	.78	.69
Enforcement of integration				
% favoring: Increase	43.8	25.5	41.9	40.8
Decrease	26.6	31.7	27.4	23.6
Same, n.c.	29.5	42.8	30.7	35.6
Support ratio	.59	.47	.57	.59
Immigration into United States				
% favoring: Increase	36.1	18.4	10.4	8.0
Decrease	27.0	29.9	52.0	44.6
Same, n.c.	36.9	51.7	37.6	47.4
Support ratio	.54	.44	.29	.32
Mean support ratios for 'Equalitarian and Human Welfare" category	.71	.50	.70	.66

Equalitarianism and Human Welfare, Tax Policy. Democratic leaders are for more eager than Republican leaders to strengthen enforcement of anti-monopoly laws and to increase regulation of public utilities and business. Indeed, the solidar-ity of Republican opposition to the regulation of business is rather overwhelming: 84 per cent want to decrease such regulation and fewer than .01 per cent say they want to increase it. Although the Democrats, on balance, also feel that

Table 2d. Comparison of Party Leaders and Followers on "Tax Policy" Issues, by Percentages and Ratios of Support

Issues	Leaders		Followers	
	Dem. (N-1788)	Repub. (N-1232)	Dem. (N-821)	Repub. (N-623)
		(%s down)		
Corporate income tax				
% favoring: Increase	32.3	4.0	32.0	23.3
Decrease	23.3	61.5	20.5	25.7
Same, n.c.	44.4	34.5	47.5	51.0
Support ratio	.54	.21	.56	.49
Tax on large incomes				
% favoring: Increase	27.0	5.4	46.6	34.7
Decrease	23.1	56.9	13.8	21.7
Same, n.c.	49.9	37.7	39.6	43.6
Support ratio	.52	.24	.66	.56
Tax on business				
% favoring: Increase	12.6	1.0	24.6	15.9
Decrease	38.3	71.1	24.1	32.6
Same, n.c.	49.1	27.8	51.3	51.5
Support ratio	.37	.15	.50	.42
Tax on middle incomes				
% favoring: Increase	2.7	0.8	4.5	3.0
Decrease	50.2	63.9	49.3	44.3
Same, n.c.	47.1	35.3	46.2	52.6
Support ratio	.26	.18	.28	.29
Tax on small incomes				
% favoring: Increase	1.4	2.9	1.6	2.1
Decrease	79.2	65.0	77.5	69.6
Same, n.c.	19.4	32.1	20.9	28.3
Support ratio	.11	.19	.12	.16
Mean support ratios for "Tax Policy" category	.36	.19	.42	.38

government controls on business should not be expanded further, the differences between the two samples on this issue are nevertheless substantial.

The two sets of leaders are also far apart on the farm issue, the Democrats preferring slightly to increase farm support, the Republicans wanting strongly to reduce them. The Republican ratio score of .20 on this issue is among the lowest in the entire set of scores. The magnitude of these scores somewhat surprised us, for while opposition to agricultural subsidies is consistent with

Republican dislike for state intervention, we had expected the leaders to conform more closely to the familiar image of the Republican as the more "rural" of the two parties.[17] It appears, however, that

---

[17] The friendlier attitude toward farmers among Democratic leaders than Republican leaders is borne out in the responses to several other questions used in the study. For example, the Republican leaders list farmers as having "too much power" far more frequently that do the Democratic leaders. Equally, the Democrats are significantly more inclined to regard farmers as having "too little power."

TABLE 2e. COMPARISON OF PARTY LEADERS AND FOLLOWERS ON "FOREIGN POLICY" ISSUES, BY PERCENTAGES AND RATIOS OF SUPPORT

Issues	Leaders		Followers	
	Dem. (*N*-1788)	Repub. (*N*-1232)	Dem. (*N*-821)	Repub. (*N*-623)
	(%s down)			
Reliance on the United Nations				
% favoring: Increase	48.9	24.4	34.7	33.4
Decrease	17.6	34.8	17.3	19.3
Same, n.c.	33.5	40.7	48.0	47.3
Support ratio	.66	.45	.59	.57
American participation in military alliance				
% favoring: Increase	41.5	22.7	39.1	32.3
Decrease	17.6	25.7	14.0	15.4
Same, n.c.	40.9	51.6	46.9	52.3
Support ratio	.62	.48	.62	.58
Foreign aid				
% favoring: Increase	17.8	7.6	10.1	10.1
Decrease	51.0	61.7	58.6	57.3
Same, n.c.	31.1	30.7	31.3	32.6
Support ratio	.33	.23	.26	.26
Defense spending [a]				
% favoring: Increase	20.7	13.6	50.5	45.7
Decrease	34.4	33.6	16.4	15.4
Same, n.c.	44.8	52.8	33.0	38.8
Support ratio	.43	.40	.67	.65
Mean support ratios for "Foreign Policy" category (excl. defense spending)	.54	.39	.49	.47

[a] See footnote 23.

the party's connection with business is far more compelling than its association with agriculture. The Republican desire to reduce government expenditures and to promote independence from "government handouts" prevails on the farm question as it does on other issues, while the Democratic preference for a more regulated economy in which government intervenes to reduce economic risk and to stabilize prosperity is equally evident on the other side. Part attitudes on this issue appear to be determined as much by ideological tendencies as by deliberate calculation of the political advantages to be gained by favoring or opposing subsidies to farmers. Comparison of our findings with Turner's earlier data on farm votes in Congress[18] suggests, in addition, that the sharp party difference on the farm issue is neither a recent development nor a mere product of the personal philosophy of the present Secretary of Agriculture.

Having implied that agricultural policies partly result from principle, we must note that on three other issues in this

[18] Turner, op. cit., p. 64.

category (trade unions, credit, and tariffs), principle seems to be over-weighed by old-fashioned economic considerations. In spite of their distaste for government interference in economic affairs, the Republicans almost unanimously favor greater regulation of trade unions and they are more strongly disposed than the Democrats toward government intervention to restrict credit and to raise tariffs. Of course, party cleavages over the credit and tariff issues have a long history,[19] which may by now have endowed them with ideological force beyond immediate economic considerations.[20] The preponderant Democratic preference for greater regulation of trade unions is doubtless a response to recent "exposures" of corrupt labor practices, though it may also signify that the party's perspective toward the trade unions is shifting somewhat.

The closer Republican identification with business, free enterprise, and economic conservatism in general, and the friendlier Democratic attitude toward labor and toward government regulation of the economy, are easily observed in the data from other parts of our questionnaire. Republican leaders score very much higher than Democratic leaders on, for example, such scales as economic conservatism, independence of government, and business attitudes. On a question asking respondents to indicate the groups from which they would be most and least likely to take advice, 41 per cent of the Democratic leaders but only 3.8 per cent of the Republican leaders list trade unions as groups from which they would seek advice. Trade unions are scored in the "least likely" category by 25 per cent of the Democrats and 63 per cent of the Republicans.

Similarly, more than 94 per cent of the Republican leaders, but 56 per cent of the Democratic leaders, name trade unions as groups that have "too much power." These differences, it should be noted, cannot be accounted for by reference to the greater number of trade union members among the Democratic party leadership, for in the 1965 conventions only 14 per cent of the Democrats belonged to trade unions and while an even smaller percentage (4 per cent) of the Republicans were trade unionists, this disparity is hardly great enough to explain the large differences in outlook. The key to the explanation has to be sought in the symbolic and reference group identifications of the two parties, and in their underlying values.

Nowhere do we see this more clearly than in the responses to the Equalitarian and Human Welfare issues. The mean difference in the ratio scores for the category as a whole is .22, a very large difference and one that results from differences in the expected direction on all six issues that make up the category. On four of these issues—federal aid to education, slum clearance and public housing, social security, and minimum wages—the leaders of the two parties are widely separated, the differences in their ratio scores ranging from .36 to .21. The percentages showing the proportions who favor increased support for these issues are even more striking. In every instance the Democratic percentages are considerably higher: 66 vs. 22 per cent (education); 78 vs. 40 per cent (slum clearance and housing); 60 vs. 23 per cent (social security); and 50 vs. 16 per cent (minimum wages). The Democratic leaders also are better disposed than the Republican leaders toward immigration: twice as many of them (36 per cent vs. 18 per cent) favor a change in policy to permit more immigrants to enter. The over-all inclination of both party elites however, is to accept the present levels of immigration, the Democratic ratio score falling slightly above, and the Republican slightly below, the mid-point.

More surprising are the differences on

[19] See John B. Johnson, Jr., *The Extent and Consistency of Party Voting in the United States Senate,* PhD. thesis, University of Chicago, 1943. By applying the Rice Index-of-Likeness to Senate votes, Johnson finds the tariff to have been the most partisan issue before the Congress in the years 1880-1940.
[20] Corinne Silverman, "The Legislator's View of the Legislative Process," *Public Opinion Quarterly,* Vol. 18 (1954-1955), p. 180.

the segregation issue, for, despite strong Southern influence, the Democratic leaders express significantly more support for enforcing integration than the Republicans do. Moreover, the difference between the two parties rises from .12 for the national samples as a whole to a difference of .18 when the southern leaders are excluded. In his study of Congress, Turner found that the Republicans gave more support to Negro rights than the Democrats did.[21] The reversal of this finding in our data does not necessarily mean that a change has occurred since Turner made his study, but only that the votes of the congressional parties do not always reflect the private feelings of the national party leadership. Then, too, Southern influence is disproportionately stronger in the Democratic congressional party than in the national Democratic organization as a whole, and disproportionately weaker in the Republican congressional party than in the Republican organization as a whole.

Examination of the actual magnitude of the ratio scores in this category reveals that the Republicans want not so much to abrogate existing social welfare or equalitarian measures as to keep them from being broadened. The Democrats, by comparison, are shown to be the party of social equality, and reform, more willing than their opponents to employ legislation for the benefit of the underprivileged. Support for these inferences and for the greater liberalism of the Democrats can be found elsewhere in our data as well. Analysis of the scale results show Republican leaders scoring higher than Democratic leaders on such measures as chauvinism, elitism, conservatism, and right-wing values, and lower on tolerance, procedural rights, and faith in democracy. No differences worth noting, however, were found for ethnocentrism, faith in freedom, or the California F scale. The Democrats had a slightly higher average score on the left-wing scale, but the number of leaders in either party who scored high on this measure was fairly small.

[21] Turner, op. cit., p. 54.

The self-images and reference group identifications of the two parties also should be noted in this connection. For example, many more Democratic than Republican leaders call themselves liberal and state that they would be most likely to take advice from liberal reform organizations, the Farmers' Union, and (as we have seen) from the trade unions; only a small number consider themselves conservative or would seek advice from conservative reform organizations, the National Association of Manufacturers, or the Farm Bureau Federation. The Republicans have in almost all instances the reverse identifications; only a handful regard themselves as liberal or would seek counsel from liberal organizations, while more than 42 per cent call themselves conservative and would look to the NAM or to conservative reform organizations for advice. Almost two-thirds of the Republicans (compared with 29 per cent of the Democrats) regard the Chamber of Commerce as an important source of advice. Businessmen are listed as having "too much power" by 42 per cent of the Democrats but by only 9 per cent of the Republicans. The Democrats are also significantly more inclined than the Republicans to consider Catholics, Jews, and the foreign born as having "too little power." While self-descriptions and reference group identifications often correspond poorly with actual beliefs— among the general population they scarcely correspond at all, in fact—we are dealing, in the case of the leaders, with a politically informed and highly articulate set of people who have little difficulty connecting the beliefs they hold and the groups that promote or obstruct those beliefs.

Our fourth category, Tax Policy, divides the parties almost as severely as do the other categories. The mean difference for the category as a whole is .20, and it would doubtless have been larger but for the universal unpopularity of proposals to increase taxes on small and middle income groups. Table 2d shows that the differences between the parties on the tax issues follow the patterns previously observed and that tax policy is for the Democrats a device for redistributing income and promoting social equality. Neither party, however, is keen about raising taxes for *any* group; even the Democrats have little enthusiasm for new taxes on upper income groups or on business and corporate enterprises. The Republican leaders are overwhelmingly opposed to increased taxes for *any* group, rich *or* poor. This can be seen in their low ratio scores on the tax issues, which range from only .15 to .24. But while they are far more eager than the Democratic leaders to cut taxes on corporate and private wealth, they are less willing to reduce taxes on the lower income groups. These differences, it should be remarked, are not primarily a function of differences in the income of the two samples. Although there are more people with high incomes among the Republican leaders, the disproportion between the two samples is not nearly great enough to account for the dissimilarities in their tax views.

Of the five categories considered, Foreign Policy shows the smallest average difference, but even on these issues the divergence between Democratic and Republican leader attitudes is significant. Except for defense spending the Democrats turn out to be more internationalist than the Republicans, as evidenced in their greater commitment to the United Nations and to American participation in international military alliances like NATO. Twice as many Democrats as Republicans want the United States to rely more heavily upon such organizations, while many more Republicans want to reduce our international involvements. Both parties are predominantly in favor of cutting back foreign aid—a somewhat surprising finding in light of Democratic public pronouncements on this subject— but more Republicans feel strongly on the subject. Our data thus furnish little support for the claim that the parties hold the same views on foreign policy or that their seeming differences are merely a response to the demands of political competition.[22]

Nevertheless, it would be incorrect to conclude that one party believes in internationalism and the other in isolationism. The differences are far too small to warrant any such inference. Traces of isolationism, to be sure, remain stronger in the Republican party than in the Democratic party—an observation buttressed by the finding that twice as many Republicans as Democrats score high on the isolationism scale. The pattern of Republican responses on both the issue and scale items signifies, however, that the leaders of that party generally accept the degree of "internationalism" now, in effect, but shrink from extending it further. Consider too, the similarities in the leaders' scores on defense spending, for despite their greater leaning toward isolationism, the Republicans are no more inclined than the Democrats to leave the country defenseless.[23]

In treating issues in the Elmira election

[22] Cf. Turner, op. cit., p. 56, in which he found differences on foreign policy difficult to assess in Congress, partly because of its tie with the executive branch; see also George Belknap and Angus Campbell, "Political Party Identification and Attitudes toward Foreign Policy," *Public Opinion Quarterly*, Vol. 15 (Winter, 1951-52), pp. 608-619.
[23] The issue of defense spending has been kept separate from the other foreign policy issues because the magnitude of the scores for some of the leaders and all of the followers were obviously inflated by the launching of Sputnik I in November, 1957. The Sputnik incident occurred between the first and second wave of the leader survey and produced an increase in the number favoring defense spending of 40 per cent for the Democrats and 33 per cent for the Republicans. While this is a fascinating testimonial to the influence sometimes exercised by events on public opinion, its effect in this case was to distort scores in such a way as to make the leader and follower samples non-comparable. With proper caution, however, comparisons can be made between the Democratic and Republican leaders since both samples were affected in roughly the same way by Sputnik. For a similar reason we can also compare the Democratic followers with the Republican followers. Comparisons between leaders and followers on this issue cannot, however, be justified from our data.

study of 1948, Berelson, Lazarsfeld, and McPhee [24] found it helpful to distinguish between "style" and "position" issues. "Style" issues principally yield symbolic, psychological or subjective gratifications, and have relatively intangible consequences; "position" issues reflect direct, personal and material interests, and have more objective consequences. According to the Elmira report, "position" issues (or what politicians might call "bread and butter" issues) divide voters more sharply than style issues. Most of the issues tested in the present study would have to be classified as "position" issues, but five of them—United Nations, international alliances, foreign aid, immigration, and segregation—could be classified as style issues. Four others—natural resources, atomic energy, education, and slum clearance—contain both symbolic and material elements and can best be described as "mixed."

Although the classification is crude, the findings it yields are generally consistent with the claims of the Elmira study. On the fourteen position issues— taxes, trade unions, tariffs, minimum wages, farm prices, social security, credit restrictions, and the regulation of business, public utilities and monopolies— Democratic and Republican leaders show an average ratio score difference of .21. On the style issues the two parties differ by .13—a significantly smaller difference. Largest of all, however, are the differences for the "mixed" issues, which average more than .30. This result should occasion little surprise, for when ideology and interest are *both* at work, partisanship is likely to be intensified. Several considerations could account for the superiority of position over style issues as causes of political cleavage: they are "bread and butter" issues, and are thus more often subject to pressure by organized interest groups; they have immediate and tangible consequences, which may lead politicians to pay greater attention to them than they do to issues whose payoff is

[24] Bernard R. Berelson, Paul F. Lazarfeld, and William N. McPhee, *Voting* (Chicago, 1954), ch. 9.

more uncertain; and, finally, they are not so likely to be part of the common core of values upon which the community structure rests.

Comparison of the magnitude of the differences between groups can be seen in Table 3, where we have ranked the issues, high to low, according to the size of the difference between the groups being compared. By presenting a rank-order of differences for the two leader groups, For the two follower groups, and for the leaders and followers of each party, this table makes it possible to observe not only which issues most and least divide the several party groups, but whether they divide the leaders and followers in the same way.

Notice that the issues commonly thought to be most divisive do not always evoke the greatest cleavage between the parties. Immigration, tariffs, civil rights, monopoly control, and credit regulation fall toward the lower end of the rank order, while farm supports, federal aid to education, slum clearance, social security, minimum wages, public housing, and issues dealing with the regulation and taxation of business fall toward the upper end. Though by no means uniformly, the older, more traditional issues appear to have been superseded as sources of controversy by issues that have come into prominence chiefly during the New Deal and Fair Deal.

IV. COMPARISONS BETWEEN FOLLOWERS

So far we have addressed ourselves to the differences between Democratic and Republican *leaders*. In each of the tables presented, however, data are included from which the two sets of party *followers* may also be compared.

The observation most clearly warranted from these data is that the rank and file members of the two parties are far less divided than their leaders. Not only do they diverge significantly on fewer issues —seven as compared with 23 for leader samples—but the magnitudes of the differences in their ratio scores are substantially smaller for every one of the 24 issues. No difference is larger than .14, and on the majority of the issues the disparity is smaller than .05. Insofar as they differ at all, however, the followers tend to divide in a pattern similar to that shown by the leaders, the correlation between their rank orders being .72. All the issues on which the followers significantly disagree are of the "bread and butter" variety, the more symbolic issues being so remotely experienced and so vaguely grasped that rank and file voters are often unable to identify them with either party. Policies affecting farm prices, business regulation, taxes, or minimum wages, by contrast, are quickly felt by the groups to whom they are addressed and are therefore more capable of arousing partisan identifications. It should also be noted that while the average differences are small for all five categories, they are smallest of all for foreign policy—the most removed and least well understood group of issues in the entire array.[25]

Democratic and Republican followers were also compared on a number of scales and reference group questions. The results, while generally consistent with the differences between the leaders, show the followers to be far more united than their leaders on these measures as well. Even on business attitudes, independence of government, and economic conservatism, the differences are small and barely significant. No differences were found on such scales as tolerance, faith in democracy, procedural rights, conservatism-liberalism

(classical), the California F scale and isolationism. The average Democrat is slightly more willing than the average Republican to label himself a liberal or to seek advice from liberal organizations; the contrary is true when it comes to adopting conservative identifications. Only in the differential trust they express toward business and labor are the two sets of followers widely separated.

These findings give little support to the claim that the "natural divisions" of the electorate are being smothered by party leaders.[26] Not only do the leaders disagree more sharply than their respective followers, but the level of consensus among the electorate (with or without regard to party) is fairly high. Inspection of the "increase" and "decrease" percentage scores (Tables 2a-c) shows that substantial differences of opinion exist among the electorate on only five of the 24 issues (credit restrictions, farm supports, segregation, and corporate and business taxes). Of course, voters may divide more sharply on issues at election time, since campaigns intensify party feeling and may also intensify opinions on issues. Availbale data from election studies allow no unequivocal conclusion on this point,[27] but even the party-linked differences found among voters during elections may largely be echoes of the opinions announced by the candidates—transient sentiments developed for the occasion and quickly forgotten.

---

[25] For comparative data on party affiliation and issue outlooks among rank and file voters, see Angus Campbell, Phillip E. Converse, Warren E. Miller, and Donald E. Stokes, *The American Voter* (in press), especially chs. 8 and 9 dealing with issues and ideology. The text of this important report on the 1956 election study carried out by the Michigan Survey Research Center unfortunately reached us too late to be used to full advantage in the present analysis. The findings of the Michigan and the PAB studies, relative to the role of issues and ideology among the general population, corroborate and supplement each other to a very great degree.

[26] Cf. Stephen K. Bailey, *The Condition of Our National Parties* (monograph), Fund for the Republic, 1959.

[27] The data reported by the Elmira study of 1948 show the supporters of the two parties to be largely in agreement on issues. See Berelson, et al., *Voting*, pp. 186, 190, 194, 211. The findings of the 1956 Michigan Survey suggest strongly that most voters, even at election time, do not know much about issues and are unable to link the parties with particular issues. Campbell and his associates conclude, for example, that "many people fail to appreciate that an issue exists; other are insufficiently involved to pay attention to recognized issues; and still others fail to make connections between issue positions and party policy." *The American Voter*, ch. 8.

VI. LEADER CONFLICT AND FOLLOWER CONSENSUS: EXPLANATIONS

Considering the nature of the differences between the leader and follower samples, the interesting question is not why the parties fail to represent the "natural division" in the electorate (for that question rests on an unwarranted assumption) but why the party elites disagree at all, and why they divide so much more sharply than their followers?

Despite the great pressure toward uniformity we have noted in American society, many forces also divide the population culturally, economically, and politically. The United States is, after all, a miscellany of ethnic and religious strains set down in a geographically large and diverse country. Many of these groups brought old conflicts and ideologies with them, and some have tried to act out in the new world, the hopes and frustrations nurtured in the old. Then, too, despite rapid social mobility, social classes have by no means been eliminated. No special political insight is needed to perceive that the two parties characteristically draw from different strata of the society, the Republicans from the managerial, proprietary, and to some extent professional classes, the Democrats from labor, minorities, low income groups, and a large proportion of the intellectuals.[28] Partly because the leaders of the two parties tend to overrespond to the modal values of the groups with which they are principally identified, they gradually grow further apart on the key questions which separate their respective supporters.[29] The Republican emphasis on business ideology is both a cause and a consequence of its managerial and proprietary support; the greater Democratic emphasis on social

justice, and on economic and social levelling, is both the occasion and the product of the support the party enjoys among intellectuals an dthe lower strata. These interrelationships are strengthened, moreover, by the tendency for a party's dominant supporters to gain a disproportionate number of positions in its leadership ranks.[30]

The differences which typically separate Democratic from Republican leaders seem also to reflect a deep-seated ideological cleavage often found among Western parties. One side of this cleavage is marked by a strong belief in the power of collective action to promote social justice, equality, humanitarianism, and economic planning, while preserving freedom; the other is distinguished by faith in the wisdom of the natural competitive process and in the supreme virtue of individualism, "character," self-reliance, frugality, and independence from government. To this cleavage is added another frequent source of political division, namely, a difference in attitude toward change between "radicals" and "moderates," between those who prefer to move quickly or slowly, to reform or to conserve. These differences in social philosophy and posture do not always coincide with the divisions in the social structure, and their elements do not, in all contexts, combine in the same way. But, however crudely, the American parties do tend to embody these competing points of view and to serve as reference groups for those who hold them.

Party cleavage in America was no doubt intensified by the advent of the New Deal, and by its immense electoral and intellectual success. Not only did it weld into a firm alliance the diverse forces that were to be crucial to all subsequent Democratic majorities, but it also made explicit the doctrines of the "welfare state" with which the party was henceforth to be inseparably identified. Because of the novelty of its program and its apparently radical threat to the familiar patterns of American political

[28] For an analysis of the connection between intellectuals and liberal politics, see Seymour M. Lipset, *Political Man* (New York, 1960), ch. 10; also Paul F. Lazasfeld and Wagner Thielens, Jr., *The Academic Mind* (Glencoe, 1958), chs. 1 and 2.

[29] Samuel P. Huntington, "A Revised Theory of American Party Politics," this *Review*, Vol. 44 (1950), p. 676.

[30] PAB data supporting this generalization will be presented in a future publication.

and economic life, it probably deepened the fervor of its Republican adversaries and drove into the opposition the staunchest defenders of business ideology. The conflict was further sharpened by the decline of left-wing politics after the war, and by the transfer of loyalties of former and potential radicals to the Democratic party. Once launched, the cleavage has been sustained by the tendency for each party to attract into its active ranks as a disproportionate number of voters who recognize and share its point of view.

Why, however, are the leaders so much more sharply divided than their followers? The reasons are not hard to understand and are consistent with several of the hypotheses that underlay the present study.

(1) Consider, to begin with, that the leaders come from the more articulate segments of society and, on the average, are politically more aware than their followers and far better informed about issues.[31] For them, political issues and opinions are the everyday currency of party competition, not esoteric matters that surpass understanding. With their greater awareness and responsibility, and their greater need to defend their party's stands, they have more interest in developing a consistent set of attitudes— perhaps even an ideology. The followers of each party, often ignorant of the issues and their consequences, find it difficult to distinguish their beliefs from those of the opposition and have little reason to be concerned with the consistency of their attitudes. Furthermore, the American parties make only a feeble effort to educate the rank and file politically, and since no central source exists for the authoritative pronouncement of party policy,[32] the followers often do not know what their leaders believe or on what issues the parties chiefly divide. In short, if we mean by ideology a coherent body of informed social doctrine, it is pos-

sessed mainly by the articulate leadership, rarely by the masses.

(2) Differences in the degree of partisan involvement parallel the differences in knowledge and have similar consequences. The leaders, of course, have more party spirit than the followers and, as the election studies make plain, the stronger to partisanship, the larger the differences on issues. The leaders are more highly motivated not only to belong to a party appropriate to their beliefs, but to accept its doctrines and to learn how it differs from the opposition party. Since politics is more salient for leaders than for followers, they develop a greater stake in the outcome of the political contest and are more eager to discover the intellectual grounds by which they hope to make victory possible. Through a process of circular reinforcement, those for whom politics is most important are likely to become the most zealous participants, succeeding to the posts that deal in the formation of opinion. Ideology serves the instrumental purpose, in addition, of justifying the heavy investment that party leaders make in political activity. While politics offers many rewards, it also makes great demands on the time, money, and energies of its practitioners—sacrifices which they can more easily justify if they believe they are serving worthwhile social goals. The followers, in contrast, are intellectually far less involved, have less personal stake in the outcome of the competition, have little need to be concerned with the "correctness" of their views on public questions, and have even less reason to learn in precisely what ways their opinions differ from their opponents. Hence, the party elites recruit members from a population stratified in some measure by ideology, while the rank and file renews itself by more random recruitment and is thus more likely to mirror the opinions of a cross section of the population.

(3) Part of the explanation for the greater consensus among followers than leaders resides in the nature and size of the two types of groups. Whereas the leader groups are comparatively small and

---

[31] For the effects of education on issue familiarity, see Campbell et al., *The American Voter*, ch. 8.

[32] E. E. Schattschneider, op cit.; *Toward A More Responsible Two Party System, passim.*

selective, each of the follower groups number in the millions and, by their very size and unwieldiness, are predisposed to duplicate the characteristics of the population as a whole. Even if the Republicans draw disproportionately from the business-managerial classes and the Democrats from the trade union movement, neither interest group has enough influence to shape distinctively the aggregate opinions of so large a mass of supporters. Size also affects the nature and frequency of interaction within the two types of groups. Because they comprise a smaller, more selectively chosen, organized, and articulate elite, the leaders are apt to associate with people of their own political persuasion more frequently and consistently than the followers do. They are not only less cross-pressured than the rank and file but they are also subjected to strong party group efforts to induce them to conform. Because their political values are continually renewed through frequent communication with people of like opinions, and because they acquire intense reference group identifications, they develop an extraordinary ability to resist the force of the opposition's arguments. While the followers, too, are thrown together and shielded to some extent, they are likely to mingle more freely with people of hostile political persuasions, to receive fewer partisan communications, and to hold views that are only intermittently and inconsistently reinforced. Since, by comparison with the leaders, they possess little interest in or information about politics, they can more easily embrace "deviant" attitudes without discomfort and without challenge from their associates. Nor are they likely to be strongly rewarded for troubling to have "correct" opinions. The followers, in short, are less often and less effectively indoctrinated than their leaders. The group processes described here would function even more powerfully in small, sectarian, tightly organized parties of the European type, but they are also present in the American party system, where they yield similar though less potent consequences.

(4) Political competition itself operates to divide the leaders more than the followers. If the parties are impelled to present a common face to the electorate, they are also strongly influenced to distinguish themselves from each other.[33] For one thing, they have a more heightened sense of the "national interest" than the followers do, even if they do not all conceive it in the same way. For another, they hope to improve their chances at the polls by offering the electorate a recognizable and attractive commodity. In addition, they seek emotional gratification in the heightened sense of brotherhood brought on by the struggle against an "out-group" whose claim to office seems always, somehow, to border upon usurpation. As with many ingroup-outgroup distinctions, the participants search for moral grounds to justify their antagonisms toward each other, and ideologies help to furnish such grounds. Among the followers, on the other hand, these needs exist, if at all, in much weaker form.

VI. LEADERS VERSUS FOLLOWERS

In comparing each party elite with its own followers we were mainly interested in seeing how closely each body of supporters shared the point of view of its leaders, in order to test the hypothesis that party affiliation, even for the rank and file, is a function of ideological agreement. In predicting that the parties would tend to attract supporters who share their beliefs, we expected, of course, to find exceptions. We knew that many voters pay little attention to the ideological aspects of politics and that, in Gabriel Almond's phrase, a party's more "esoteric doctrines" are not always known to its followers.[34] Nevertheless we were not prepared for the findings turned up by this phase of the inquiry, for the differences

---

[33] See E. E. Schattschneider, *Party Government*, p. 192.

[34] Gabriel Almond, *The Appeals of Communism* (Princeton, 1954), pp. 5-6, and ch. 3.

between leaders and followers—among the Republicans at least—are beyond anything we had expected. Indeed, the conclusion is inescapable that the views of the Republican rank and file are, on the whole, much closer to those of the Democratic leaders than to those of the Republican leaders. Although conflict in outlook also exist between Democratic leaders and followers, they are less frequent or severe.

If we turn once again to the table of rank order differences, we see that the Democratic followers differ significantly from their leaders on twelve of the 23 issues, and that the average difference in the ratio scores of the two samples is .07. Democratic leaders and Republican followers differ significantly on only eleven of the 23 issues, with an average difference between them of only .08. Notice, by contrast, that Republican leaders and followers diverge significantly on 18 of the 23 issues, and show an average difference of .16. To complete the comparison, the Republican leaders and Democratic followers were in disagreement on 19 of the 23 issues, their average difference being .20. As these comparisons make plain, there is substantial consensus on national issues between Democratic leaders and Democratic and Republican followers, while the Republican leaders are separated not only from the Democrats but from their own rank and file members as well.

Examination of the Democratic scores shows the leaders to be slightly more "progressive" than their followers on most of the issues on which differences appear. The leaders are, for example, more favorable to public ownership of natural resources, to regulation of monopolies and public utilities, to a reduction of tariffs, and to a liberalized credit policy. They are more internationalist on the foreign aid and United Nations issues and substantially more sympathetic to the maintenance and expansion of immigration. The results showing the relative radicalism of the two samples are not unequivocal, however, for on several issues— federal aid to education, minimum wages,

and taxes on business enterprise and large incomes—the followers take the more radical view. Nor are the differences significant on such issues as atomic energy, slum clearance, segregation, farm price supports, government control of business and trade unions, and taxes on middle and small income groups. In general, the followers turn out more radical chiefly on a few of the bread and butter issues—a reflection, no doubt, of their lower socio-economic status. When we control for occupation, the differences between Democratic leaders and followers on these issues largely disappear.

Consideration of the scores of Republican leaders and followers shows not only that they are widely separated in their outlooks but also that the leaders are uniformly more conservative than their followers. Only on the immigration issue is this trend reversed. The followers hold the more "radical" ideas on the two public ownership issues, on five of the six equalitarian and human welfare issues, on four of the seven regulation-of-the-economy issues, and on four of the five tax policy issues. They are also more willing to place greater reliance upon the U.N. and upon international military alliances. Observe that the largest differences occur on those issues which have most sharply separated New Deal-Fair Deal spokesmen from the hard core of the Republican opposition—federal aid to education, redistribution of wealth through taxes on business, corporations and the wealthy, public ownership of natural resources, public housing, regulation of business, social security, farm price supports, minimum wages, and trade union regulations.

In short, whereas Republican leaders hold to the tenets of business ideology and remain faithful to the spirit and intellectual mood of leaders like Robert A. Taft, the rank and file Republican supporters have embraced, along with their Democratic brethren, the regulatory and social reform measures of the Roosevelt and Truman administrations. This inference receives further support from the scores on our Party Ideology scale

TABLE 3. RANK ORDER OF DIFFERENCES IN THE SUPPORT-RATIO SCORES OF PARTY AND FOLLOWERS[a]

#	Democratic vs. Republican Leaders — Issues	Diff. Between Ratio Scores[c]	Democratic vs. Republican Followers — Issues	Diff. Between Ratio Scores	Democratic Leaders vs. Followers — Issues	Diff. Between Ratio Scores	Republican Leaders vs. Followers — Issues	Diff. Between Ratio Scores
1.	Natural resources	+.39	Farm supports	+.14	Immigration	+.25	Fed. aid to edu.	−.39
2.	Farm supports	+.38	Gov't reg. of business	+.12	Anti-monopoly	+.15	Taxes—large income	−.32
3.	Fed. aid to edu.	+.37	Taxes—large income	+.10	Taxes—large income	−.15	Taxes—corp.	−.28
4.	Taxes—corp.	+.33	Minimum wages	+.09	Taxes—Business	+.13	Taxes—business	−.27
5.	Reg.—business	+.33	Taxes—business	+.09	Reg. pub. util.	−.13	Natural resources	−.25
6.	Taxes—large inc.	+.28	Reg. pub. util.	+.07	Tariffs	+.12	Pub. housing	−.23
7.	Pub. housing	+.27	Taxes—corp.	+.07	Restrict. credit	−.11	Reg. business	−.22
8.	Reg. pub. util.	+.26	Fed. aid to edu.	+.07	Natural resources	−.09	Social security	−.22
9.	Social security	+.23	Social security	+.06	Fed. aid to edu.	+.09	Farm supports	−.22
10.	Taxes—business	+.22	Reg. trade unions	−.05	Foreign aid	−.08	Minimum wages	−.18
11.	Minimum wages	+.21	Natural resources	+.05	Reliance on U.N.	+.08	Reg. trade unions	−.17
12.	Reliance on U.N.	+.21	Public housing	+.05	Minimum wages	+.07	Immigration	+.17
13.	Anti-monopoly	+.20	Taxes—small income	−.04	Social security	−.05	Reliance on U.N.	−.13
14.	Atomic energy control	+.18	American participation, NATO	+.04	Reg. trade unions	+.05	Enforce integration	−.12
15.	Reg. trade unions	−.18	Atomic energy control	+.04	Atomic energy control	+.04	Taxes—middle income	−.11
16.	American participation, NATO	+.13	Immigration	−.03	Farm supports	+.02	Atomic energy control	−.10
17.	Enforce integration	+.12	Defense spending	+.02	Reg. business	−.02	American participation, NATO	−.10
18.	Tariffs	−.11	Taxes—middle income	−.02	Enforce integration	+.01	Reg. public util.	−.07
19.	Foreign aid	+.10	Reliance on U.N.	+.02	Taxes—middle income	−.01	Anti-monopoly	−.04
20.	Increase immigration	+.10	Tariffs	−.01	Taxes—corp.	−.01	Foreign aid	−.03
21.	Taxes—small income	−.08	Enforce integration	−.01	Taxes—small income	−.01	Taxes—small income	+.03
22.	Taxes—middle income	+.08	Restriction credit	+.01	American participation, NATO	−.01	Restriction credit	−.01
23.	Restriction credit	−.07	Foreign aid	−.01	Public housing	.00	Tariffs	−.01
24.	Defense spending	+.03	Anti-monopoly	+.00	Defense spending	[b]	Defense spending	[b]

N's. Democratic Leaders: 1788; Republican Leaders: 1232; Democratic Followers: 821; Republican Followers: 623.

[a] The plus sign means that the first group listed in the heading is more favorable to the issue named than the second group; the minus sign means that the second group is the more favorable.

[b] Leaders and Followers cannot be compared on defense spending, for reasons given in footnote to Table 2e.

[c] Size of difference required for differences to be significant at .01 level: Democratic Leaders vs. Republican—.048; Democratic Followers vs. Republican Followers—.068; Democratic Leaders vs. Democratic Followers—.054; Republican Leaders vs. Republican Followers—.063.

where, on a variety of attitudes and values which characteristically distinguish the leaders of the two parties, the Republican followers fall closer to the Democratic than to the Republican side of the continuum. Thus, in addition to being the preferred party of the more numerous classes, the Democrats also enjoy the advantages over their opponents of holding views that are more widely shared throughout the country.

Assuming the findings are valid, we were obviously wrong to expect that party differentiation among followers would depend heavily upon ideological considerations.[35] Evidently, party attachment is so much a function of other factors (e.g. class and primary group memberships, religious affiliation, place of residence, mass media, etc.) that many voters can maintain their party loyalties comfortably even while holding views that contradict the beliefs of their own leaders.

Still, we are not entitled to conclude that issues outlook has no effect on the party affiliation of ordinary members. It is conceivable, for example, that the Republican party has come to be the minority party partly because the opinions of its spokesmen are uncongenial to a majority of voters. We have no way of knowing from our data—collected at only a single point in time—how many "normally" Republican voters, if any, have defected to the Democrats or fled into independency because they disapprove of Republican beliefs. At the present stage of the analysis, we have no grounds for going beyond the proposition that political affiliation without conformity on issues is possible on a wide scale. In future analyses we shall attempt to learn more about the nature of the relationship between belief and party affiliation by stratifying voters according to the frequency with which they conform to the beliefs of their party leaders. We hope, in this way, to discover whether

those who conform least are also less firm in their party loyalties.

VII. THE HOMOGENEITY OF SUPPORT FOR LEADERS AND FOLLOWERS

So far we have only considered conflict and agreement *between* groups. We should now turn to the question of consensus *within* groups. To what extent is each of our samples united on fundamental issues?

In order to assess homogeneity of opinion within party groups, standard deviation scores were computed on each issue for each of the four samples. The higher the standard deviation, of course, the greater the disagreement. The range of possible sigma scores is from 0 (signifying that every member of the sample has selected the same response) to .500 (signifying that all responses are equally divided between the increase" and "decrease" alternatives). If we assume that the three alternative responses had been randomly (and therefore equally) selected, the standard deviations for the four samples would fall by chance alone around .410. Scores at or above this level may be taken to denote extreme dispersion among the members of a sample while scores in the neighborhood of .300 or below suggest that unanimity within the sample is fairly high. By these somewhat arbitrary criteria we can observe immediately (Table 4) that consensus within groups is greater on most issues than we would expect by chance alone, but that it is extremely high in only a few instances. Although the Republican leaders appear on the average to be the most united and the Democratic leaders the least united of the four groups, the difference between their homogeneity scores (.340 vs. .310) is too small to be taken as conclusive. The grounds are somewhat better for rejecting the belief that leaders are more homogeneous in their outlooks than their followers, since the hypothesis holds only for one party and not for the other.

---

[35] See the discussion bearing on this conclusion in Campbell et al., op. cit., chs. 8 and 9. Also, Avery Leiserson, *Parties and Politics, An Institutional and Behavioral Approach* (New York, 1958), pp. 162-166.

TABLE 4. CONSENSUS WITHIN PARTY GROUPS: RANK ORDER OF
HOMOGENEITY OF SUPPORT ON TWENTY-FOUR ISSUES

Average Rank Order [a]	Issues	Democratic Leaders		Republican Leaders		Democratic Followers		Republican Followers	
		Rank Order	Sigma	Rank Order	Sigma	Rank Order	Sigma	Rank Order	Sigma
1	Tax on small incomes	1	.220	6	.270	1	.224	1	.250
2	Tax in middle incomes	3	.276	4	.248	6	.292	2	.278
3	Social security benefits	5	.282	8	.296	2	.266	3	.286
4	Minimum wages	6	.292	5	.268	4	.276	4	.294
5	Enforcement of anti-monopoly	2	.246	13	.321	8	.324	7	.314
6	Regulation of public util.	8	.307	10	.300	10	.336	5.5	.310
7	Slum clearance	4	.276	23	.386	3	.274	5.5	.310
8	Regulation of trade unions	12	.356	3	.240	9	.331	15	.345
9	Government regulation of business	17	.376	1	.192	20	.363	8	.315
10	Tax on business	9	.338	2	.236	19	.362	16	.348
11	Level of tariffs	10	.350	16	.344	11	.338	9	.316
12	Public control of atomic energy	7	.302	20	.362	7	.312	13	.340
13	Federal aid to edu.	13	.360	24	.394	5	.283	11	.322
14	Foreign aid	19	.383	12	.317	12.5	.340	12	.340
15	Tax on large incomes	11	.356	9	.298	17	.358	22	.379
16	American participation in military alliances, NATO	14	.370	18	.351	14	.350	14	.344
17	Immigration into U.S.	21	.399	17	.345	12.5	.340	10	.318
18	Corporate income tax	16	.375	7	.284	21	.371	17	.361
19	Restrictions on credit	22	.400	14	.324	16	.358	18	.362
20	Defense spending	15	.371	14	.334	22	.380	21	.366
21	Public ownership of natural resources	20	.393	19	.354	15	.352	19	.362
22	Reliance on U.N.	18	.380	22	.384	18	.359	20	.365
23	Level of farm supports	24	.421	11	.306	23	.414	23	.397
24	Enforce integration	23	.416	21	.382	24	.418	24	.399

[a] The range of sigma scores is from .192 to .421, out of a possible range of .000 (most united) to .500 (least united.) Hence, the lower the rank order the greater the unity on the issue named.

While generalizations about the relative unity of the four samples seem risky, we can speak more confidently about the rank order of agreement *within* samples. In Table 4 we have ranked the issues according to the degree of consensus exhibited toward them by the members of each of the four party groups. There we see that the leaders of the Republican party are most united on the issues that stem from its connections with business— government regulation of business, taxes (especially on business), regulation of trade unions and minimum wages. The Democratic leaders are most united on those issues which bear upon the support the party receives from the lower and middle income groups—taxes on small and middle incomes, anti-monopoly, slum clearance, social security, and minimum wages. The Republican leaders divide most severely on federal aid to education, slum clearance, U.N. support, segregation, and public control of atomic energy and natural resources; the Democratic leaders are most divided on farm prices, segregation, credit restrictions, imigration, and the natural resources issue. Among the followers the patterns of unity and division are very similar, as attested by the high correlation of .83 between the rank orders of their homogeneity scores. Both Republican and Democratic followers exhibit great cohesion, for example, on taxes on small and middle incomes, social security, slum clearance, and minimum wages. Both divide rather sharply on segregation, farm price supports, defense spending, U.N. support, and taxes on large incomes. The two sets of followers, in short, are alike not only in their opinions on issues but in the degree of unanimity they exhibit toward them.

Inspection of the homogeneity data furnishes additional evidence on the between-group comparisons made earlier. Whereas Democratic and Republican followers divide on issues in approximately the same way, the two sets of leaders differ from each other in this respect also (the correlation between their rank orders on homogeneity is only .28). Democratic leaders and followers tend to unite or divide on the same issues for the most part (*r* equals .77), but Republican leaders and followers are not parallel in this respect either (*r* equals .30). The pattern of homogeneity and dispersion among Republican followers is, in fact, much closer to that of the Democratic leaders (*r* equals .75).

In computing scores for homogeneity we were in part concerned to test the belief that political parties develop greatest internal solidarity on those questions which most separate them from their opponents. According to this hypothesis, external controversy has the effect of uniting the members further by confronting them with a common danger. Whether or not this hypothesis would be borne out in a study of small, sectarian parties we cannot say, but it receives no support from the present study of the American mass parties. Comparisons of the rank order data in Tables 3 and 4 show that there is no consistent connection between interparty conflict and intra-party cohesion. The correlations between the rank orders of difference and the rank orders of homogeneity are in every case insignificant.[36]

SUMMARY AND CONCLUSIONS

The research described in this paper— an outgrowth of a nationwide inquiry into the nature and sources of political affiliation, activity, and belief—was principally designed to test a number of hypotheses about the relation of ideology to party membership. Responses from large samples of Democratic and Republican leaders and followers were compared on twenty-four key issues and on a number of attitude questions and scales. Statistical operations were carried out to assess conflict and consensus among party groups and to estimate the size and signifi-

[36] For an interesting set of comparative data on the relation of internal party cohesion to issue outlook, see Morris Davis and Sidney Verba, "Party Affiliation and International Opinions in Britain and France, 1947-56." *Public Opinion Quarterly,* Winter 1960-61 (forthcoming).

cance of differences. From the data yielded by this inquiry, the following inferences seem most warranted:

1. Although it has received wide currency, especially among Europeans, the belief that the two American parties are identical in principle and doctrine has little foundation in fact. Examination of the opinions of Democratic and Republican leaders shows them to be distinct communities of co-believers who diverge sharply on many important issues. Their disagreements, furthermore, conform to an image familiar to many observers and are generally consistent with differences turned up by studies of Congressional roll calls. The unpopularity of many of the positions held by Republican leaders suggests also that the parties submit to the demands of their constituents less slavishly than is commonly supposed.

2. Republican and Democratic leaders stand furthest apart on the issues that grow out of their group identification and support—out of the managerial, proprietary, and high-status connections of the one, and the labor, minority, low-status, and intellectual connections of the other. The opinions of each party elite are linked less by chance than by membership in a common ideological domain. Democratic leaders typically display the stronger urge to elevate the lowborn, the uneducated, the deprived minorities, and the poor in general; they are also more disposed to employ the nation's collective power to advance humanitarian and social welfare goals (e.g., social security, immigration, racial integration, a higher minimum wage, and public education). They are more critical of wealth and big business and more eager to bring them under regulation. Theirs is the greater faith in the wisdom of using legislation for redistributing the national product and for furnishing social services on a wide scale. Of the two groups of leaders, the Democrats are the more "progressively" oriented toward social reform and experimentation. The Republican leaders, while not uniformly differentiated from their opponents, subscribe in greater measure to the symbols and practices of individualism, *laissez-faire*, and national independence. They prefer to overcome humanity's misfortunes by relying upon personal effort, private incentives, frugality, hard work, responsibility, self-denial (for both men and government), and the strengthening rather than the diminution of the economic and status distinctions that are the "natural" rewards of the differences in human character and fortunes. Were it not for the hackneyed nature of the designation and the danger of forcing traits into a mold they fit only imperfectly, we might be tempted to describe the Republicans as the chief upholders of what Max Weber has caled the "Protestant Ethic."[37] Not that the Democrats are insensible to the "virtues" of the Protestant-capitalistic ethos, but they embrace them less firmly or uniformly. The differences between the two elites have probably been intensified by the rise of the New Deal and by the shift of former radicals into the Democratic party following the decline of socialist and other left-wing movements during and after the war.

3. Whereas the leaders of the two parties diverge strongly, their followers differ only moderately in their attitudes toward issues. The hypothesis that party beliefs unite adherents and bring them into the party ranks may hold for the more active members of a mass party but not for its rank and file supporters. Republican followers, in fact, disagree far more with their own leaders than with the leaders of the Democratic party. Little support was found for the belief that deep cleavages exist among the electorate but are ignored by the leaders. One might, indeed more accurately assert the contrary, to wit: that the natural cleavages between the leaders are largely ignored by the voters. However, we cannot presently conclude that ideology exerts no influence over the habits of party support, for the followers do differ significantly and in the predicted directions on some issues. Furthermore, we do not know how many followers may previously have

[37] Max Weber, *Protestant Ethic and the Spirit of Capitalism* (London, 1948), ch. V.

been led by doctrinal considerations to shift their party allegiances.

4. Except for their desire to ingratiate themselves with as many voters as possible, the leaders of the two parties have more reason than their followers to hold sharply opposing views on the important political questions of the day. Compared with the great mass of supporters, they are articulate, informed, highly partisan, and involved; they comprise a smaller and more tightly knit group which is closer to the well-springs of party opinions, more easily rewarded or punished for conformity or deviation, and far more affected, politically and psychologically, by engagement in the party struggle for office. If the leaders of the two parties are not always candid about their disagreements, the reason may well be that they sense the great measure of consensus to be found among the electorate.

5. Finding that party leaders hold contrary beliefs does not prove that they *act* upon those beliefs or that the two parties are, in practice, governed by different outlooks. In a subsequent paper we shall consider these questions more directly by comparing platform and other official party pronouncements with the private opinions revealed in this study. Until further inquiries are conducted, however, it seems reasonable to assume that the views held privately by party leaders can never be entirely suppressed but are bound to crop out in hundreds of large and small ways—in campaign speeches, discussions at party meetings, private communications to friends and sympathizers, statements to the press by party officials and candidates, legislative debates, and public discussions on innumerable national, state, and local questions.

If, in other words, the opinions of party leaders are as we have described them, there is every chance that they are expressed and acted upon to some extent. Whether this makes our parties "ideological" depends, of course, on how narrowly we define that term. Some may prefer to reserve that designation for parties that are more obviously preoccupied with doctrine, more intent upon the achievement of a systematic political program, and more willing to enforce a common set of beliefs upon their members and spokesmen.

6. The parties are internally united on some issues, divided on others. In general, Republican leaders achieve greatest homogeneity on issues that grow out of their party's identification with business, Democratic leaders on issues that reflect their connection with liberal and lower-income groups. We find no support for the hypothesis that the parties achieve greatest internal consensus on the issues which principally diivde them from their opponents.

In a sequel to this paper we shall offer data on the demographic correlates of issue support, which show that most of the differences presented here exist independently of factors like education, occupation, age, religion, and sectionalism. Controlling for these influences furnishes much additional information and many new insights but does not upset our present conclusions in any important respect. Thus, the parties must be considered not merely as spokesmen for other interest groups but as reference groups in their own right, helping to formulate, to sustain and to speak for a recognizable point of view.

Public Opinion and Democratic Politics

V. O. KEY

The exploration of public attitudes is a pursuit of endless fascination—and frustration. Depiction of the distribution of opinions within the public, identification of the qualities of opinion, isolation of the odd and of the obvious correlates of opinion, and ascertainment of the modes of opinion formation are pursuits that excite human curiosity. Yet these endeavors are bootless unless the findings about the preferences, aspirations, and prejudices of the public can be connected with the workings of the governmental system. The nature of that connection has been suggested by the examination of the channels by which governments become aware of public sentiment and the institutions through which opinion finds more or less formal expression.

When all these linkages are treated, the place of public opinion in government has still not been adequately portrayed. The problem of opinion and government needs to be viewed in an even broader context. Consideration of the role of public opinion drives the observer to the more fundamental question of how it is that democratic governments manage to operate at all. Despite endless speculation on that problem, perplexities still exist about what critical circumstances, beliefs, outlooks, faiths, and conditions are conducive to the maintenance of regimes under which public opinion is controlling, at least in principle, and is, in fact, highly influential.

1. A MISSING PIECE OF THE PUZZLE

Though the preceding analyses did not uncover the secret of the conditions pre-cedent to the practice of democratic politics, they pointed to a major piece of the puzzle that was missing as we sought to assemble the elements that go into the construction of a democratic regime. The significance of that missing piece may be made apparent in an indirect manner. In an earlier day public opinion seemed to be pictured as a mysterious vapor that emanated from the undifferentiated citizenry and in some way or another enveloped the apparatus of government to bring it into conformity with the public will. These weird conceptions, some of which were mentioned in our introductory chapter, passed out of style as the technique of the sample survey permitted the determination, with some accuracy, of the distribution of opinions within the population. Vast areas of ignorance remain in our information about people's opinions and aspirations; nevertheless, a far more revealing map of the gross topography of public opinion can now be drawn than could have been a quarter of a century ago.

Despite their power as instruments for the observation of mass opinion, sampling procedures do not bring within their range elements of the political system basic for the understanding of the role of mass opinion within the system. Repeatedly, as we have sought to explain particular distributions, movements, and qualities of mass opinion, we have had to go beyond the survey data and make assumptions and estimates about the role and behavior of that thin stratum of persons referred to variously as the political elite, the political activists, the leadership echelons, or the influentials. In the normal operation of surveys designed to obtain tests of mass sentiment, so few persons from this activist stratum fall into the sample that they cannot well be differentiated, even in a static description, from those persons less involved politically. The data tell us almost nothing about the dynamic relations between the upper layer of activists and mass opinion. The missing piece of our puzzle is this elite element of the opinion system. That these political influentials both affect mass opinion and are conditioned in their behavior by it is obvious. Yet systematic knowledge of the composition, distribution in the social structure, and patterns of behavior of this sector of the political system remains far from satisfactory.

The longer one frets with the puzzle of how democratic regimes manage to function, the more plausible it appears that a substantial part of the explanation is to be found in the motives that actuate the leadership echelon, the values that it holds, in the rules of the political game to which it adheres, in the expectations which it entertains about its own status in society, and perhaps in some of the objective circumstances, both material and institutional, in which it functions. Focus of attention on this sector of the opinion system contrasts with the more usual quest for the qualities of the people that may be thought to make democratic practices feasible. That focus does not deny the importance of mass attitudes. It rather emphasizes that the pieces of the puzzle are different in form and function, and that for the existence of a democratic opinion-oriented system each piece must possess the characteristics necessary for it to fit together with the others in a working whole. The superimposition over a people habituated to tyranny of a leadership imbued with democratic ideals probably would not create a viable democratic order.

VALUES AND MOTIVES OF THE ACTIVIST SUBCULTURE

The traits and characteristics of political activists assume importance in the light of a theory about why the leadership and governing levels in any society behave as they do. That theory amounts to the proposition that these political actors constitute in effect a subculture with its own peculiar set of norms of behavior,

motives, and approved standards. Processes of indoctrination internalize such norms among those who are born to or climb to positions of power and leadership; they serve as standards of action, which are reinforced by a social discipline among the political activists. In some regimes the standards of the ruling groups prescribe practices of firmness toward the governed who are regarded as menials with no rights; they deserve no more than the rough and arbitrary treatment they receive. The rules of the game may prescribe that the proper practice for rulers is to maximize their own advantage as well as the correlative deprivations of the ruled. The ignorant, the poor, and the incompetent may be seen as entitled to what they get, which is very little. Or the rules of the game of a regime may mitigate the harshness of these outlooks by a compassionate attitude toward the wretched masses who cannot help themselves. Hence, we may have little fathers of the people. The point is that the politically active classses may develop characteristic norms and practices that tend to guide their behavior. In a loose sense these may be the norms of a subculture, that of the specialists in politics and government. Beliefs generally accepted among these persons tend to establish habits and patterns of behavior with considerable power of self-maintenance or persistence through time.

While the ruling classes of a democratic order are in a way invisible because of the vagueness of the lines defining the influentials and the relative ease of entry to their ranks, it is plain that the modal norms and standards of a democratic elite have their peculiarities. Not all persons in leadership echelons have precisely the same basic beliefs; some may even regard the people as a beast. Yet a fairly high concentration prevails around the modal beliefs, even though the definition of those beliefs must be imprecise. Fundamental is a regard for public opinion, a belief that in some way or another it should prevail. Even those who cynically humbug the people make a great show of deference to the populace. The basic doctrine goes further to include a sense of trusteeship for the people generally and an adherence to the basic doctrine that collective efforts should be dedicated to the promotion of mass gains rather than of narrow class advantage; elite elements tethered to narrow group interest have no slack for maneuver to accommodate themselves to mass aspirations. Ultimate expression of these faiths comes in the willingness to abide by the outcome of popular elections. The growth of leadership structures with beliefs including these broad articles of faith is probably accomplished only over a considerable period of time, and then only under auspicious circumstances.

If an elite is not to monopolize power and thereby to bring an end to democratic practices, its rules of the game must include restraints in the exploitation of public opinion. Dimly perceptible are rules of etiquette that limit the kinds of appeals to public opinion that may be properly made. If it is assumed that the public is manipulable at the hands of unscrupulous leadership (as it is under some conditions), the maintenance of a democratic order requires the inculcation in leadership elements of a taboo against appeals that would endanger the existence of democratic practices. Inflammation of the sentiments of a sector of the public disposed to exert the tyranny of an intolerant majority (or minority) would be a means of destruction of a democratic order. Or by the exploitation of latent differences and conflicts within the citizenry it may at times be possible to paralyze a regime as intense hatreds among classes of people come to dominate public affairs. Or by encouraging unrealistic expectations among the people a clique of politicians may rise to power, a position to be kept by repression as disillusionment sets in.[1] In an experienced democracy such tactics may be "unfair" competition among members of the politically active class. In short, certain restraints on political competition help keep competition within tolerable limits. The observation of a few American political campaigns might lead one to the conclusion that there are no restraints on politicians as they attempt to humbug the people. Even so, admonitions ever recur against arousing class against class, against stirring the animosities of religious groups, and against demagoguery in its more extreme forms. American politicians manifest considerable restraint in this regard when they are tested against the standards of behavior of politicians of most of those regimes that have failed in the attempt to establish or maintain democratic practices.

The norms of the practice of politics in an order that has regard for public opinion include broad rules of etiquette governing relations among the activists, as well as rules governing the relations of activists with the public. Those rules, in their fundamental effect, assure the existence of a minority among the political activists; if those who control government can suppress opposition activists, an instrument essential for the formation and expression of public opinion is destroyed. A body of customs that amounts to a policy of "live and let live" must prevail. In constitutional democracies some of these rules are crystallized into fundamental law in guarantees such as those of freedom of speech, freedom of press, and the right to appeal to the electorate for power. Relevant also are procedures for the protection of property rights; a political opposition may be destroyed by expropriation as well as by execution.[2] While such rules extend in their application to the entire population, one of their major functions is to prevent politicians from putting each other into jail or from destroying each other in the ordinary course of their competitive endeavors. All these elements of the rules of the game gain strength, not

---

[1] The politicians of some of the new democracies have installed new regimes as they took the unfortunate step of arousing popular expectations beyond hope of early fulfillment.

[2] Rules against the use of public authority for the private advantage of officials also have their political bearing. Officials who build huge fortunes or enterprises by the abuse of official position can yield power only at enormous cost.

from their statement in the statutes and codes, but from their incorporation into the norms that guide the behavior of the political activists.[3]

FORM AND STRUCTURE

Certain broad structural or organizational characteristics may need to be maintained among the activists of a democratic order if they are to perform their functions in the system. Fundamental is the absence of sufficient cohesion among the activists to unite them into a single group dedicated to the management of public affairs and public opinion. Solidification of the elite by definition forecloses opportunity for public choice among alternative governing groups and also destroys the mechanism for the unfettered expression of public opinion or of the opinions of the many subpublics. Maintenance of division and competition among political activists requires the kinds of etiquette that have been mentioned to govern their relations among themselves. Those rules, though, do not create the cleavages among the activists. Competitive segments of the leadership echelons normally have their roots in interests or opinion blocs within society. A degree of social diversity thus may be, if not a prerequisite, at least helpful in the construction of a leadership appropriate for a democratic regime. A series of independent social bases provide the foundations for a political elite difficult to bring to the state of unification that either prevents the rise of democratic processes or converts them into sham rituals.

At a more earthy level, maintenance of a multiplicity of centers of leadership and political activism requires arrangements by which men may gain a livelihood despite the fact that they are out of power. Consider the consequences for the structure of opinion leadership of a socio-economic system in which those skilled in the arts of governance have open to them no way of obtaining a livelihood save by the exercise of those skills. In the United States the high incidence of lawyers among the politically influential provides a base of economic independence; the defeated politician can always find a few clients. Extensive reliance on part-time, amateur politicians in respresentative bodies and in many governing commissions has assured an economic cushion for many political activists. The custom of making many such offices economically unattractive has, in effect, required that they be filled by persons with an economic base independent of the public treasury. Opinion leaders and managers often find economic independence in posts with business associations and other voluntary societies. Communications enterprises, important in the operation of democracies, gain independence from government by their commercial position. The structure of government itself, through its many independent units and agencies, assures havens of some security for spokesmen for a variety of viewpoints. All this may boil down to the contention that development and maintenance of the type of leadership essential for the operation of a democratic political order is facilitated by the existence of a social system of some complexity with many centers that have some autonomy and economic independence. Perhaps a safer formulation would be that societies that do not meet these requisites may encounter difficult problems in the support of a fractionalized stratum of political activists; they need to construct functional equivalents of the means we have been describing to assure the maintenance of competing centers of leadership.[4]

When viewed from another angle, these comments about the utility of independent foundations for competing sectors of the political elite relate to the more general proposition that regimes deferential to public opinion may best flourish when the

---

[3] Probably a critical stage in the evolution toward democracy occurs at the moment when those in authority conclude that their acceptance of the unfavorable outcome of an election would not result in grievous harm to them. Genetic analyses of democracies with a focus of attention on this point would be instructive.

[4] Consider the problem of a regime that seeks to carry out economic development in large measure through governmental enterprise.

deprivations contingent upon the loss of an election are limited. The structure of government itself may also contribute to that loss limitation. In federal regimes and in regimes with extensive devolution to elective local governmental authorities the prospect of loss of a national election may be faced with some equanimity, for the national minority may retain its position in many subordinate units of the nation and remain in a measure undisturbed by the alternations of control within the nation as a whole. The same function of loss limitation may be served by constitutional and customary expectations that limit the permissible range of governmental action.

Another characteristic may be mentioned as one that, if not a prerequisite to government by public opinion, may profoundly affect the nature of a democratic order. This is the distribution through the social structure of those persons highly active in politics. By various analyses, none founded on completely satisfactory data, we have shown that in the United States the political activists—if we define the term broadly—are scattered through the socio-economic hierarchy. The upper-income and occupational groups, to be sure, contribute disproportionately; nevertheless, individuals of high political participation are sprinkled throughout the lesser occupational strata. Contrast the circumstances when the highly active political stratum coincides with the high socio-economic stratum. Conceivably the winning of consent and the creation of a sense of political participation and of sharing in public affairs may be far simpler when political activists of some degree are spread through all social strata. The alternative circumstance may induce an insensitivity to mass opinion, a special reliance on mass communications, and a sharpened sense of cleavage and separatism within the political order. The contention made here amounts to more than the axiom that democracies can exist only in societies that possess a well-developed middle class. In a modern industrial society with universal suffrage the chances are that a considerable sprinkling of po-

litical activists needs to exist in groups below the "middle class," however that term of vague referent may be defined. The correct general proposition may be that the operation of democratic processes may be facilitated by the distribution of persons participating in the order through all strata of the electorate. When the belief that democracy depended upon the middle class flourished, a comparatively narrow suffrage prevailed.

Allied with these questions is the matter of access to the wider circles of political leadership and of the recruitment and indoctrination of these political activists. Relative ease of access to the arena of active politics may be a preventive of the rise of intransigent blocs of opinion managed by those denied participation in the regularized processes of politics. In a sense, ease of access is a necessary consequence of the existence of a somewhat fragmented stratum of political activists. Systems built on rigid class lines or on the dominance of clusters of families may be especially prone to the exclusion of those not to the proper status born—or married. Yet ease of access does not alone suffice. It must be accompanied by means, either deliberate or informal, for the indoctrination of those admitted in the special mores and customs of the activist elements of the polity. Otherwise, ease of access may only facilitate the depredations of those alienated from the values of the political order. By their nature democratic political systems have large opportunity—if there is the necessary will—to extend widely opportunities for political participation in lesser capacities and thereby to sift out those capable of achieving access to the more restricted circles of influentials. Whether the builders of political orders ever set about deliberately and systematically to tackle such problems of recruitment and indoctrination may be doubtful. Those problems may be solved, when they are solved, by the unconscious and unwilled processes of evolutionary adaptation of social systems.

This discussion in terms of leadership echelons, political activists, or elites falls painfully on the ears of democratic romantics. The mystique of democracy has in it no place for ruling classes. As perhaps with all powerful systems of faith, it is vague on the operating details. Yet by their nature governing systems, be they democratic or not, involve a division of social labor. Once that axiom is accepted, the comprehension of democratic practices requires a search for the peculiar characteristics of the political influentials in such an order, for the special conditions under which they work, and for the means by which the people keep them in check. The vagueness of the mystique of democracy is matched by the intricacy of its operating practices. If it is true that those who rule tend sooner or later to prove themselves enemies of the rights of man—and there is something to be said for the validity of this proposition—then any system that restrains that tendency however slightly can excite only awe.

2. MASS OPINION: VARIATIONS IN NATURE AND FUNCTION

The demarcation between the political activists and the "mass" must be regarded as a zone of gray rather than as a sharp line, but we may make a distinction between the two types of people with respect to their roles in a system in which public opinion conditions governmental action. The assumption of the preceding paragraphs has been that political activists must possess certain modal characteristics if a political system is to be a viable democracy. Without an imposing foundation of empirical data, an attempt was made to specify some of these characteristics of the activist stratum. Presumably the mass of the people must also possess attitudes and behavioral tendencies congenial to the necessities of a democratic order. That assumption involves us in a process of some circularity, for it has been repeatedly noted that the political activists may shape the opinions of the rest of the people. If the activists control, there is no need to consider mass opinion.

Yet the remolding of popular attitudes is not the work of a day; they have a considerable viscosity. Hence, it is permissible to speak of the mass of the people as independent in their characteristics of the activist stratum and as one of the elements that combine with appropriate types of leadership behavior to create a functioning system. Specification of what modal qualities or attitudes should characterize the mass of the people if a society is to have a working democracy presents its difficulties. Although the survey data tell us a great deal about mass opinion, the available materials still leave wide gaps in the information relevant to the broad question that concerns us at the moment. Nevertheless, from what is known and surmised about mass opinion, we may grope toward an identification of those characteristics that may make it compatible with the practice of democracy.

DIFFERENTIATIONS WITHIN THE PUBLIC: CLUES TO DEMOCRATIC CAPABILITIES.

Students of public opinion quickly learn that it is not illuminating to speak of "the public." In their biological characteristics men are animals of endless diversity; in their political behavior they may be equally varied. To bring that diversity within our comprehension, students of public opinion often attempt broad classifications of the citizenry. Thus, we have differentiations according to kinds of participation in political matters, ranging from the sector of the public with a continuing interest in public affairs and an inclination to write their congressman at the drop of a hat to those persons who pay virtually no attention to politics and rarely bother even to vote. The relevance of such categories at this point lies in the possibility that they may provide clues as we search for those qualities of outlook and behavior of the mass of the people or of large sectors of the public that are congenial to the workings of a democratic order—that help make possible the existence of a regime in which public opinion plays a role.

A recurring classification is that of the attentive public (or publics) and the inattentive public. So crude a statement conceals a variety in the objects as well as in the degrees of attention. Our data have identified, for example, variations in attention to presidential campaigns through any of the media, while at the opposite end of the scale are others who follow the campaigns through all the media and entertain a deep concern about their outcome.

Doubtless those who manifest high interest in campaigns also maintain a continuing interest in the flow of action between campaigns. Their focus of attention on the stream of events certainly has its consequences at the next election, not only in their votes but in their influence on the less attentive to whom they communicate their views. Beyond this audience with its focus of attention on a range of political events generally, there exists a complex population of special publics whose attentions center more or less continuously on specific governmental agencies or fields of policy. We lack surveys to define the dimensions of these publics, the objects of their attention, or the extent to which they overlap. Nevertheless, some types of such publics can be indicated. The most obvious attentive publics consist of those with a direct concern in particular policies or actions. That concern may rest, though not necessarily, on an economic self-interest. In any case, these special publics extend considerably beyond the leaders and spokesmen of formalized organizations. For example, farmers make up an attentive public; to be sure, not all farmers earn a place in that public, but the better-informed and more alert of them center attention on farm policy and its administrators, and have their views both solicited and taken into account by officialdom. Or consider the old folks. With both the leisure and the motivation of interest, many of them a familiarity with policies and practices with respect to benefits for the aged as well as an eager eye for helpful new proposals. Congressmen are likely to hear from them.

Veterans constitute another attentive public whose attention seems to be especially capable of producing a feedback into the halls of government. Another attentive public keeps a continuing watch over policy toward education: teachers associations and PTA's are the more prominent spokesmen for this public, but many (sometimes, one suspects, too many) people consider themselves to be experts on education and do not hesitate to give confident vent to their assured views. One could identify for almost every governmental function comparable attentive publics varying both in size and in intensity of their concern. Not all such publics are motivated by a direct self-interest. Consider the public attentive to foreign policy. Sprinkled over the land are societies, associations, circles, and study groups whose members give attention to international affairs, entertain visiting ambassadors, advise both the government and their fellow citizens on recondite issues of foreign policy, and look down generally on those clods among their fellow men who do not pay heed to the really important questions of the world.

Another type of attentive public, probably of special influence, consists of professional groups. Professions develop their own codes of ethics as well as their standards of practice. Members of the professions who deviate from the norms of their group may be cold-shouldered by their breathren and under some circumstances even deprived of the right to earn a livelihood by the practice of their trade. Members of the professions who occupy official positions carry on their functions under the scrutiny of the nongovernmental members of the profession and are thus subjected to the gaze of an attentive public equipped with standards of appraisal of some precision. Consider the relations between the bench and the bar. Judges may have the last word with attorneys who practice before them, but they are not unmindful of the expectations of the bar generally. Their work is open to the criticism of their professional peers. Engineers are equipped with greater technical precision than lawyers but with a less compelling system of professional ethics. Nevertheless, engineers in public posts, when they botch a job, incur the disapproval of the attentive public of engineers. Medical men in public posts are not beyond the pull of their professional norms even as they develop public policy on medical care. Among persons engaged in general administration professional norms seem to be in the process of development, and these group standards emerge from an attentive public which is largely, but not entirely, intragovernmental.[5]

This kind of differentiation between the attentive and nonattentive public is a commonplace of speculation about the place of the citizenry in a democracy. It is often accompanied by attempts to estimate the proportions of the public that share varying degrees and kinds of attentiveness, estimates often unsupported by the data of observation. But surely the highly attentive and active public of which we have been speaking constitutes normally no more than 10 to 15 per cent of the adult population, although at times of crisis far higher proportions may focus their attention on particular actions of government.

The reason, though, for the introduction here of the question of political differentiations among people was the hope that it might suggest popular characteristics conducive to, if not essential for, the existence of democratic practices. Obviously the highly attentive publics, as they monitor the actions of government and let their judgments be known, play a critical role in assuring a degree of responsiveness of government to nongovernmental opinion. For these publics to perform that function, though, an understanding and acceptance of their role must prevail among many people. The

belief must exist that it is the public's business to engage in such activities of surveillance and criticism of government. Societies have existed and do exist in which there is a radically different role system; it may be improper for private persons to concern themselves with the business of officials. For lack of adequate comparative data, it is difficult to make vivid the significance of behaviors we regard as commonplace.[6] It is sufficient to note that there is nothing in human nature to assure that the attentive publics will act as they do. Development of understandings of roles and of appropriate behaviors among large numbers of people requires considerable time and a good deal of trial and error; this is one reason why democracies are not created by decree but, rather, evolve.[7]

Attentiveness with its correlative behaviors will wane unless it is associated with a belief that watchfulness and articulateness ultimately have some bearing on what government does or does not do. That belief can be engendered only if it has some foundation in reality. In turn, that reality depends upon the outlooks of those persons who constitute the highly activist element—the officials, the occupants of points of nongovernmental power, the persons who may next occupy points of private and public power. That is, each of the elements of the political system must have characteristics that make it possible for them to fit together. Thus, democratic politicians defer to expressions of opinion. They listen with patience to the crackpot and even maintain their composure in the face of unfair and uninformed criticism—especially when it comes from an influential constituent. In all this there is a core of

[5] An interesting question relevant to the relation of attentive publics and government is the effect of the competition of different areas of public activity for attention. For example, some of the troubles of urban government may come from the fact that the more dramatic activities of the federal government divert to it the attention of those persons who might, under other conditions, constitute the watchful audience for the conductors of municipal affairs.

[6] Probably what all this boils down to is that in a democratic order the indignant private citizen regards it as proper to raise a popular commotion. When he does so, he acts with the expectation that he will not be jailed, but that he will be heard with courtesy and that his views may have some effect.

[7] One way in which the understanding and behaviors appropriate for national democracies may develop is through widespread participation in the relatively simple affairs of local government.

genuine concern about public opinion even though impracticable and intemperate expressions of opinion may be greeted with a ceremonial courtesy devoid of substantive deference. All these observations may amount to is the contention that if a democracy is to exist, the belief must be widespread that public opinion, at least in the long run, affects the course of public action. In a technical sense that belief may be a myth, an article of faith, yet its maintenance requires that it possess a degree of validity. It seems even that those clerics who most successfully perpetuate their myths are those who can turn up a miracle for their communicants now and then.

Political involvement is another type of differentiation among the citizenry that may provide clues to those characteristics of people which are congenial to the workings of a democracy. Variations in the degree of psychological "care" and "interest" in campaigns have served as a crude but useful index for many of our analyses. Almost by definition there must exist a fairly widespread psychological involvement in political affairs if a society is to operate by democratic procedures. Involvement probably carries with it at least a degree of attention to political affairs. Yet as we move from the most highly attentive and most highly involved sector of society, involvement may take on rather special dimensions. A substantial proportion of the citizenry may not belong to the highly attentive sector of the public of which we have spoken but may pay a routine heed to politics, may "care" about how elections come out, and may have an "interest" in campaigns. This involvement tends to carry with it some sense of sharing in the political process, some belief that participation makes a difference, some faith in the reality of the dogmas of democracy. Yet the activities associated with this sense of involvement are of a different order from those of the highly attentive publics whose members may be especially well informed and fairly closely in touch with political processes.

The psychological involvement of a substantial sector of the populace represents, of course, an acquired cultural characteristic. It takes some learning and habituation for a people to acquire a sense of participation, a sense of sharing in a political order.[8] Yet this sense of involvement may be of prime significance. It is basic for any popular participation in governmental processes. Beyond this, the sense of involvement may be a fundamental means by which discontents may occur in any order. The practical question is how large such blocs of sentiment need to be and what circumstances need to exist for them to become destructive of the normal democratic processes.[9]

LOYALTIES, ORIENTATIONS, EXPECTATIONS

In the division of labor in a democratic order the highly attentive publics, a comparatively small sector of the whole, need to develop an understanding of their special role in the workings of the system. Other kinds of understandings and outlooks, which may be associated with considerably less in the way of overt participation, must permeate most of the population. To specify those understandings and outlooks requires that we grope beyond data that can be neatly set forth in demonstrative tables.

A basic prerequisite is that the population be pervaded by a national loyalty. Or, perhaps more accurately, that the population not consist of segments each with its own sense of separateness. The condition is best illustrated by synthetic nations consisting of blocs with their own

[8] Hence, one may express some pessimism about the outcome when a society that is attempting to move almost from the Stone Age to the Atomic Age overnight immediately franchises all its people. None of the more mature democracies acquired the habit patterns of democratic governance at so rapid a rate.

[9] For a sense of political involvement to be widespread within the population, the conditions of life must be such that the struggle for subsistence does not monopolize the efforts of most men. In a random sample of the American population a few respondents are found whose struggle for the bare necessities of life so occupy their time and energy that their political involvement is at a zero level.

history, language, culture, and memories of, if not aspirations for, a separate national identity. Students of public opinion long ago noted the incompatibility of these circumstances with democratic processes. That incompatibility comes not so much from the psychological characteristics of the mass of the people as from the fact that those characteristics invite exploitation by elements of leadership. Reckless leaders can disrupt the processes of government by diversionary appeals that weaken or destroy the foundations of national unity. Regimes with tight discipline in the ranks of political leadership—dictatorships, semidictatorships, monarchies—can restrain those who would activate the latent or not so latent divisive animosities of the mass of people. Democratic elites ordinarily have less capacity to restrain their irresponsible elements. Hence, mass attitudes that yield readily to divisive appeals create special difficulties for democratic orders.[10]

Closely related to this acceptance of the regime is what might be called a sense of the collectivity or of the community. Probably for the existence of an order deferential to public opinion the mass of people must share some sense of the legitimacy of the collectivity, in contrast with a situation in which large sectors of the population have no sense of a community of interest but center their attachments upon group, class, or even upon some smaller subnational entity. Perhaps a shadow of this sentiment of commonality was captured by the survey questions analyzed earlier about the influence on government of big business and trade unions. People of all occupational and income levels tended to think that both these interests should be kept in their place, that each should have its say but

neither should have too much power. The view among the articulate seemed to be that some greater common interest should prevail. The same sense of the collectivity may manifest itself when people say that they have "something in common" with their fellow citizens of other social classes. It appears again on policy question after policy question as people of all sorts share attitudes on issues that might be expected, on a simple calculus of self-interest, to draw sharp class cleavages.

The bearing of this sense of community or of commonality upon democratic processes can best be surmised by estimates of what occurs when it is absent. If mass attachments are to subdivisions of the nation and if elements of the leadership both exploit those attachments and become anchored to them, the basis exists for national paralysis, since there is no freedom for a quest for common interest.[11] Sooner or later people, or some of them, may weary of the democratic game and resort to nondemocratic steps to attain their ends.

How people acquire this sense of political community is not clear. Doubtless, as with all basic social outlooks, the development of these attitudes is the product of a prolonged process. While all the apparatus of civic education plays a part, the sense of community must also be in part a product of public policy; that is, without appropriate practices in leadership echelons to give it a basis in reality the sense of community may languish.

The observations resemble the proposition that a consensus needs to prevail for democracy to exist; yet they should not

---

[10] Federal regimes may, to some extent, overcome the difficulties of cultural diversity but even so a price must be paid. Thus, the Canadian system, as it took form under the protection of the British Crown, developed a political elite with norms appropriate to the mixed culture of the Commonwealth. Yet the cost of unity includes both constitutional and customary restraints on governmental action.

[11] In the preceding chapters demonstrations recur of the incohesiveness of subnational interests on the American scene. Social researchers give great emphasis to manifestations of solidarity of subsectors of the nation, but the fact of greater import for the nature of the political system is the relative weakness of such solidarity. Group cohesiveness, always something less than complete, waxes and wanes as considerations transcending group concerns assume greater or lesser salience.

be taken as the equivalent of that proposition. Perhaps among the upper-activist stratum a consensus does need to prevail on the technical rules of the game by which the system operates. What kind of consensus, if any, extends throughout the population beyond a general acceptance of the regime remains problematic. In the main, the notion of consensus has sprung from the inventive minds of theorists untainted by acquaintance with mass attitudes. Knowledge of the relevant mass attitudes is slight, but such as it is does not give much comfort to those who suppose that most people carry around in their heads the elements of democratic theory even in the most attenuated form. Nevertheless, the mass may possess outlooks that permit the regime to function as if a consensus prevailed, though precisely what those outlooks are is another question.

Another psychological characteristic of the mass of people that probably bears upon the workability of democratic processes relates to popular expectations. We may differentiate level and focus of expectations. Some optimum level of expectation may render a populace susceptible to the wiles of the high bidder whose unrealistic promises may sweep him to power and bring only disillusionment to the people. Governmental instability may develop as the bids are raised and one set of rulers replaces another. At the other pole, an extremely low level of expectation may be a reflection of mass cynicism and alienation from democratic processes. Doubtless, a good deal of experience and political indoctrination must go into the formation of mass attitudes characterized by the appropriate mixture of realism and optimism, of patience and eagerness. Good faith on the part of the leadership echelons is essential for this state of mind to exist in the mass of people; there also must be sprinkled through the population a substantial number of persons with sufficient understanding of the limitations and possibilities of politically induced social change to generate an optimum level of epectation in the mass.[12]

The question of the focus of mass expectations raises a problem different from that of their level. People's expectations may center on political or nonpolitical sources of fulfillment. Since one set of expectations tends to be fullfilled (except in a rapidly expanding economy) at the expense of others, it might plausibly be expected that a sustained high level of expectation associated with a focus upon government for fulfillment would tend to generate high stresses within a society.[13] On the contrary, with the focus of expectations diffused—upon the self, upon the family, upon business corporations, upon trade unions, and upon other nonpolitical institutions—the stakes of the political game might be expected to be more readily kept within those limits that make defeat tolerable. This is, in effect, a translation of the hackneyed question of whether democracy is feasible only under some variant of capitalism. When government decree controls almost completely the allocation of the social product as well as the assignment of resources, human and material, to productive tasks, the stakes of politics become enormous indeed. The easy answer to the problem is that mass tensions that could be stirred

[12] The reader has doubtless observed that in these characterizations of mass prerequisites for democratic processes we have moved far away from hard data. The kinds of problems of which we speak here have not been explored by the use of sample surveys which have centered mostly on more manageable problems such as the explanation of voting behavior. Yet it seems clear that appropriate use of survey procedures could bring far more understanding of mass political attitudes than we have.

[13] Democratic politicians, though, are skilled in the contrivance of formal actions that fulfill expectations at a verbal level but are cushioned in the reality of their application. Thus, though the American progressive income tax in form heavily taxes the rich, in fact the statutes are such that most men of wealth, with the advice of a competent tax lawyer, can greatly mitigate the impact of the high rates in the upper brackets. See Murray Edelman: "Symbols and Political Quiescence," *American Political Science Review*, **LIV** (1960), 695-704.

over such questions by competing factions of the political elite make it impossible for the struggle to be contained within the bounds of the easy give-and-take of democratic processes. The correct answer, though, may be that under the conditions described the development of democratic practices require the creation of rules of the game among the political activists together with expectations among the masses of the people appropriate to the special requirements of a socialist economy. Though such an evolution of behavioral patterns would have to surmount formidable obstacles, the possibility of its occurrence should not be excluded, for political man is a malleable creature.[14]

3. INTERACTION AND DISCRETION

Analytically it is useful to conceive of the structure of a democratic order as consisting of the political activists and the mass of people. Yet this differentiation becomes deceptive unless it is kept in mind that the democratic activists consist of people arranged along a spectrum of political participation and involvement, ranging from those in the highest posts of official leadership to the amateurs who become sufficiently interested to try to round up a few votes for their favorite in the presidential campaign. In the preceding discussion we sought to isolate some of the characteristics of both activists and mass that appear to be compatible with, if not essential for, the operation of a democratic order, thus setting up a static picture of two broad political strata. It is in the dynamics of the system, the interactions between these

[14] The problem mentioned in the text is not hypothetical but a pressing reality in young and underdeveloped countries with democratic aspirations. If our broad analysis of the conditions requisite for the rise of democratic practice has validity, these nations, as they attempt to install such practices, work under the most favorable circumstances. Whatever evolves will probably diverge markedly from the patterns of the mature western democracies.

strata, that the import of public opinion in democratic orders becomes manifest. Between the activists and the mass there exists a system of communication and interplay so complex as to defy simple description; yet identification of a few major features of that system may aid in our construction of a general conception of democratic processes.

OPINION DIKES

In the interactions between democratic leadership echelons and the mass of people some insight comes from the conception of public opinion as a system of dikes which channel public action or which fix a range of discretion within which government may act or within which debate at official levels may proceed. This conception avoids the error of personifying "public opinion" as an entity that exercises initiative and in some way functions as an operating organism to translate its purposes into governmental action.

In one of their aspects the dikes of opinion have a substantive nature in that they define areas within which day-to-day debate about the course of specific action may occur. Some types of legislative proposals, given the content of general opinion, can scarcely expect to attract serious attention. They depart too far from the general understandings of what is proper. A scheme for public ownership of the automobile industry, for example, would probably be regarded as so far outside the area of legitimate public action that not even the industry would become greatly concerned. On the other hand, other types of questions arise within areas of what we have called permissive consensus. A widespread, if not a unanimous, sentiment prevails that supports action toward some general objective, such as the care of the ill or the mitigation of the economic hazards of the individual. Probably quite commonly mass opinion of a permissive character tends to develop in advance of governmental action in many areas of domestic policy. That opinion grows out of public discussion against the background of the modal aspirations and values of people generally. As it takes shape, the time becomes ripe for action that will be generally acceptable or may even arouse popular acclaim for its authors.

The qualities of this substantive opinion doubtless differ widely from issue to issue and from person to person. On some issues opinion may be oriented favorably toward broadly defined objectives; on others, perhaps extremely few, opinion may become focused on sharply defined issues; others may have broad preferences—for example, something ought to be done for the farmers but not too much.

Opinion dikes may bear on the manner as well as on the substance of action. And it may be that in a democratic order those opinions that control or guide the mode of action may be of special importance as substantive action moves into areas where it encounters formidable opposition. Action taken in a seemingly fair and equitable manner may be acceptable, but arbitrary action to the same effect may be regarded as intolerable. The procedural content of American public opinion has been little explored. The division of opinion and the spontaneous comment on the proposition that government employees accused of communism ought to be fired even though the charge is not proved suggest that notions of fair play may be widely held within the population. Doubtless other procedural notions have wide popular acceptance that could be demonstrated by survey methods.

The idea of public opinion as forming a system of dikes which channel action yields a different conception of the place of public opinion than does the notion of a government by public opinion as one in which by some mysterious means a referendum occurs on every major issue. In the former conception the articulation between government and opinion is relatively loose. Parallelism between action and opinion tends not to be precise in matters of detail; it prevails rather with respect to broad purpose. And in the correlation of purpose and action time lags may occur between the crystallization

of a sense of mass purpose and its fulfillment in public action. Yet in the long run majority purpose and public action tend to be brought into harmony.

MODIFICATIONS OF THE OPINION CONTEXT

The content of mass opinion changes through time; it is perhaps in such alterations that the power of mass opinion is made manifest. Though changes in opinion content occur continuously, at some moments combinations of events, imaginative leadership, and action induce relatively rapid and marked changes in popular preferences and expectations. These episodes may bring new opinion orientations, which in turn become rather rigid elements of the pattern of popular attitudes.

The movement of opinions and the expectations atht accompanied the fulfillment of the program of the New Deal illustrate well the process of change and its consequences for governmental action. A spirited leadership with programs of action deviating markedly from past practice won approval and generated a new set of popular expectations about governmental action. The "power" of public opinion manifested itself in a negative way. Those candidates and leaders tainted with the suspicion that they wanted to turn the clock back had hard sledding for years. Until they could make a show of acceptance of changes they could not capture control of the government. Thus, through elections opinion ratified past reforms by its rejection of those who appeared to be at odds with the new balance of public sentiment.

Similarly, in the area of foreign policy World War II brought with it a reorientation of the context of public opinion, which became more supportive of involvement in international politics. Probably the body of popular opinion in this area has a less solid base and a less constricting effect upon public action than does opinion on domestic welfare policy. The radically changed position of the United States in world affairs creates new problems not only for a government that rests on public opinion, but also for those who seek to inform and to lead that opinion. The conduct of domestic debates over foreign policy carries hazards for external policy. On the other hand, repression of debate results in a failure to inform the people of incompetence in the conduct of foreign affairs.[15]

Mass opinions, aspirations, and expectations change as the political system moves through time. It is in this moving situation that the power of mass opinion makes itself manifest in its interactions with democratic leadership—chiefly in its rejection of leadership factions whose outlook lags notably behind or strikes out markedly ahead of the moving average of opinion. Those wish to turn the clock back, to reverse decisions already rooted in popular acceptance, gradually learn their lesson as they meet rebuff after rebuff. Those too far ahead of opinion, though they may contribute to the forces impelling alteration of the opinion context, likewise find themselves rejected. Deviants from dominant opinion, though, play a critical role in the preservation of the vitality of a democratic order as they urge alterations and modifications better to achieve the aspirations of men. Hence the fundamental significance of freedom of speech and agitation. Those activists closest to the core of power may hesitate to assume the risks of political entrepreneurship, but others, with less to lose, may be their efforts gradually make the endeavor that is not "practical politics" today feasible tomorrow.

---

[15] The dilemma which the circumstances of a garrison state create for democracies leads some scholars to advocate fundamental reconstruction of the structure of government. The fixed term of the president makes it impossible for a bumbling administration to be thrown out of power until the date for the next presidential election rolls around. The limitations on debate and discussion imposed by the necessities of external unity and by diplomatic secrecy make it difficult adequately to inform the electorate. The remedy urged by some scholars is some variant of the cabinet system by which Congress, a body better informed that the electorate, could cast out an incompetent administration.

OPINION CONTEXT AND GOVERNMENTAL DISCRETION

This discussion of the anchorage of leadership to public opinion should not be taken to mean that wide ranges of discretion do not exist within which a creative role may be played by popular leadership. Glum political philosophers mediate in their melancholy fashion about how the pursuit of the good of the Republic is frustrated as the mass pulls superior men down to its own mean and grasping material level. The long-run good of the polity, the argument goes, must be neglected as leadership is compelled to cater to the greed and to the ignorance of the masses. Measures that obviously promote the greater public good cannot be undertaken because of mass opposition and misunderstanding.

That at times mass opinion may handicap desirable action cannot be denied. Yet as one puzzles over the nature of interactions between government and mass opinion and ponders such empirical data as can be assembled on the matter, he can arrive only at the conclusion that a wide range of discretion exists for whatever wisdom leadership echelons can muster in the public service. The generality of public preferences, the low intensity of the opinions of many people, the low level of political animosities of substantial sectors of the public, the tortuousness of the process of translation of disapproval of specific policies into electoral reprisal, and many other factors point to the existence of a wide latitude for the exercise of creative leadership. While the winning of consent for innovation may require skill in popular exposition and in political technique, those political leaders who shirk the task of popular education are misfits who do not understand the responsibilities of their jobs. And those leaders who act as if they thought the people to be fools responsive only to the meanest appeals deserve only scorn.

THE BASIC WEAPON OF PUBLIC OPINION

These concluding observations about the interaction of the activists and the mass take on an ethereal tenor, and they should be tied to their referent in institutional reality, which is the party system. In the give-and-take between the leadership echelons, with their intense policy drives and attachments, and the mass of people, the ultimate weapon of public opinion is the minority party. The effect of opinion on the grand course of public opinion depends on the existence of a crowd of outs who can be elevated to power—and the capacity to boot the ins from office. The mechanism is cumbersome and produces no minute fit of public preference and public policy. At times the remedy to the public becomes effective only over the long run, for the outs may offer no alternative congruent with the dissatisfactions against the ins. Yet the party system introduces the possibility of a fluidity in the political order to offset the policy myopia of governments long secure in their position. Paradoxically the party system may also introduce a saving degree of stability into orders dependent upon public opinion. It creates among many people loyalties that transcend and neutralize the vagaries of the opinion of the moment. It introduces traditional and stable policy outlooks with strength but susceptible of modification as they are abraded by their moving contact with the future. It provides ways and means of recruitment of leadership and for its indoctrination with the basic values and working habits of the political order.

INEVITABILITY OF THE DECAY OF DEMOCRACIES?

Our exposition of the interactions between leadership and mass opinion enables us better to understand the argument that democracies, by their inner logic, tend toward decay. That in the long sweep of time all regimes tend toward decay is a proposition at least not negated by the annals of recorded history. Yet the contention, advanced by respectable authorities, is that democracies possess within themselves defects that inevitably lead to their decay in a manner peculiar to democracies.

The fatal weakness of modern mass democracies, so the argument goes, rests in the subjection of government to a public opinion whose mandates are certain to be destructive of the order. Implicit in that proposition is the assumption that mass opinion in the long run tends toward positions incompatible with the demands of the health of the order and that mass opinion tends to pull governments into harmony with those positions. Thus, we have the picture of a mass opinion animated by greed and by a disregard for the rights of man. Politicians must, the conclusion is, sooner or later adopt the view and in the process ultimately create a dictatorship of a majority dedicated to the reduction of all men to a drab equality, an action to be maintained only by a destruction of freedom. Or the argument is that governments accountable to democratic masses invariably tend to take the easy route, to dodge the hard decisions, to avoid at moments of crisis demands for the sacrifices by the populace necessary for the maintenance of the system. Governments, by their subjection to mass opinion, lose decisiveness and are bereft of the will to act, a condition creative of special dangers for the democracy that exists in a hostile international environment. All these consequences flow inevitably from the interaction between leadership and mass opinion as cliques of leaders seek power and, in so doing, are compelled to appeal to mass opinions that contain within themselves the seeds of national destruction. By a kind of Gresham's law, those leadership cliques with a wisdom greater than that of mass opinion either perish or embrace the follies of the mass.[16]

What can we say about this melancholy hypothesis? For a certainty, there are democracies and democracies. Perhaps in some situations the hypothesis fits the facts, but our analyses of the American

[16] An argument to the effect of this paragraph but in a far more sophisticated form is put in Walter Lippmann: *The Public Philosophy* (Boston: Little, Brown, 1955), especially ch. 3-5. See the perceptive comment on Lippmann's analysis in David B. Truman: "The American System in Crisis," *Political Science Quarterly*, LXXIV (1959), 481-97.

scene caution us against easy acceptance of so glib a theory of the dynamics of democratic self-destruction. We have pictured public opinion as the product of an interaction between political influentials and the mass of the people, an interaction that may produce alterations in mass opinion. In the course of time that interaction may also alter the modal position of the influentials as a novel doctrine asserted by one sector of the influentials gains acceptance among the masses. Mass opinion is not self-generating; in the main, it is a response to the cues, the proposals, and the visions propagated by the political activisits.

If this conception of the formation of opinion has validity, democracies decay, if they do, not because of the cupidity of the masses, but because of the stupidity and self-seeking of leadership echelons. Politicians often make of the public a scapegoat for their own shortcomings; their actions, they say, are a necessity for survival given the state of public opinion. Yet that opinion itself results from the preachings of the influentials, of this generation and of several past generations.

Moreover, even if mass opinion assumes forms incompatible with the national interest, the articulation between government and mass opinion is so loose that politicians enjoy a considerable range of discretion within which to exercise prudence and good sense. Our explora-tions into the nature and form of mass opinion leave no doubt that its directives tend toward generality rather than specificity. Even on broad issues on which opinion becomes fairly well crystallized room may remain for choice among a variety of specific actions. Furthermore, translation of opinion into actions of electoral punishment or reward is a torturous and uncertain procedure. The predictability of electoral response to a particular action remains so uncertain that the avoidance of a sensible decision because it will lose votes is usually the work of a man whose anxieties outweigh his capacities of prediction.

The argument amounts essentially to the position that the masses do not corrupt themselves; if they are corrupt, they have been corrupted. If this hypothesis has a substantial strain of validity, the critical element for the health of a democratic order consists in the beliefs, standards, and competence of those who constitute the influentials, the opinion-leaders, the political activists in the order. The group, as has been made plain, refuses to define itself with great clarity in the American system; yet analysis after analysis points to its existence. If a democracy tends toward indecision, decay, and disaster, the responsibility rests here, not in the mass of the people.[17]

---

[17] This analysis and its implications should be pondered well by those young gentlemen in whose education the Republic has invested considerable sums.

CHAPTER 3

Values and Ideology

WHAT are the political values and beliefs of people at the various class levels of American society? To what extent do they share convictions supportive of democratic processes, or of the present American political system? The three selections in this chapter represent different approaches to answering these questions.

Professors James Prothro and Charles R. Grigg employ a comparative approach at the local level, searching for those features that are common and those that are different in two geographically widely separated cities. Professor Prothro is a political scientist and teaches at the University of North Carolina and Professor Grigg is a sociologist at Florida State University.

Professor McClosky's article is another major contribution, offering a comparison of elite and mass views on basic political values on a national basis.

Professor Lane's approach is distinctive in that he employs depth interviewing of a small number of persons, rather than large-scale surveys, to explore political attitudes and their roots. He is a political scientist specializing in public opinion research and teaches at Yale University. His books include *Political Ideology* (1962), *Political Life* (1959), and *Public Opinion* (1964).

A selected bibliography follows Chapter 5.

Fundamental Principles of Democracy: Bases of Agreement and Disagreement

JAMES W. PROTHRO AND CHARLES M. GRIGG

The idea that consensus on fundamental principles is essential to democracy is a recurrent proposition in political theory. Perhaps, because of its general acceptance, the proposition has never been formulated in very precise terms. When authoritative sources state, for example, that "a successful democracy requires the existence of a large measure of consensus in society," exactly what is meant? We assume that the term "successful democracy," although far from precise, carries a widely shared meaning among political scientists. But we are not told in this typical assertion on what *issues* or *problems* consensus must exist. Presumably they are the basic issues about how political power should be won. Nor are we told what degree of agreement democracy requires. Since the word "consensus" is used to refer to "general agreement or concord," however, a "large measure of consensus" presumably falls somewhere close to 100 per cent.[1] For

the purpose of examining the proposition as it is generally formulated, then, we interpret it as asserting: a necessary condition for the existence of a democratic government is widespread agreement (approaching 100 per cent) among the adult members of society on at least the basic questions about how political power is won. Specifically, we propose to submit this proposition to empirical examination in an effort to give it more precise meaning and to discover bases of agreement and/or disagreement on fundamental principles.

A recent symposium by three leading political theorists illustrates both the widespread assumption that consensus is necessary and the lack of precision with which the concept of consensus is discussed. In considering the cultural prerequisites of democracy, they all assume the necessity of agreement on basic values, differing only as to the underlying sources of "the attitudes we regard as cultural prerequisites."[2] Ernest S. Griffith supplies an initial list of "the necessary attitudes to sustain democratic institutions," but he is not clear on whether an actual consensus is necessary: ". . .I believe that they must be sufficiently widespread to be accepted as *norms* of desirable conduct, so that deviations

SOURCE. Reprinted from *The Journal of Politics*, Vol. 22, 1960, by permission of the author and publisher. Copyright 1960 by *The Journal of Politics*.

[1] The consensus of Quaker meetings seems to mean unanimity; although no formal vote is recorded, discussion continues until a position emerges on which no dissent is expressed. Similarly, the literature on the family refers to "family consensus" in a way that suggests unanimity; in a family of three or four people, even one dissenter would make it impossible to speak of consensus. At a different extreme, some students of collective behavior employ a functional definition of consensus, taking it to mean that amount of agreement in a group which is necessary for the group to act. Political scientists clearly do not have such limited agreement in mind when they speak of consensus as necessary to democracy. Majorities as large as three-fourths are required by the Constitution (in ratifying amendments), but such a large majority is

no more thought of as consensus than a majority of 50 per cent plus one. Our purpose here is not to develop a general definition of consensus. We interpret the vague usage of the term to suggest agreement approaching unanimity. And, since our study actually found agreement as great as 98 per cent on some questions, we regard any degree of agreement that falls significantly below this figure to be less than consensus.

[2] Ernest S. Griffith, John Plamenatz and J. Roland Pennock, "Cultural Prerequisites to a Successfully Functioning Democracy: A Symposium," *The American Political Science Review*, L (March, 1956), 101.

therefrom are subject to questioning and usually social disapproval."[3]

John Plamenatz emphasizes individualism as "the sentiment which must be widespread and strong if democracy is to endure," and adds that individualism "has a less general, a less abstract side to it" than the vague "right of every man to order his life as he pleases provided he admits the same right in others." Here the requisite attitudes must be *strong* as well as *widespread,* but when Plamenatz shifts to the specific side he refers to "the faith of the *true* democrat," a somewhat less inclusive reference.[4]

J. Roland Pennock says, "We are in agreement that certain attitudes are essential to democracy," and his initial quantitative requirements are similar to the "widespread" and "strong" criteria: "Unless the *bulk of the society* is committed to a high valuation of these ideals [liberty and equality] it can hardly be expected that institutions predicated upon them will work successfully or long endure."[5] But when he turns to the idea of consensus as such, he withdraws all precision from the phrase "the bulk of the society": "Of course democracy, like other forms of government but to a greater extent, must rest upon a measure of consensus. . . . But can we say with any precision what must be the nature or extent of this consensus, what matters are so fundamental that they must be the subject of general agreement? doubt it."[6] Here consensus appears necessary as a matter "of course," but we cannot say on what matters it must exist (Pennock cites two opposing views—the necessity of agreement on the substance of policy versus the necessity of agreement on procedures for determining policy); nor need consensus have a great "extent," which presumably means that it can vary from

the "great bulk" to even greater portions of society.[7]

Other theorists take similar positions. William Ebenstein, for example, submits that "the *common agreement on fundamentals* is a . . . condition indispensable to . . . political democracy."[8] Bernard R. Berelson asserts, "For political democracy to survive . . . a basic consensus must bind together the contending parties."[9] The same assumption is implicit in Harry V. Jaffa's more specific formulation of the content of consensus: "To be dedicated to this proposition [that 'all men are created equal'], whether by the preservation of equal rights already achieved, or by the preservation of the hope of an equality yet to be achieved, was the 'value' which was the *absolutely necessary condition* of the democratic process."[10]

---

[7] If the term consensus has any meaning, it is in a great extent of agreement; Pennock's reference to the varying "extent" of consensus must accordingly mean variations from large to even larger majorities.

[8] *Today's Isms* (Englewood Cliffs, 1954), p. 99. Italics are his.

[9] Bernard R. Berelson, Paul F. Lazarsfeld and William N. McPhee, *Voting: A Study of Opinion Formation in a Presidential Election* (Chicago, 1954), p. 313. Although not a political theorist, Berelson was speaking here on the "theoretical" aspects of "Democratic Practice and Democratic Theory."

[10] " 'Value Consensus' in Democracy: The Issue in the Lincoln-Douglas Debates," *The American Political Science Review,* LII (September, 1958), 753. Italics are added. Among the other theorists who have offered similar conclusions is Norman L. Stamps: "Democracy is a delicate form of government which rests upon conditions which are rather precarious. . . . It is impossible to overestimate the extent to which the success of parliamentary government is dependent upon a considerable measure of agreement on fundamentals." *Why Democracies Fail: A Critical Evaluation of the Causes of Modern Dictatorship* (Notre Dame, Indiana, 1957), pp. 41-42. Walter Lippmann, in explaining "the decline of the West," cites "the disappearance of the public philosophy—and of a consensus on the first and last things. . . ." *Essays in the Public Philosophy* (Boston, 1955), p. 100. Joseph A. Schumpeter submits: ". . . democratic government will work to full advantage only if all the interests that matter are practically unanimous not only in their allegiance to the

---

[3] *Ibid.,* pp. 103-104. Italics are his.

[4] *Ibid.,* p. 118. Italics are added.

[5] *Ibid.,* pp. 129-131. Italics are added.

[6] *Ibid.,* p. 132.

All of these theorists thus assume the necessity of consensus on some principles but without giving the term any precise meaning.[11] In specifying the principles on which agreement must exist, some differences appear. Although, as Pennock notes, some have gone so far as to argue the need for agreement on the substance of policy, the general position is that consensus is required only on the procedures for winning political power. At the broadest level Ebenstein says that "the most important agreement . . . is the common desire to operate a democratic system,"[12] and Pennock begins his list with "a widespread desire to be self-governing."[13] In addition to this highly general commitment, most theorists speak of consensus on the general values of liberty, equality, individualism, compromise, and acceptance of procedures necessary to majority rule and minority rights. For most of these general principles, the existence (and therefore perhaps the necessity) of consensus is supported by "common sense" observation, by logic, and by opinion survey results. Consensus certainly seems to exist among the American people on the desirability of operating "a democratic system" and on such abstract principles as the idea that "all men are created equal."[14]

But for some of the principles on which agreement is said (without empirical

support) to be necessary, the certainty of consensus cannot so easily be taken for granted. Ernest S. Griffith, in maintaining that the essential attitudes of democracy stem from the Christian and Hebrew religions, submits: "Moreover, it would appear that it is these faiths, and especially the Christian faith, that perhaps alone can *cloak such attitudes with the character of 'absolutes'*—a character which is not only *desirable,* but perhaps even *necessary* to democratic survival."[15] Rather than taking absolutist attitudes as desirable or necessary for democracy, Ebenstein asserts that an opposite consensus is necessary: "The dogmatic, totalitarian viewpoint holds that there is only one Truth. The democratic viewpoint holds that different men perceive different aspects of truth . . . and that there will be at least two sides to any major question."[16] At least one of these positions must be incorrect. Does democracy in fact require rejection or acceptance of the "one Truth" idea? In the survey reported in this paper, neither position appears correct: both Midwestern and Southern Americans were found to be closer to a complete absence of consensus than to common agreement in either accepting or rejecting the "one Truth" idea.[17]

Not only do political theorists speak of consensus on abstract principles where none exists, but they also suggest the need for consensus on more specific principles without empirical support. Griffith, for example, insists that the individualistic "view of the nature of individual personality leads straight to true equality of opportunity and treatment as well as to liberty."[18] And this "true equality" must include dedication not only to the old

---

country but also in their allegiance to the structural principles of the existing society." *Capitalism, Socialism, and Democracy,* 3rd ed., (New York, 1950), p. 296.

[11] In Pennock's case, the lack of precision is deliberate, reflecting a well-defined position that the necessary amount of consensus on fundamentals varies according to the strength of two other prerequisites of democracy—"willingness to compromise" and "respect for rules and set procedures." *Op. cit.,* p. 132.

[12] *Op cit.,* p. 99.

[13] *Op. cit.,* p. 129.

[14] For findings of overwhelming endorsement of the general idea of democracy, see Herbert H. Hyman and Paul B. Sheatsley, "The Current Status of American Public Opinion," in Daniel Katz *et al.* (eds.), *Public Opinion and Propaganda* (New York, 1954), pp. 33-48, reprinted from the *National Council for Social Studies Yearbook,* 1950, Vol. XXI, pp. 11-34.

[15] *Op. cit.,* p. 103. Italics are added.

[16] *Op. cit.,* p. 101.

[17] This item is not included in the results below because we report only on those propositions that relate directly to the question of how political power is gained. The recognition of "different aspects of truth" logically underlies the ideas of majority rule and minority rights, but it is not as directly connected with them as the propositions on which we report.

[18] *Op. cit.,* p. 105.

inalienable rights such as freedom of speech, but also to "the right of each one to be treated with dignity as befits a free person—without regard to sex or creed or race or class."[19] As we shall see, the findings below do not support the assumption of general agreement on "true equality" even in such spheres as freedom of speech. And the same is true of the specific proposition that Pennock uses to illustrate the values on which "the bulk of the society" must be agreed—"The proposition that each vote should count for one and none for more than one is doubtless sufficiently implied by the word 'equality'."[20] "True believers" in democracy may be able to make an unimpeachable case for this proposition, but it is not accepted by the bulk of the society.

The discovery that consensus on democratic principles is restricted to a few general and vague formulations might come as a surprise to a person whose only acquaintance with democracy was through the literature of political theory; it will hardly surprise those who have lived in a democracy. Every village cynic knows that the local church-goer who sings the creed with greatest fervor often abandons the same ideas when they are put in less lyrical form. Political scientists are certainly not so naive as to expect much greater consistency in the secular sphere. The theorists who argue the necessity of consensus on such matters as the existence of absence of multi-faceted truth, true equality in the right of free speech, and dedication to an equal vote for every citizen are no doubt as aware of these human frailties as the village cynic.[21] But we tend to regard that which seems a *logically necessary* belief in the light of democratic processes as being *empirically necessary* to the existence of those processes. We assume, in a two-step translation, that what people *should* (logically) believe is what they *must* be-

lieve (this being a democracy), and that what they *must* believe is what they *do* believe.

In undertaking to discover what kind of consensus actually exists, we assumed that we would find the anticipated agreement on the basic principles of democracy when they were put in a highly abstract form, but that consensus would not be found on more concrete questions involving the application of these principles. We further assumed that regional and class-related variations would be found on the specific formulation of democratic principles. In pinning down these assumptions, we are no doubt demonstrating the obvious—but such a demonstration appears necessary if the obvious is to be incorporated into the logic of political theory. With empirical support for these two assumptions, we can put the proposition about consensus in more precise form and test the following hypothesis: consensus in a meaningful sense *(at both the abstract and specific levels) exists among some segment(s) of the population (which can be called the "carriers of the creed")*. Should our findings support this hypothesis, we could reformulate the proposition about democratic consensus with reference to a smaller group than the total population, whereupon it could be tested more fully, both in the United States and in other democracies, for further refinement.

PROCEDURE

Our research design was based upon the major assumption that the United States is a democracy. Taking this point for granted, we prepared an interviewing schedule around the presumably basic principles of democracy and interviewed samples of voters in two American cities to elicit their attitudes toward these principles.

While the general research design was thus quite simple, the preparation of a questionnaire including the basic points on which agreement is thought to be

---

[19] *Ibid.*

[20] *Op. cit.,* 131.

[21] That the awareness is so consistently forgotten attests to the need of uniting research in political theory with research in public opinion.

necessary was a difficult and critical step. From the literature on consensus cited above and from general literature on democracy, however, we conclude that the principles regarded as most essential to democracy are majority rule and minority rights (or freedom to dissent). At the abstract level, then, our interviewers asked for expressions of agreement or disagreement on the following statements:

PRINCIPLE OF DEMOCRACY IT-SELF

Democracy is the best form of government.

PRINCIPLE OF MAJORITY RULE

Public officials should be chosen by majority vote. Every citizen should have an equal chance to influence government policy.

PRINCIPLE OF MINORITY RIGHTS

The minority should be free to criticize majority decisions. People in the minority should be free to try to win majority support for their opinions.

From these general statements, specific embodiments of the principles of democracy were derived.

PRINCIPLE OF MAJORITY RULE IN SPECIFIC TERMS

1. In a city referendum, only people who are well informed about the problem being voted on should be allowed to vote.
2. In a city referendum deciding on tax-supported undertakings, only taxpayers should be allowed to vote.
3. If a Negro were legally elected mayor of this city, the white people should not allow him to take office.
4. If a Communist were legally elected mayor of this city, the people should not allow him to take office.
5. A professional organization like the AMA (the American Medical Association) has a right to try to increase the influence of

doctors by getting them to vote as a bloc in elections.

PRINCIPLE OF MINORITY RIGHTS IN SPECIFIC TERMS

6. If a person wanted to make a speech in this city against churches and religion, he should be allowed to speak.
7. If a person wanted to make a speech in this city favoring government ownership of all the railroads and big industries, he should be allowed to speak.
8. If an admitted Communist wanted to make a speech in this city favoring Communism, he should be allowed to speak.
9. A Negro should not be allowed to run for mayor of this city.
10. A Communist should not be allowed to run for mayor of this city.

These specific propositions are designed to embody the principles of majority rule and minority rights in such a clear fashion that a "correct" or "democratic" response can be deduced from endorsement of the general principles. The democratic response to statements 1 and 2 are negative, for example, since a restriction of the franchise to the well-informed or to taxpayers would violate the principle that "Every citizen should have an equal chance to influence government policy."[22] The same general principle requires an affirmative answer to the fifth statement, which applies the right of people to "influence government policy" to the election efforts of a specific professional group. The correct responses to statements 3 and 4 are negative because denial of an office to any person "legally elected" would violate the principle that "public

[22] We are not arguing, of course, that these propositions are incorrect in any absolute sense. Good arguments can no doubt be advanced in support of each of the positions we label as "incorrect." Our point is simply that they are incorrect *in the sense* of being undemocratic, *i.e.,* inconsistent with general principles of democracy.

officials should be chosen by majority vote."

Of the five statements derived from the broad principle of minority rights, 6, 7, and 8 put the right of "the minority . . . to criticize majority decisions" and "to try to win majority support for their opinions" in terms of specific minority spokesmen; agreement is therefore the correct or democratic answer. Disagreement is the correct response to statements 9 and 10, since denial of the right to seek office to members of minority ethnic or ideological groups directly violates their right "to try to win majority support for their opinions."

Since the proposition being tested asserts the existence of consensus, the interviewing sample could logically have been drawn from any group of Americans. Because we assume regional and class differences, however, we could not rely on the most available respondents, our own college students. The registered voters of two academic communities, Ann Arbor, Michigan, and Tallahassee, Florida, were selected as the sampling population, primarily because they fitted the needs of the hypothesis, and partly because of their accessibility. Although a nation-wide survey was ruled out simply on the ground of costs, these atypical communities offer certain advantages for our problem. First, they do permit at least a limited regional comparison of attitudes on democratic fundamentals. Second, they skew the sample by over-representing the more highly educated, thus permitting detailed comparison of the highly educated with the poorly educated, a comparison that could hardly be made with samples from more typical communities.

The over-representation of the highly educated also served to "stack the cards" in favor of the proposition on consensus. Since our hypothesis holds that consensus is limited, we further stacked the cards against the hypothesis by choosing the sample from registered voters rather than all residents of the two communities. Although the necessity of consensus is stated in terms of the society as a whole, a line of regression is available in the argument

that it need exist only among those who take part in politics. Hence our restriction of the sample to a population of registered voters.

In each city the sample was drawn by the system of random numbers from the official lists of registered voters. The sample represents one per cent of the registered voters from the current registration list in each of the two communities. In a few cases the addresses given were incorrect, but if the person selected could be located in the community, he was included in the sample. A few questions on a limited number of individuals were not recorded in usable form, which accounts for a slight variation in the totals in the tables presented in the paper.

FINDINGS: THE CONSENSUS PROBLEM

In the two communities from which our samples were drawn, consensus can be said to exist among the voters on the basic principles of democracy when they are put in abstract terms. The degree of agreement on these principles ranges from 94.7 to 98.0 per cent, which appears to represent consensus in a truly meaningful sense and to support the first of our preliminary assumptions. On the generalized principles, then, we need not look for "bases of disagreement"—the agreement transcends community, educational, economic, age, sex, party, and other common bases of differences in opinion.[23] We may stop with the conclusion that opinions on these abstract principles have a cultural base.

When these broad principles are translated into more specific propositions, however, consensus breaks down completely. As Table 1 indicates, agreement does not reach 90 per cent on any of the ten propositions, either from the two samples combined or from the communities considered separately. Indeed, respondents in both communities are closer to perfect

[23] See Angus Campbell and Homer C. Cooper, *Group Differences in Attitudes and Votes* (Ann Arbor, 1956).

TABLE 1. PERCENTAGE OF "DEMOCRATIC" RESPONSES TO BASIC PRINCIPLES OF DEMOCRACY AMONG SELECTED POPULATION GROUPS

	Total (N = 244)	Education [c]		Ann Arbor (N = 144)	Talla-hassee (N = 100)	Income [d]	
		High (N = 137)	Low (N = 106)			High (N = 136)	Low (N = 99)
Majority rule							
1. Only informed vote [a]	49.0	61.7	34.7	56.3	38.4	56.6	40.8
2. Only tax-payers vote [a]	21.0	22.7	18.6	20.8	21.2	20.7	21.0
3. Bar Negro from office [a]	80.6	89.7	68.6	88.5	66.7	83.2	77.8
4. Bar Communist from office [a]	46.3	56.1	34.0	46.9	45.5	48.9	43.0
5. AMA right to bloc voting [b]	45.0	49.6	39.2	44.8	45.5	45.5	44.4
Minority rights							
6. Allow anti-religious speech [b]	63.0	77.4	46.5	67.4	56.6	72.8	52.1
7. Allow socialist speech [b]	79.4	90.2	65.7	81.3	76.8	83.8	73.7
8. Allow Communist speech [b]	44.0	62.9	23.5	51.4	33.3	52.2	36.7
9. Bar Negro from candidacy [a]	75.5	86.5	60.2	85.6	58.0	78.6	71.1
10. Bar Communist from candidacy [a]	41.7	48.1	30.3	44.1	38.2	44.8	34.4

[a] For these statements, disagreement is recorded as the "democratic" response.
[b] For these statements, agreement is recorded as the "democratic" response.
[c] "High education" means more than 12 years of schooling; "low education," 12 years or less.
[d] "High income" means an annual family income of $6,000 or more; "low income," less than $6,000.

discord than to perfect consensus on over half the statements. If we keep in mind that a 50-50 division represents a total absence of consensus, then degrees of agreement ranging from 25 to 75 per cent can be understood as closer to the total absence of consensus (50 per cent agreement) than to its perfect realization (100 per cent agreement). Responses from voters in both communities fall in this "discord" range on six of the statements (1, 4, 5, 6, 8, and 10); voters in the Southern community approach maximum discord on two additional statements (3 and 9), both of which put democratic principles in terms of Negro participation in public office. These findings strongly support the second of our preliminary assumptions, that consensus does not exist on more concrete questions involving the application of democratic principles.

Three of the statements that evoke more discord than consensus deal with the extension of democratic principles to Communists, a highly unpopular group in the United States. But it should be noted that these statements are put in terms of generally approved behaviors (speaking and seeking public office), not conspiratorial or other reprehensible activities. And the other statements on which discord exceeds consensus refer to groups (as well as activities) that are not in opposition to the American form of government: the right of all citizens to vote, the right of a professional group to maximize its voting strength, and the right to criticize churches and religion.

The extent to which consensus breaks down on the specific formulation of democratic principles is even greater than suggested by our discussion of the range of discord. To this point we have ignored the content of the opinions on these priniciples, which would permit an overwhelming *rejection* of a democratic principle to be accepted as consensus. Specifically, responses to statement 2 were not counted as falling in the "discord" category but the approach to consensus in this case lies in rejection of the democratic principle of the "majority vote" with an "equal chance" for "every

citizen." But the proposition about consensus holds, of course, that the consensus is in favor of democratic principles. On four statements (2, 4, 5, and 10) a majority of the voters in Ann Arbor express "undemocratic" opinions; and on six statements (1, 2, 4, 5, 8, and 10) a majority of the voters in Tallahassee express "undemocratic" opinions.

However the reactions to our specific statements are approached, they run counter to the idea of extended consensus. On none of them is there the real consensus that we found on the abstract form of the principles; responses to over half of the statements express the "wrong" answers. Unlike the general statements, then, the specific propositions call for an appraisal of bases of agreement and disagreement.

FINDINGS: BASES OF AGREEMENT AND DISAGREEMENT

The report of findings on the consensus problem has already suggested that regional subcultures are one basis of differences in opinions on democratic principles. Table 1 also shows differences along educational and income lines. Not included are other possible bases of disagreement that were found to have only a negligible effect, *e.g.*, age, sex and party.

Community, education and income all have an effect on opinions about democratic principles. More "correct" responses came from the Midwestern than from the Southern community, from those with high education than from those with less education, and from those with high income than from those with low income. The systematic nature of these differences supports the assumption that regional and class-related factors affect attitudes toward democratic principles when they are put in specific terms.

Which of these variables has the greatest effect on attitudes toward basic principles of democracy? Table 1 suggests that education is most important on two counts: (1) for every statement, the greatest difference in opinions is found in the high education-low education dichotomy; (2) for every statement, the grouping with the most "correct" or "democratic" responses is the high education category. Before education can be accepted as the independent variable in relation to democratic attitudes, however, the relationship must be examined for true independence. Since more Ann Arbor than Tallahassee respondents fall in the high education category, and since more high income than low income respondents have high education, the education variable might prove to be spurious—with the concealed community and income factors accounting for its apparent effect. Tables 2 and 3 show that when we control for community and income, differences between the high and low education respondents remain. When we control for education, on the other hand, the smaller differences reported in Table 1 by community and income tend to disappear.[24]

Since educational differences hold up consistently when other factors are "partialled out," education may be accepted as the most consequential basis of opinions on basic democratic principles.[25] Regardless of their other group identifications, people with high education accept democratic principles more than any other grouping. While the highly educated thus come closest to qualifying as the carriers of the democratic creed, the data do not support our hypothesis; consensus in a meaningful sense (on both the abstract and the specific principles) is not found even among those with high education. On only three of the ten specific statements (3, 7, and 9) does agreement among those with high education reach 90 per cent in Ann Arbor, and in Tallahassee it fails to reach 90 per cent on any of the statements. On the proposition that the vote should be restricted to tax-

payers in referenda deciding on tax-supported undertakings, 75.8 per cent of the highly educated in Ann Arbor and 81.5 per cent in Tallahassee reject the democratic principle of an equal vote for every citizen. And on five statements (1, 4, 5, 8, and 10) the highly educated in both communities are closer to perfect discord than to prefect harmony. Even when the necessity of consensus is reformulated in terms of the group most in accord with democratic principles, then, consensus cannot be said to exist.

SUMMARY AND CONCLUSIONS

The attitudes of voters in selected Midwestern and Southern communities offer no support for the hypothesis that democracy requires a large measure of consensus among the carriers of the creed, *i.e.*, those most consistently in accord with democratic principles. As expected, general consensus was found on the idea of democracy itself and on the broad principles of majority rule and minority rights, but it disapeared when these principles were put in more specific form. Indeed, the voters in both communities were closer to complete discord than to complete consensus; they did not reach consensus on any of the ten specific statements incorporating the principles of majority rule and minority rights; and majorities expressed the "undemocratic" attitude on about half of the statements.

In trying to identify the carriers of the creed, the expected regional and class-related variations were found in attitudes toward democratic principles in specific form, with education having the most marked effect. While attitudes on democratic fundamentals were not found to vary appreciably according to age, sex or party affiliation, they did vary according to education, community, and income. The greatest difference on every statement was between the high-education group and the low-education group, and the high-education group gave the most democratic response to every question, whether compared with other educational, com-

---

[24] Those statements with particular salience for one of the regional subcultures (Southern anti-Negro sentiment) constitute an exception.

[25] For a discussion of this approach to controlling qualitative data, see Herbert Hyman, *Survey Design and Analysis* (Glencoe, 1955), Ch. 7.

TABLE 2. PERCENTAGE OF "DEMOCRATIC" RESPONSES TO BASIC PRINCIPLES OF DEMOCRACY BY EDUCATION, WITH INCOME CONTROLLED

Statement	High-Low Education Differences (N = 134)(N = 101)	Low income			High Income		
		High Education (N = 42)	Low Education (N = 58)	Difference	High Education (N = 92)	Low Education (N = 43)	Difference
1	27.0	67.5	22.4	45.1	59.1	51.2	7.9
2	4.1	20.0	22.0	−2.0	23.9	14.0	9.9
3	21.1	94.4	64.4	30.0	87.8	73.2	14.6
4	22.1	55.0	35.0	20.0	56.5	32.6	23.9
5	10.4	52.5	39.0	13.5	48.4	39.5	8.9
6	30.9	67.5	41.1	26.4	81.7	53.5	28.2
7	24.5	87.5	64.4	23.1	91.4	67.4	24.0
8	39.4	59.0	22.0	37.0	64.5	25.6	38.9
9	26.3	86.1	59.6	26.5	86.7	61.0	25.7
10	17.8	41.0	39.8	11.2	51.1	31.0	20.1

Table 3. Percentage of "Democratic" Responses to Basic Principles of Democracy by Education, with Community Controlled

Statement	High-Low Education Differences (N = 137)(N = 106)	Ann Arbor			Tallahassee		
		High Education (N = 92)	Low Education (N = 52)	Difference	High Education (N = 45)	Low Education (N = 54)	Difference
1	27.0	63.7	42.3	21.4	57.1	26.5	30.6
2	4.1	24.2	15.4	8.8	19.5	22.0	−2.5
3	21.1	94.4	77.6	16.8	78.4	56.8	21.6
4	22.1	56.7	28.8	27.9	54.8	39.2	15.6
5	10.4	48.4	38.5	9.9	53.3	38.9	14.4
6	30.9	80.2	47.1	33.1	71.4	45.8	25.6
7	24.5	92.3	61.5	30.8	85.7	70.0	15.7
8	39.4	67.0	23.1	43.9	53.7	24.5	29.2
9	26.3	96.6	65.3	31.3	62.2	53.8	8.4
10	17.8	48.9	34.6	14.3	46.4	25.5	20.9

munity or income groupings. Education, but not community or income, held up consistently as a basis of disagreement when other factors were controlled. We accordingly conclude that endorsement of democratic principles is not a function of class as such (of which income is also a criterion), but of greater acquaintance with the logical implications of the broad democratic principles. Note, for example, that the highly educated renounce in much greater degree than any other group the restriction of the vote to the well-informed, a restriction that would presumably affect them least of all.

Although high education was the primary basis of agreement on democratic principles, actual consensus was not found even among this segment of the voting population. The approach to consensus is closer among the highly educated in Ann Arbor, where greater agreement exists on the extension of democratic rights to Negroes, but in both communities the highly educated are closer to discord than consensus on half of the statements. On the basis of these findings, our hypothesis appears to be invalid.

Our failure to find a more extended consensus may, of course, be attributed to the possibility that the statements we formulated do not incorporate the particular "fundamentals" that are actually necessary to democracy.[26] When the approach to consensus is in the "undemocratic" direction—as in the question about restricting the vote to tax-payers—two possible objections to our interviewing schedule are suggested. First, perhaps the question is not a logical derivation from the basic principles with which we began. Second, perhaps the respondents are not interpreting the questions in any uniform way.

On the first point, the logical connection of the specific proposition with the general proposition is virtually self-evident. In syllogistic terms, we have: major premise—every citizen should have an equal chance to influence government policy; minor premise—nontax-payers are citizens; conclusion—nontax-payers should be allowed to vote in a city referendum deciding on tax-suppotred undertakings. Since decisions on tax-supported undertakings are clearly matters of government policy, rejection of the conclusion is inconsistent with acceptance of the major premise. As a matter of policy, perhaps the vote should be restricted—as it often is—under the circumstances indicated. We simply note that such a position is inconsistent with the unqualified major premise.

As to the second apparent difficulty, varying interpretations of the questions undoubtedly influenced the results. As our pre-test of the questionnaire indicated, the wordings finally chosen conveyed common meanings but tapped different attitudes embedded in different frames of reference. In surveys, as in real political situations, citizens are confronted with the need for making decisions about questions to which they attribute varying implications. We can infer, for example, that the respondents who repudiate free speech for Communists are responding in terms of anti-Communist rather than anti-free speech sentiments, especially since they endorse the idea of free speech in general. Conversely, those who endorse free speech for Communists are presumably reflecting a more consistent dedication to free speech rather than pro-Communist sentiments. But our concern in this study is with the opinions themselves rather than with the varying functions that a given opinion may perform for different individuals.[27] The significant fact is that the opinions (and presumably the frames of reference that produce them) vary systematically from group to group, not randomly or on a meaninglessly idiosyncratic basis.

Assuming that the United States is a

---

[26] The lack of extended consensus cannot, however, be attributed to the possibility that the responses classified as "correct" are actually "incorrect," for we found consensus neither in acceptance nor in rejection of the statements.

[27] The latter approach is, of course, a fruitful type of investigation, but it is not called for by our problem. For a functional analysis of opinions, see M. Brewster Smith, Jerome S. Bruner and Robert W. White, *Opinions and Personality* (New York, 1956).

democracy, we cannot say without qualification that consensus on fundamental principles is a necessary condition for the existence of democracy. Nor does it appear valid to say that, although consensus need not pervade the entire voting population, it must exist at least among the highly educated, who are the carriers of the creed. Our data are not inconsistent, of course, with the qualified proposition that consensus on fundamental principles in a highly abstract form is a necessary condition for the existence of democracy. But the implication of political theory that consensus includes more specific principles is empirically invalid. Our findings accordingly suggest that the intuitive insights and logical inferences of political theorists need to be subjected more consistently to empirical validation.

Discussions of consensus tend to overlook the functional nature of apathy for the democratic system. No one is surprised to hear what people *say* they *believe* and what they *actually* do are not necessarily the same. We usually assume that verbal positions represent a higher level—a more "democratic" stance—than non-verbal behavior. But something close to the opposite may also be true: many people express undemocratic principles in response to questioning but are too apathetic to act on their undemocratic opinions in concrete situations. And in most cases, fortunately for the democratic system, those with the most undemocratic principles are also those who are least likely to act. A sizeable number (42.0 per cent) of our Southern respondents said, for example, that "a Negro should not be allowed to run for mayor of this city," but a few months before the survey a Negro actually did conduct an active campaign for that office without any efforts being made by the "white" people to obstruct his candidacy.

In this case, the behavior was more democratic than the verbal expressions. If the leadership elements—the carriers of the creed—had encouraged undemocratic action, it might have materialized (as it did in Little Rock in the school desegregation crisis). But, in fact, people with basically undemocratic opinions either abstained from acting or acted in a perfectly democratic fashion. "The successful working of the system is not deliberately aimed at by those who work it," John Plamenatz says, "but is the result of their behaving as they do."[28] As J. Roland Pennock puts it, democracy can tolerate less conscious agreement on principles if people are willing to compromise and to follow set rules and procedures.[29] Loose talk of consensus as a self-evident requirement of democracy should have no place beside such insightful observations as these. Carl J. Friedrich appears to have been correct in asserting, eighteen years ago, that democracy depends on habitual patterns of behavior rather than on conscious agreement on democratic "principles."[30] His argument has been largely ignored because, like the position from which he dissented, it was advanced without the support of directly relevant research findings. Our results are offered as a step toward settling the question on empirical grounds.

---

[28] *Op. cit.,* p. 123.
[29] *Op. cit.,* p. 132.
[30] *The New Belief in the Common Man* (Boston, 1942).

Consensus and Ideology
in American Politics*

HERBERT MCCLOSKY

The belief that consensus is a prerequisite of democracy has, since deTocqueville, so often been taken for granted that it is refreshing to find the motion now being challenged. Prothro and Grigg,[1] for example, have questioned whether agreement on "fundamentals" actually exists among the electorate, and have furnished data which indicate that it may not. Dahl,[2] reviewing his study of community decision-makers, has inferred that political stability does not depend upon widespread belief in the superiority of democratic norms and procedures, but only upon their *acceptance*. From the findings turned up by Stouffer,[3] and by Prothro and Grigg, he further conjectures

that agreement on democratic norms is greater among the politically active and aware—the "political stratum" as he calls them—than among the voters in general. V. O. Key,[4] going a step further, suggests that the viability of a democracy may depend less upon popular opinion than upon the activities and values of an "aristocratic" strain whose members are set off from the mass by their political influence, their attention to public affairs, and their active role as society's policy makers. "If so, any assessment of the vitality of a democratic system should rest on an examination of the outlook, the sense of purpose, and the beliefs of this sector of society."

Writers who hold consensus to be necessary to a free society have commonly failed to define it precisely or to specify what it must include. Even Tocqueville[5] does not go deeply enough into the matter to satisfy these needs. He tells us that a society can exist and, *a fortiori* prosper only when "the minds of all the citizens (are) rallied and held together by certain predominant ideas; . . . when a great number of men consider a great number of things from the same aspect, when they hold the same opinions upon many subjects, and when the same occurrences suggest the same thoughts and impressions to their minds"—and he follows this pronouncement with a list of general

SOURCE. Reprinted from *The American Political Science Review*, Vol. 58, 1964, by permission of the author and publisher. Copyright 1964, The American Political Science Association.

* This is a revised version of a paper initially prepared for delivery at the Annual Meeting of the American Political Science Association, Washington D.C., September 1962. The research on which it is based has been processed and analyzed through the Survey Research Center, University of California, Berkeley. Major support for the research was made available by the Social Science Research Council; supplementary support was given by the Rockefeller Foundation and the Institute of Social Sciences, University of California. I am indebted to my research assistant, Beryl L. Crowe, for assistance in the preparation of the research materials. This article may be referred to as number A22 in the Survey Research Center's publication series.

[1] James W. Prothro and C. W. Grigg, "Fundamental Principles of Democracy: Bases of Agreement and Disagreement," *Journal of Politics*, Vol. 22 (Spring, 1960), pp. 276-94.
[2] Robert A. Dahl, *Who Governs?* (New Haven, 1961), ch. 28.
[3] Samuel A. Stouffer, *Communism, Conformity, and Civil Liberties* (New York, 1955).

[4] V. O. Key, "Public Opinion and the Decay of Democracy," *Virginia Q. Rev.*, Vol. 37 (Autumn, 1961), pp. 481-94. See also David B. Truman, "The American System in Crisis," *Political Science Quarterly*, Vol. 74 (Dec., 1959), pp. 481-97. John Plamenatz, "Cultural Prerequisites to a Successfully Functioning Democracy: a Symposium," this *Review*, Vol. 50 (March, 1956), p. 123.
[5] Alexis deTocqueville, *Democracy in America*, ed. Phillips Bradley (New York, 1945),

principles he believes Americans hold in common. Elsewhere, he speaks of the "customs" of the American nation (its "habits, opinions, usages, and beliefs") as "the peculiar cause which renders that people able to support a democratic government." But nowhere does he set forth explicitly the nature of the agreement upon which a democratic society presumably depends.

Later commentators have not clarified matters much. Some, like A. Lawrence Lowell,[6] have avoided Tocqueville's emphasis upon shared ideas, customs, and opinions in favor of the less demanding view that popular government requires agreement mainly "in regard to the legitimate character of the ruling authority and its right to decide the questions that arise." Consensus in this view, becomes merely a synonym for legitimacy. Others speak of consensus as a sense of solidarity or social cohesion arising from a common ethos or heritage, which unites men into a community.[7] Political scientists have most frequently employed the term to designate a state of agreement about the "fundamental values" or "rules of the game" considered essential for constitutional government. Rarely, however, have writers on consensus attempted to state what the fundamentals must include, how extensive the agreement must be, the *who* must agree. Its agreement required among

---

II, p. 8; I, pp. 392, 322. The difficulty of specifying the values which underly democracy, and on which consensus is presumed to be required, is illustrated in the exchange between Ernest S. Griffith, John Plamenatz, and J. Roland Pennock, cited above, pp. 101-37. The problem of certifying the "fundamentals" of democratic consensus is directly discussed by Pennock, pp. 132-3. See also Peter Bachrach, "Elite Consensus and Democracy," *Journal of Politics*, Vol. 24 (August, 1962), pp. 449-52.

[6] A. L. Lowell, *Public Opinion and Popular Government* (New York, 1926), p. 9.

[7] Cf., for example, Louis Wirth, *Community Life and Social Policy* (Chicago, 1956), pp. 201-3, 381-2. For a critique of "consensus theory" and the several definitions of consensus see Irving L. Horowitz, "Consensus, Conflict, and Cooperation: A Sociological Inventory," *Social Forces*, Vol. 41 (Dec., 1962), pp. 177-188.

all men or only among certain of them? Among the entire electorate or only those who actively participate in public affairs? Is the same type of consensus essential for democracies at all times, or is a firmer and more sweeping consensus needed for periods of crisis than for periods of calm, for newer, developing democracies than for older stable ones?

While certain of these questions are beyond the scope of this paper (no one, in any event, has done the systematic historical and comparative research to answer them satisfactorily), something might be learned about the relation of ideological consensus to democracy by investigating the subject in at least one major democracy, the United States. In the present paper I wish to explore further some of the questions raised by the writers I have cited and to present research findings on several hypotheses relating to those questions.

I. HYPOTHESES AND DEFINITIONS

We expected the data to furnish support for the following hypotheses, among others:

That the American electorate is often divided on "fundamental" democratic values and procedural "rules of the game" and that its understanding of politics and of political ideas is in any event too rudimentary at present to speak of ideological "consensus" among its members.

That, as Prothro and Grigg report for their samples, the electorate exhibits greater support for general, abstract statements of democratic belief than for their specific applications.

That the constituent ideas of American democratic ideology are principally held by the more "articulate" segments of the population, including the political influentials; and that people in these ranks will exhibit a more meaningful and far reaching consensus on democratic and constitutional values than will the general population.

That consensus is far from perfect even among the articulate classes, and will be evidenced on political questions more than on economic ones, on procedural rights more than on public policies, and on freedom more than equality.

That whatever increases the level of political articulateness—education, S.E.S., urban residence, intellectuality, political activity, etc.—strengthens consensus and support for American political ideology and institutions.

Whether a word like ideology can properly be employed in the American context depends, in part, on which of its many connotations one choose to emphasize. Agreement on the meaning of the term is far from universal, but a tendency can be discerned among contemporary writers to regard ideologies as *systems* of belief that are elaborate, integrated, and coherent, that justify the exercise of power, explain and judge historical events, identify political right and wrong, set forth the interconnections (causal and moral) between politics and other spheres of activity, and furnish guides for action.[8] While liberal democracy does not fulfill perfectly the terms of this definition, it comes close enough, in my opinion, to be considered an ideology.[9] The elements of liberal democratic

[8] Cf. Daniel Bell, *The End of Ideology* (Glencoe, 1960), pp. 369-75; Edward Shils, "Ideology and Civility: on the Politics of the Intellectual," *Sewanee Review*, Vol. 66 (Summer, 1958), pp. 450-1; Louis Wirth, op. cit., pp. 202-3.

[9] A persuasive case for considering liberal democracy as an ideology is made by Bernard Williams, "Democracy and Ideology," *Political Science Quarterly*, Vol. 32 (October-December, 1961), pp. 374-84. The nature of ideology in America and some of the other questions addressed in the present paper are discussed by Robert G. McCloskey, "The American Ideology," in Marian D. Irish (ed.), *Continuing Crisis in American Politics* (Englewood Cliffs, N.J., 1963), pp. 10-25.

thought are not nearly so vague as they are sometimes made out to be, and their coalescence into a single body of belief is by no means fortuitous. American democratic "ideology" possesses an elaborately defined theory, a body of interrelated assumptions, axioms, and principles, and a set of ideals that serve as guides for action. Its tenets, postulates, sentiments, and values inspired the great revolutions of the seventeenth and eighteenth centuries, and have been repeatedly and explicitly set forth in fundamental documents, such as the Constitution, the Declaration, and the Federalist Papers. They have been restated with remarkable unanimity in the messages of Presidents, in political speeches, in the pronouncements of judges and constitutional commentators, and in the writings of political theorists, historians, and publicists. They are so familiar that we are likely to see them not as a coherent union of ideas and principles embodying a well-defined political tendency, but as a miscellany of slogans and noble sentiments to be trotted out on ceremonial occasions.

Although scholars or Supreme Court justices might argue over fine points of interpretation, they would uniformly recognize as elements of American democratic ideology such concepts as consent, accountability, limited or constitutional government, representation, majority rule, minority rights, the principle of political opposition, freedom of thought, speech, press, and assembly, equality of opportunity, religious toleration, equality before the law, the rights of juridical defense, and individual self-determination over a broad range of personal affairs. How widely such elements of American liberal democracy are approved, by whom and with what measure of understanding, is another question—indeed, it is the central question to be addressed in this paper. But that they form an integrated body of ideas which has become part of the American inheritance seems scarcely open to debate.[10]

The term consensus will be employed in this paper to designate a state of agreement concerning the aforementioned values. It has principally to do with shared beliefs and not with feelings of solidarity, the willingness to live together, to obey the laws, or to accept the existing government as legitimate. Nor does it refer to an abstract or universal state of mind, but to a measurable state of concurrence around values that can be specified. Consensus exists in degree and can be expressed in quantitative form. No one, of course, can say how close one must come to unanimity before consensus is achieved, for the cutting point, as with any continuous variable, is arbitrary. Still, the term in ordinary usage has been reserved for fairly substantial measures of correspondence, and we shall take as a minimal requirement for consensus a level of agreement reaching 75 per cent. This figure, while also arbitrary, recommends itself by being realistically modest (falling as it does midway between a bare majority and unanimity), and by having been designated in this country and elsewhere as the extraordinary majority required for certain constitutional purposes.

Since I shall in subsequent pages frequently (and interchangeably) employ such terms as the "articulate minority," the "political class," the "political elite," the "political influentials," and the "political stratum," I should also clarify what

[10] See Gunnar Myrdal, *An American Dilemma: The Negro Problem and American Democracy* (New York, 1944), ch. 1. For a comprehensive review of the American value system and evidence concerning its stability over time, see Clyde Kluckhohn, "Have There Been Discernible Shifts in American Values during the Past Generation?" in E. E. Morison (ed.), *The American Style: Essays in Value and Performance* (New York, 1958), pp. 145-217. Kluckhohn concludes (p. 152) that despite some changes, the American value system has been "remarkably stable" since the 18th century and remains "highly influential in the life of the United States."

they are intended to signify. I mean them to refer to those people who occupy themselves with public affairs to an unusual degree, such as government officials, elected office holders, active party members, publicists, officers of voluntary associations, and opinion leaders. The terms do not apply to any definable social class in the usual sense, nor to a particular status group or profession. Although the people they designate can be distinguished from other citizens by their activity and concerns, they are in no sense a community, they do not act as a body, and they do not necessarily possess identical or even harmonious interests. "Articulates" or "influentials" can be found scattered throughout the society, at all income levels, in all classes, occupations, ethnic groups, and communities, although some segments of the population will doubtless yield a higher proportion of them than others. I scarcely need to add that the line between the "articulates" and the rest of the population cannot always be sharply drawn, for the qualities that distinguish them vary in form and degree and no single criterion of classification will satisfy every contingency.

The data for the present inquiry have been taken from a national study of political actives and supporters carried out in 1957-58. I have in a previous paper described the procedures of that study in some detail,[11] and will not trouble to repeat that description here. Perhaps it will suffice for present purposes merely to note the following: national surveys were carried out on two separate samples, the first a sample of over 3,000 political "actives" or "leaders" drawn from the delegates and alternates who had attended the Democratic and Republican conventions of 1956; the second a representative

[11] Herbert McClosky, Paul J. Hoffmann, and Rosemary O'Hara, "Issue Conflict and Consensus Among Party Leaders and Followers," this *Review,* Vol. 44 (June, 1960), pp. 406-27.

national sample of approximately 1,500 adults in the general population drawn by the American Institute of Public Opinion (Gallup Poll). Gallup interviewers also delivered and introduced the questionnaire to all respondents, discussed its contents with them, and furnished both oral and written instructions for its self-administration and completion. (For sample characteristics, see Appendix B.)

The party actives may be considered an especially pure sample of the "political stratum," for every person in the sample has marked himself off from the average citizen by his greater political involvement. Although the general population sample may be regarded as a sample of "inarticulates," to be compared with the sample of leaders, there are within it, of course, many persons who by virtue of education, profession, organizational activities, etc. can be classified as "articulates." We shall for certain purposes consider them in this light in order to provide further tests for our hypotheses.

Both samples received the same questionnaire—a lengthy instrument containing questions on personal background, political experience, values, attitudes, opinions, political and economic orientation, party outlooks, and personality characteristics. Many of the questions were direct inquiries in the standard form, but most were single sentence "items" with which the respondent was compelled to express his agreement or disagreement. While each of these items can stand alone and be regarded in its own right as an indicator of a person's opinions or attitudes, each of them is simultaneously an integral element of one of the 47 "scales" that was expressly fashioned to afford a more refined and reliable assessment of the attitude and personality predispositions of every respondent. Each of the scales (averaging approximately nine items) has been independently validated either by empirical validation procedures employing approximate criterion groups, or by a modified Guttman reproducibility procedure (supplemented in some instances, by a "face validity" procedure utilizing item ratings by experts).

Data on the *scale* scores are presented in Table 4 and are to be distinguished from the "percentage agree" scores for *individual items* presented in the remaining tables.

II. FINDINGS

"RULES OF THE GAME" AND DEMOCRATIC VALUES

Although the so-called "rules of the game" are often separated from other democratic values, the distinction is to some extent arbitrary. One might, for example, reasonably regard as "rules of the game" many of the norms governing free speech, press, social and political equality, political toleration, and the enforcement of justice. For convenience, nevertheless, we shall treat separately those responses that stand out from the general body of democratic attitudes by their particular emphasis upon fair play, respect for legal procedures, and consideration for the rights of others. A sample of items expressing these values is presented in Table 1.

The responses to these items show plainly that while a majority of the electorate support the "rules of the game," approval of such values is significantly greater and more uniform among the influentials. The latter have achieved consensus (as we have defined it) on eight of the twelve items and near consensus on three of the remaining four items. The electorate, by contrast, does not meet the criterion for consensus on a single item.

Although the *scales* (as distinguished from individual *items*) cannot appropriately be used to measure *consensus*, comparison of the scores on those scales which most nearly embody the "rules of the game" furnishes additional evidence that the political class responds to such norms more favorably than does the electorate. The proportion scoring high[12] on

---

[12] "High" refers to a score made by the upper third of the popular distribution on the scale in question. For example, in the case of the "political indulgence" scale approximately one-third (actually 30.6%) re-

Table 1. Political Influentials vs. the Electorate: Response to Items Expressing "Rules of the Game"[a]

Items	Political Influentials (N-3020)	General Electorate (N-1484)
	% Agree	
There are times when it almost seems better for the people to take the law into their own hands rather than wait for the machinery of government to act.	13.3	26.9
The majority has the right to abolish minorities if it wants to.	6.8	28.4
We might as well make up our minds that in order to make the world better a lot of innocent people will have to suffer.	27.2	41.6
If congressional committees stuck strictly to the rules and gave every witness his rights, they would never succeed in exposing the many dangerous subversives they have turned up.	24.7	47.4
I don't mind a politician's methods if he manages to get the right things done.	25.6	42.4
Almost any unfairness or brutality may have to be justified when some great purpose is being carried out.	13.3	32.8
Politicians have to cut a few corners if they are going to get anywhere.	29.4	43.2
People ought to be allowed to vote even if they can't do so intelligently.	65.6	47.6
To bring about great changes for the benefit of mankind often requires cruelty and even ruthlessness.	19.4	31.3
Very few politicians have clean records, so why get excited about the mudslinging that sometimes goes on?	14.8	38.1
It is alright to get around the law if you don't actually break it.	21.2	30.2
The true American way of life is disappearing so fast that we may have to use force to save it.	12.8	34.6

[a] Since respondents were forced to make a choice on each item, the number omitted or "don't know" responses was, on the average, fewer than one percent, and thus has little influence on the direction or magnitude of the results reported in this and subsequent tables.

a scale of "faith in direct action" (a scale measuring the inclination to take the law into one's own hands) is 26.1 per cent for the active political minority and 42.5 percent for the general population.

ceived scores of five or above. Hence, anyone making a score of five or above on this scale is considered to have scored high in "political indulgence." "Low" refers to scores made by the lower third of the distribution.

On a scale assessing the willingness to flout the rules of political integrity, the proportions scoring high are 12.2 per cent and 30.6 per cent respectively. On "totalitarianism," a scale measuring the readiness to subordinate the rights of others to the pursuit of some collective political purpose, only 9.7 per cent of the political actives score high compared with 33.8 per cent of the general population.

These and other results which could be cited support the claim advanced by earlier investigators like Prothro and Grigg, and Hyman and Sheatsley,[13] that a large proportion of the electorate has failed to grasp certain of the underlying ideas and principles on which the American political system rests. Endorsement of these ideas is not unanimous among the political elite either, but is in every instance greater than that exhibited by the masses.

The picture changes somewhat when we turn from "rules of the game" to items which in a broad, general way express belief in freedom of speech and opinion. As can be seen from Table 2,

support for these values is remarkably high for both samples. Both groups, in fact, respond so overwhelmingly to abstract statements about freedom that one is tempted to conclude that for these values, at least, a far-reaching consensus has been achieved.[14] These results become even more striking when we consider that the items in the table are not mere cliches but statements which in some instances closely paraphrase the arguments developed in Mill's essay, On Liberty. We cannot, therefore, dismiss them as mere responses to familiar, abstract sentiments which commit the respondent to nothing in particular.

Still, as can readily be discerned from the items in Table 3, previous investigators have been partially correct, at least,

[13] Prothro and Grigg, loc. cit.; Herbert Hyman and Paul B. Sheatsley, "The Current Status of American Public Opinion," in Daniel Katz et al. (eds.), Public Opinion and Propaganda (New York, 1954), pp. 33-48.

[14] CF. Robert Lane's report on his "Eastport" sample, in Political Ideology (New York, 1962), pp. 461-2.

TABLE 2. POLITICAL INFLUENTIALS VS. THE ELECTORATE: RESPONSES TO ITEMS EXPRESSING SUPPORT FOR GENERAL STATEMENTS OF FREE SPEECH AND OPINION

Items	Political Influentials (N-3020)	General Electorate (N-1484)
	% Agree	
People who hate our way of life should still have a chance to talk and be heard.	86.9	81.8
No matter what a person's political beliefs are, he is entitled to the same legal rights and protections as anyone else.	96.4	94.3
I believe in free speech for all no matter what their views might be.	89.4	88.9
Nobody has a right to tell another person what he should and should not read.	81.4	80.7
You can't really be sure whether an opinion is true or not unles people are free to argue against it.	94.9	90.8
Unless there is freedom for many points of view to be presented, there is little chance that the truth can ever be known.	90.6	85.2
I would not trust any person or group to decide what opinions can be freely expressed and what must be silenced.	79.1	64.6
Freedom of conscience should mean freedom to be an atheist as well as freedom to worship in the church of one's choice.	87.8	77.0

Table 3. Political Influentials vs. the Electorate: Response to Items Expressing Support for Specific Applications of Free Speech and Procedural Rights

Items	Political Influentials (N-3020)	General Electorate (N-1484)
	% Agree	
Freedom does not give anyone the right to teach foreign ideas in our schools.	45.5	56.7
A man oughtn't to be allowed to speak if he doesn't know what he's talking about.	17.3	36.7
A book that contains wrong political views cannot be a good book and does not deserve to be published.	17.9	50.3
When the country is in great danger we may have to force people to testify against themselves even if it violates their rights.	28.5	36.3
No matter what crime a person is accused of, he should never be convicted unless he has been given the right to face and question his accusers.	90.1	88.1
If a person is convicted of a crime by illegal evidence, he should be set free and the evidence thrown out of court.	79.6	66.1
If someone is suspected of treason or other serious crimes, he shouldn't be entitled to be let out on bail.	33.3	68.9
Any person who hides behind the laws when he is questioned about his activities doesn't deserve much consideration.	55.9	75.7
In dealing with dangerous enemies like the Communists, we can't afford to depend on the courts, the laws and their slow and unreliable methods.	7.4	25.5

in observing that the principles of freedom and democracy are less widely and enthusiastically favored when they are confronted in their specific, or applied forms.[15] As Dahl remarks, it is a "common tendency of mankind . . . to qualify universals in application while leaving them intact in rhetoric."[16] This observation, of course, also holds for the political articulates, but to a lesser degree. Not only do they exhibit stronger support for democratic values than does the electorate, but they are also more consistent in applying the general principle to the specific instance.[17] The average citizen has greater difficulty appreciating the importance of certain procedural or juridical rights, especially when he believes the country's internal security is at stake.

Findings which underscore and amplify these conclusions are yielded by a comparison of the scale scores. The data presented in Table 4 confirm that the influentials not only register higher scores on all the pro-democratic scales (faith in freedom, faith in democracy, procedural rights, tolerance), but are more likely to reject antidemocratic sentiments as well.

[15] See Hyman and Sheatsley, op. cit., pp. 40-2; Prothro and Grigg, op. cit.

[16] Robert A. Dahl, loc. cit. For data on the failure of some people to perceive the relevance of democratic principles for concrete situations see G. D. Wiebe, "The Army-McCarthy Hearings and the Public Conscience," *Public Opinion Quarterly*, Vol. 22 (Winter 1958-59), pp. 490-502.

[17] See also Stouffer, op. cit., ch. 2.

TABLE 4. POLITICAL INFLUENTIALS VS. THE ELECTORATE: PERCENTAGE SCORING HIGH AND LOW ON DEMOCRATIC AND ANTI-DEMOCRATIC ATTITUDE SCALES[a]

Scale	Political Influentials (N-3020)	General Electorate (N-1484)
	(%s down)	
Faith in democracy		
% High*	40.1	18.5
% Low	14.4	29.7
Procedural rights		
% High	58.1	24.1
% Low	12.3	31.3
Tolerance		
% High	61.3	43.1
% Low	16.4	33.2
Faith in freedom		
% High	63.0	48.4
% Low	17.1	28.4
Ethnocentrism		
% High	27.5	36.5
% Low	46.9	36.3
Elitism		
% High	22.8	38.7
% Low	41.0	22.4
Totalitarianism		
% High	9.7	33.8
% Low	60.1	28.4
Right wing		
% High	17.5	33.1
% Low	45.3	28.9
Left wing		
% High	6.7	27.8
% Low	68.7	39.3
California F-scale		
% High	14.7	33.5
% Low	48.0	23.5

[a] For explanation of % High and Low see footnote 12. The middle group has been omitted from this table. Differences between the influentials and the electorate on all the scales in this table are, by Kolmogorov-Smirnov and chi-square tests, statistically significant at or beyond the .01 percent level of significance.

Although they are themselves an elite of a sort, they display greater faith in the capacity of the mass of men to govern themselves, they believe more firmly in political equality, and they more often disdain the "extreme" beliefs embodied in the Right Wing, Left Wing, totalitarian, elitist, and authoritarian scales. Their repudiation of anti-democratic attitudes is by no means unanimous either, but their responses are more uniformly democratic than are those expressed by the electorate.

EQUALITARIAN VALUES

If Americans concur most strongly about liberty in the abstract, they disagree most strongly about equality. Examples of equalitarian values are presented in Table 5. Both the political stratum and the public divide sharply on these values, a finding which holds for political, as well are for social and economic equality. Both are torn not only on the empirical question of whether men are *in fact* equal but also on the normative issue of whether they should be *regarded* as equal. Neither comes close to achieving consensus on such questions as the ability of the people to rule themselves, to know their best interests in the long run, to understand the issues, or to pick their own leaders wisely. Support for these equalitarian features of "popular" democracy, however, is greater among the elite than among the masses.

The reverse is true for the values of economic equality. Among the political stratum, indeed, the weight of opinion is against equality—a result strongly though not exclusively influenced by the pronounced economic conservatism of the Republican leaders in the sample. Support for economic equality is only slightly greater among the electorate. The pattern, furthermore, is extremely spotty, with some policies strongly favored and others as strongly rejected. Thus approval is widespread for public policies (such as social security) that are designed to overcome gross inequalities, but is equally strong for certain features of economic life that promote inequality, such as

TABLE 5. POLITICAL INFLUENTIALS VS. THE ELECTORATE: RESPONSES TO ITEMS EXPRESSING BELIEF IN EQUALITY

Items	Political Influentials (N-3020)	General Electorate (N-1484)
	% Agree	
Political equality		
The main trouble with democracy is that most people don't really know what's best for them.	40.8	58.0
Few people really know what is in their own best interest in the long run.	42.6	61.1
"Issues" and "arguments" are beyond the understanding of most voters.	37.5	62.3
Most people don't have enough sense to pick their own leaders wisely.	28.0	47.8
It will always be necessary to have a few strong, able people actually running everything.	42.5	56.2
Social and ethnic equality		
We have to teach children that all men are created equal but almost everyone knows that some are better than others.	54.7	58.3
Just as is true of fine race horses, some breeds of people are just naturally better than others.	46.0	46.3
Regardless of what some people say, there are certain races in the world that just won't mix with Americans.	37.2	50.4
When it come to the things that count most, all races are certainly not equal.	45.3	49.0
The trouble with letting certain minority groups into a nice neighborhood is that they gradually give it their own atmosphere.	49.8	57.7
Economic equality		
Labor does not get its fair share of what it produces.	20.8	44.8
Every person should have a good house, even if the government has to build it for him.	14.9	28.2
I think the government should give a person work if he can't find another job.	23.5	47.3
The government ought to make sure that everyone has a good standard of living.	34.4	55.9
There will always be poverty, so people might as well get used to the idea.	40.4	59.4

private enterprise, economic competition, and unlimited pursuit of profit.[18] On social and ethnic equality, both samples are deeply split.

In short, both the public and its leaders are uncertain and ambivalent about equality. The reason, I suspect, lies partly in the fact that the egalitarian aspects of democratic theory have been less adequately thought through than other aspects, and partly in the complications connected with the concept itself. One such complication arises from the historical association of democracy with capitalism, a commingling of egalitarian and inegalitarian elements that has never been (and perhaps never can be) perfectly reconciled. Another complication lies in the diffuse and variegated nature of the concept, a result of its application to at least four separate domains: political (e.g., universal suffrage), legal (e.g., equality before the law), economic (e.g., equal distribution of property or opportunity), and moral (e.g., every man's right to be treated as an end and not as a means). Accompanying these are the confusions which result from the common failure to distinguish equality as a *fact* from equality as a *norm*. ("All men are created equal," for example, is taken by some as an empirical statement, by others as a normative one.) Still other complications arise from the differential rewards and opportunities inevitable in any complex society, from the differences in the initial endowment individuals bring into the world, and from the symbolism and fears that so often attend the division of men into ethnic compartments. All these confound the effort to develop a satisfactory theory of democratic equality, and

further serve to frustrate the realization of consensus around egalitarian values.

FAITH IN THE POLITICAL SYSTEM

Another perspective on the state of ideology and consensus in America may be obtained by observing how people respond to the political system. How do Americans feel about the political and social institutions by which they are ruled? Do they perceive the system as one they can reach and influence? Are they satisfied that it will govern justly and for the common good?

Sample items relating to these questions are contained in Tables 6 and 7. An assessment of the responses, however, is confounded by an ambivalence in our tradition. Few will question that Americans are patriotic and loyal, that they accept the political system as legitimate, and that they are inclined to shy away from radical or extreme movements which aim to alter or to overthrow the constitutional foundations of the system. Yet Americans are also presumed to have a longstanding suspicion of government— a state of mind which some historians trace back to the depredations of George III and to the habits of self-reliance forced upon our ancestors by frontier life.[19]

It is impossible in the present context to determine the extent to which the scores contained in these tables signify genuine frustration and political disillusionment and the extent to which they represent familiar and largely ritualistic responses. It is plain, however, that Americans are, verbally at least, both confused and divided in their reactions to the political system. Many feel themselves

---

[18] These inferences are drawn not only from the few items presented in Table 5, but from data previously reported by H. McClosky, P. J. Hoffmann, and R. O'Hara, op. cit., p. 413; and from the responses to dozens of items in the present study that express attitudes and opinions toward the private enterprise system, taxes, private property, profits, socialism, etc. On the whole, little enthusiasm is registered among either the elite or the masses for a drastic revision of the economy or a major redistribution of the wealth.

[19] Evidence is accumulating that the distrust of politics, often thought to be peculiar to the United States, is also found in many other countries. In fact, Gabriel Almond and Sidney Verba report in their cross-cultural study of citizenship that political interest is higher in the United States than it is in the four other countries they studied (United Kingdom, West Germany, Italy, and Mexico); and that Americans, if anything, are less negative toward politics than are the citizens of the other countries. See *The Civic Culture* (1963), chs. II-IV.

TABLE 6. POLITICAL INFLUENTIALS VS. THE ELECTORATE: RESPONSES TO ITEMS EXPRESSING CYNICISM TOWARD GOVERNMENT AND POLITICS

Items	Political Influentials (N-3020)	General Electorate (N-1484)
	% Agree	
Most politicians are looking out for themselves above all else.	36.3	54.3
Both major parties in this country are controlled by the wealthy and are run for their benefit.	7.9	32.1
Many politicians are bought off by some private interest.	43.0	65.3
I avoid dealing with public officials as much as I can.	7.8	39.3
Most politicians can be trusted to do what they think is best for the country.	77.1	58.9
I usually have confidence that the government will do what is right.	81.6	89.6
The people who really "run" the country do not even get known to the voters.	40.2	60.5
The laws of this country are supposed to benefit all of us equally, but the fact is that they're almost all "rich man's laws."	8.4	33.3
No matter what the people think, a few people will always run things anyway.	30.0	53.8
Most politicians don't seem to me to really mean what they say.	24.7	55.1
There is practically no connection between what a politician says and what he will do once he gets elected.	21.4	54.0
A poor man doesn't have the chance he deserves in the law courts.	20.3	42.9
Most political parties care only about winning elections and nothing more.	28.3	46.2
All politics is controlled by political bosses.	15.6	45.9

hopelessly ineffectual politically. Approximately half perceive government and politicians as remote, inaccessible, and largely unresponsive to the electorate's needs of opinions.[20] About the same proportion regard politics as squalid and seamy, as an activity in which the participants habitually practice deception, expediency, and self-aggrandizement. Yet by a curious inconsistency which so frequently frustrates the investigator searching the data for regularities, 89.6 per cent express confidence that the government will do what is right. However strongly they mistrust the men and the procedures through which public policies are fashioned, most voters seem not to be greatly dissatisfied with the outcome. They may be cynical about the operation of the political system, but they do not question its legitimacy.[21]

[20] See also the Michigan data on voters' sense of "political efficacy" in Angus Campbell, Gerald Gurin, and Warren E. Miller, *The Voter Decides* (Evanston, 1954), pp. 187-94.

[21] For other data on ambivalent attitudes toward government, see Hyman and Sheatsley, op. cit.

TABLE 7. POLITICAL INFLUENTIALS VS. THE ELECTORATE: RESPONSES TO ITEMS EXPRESSING A SENSE OF POLITICAL FUTILITY

Items	Political Influentials (N-3020)	General Electorate (N-1484)
	% Agree	
It's no use worrying my head about public affairs; I can't do anything about them anyhow.	2.3	20.5
The people who really "run" the country do not even get known to the voters.	40.2	60.5
I feel that my political leaders hardly care what people like myself think or want.	10.9	39.0
Nothing I ever do seems to have any effect upon what happens in politics.	8.4	61.5
Political parties are so big that the average member hasn't got much to say about what goes on.	37.8	67.5
There doesn't seem to be much connection between what I want and what my representative does.	24.0	43.7
It seems to me that whoever you vote for, things go on pretty much the same.	21.1	51.3

Although the influentials do not unanimously endorse American political practices either, they are substantially less suspicious and cynical than is the electorate. Indeed, they have achieved consensus or come close to achieving it on most of the items in the two tables. These results are further borne out by the *scale* scores: only 10.1 per cent of the articulates score "high" on the political cynicism scale, as contrasted with 31.3 per cent of the general population; on political suspiciousness the scores are 9.0 per cent high versus 26.7 per cent; on pessimism they are 12.6 per cent versus 26.7 per cent; and on sense of political futility the influentials score (understandably enough) only 3.1 per cent high compared with 30.2 per cent high for the electorate. The active minority also exhibits a stronger sense of social responsibility than the people do (their respective percentage high scores are 40.7 per cent versus 25.8 per cent) and, as previously noted, they are less tolerant of infractions against ethical political procedures.

Should we not, however, have expected these results as a matter of course, considering that the influentials were selected for study precisely because of their political experience and involvement? Possibly, except that similar (though less pronounced) differences emerge when we distinguish articulates from inarticulates by criteria other than actual political activity. Voters, for example, who have been to college, attained high status occupations or professions, or developed strong intellectual interests are, by a significant margin, also likely to possess more affirmative attitudes toward government, politics and politicians.[22] They display a greater sense of social and political responsibility, are more optimistic, and are less indulgent of shoddy political methods. The political actives who are highly educated exhibit these attitudes even more strongly. Familiarity, it seems, far from breeding contempt, greatly increases respect, hope and support for the

---

[22] Similar findings are reported by Robert E. Agger, Marshall N. Goldstein and Stanley A. Pearl, "Political Cynicism: Measurement and Meaning," *Journal of Politics*, Vol. 23 (1961), pp. 477-506.

nation's political institutions and practices. Inferential support for this generalization is available from the findings turned up by Almond and Verba in all five countries they investigated in their comparative study of citizenship.[23]

COHERENCE AND CONSISTENCY OF ATTITUDES

So far we have explored the question of ideology and consensus mainly from the point of view of agreement on particular values. This, however, is a minimum criterion. Before one can say that a class or group or nation has achieved consensus around an idelogy, one should be satisfied that they understand its values in a coherent and correct way. It is a poor consensus in which generalities and slogans are merely echoed with little appreciation of their significance. It seemed appropriate, therefore, to compare the influentials and voters concerning their information and understanding, the relation of their opinions to their party preferences, and the consistency of their view on public affairs.

To begin with, the influentials are more likely than the electorate to have opinions on public questions. For example, 28 per cent of the public are unable (though a few may only be *unwilling*) to classify themselves as liberal, middle of the road, or conservative; while only 1.1 per cent of the articulates fail to make this classification. Forty-eight per cent of the voters, compared to 15 percent of the actives, do not know in which direction they would turn if the parties were reorganized to reflect ideological differences more clearly. Forty-five per cent of the electorate but only 10.2 per cent of the influentials cannot name any issue that divides the parties. By ratios of approximately three or four to one the

electorate is less likely to know which level of government they are mainly interested in, whether they prefer their party to control Congress or the presidency, whether they believe in party discipline and of what type, whether control of the parties should rest at the national or local levels, and so on.

As these and other of our findings suggest, active political involvement heightens one's sense of intellectual order and commitment. This inference is further supported by the data on partisanship. One example may suffice to illustrate the point: when the articulates and the electorate are ranged on a scale assessing their orientation toward 14 current liberal-conservative issues, the political actives tend to bunch up at the extreme ends of the distribution (the Democratic actives at the "liberal" end, the Republican actives at the "conservative" end), while the rank and file supporters of both parties fall more frequently into the middle or conflicted category. The political influentials, in short, display issue orientations that are more partisan and more consistent with their party preferences.

Essentially the same effect is achieved among the general population by increases in education, economic status, or other factors that raise the level of articulateness. College-educated Democrats and Republicans, for example, disagree more sharply on issue than grade school Democrats and Republicans do. Partisan differences are greater between the informed than between the uninformed, between the upper-class supporters of the two parties than between the lower-class supporters, between the "intellectuals" in both parties than between those who rank low on "intellectuality."

Increases in political knowledge or involvement, hence, cause men not so much to waver as to choose sides and to identify more unswervingly with one political tendency or its opposite. Inarticulateness and distance from the sources of political decision increase intellectual uncertainty and evoke political responses that are random rather than systematic. We are thus led by the findings to a pair of

---

[23] Almond and Verba, op. cit., ch. IV. One can, of course, imagine circumstances, such as political disorganization or revolutionary crises, in which the generalization would not hold—in which, indeed, the political elite might lead the struggle *against* the existing governing institutions. I am speaking, in the present context, of politics under "normal" conditions in established democracies.

conclusions that may at first appear contradictory but that in reality are not: the political class is more united than the electorate on fundamental political values but divides more sharply by party affiliation on the issues which separate the two parties.[24] Both facts—the greater consensus in the one instance and the sharper cleavage in the other—testify to its superior ideological sophistication.

Not only are the articulates more partisan, but they are also more consistent in their views. Their responses to a wide range of political stimuli are to a greater extent intellectually patterned and informed. They are, for example, better able to name reference groups that correspond with their party affiliation and doctrinal orientation: approximately twice as many active Democrats as ordinary Democratic voters name liberal, Democratically oriented organizations as groups they would seek advice from (e.g., trade unions, Farmers Union, etc.); and by equally large or larger ratios they *reject* as sources of advice such conservative or Republican oriented organizations at the NAM, the Farm Bureau, and the Chamber of Commerce. With some variations, similar findings emerge when Republican leaders are compared with Republican voters. If we also take into account the liberal or conservative issue-orientation of the respondents, the differential ability of party leaders and followers to recognize reference groups becomes even more pronounced. Clearly, the political stratum has a better idea than the public has of who its ideological friends and enemies are. The capacity to recognize sympathetic or hostile reference groups is not highly developed among the public at large.

Compared with the influentials, ordinary voters also show up poorly in their ability to classify themselves politically. For example, among Democratic actives who score as "liberals" in their views on issues, 82.2 per cent correctly describe themselves as "liberals," while 16.7 per cent call themselves "middle of the road-

ers" and only 1.1 per cent misclassify themselves as "conservatives." Among Democratic *voters* who actually hold liberal views, only 37.0 per cent are able to label themselves correctly. The disparity is less striking between Republican leaders and followers but bears out no less conclusively that most voters lack the sophistication to recognize and label accurately the tendency of their own political views. Even their choice of party is frequently discrepant with their actual ideological views: as we reported in a previous paper,[25] not only do Democratic and Republican voters hold fairly similar opinions on issues, but the latter's opinions are closer to the opinions of Democratic leaders than to those of their own leaders.

Data we have gathered on patterns of support for individual political leaders yield similar conclusions: the articulates are far better able than the electorate to select leaders whose political philosophy they share. Often, in fact, voters simultaneously approve of two or more leaders who represent widely different outlooks—for example, Joseph McCarthy and Dwight D. Eisenhower. In a similar vein, a surprisingly large number of voters simultaneously score high on a Right Wing scale and a liberal issues scale, or hold other "discrepant" outlooks. Such inconsistencies are not unknown among the political actives either, but they are much less frequent. Not only does the public have less information than the political class but it does not succeed as well in sorting out and relating the information it does possess.[26]

Most of the relationships reported in the foregoing have been tested with education, occupation, and sometimes with other demographic variables controlled, but the introduction of these factors does not change the direction of the findings,

---

[24] See also V. O. Key, *Public Opinion and Democracy* (New York, 1961), pp. 51-2.

[25] McClosky, Hoffmann, and O'Hara, op. cit.
[26] For other findings on the state of ideological development among the electorate, see Angus Campbell, Philip E. Converse, Warren E. Miller and Donald E. Stokes, *The American Voter* (New York, 1960), chs. 8-10.

although it sometimes affects the magnitude of the scores.

Comparisons of scores for the two samples have also been made with "acquiescent" response-set controlled. Acquiescence affects the results, but does not eliminate the differences reported or alter the direction or significance of the findings. (See Appendix A.)

III. SUMMARY AND DISCUSSION

Several observations can be offered by way of summarizing and commenting upon the data just reported:

1. American politics is widely thought to be innocent of ideology, but this opinion more appropriately describes the electorate than the active political minority. If American ideology is defined as that cluster of axioms, values and beliefs which have given form and substance to American democracy and the Constitution, the political influentials manifest by comparison with ordinary voters a more developed sense of ideology and a firmer grasp of its essentials. This is evidenced in their strong approval of democratic ideas, their greater tolerance and regard for proper procedures and citizen rights, their superior understanding and acceptance of the "rules of the game," and their more affirmative attitudes toward the political system in general. The electorate displays a substantial measure of unity chiefly in its support of freedom in the abstract; on most other features of democratic belief and practice it is sharply divided.

The political views of the influentials are relatively ordered and coherent. As liberals and conservatives, Democrats and Republicans, they take stands on issues, choose reference groups, and express preferences for leaders that are far more consistent than the attitudes and preferences exhibited by the electorate. The latter's opinions do not entirely lack order but are insufficiently integrated to meet the requirements of an ideology.[27] In contrast to the political elite, which tends to be united on basic values but divided on issues by party affiliation (both of which testify to a measure of ideological sophistication), the voters diivde on many basic political values and adopt stands on issues with little reference to their party affiliation.

The evidence suggests that it is the articulate classes rather than the public who serve as the major repositories of the public conscience and as the carriers of the Creed. Responsibility for keeping the system going, hence, falls most heavily upon them.[28]

2. Why should consensus and support for democratic ideology be stronger among the political stratum than among the electroate? The answer plainly has to do with the differences in their political activity, involvement and articulateness.

Some observers complain that Americans have little interest in political ideas because they are exclusively concerned with their own personal affairs. Evidence is becoming available, however, that political apathy and ignorance are also widespread among the populations of other countries and may well be endemic in all societies larger than a city-state. It is difficult to imagine any circumstance, short of war or revolutionary crisis, in which the mass of men will evince more interest in the community's affairs than in their own concerns. This is not because they are selfish, thoughtless, or morally deficient, but because the stimuli they receive from public affairs are rela-

---

[27] For a similar conclusion on this point, see V. O. Key, *Public Opinion and American Democracy* (New York, 1961), pp. 41, 49. The second chapter of this volume contains an excellent discussion of opinion consensus among the electorate, and touches on a number of the points dealt with in this paper. Evidence on the infrequency of "ideological" thinking among the voters is presented in Campbell, Converse, Miller and Stokes, op. cit., p. 249. By the criteria used the authors were able to classify only 3.5% of the voters as "ideologues" and 12% as "near-idealogues."

[28] V. O. Key, "Public Opinion and the Decay of Democracy," loc. cit.

tively remote and intangible. One can scarcely expect ordinary men to respond to them as intensely as they respond to the more palpable stimuli in their own everyday lives, which impinge upon them directly and in ways they can understand and do something about. The aphorism which holds man to be a political animal may be supportable on normative grounds but is scarcely defensible as a description of reality. Political apathy seems for most men the more "natural" state. Although political matters are in a sense "everyone's concern", it is just as unreasonable to hope that all men will sustain a lively interest in politics as it would be to expect everyone to become addicted to chamber music, electronics, poetry, or baseball. Since many voters lack education, opportunity, or even tangible and compelling reasons for busying themselves with political ideas, they respond to political stimuli (if they respond at all) without much reflection or consistency. Their life-styles, furthermore, tend to perpetuate this state of affairs, for they are likely to associate with people like themselves whose political opinions are no more informed or consistent than their own. As inarticulates, they are also inclined to avoid the very activities by which they might overcome their indifference and develop a more coherent point of view.

Many voters, in addition, feel remote from the centers of political decision and experience an acute sense of political futility. They know the political world only as a bewildering labyrinth of procedures and unceasing turmoil in which it is difficult to distinguish the just from the wicked, the deserving from the undeserving. The political questions about which they are asked to have opinions are complex and thorny; every solution is imperfect and exacts its price; measures that benefit some groups invariably aggrieve others. The principles which govern the political process seem vague, recondite and impossible to relate to actual events. All this obviously deters voters from developing ideologically, from acquiring insights into the subtleties

of the democratic process, and from achieving consensus even on fundamental values.

Although the influentials face some of the same obstacles, they are better able to overcome them. As a group they are distinguished from the mass of the electorate by their above-average education and economic status, their greater political interest and awareness, and their more immediate access to the command posts of community decision. Many of them participate not only in politics but in other public activities as well. This affords them, among other benefits, a more sophisticated understanding of how the society is run and a more intimate association with other men and women who are alert to political ideas and values. Political concepts and abstratcions, alien to the vocabulary of many voters, are, for the elite familiar items of everyday discourse.

Consider also that the political stratum is, by almost every social criterion we have examined, more homogeneous than the electorate. This promotes communication among them and increases their chances of converging around a common body of attitudes.[29] As Newcomb[30] has remarked, "The actual consequences of communication, as well as the intended ones, are consensus—increasing." Among many segments of the general population, however, communication on matters of political belief either occurs not at all or is so random and cacophonous as to have little utility for the reinforcement of political values. If Louis Wirth is correct in observing that "the limits of consensus are marked by the range of effective communication,"[31] it becomes easier to under-

---

[29] For additional data on the homogeneity of social characteristics and values among American elite groups, see James N. Rosenau, "Consensus-Building in the American National Community: Hypotheses and Supporting Data," *Journal of Politics*, Vol. 24 (November, 1962), pp. 639-661.

[30] Theodore M. Newcomb, "The Study of Consensus," in R. K. Merton et al. (eds.), *Sociology Today* (New York, 1959), pp. 277-92.

[31] Op. cit., p. 201.

stand why the active minority achieves consensus more often than the voters do.

Compared with the electorate, whose ordinary members are submerged in an ideological babble of poorly informed and discordant opinions, the members of the political minority inhabit a world in which political ideas are vastly more salient, intellectual consistency is more frequently demanded, attitudes are related to principles, actions are connected to beliefs, "correct" opinions are rewarded and "incorrect" opinions are punished. In addition, as participants in political roles, the actives are compelled (contrary to stereotype) to adopt opinions, to take stands on issues, and to evaluate ideas and events. As *articulates* they are unavoidably exposed to the liberal democratic values which form the main current of our political heritage. The net effect of these influences is to heighten their sensitivity to political ideas and to unite them more firmly behind the values of the American tradition. They may, as a result, be better equipped for the role they are called upon to play in a democracy than the citizens are for *their* role.

The findings furnish little comfort for those who wish to believe that a passion for freedom, tolerance, justice and other democratic values springs spontaneously from the lower depths of the society, and that the plain, homespun, uninitiated yeoman, worker and farmer are the natural hosts of democratic ideology. The mystique of the simple, unworldly, "natural" democrat has been with us since at least the rise of Christianity, and has been assiduously cultivated by Rousseau, Tolstoy, Marx, and numerous lesser writers and social reformers. Usually, the simpler the man, the lower his station in life, and the greater his objective need for equality, the more we have endowed him with a capacity for understanding democracy. We are thus inclined to give the nod to the farmer over the city man, the unlearned over the educated, the poor man over the man of wealth, the "people" over their leaders, the unsophisticated over the sophisticated. Yet everyone of these intuitive expectations turns out, upon in-

vestigation, to be questionable or false. Democratic beliefs and habits are obviously not "natural" but must be learned; and they are learned more slowly by men and women whose lives are circumscribed by apathy, ignorance, provincialism and social or physical distance from the centers of intellectual activity. In the absence of knowledge and experience—as we can readily observe from the fidgety course of growth in the newly emerging nations—the presuppositions and complex obligations of democracy, the rights it grants and the self-restraints it imposes, cannot be quickly comprehended. Even in a highly developed democratic nation like the United States, millions of people continue to possess only the most rudimentary understanding of democratic ideology.

3. While the active political minority affirms the underlying values of democracy more enthusiastically than the people do, consensus among them is far from perfect, and we might well inquire why this is so.

Despite the many forces impelling influentials toward agreement on basic ideological values, counteracting forces are also at work to divide them. Not all influentials are able to comprehend democratic ideas, to apply them to concrete contexts, or to thread their way through the complexities of modern political life. Nor is communication perfect among them either, despite their greater homogeneity. Many things divide them, not least of which are differences in education, conflicting economic and group interests, party competition, factional cleavages and personal political ambitions.

In demonstrating that the influentials are better prepared than the masses to receive and reflect upon political ideas, we run the risk of overstating the case and of exaggerating their capacity for ideological reasoning. Some members of the political class obviously have no more intellectual concern with politics than the masses do; they are in it for "the game," for personal reasons, or for almost any reason except ideology.

Then, too, while most democratic ideas are in their most general form simple enough for almost all members of the elite to understand, they become considerably more puzzling when one sets out to explicate them, to relate them to each other, or to apply them to concrete cases. Only a few of the complications need to be cited to illustrate the point: several of the ideas, such as equality, are either inherently vague or mean different things in different contexts. Some democratic (or constitutional) values turn out in certain situations to be incompatible with other democratic values (e.g., the majority's right to make and enforce the laws at times clashes with individual rights, such as the right to stand on one's religious conscience). As this suggests, democratic ideas and rules of the game are ordinarily encountered not in pure form or in isolation but in substantive contexts that are bound to influence the ways in which we react to them.[32] Many businessmen who consider the regulation of business as an unconstitutional invasion of freedom look upon the regulation of trade unions as a justifiable curb upon lawlessness; trade unionists, needless to say, lean to the opposite view.

Consider, too, what a heavy burden we place upon a man's normal impulses by asking him to submit unconditionally to democratic values and procedures. Compliance with democratic rules of the game often demands an extraordinary measure of forbearance and self-discipline, a willingness to place constraints upon the use of our collective power and to suffer opinions, actions, and groups we regard as repugnant. The need for such self-restraint is for many people intrinsically difficult to comprehend and still more difficult to honor. Small wonder, then, that consensus around democratic values is imperfect, even among the political influentials who are well situated to appreciate their importance.

4. We turn now to the most crucial question suggested by the research findings, namely, what significance must be assigned to the fact that democratic ideology and consensus are poorly developed among the electorate and only imperfectly realized among the political influentials?

Our first and most obvious conclusion is that, contrary to the familiar claim, a democratic society can survive despite widespread popular misunderstanding and disagreement about basic democratic and constitutional values. The American political system survives and even flourishes under precisely these conditions, and so, we have reason to think, do other viable democracies. What makes this possible is a more conjectural question, though several observations can be offered by way of answering it.

Democratic viability is, to begin with, saved by the fact that those who are most confused about democratic ideas are also likely to be politically apathetic and without significant influence. Their role in the nation's decision process is so small that their "misguided" opinions or non-opinions have little practical consequence for stability. If they contribute little to the vitality of the system, neither are they likely to do much harm. Lipset[33] has pointed out that "apathy undermines consensus," but to this one may add the corollary observation that apathy also furnishes its own partial corrective by keeping the doubters from acting upon their differences. In the United States, at least, their disagreements are *passive* rather than *active,* more the result of political ignorance and indifference than of intellectual conviction or conscious identification with an "alien" political tendency. Most seem not even to be aware of their deviations from the established values. This suggests that there

---

[32] For a discussion of this point, see Peter Bachrach, "Elite Consensus and Democracy," *Journal of Politics,* Vol. 24 (August, 1962), pp. 439-52.

[33] Seymour Martin Lipset, *Political Man,* (New York, 1960), p. 27. Chapter I of this volume provides a stimulating and valuable discussion of the relation of conflict and consensus to the operation of democracy.

may, after all, be some utility in achieving agreement on large, abstract political sentiments, for it may satisfy men that they share common values when in fact they do not. Not only can this keep conflicts from erupting, but it also permits men who disagree to continue to communicate and thus perhaps to convert their pseudo-consensus on democratic values into a genuine consensus.

I do not mean to suggest, of course, that a nation runs no risks when a large number of its citizens fail to grasp the essential principles on which its constitution is founded. Among Americans, however, the principal danger is not that they will reject democratic ideals in favor of some hostile ideology, but that they will fail to understand the very institutions they believe themselves to be defending and may end up undermining rather than safeguarding them. Our research on "McCarthyism," for example, strongly suggests that popular support for the Senator represented less a conscious rejection of American democratic ideals than a misguided effort to defend them. We found few McCarthy supporters who genuinely shared the attitudes and values associated with his name.[34]

Whether consensus among the influentials is either a necessary or sufficient condition for democratic stability is not really known. Since the influentials act, make public decisions, are more organized, and take political ideas more seriously, agreement among them on constitutional values is widely thought to be essential for viability. At present, however, we do not have enough information (or at least we do not have it in appropriately organized form) to state with satisfactory precision what the actual relation is between elite consensus and democratic stability. Some democratic governments, e.g., Weimar Germany, crumbled when faced with ideological conflicts among their political classes;

others, e.g., post-war Italy and France, have until now managed to weather pronounced ideological cleavages. The opinion has long prevailed that consensus is needed to achieve stability, but the converse may be the more correct formulation, i.e., that so long as conditions remain stable, consensus is not required; it becomes essential only when social conditions are disorganized. Consensus may strengthen democratic viability, but its absence in an otherwise stable society need not be fatal or even particularly damaging.

It should also be kept in mind that the existence of intellectual disagreements— even among the influentials—does not necessarily mean that they will be expressed or acted upon. In the United States (and doubtless elsewhere as well), numerous influences are at work to prevent ideological cleavages from assuming an important role in the nation's political life. This is certainly the tendency of such political institutions as federalism, checks and balances, separation of powers, bicameralism, the congressional committee system, the judiciary's practice of accommodating one discrepant law to another, and a system of elections more often fought around local issues and personalities than around urgent national questions. Our two-party syetsm also functions to disguise or soften the genuine disagreements that distinguish active Democrats from active Republicans. The American social system contributes to the same end, for it is a model of the pluralistic society, a profuse collection of diverse groups, interests and organizations spread over a vast and variegated territory. Consensus in such a society becomes difficult to achieve, but by the same token its absence can also more easily be survived. The complexities of a highly pluralistic social and political order tend to diminish the impact of intellectual differences, to compel compromise, and to discourage the holders of divergent views from crystalizing into intransigent doctrinal camps. Thus it seems, paradoxically enough, that the need for consensus on democratic rules of the game increases as the conflict

---

[34] Herbert McClosky, "McCarthyism: The Myth and the Reality," unpublished paper delivered at the American Psychological Association, New York, September, 1957. See also Wiebe, loc. cit.

among competing political tendencies becomes sharper, and declines as their differences become more diffused. Italy, by this reasoning, has greater need of consensus than the United States, but has less chance of achieving it. A democratic nation may wisely prefer the American model to the Italian, though what is ideally desired, as Lipset observes,[35] is a balance between cleavage and consensus —the one to give reality and force to the principle of opposition, the other to furnish the secure framework within which that principle might be made continuously effective. Countervailing power within a structure of shared political values would, by this logic, be the optimal condition for the maintenance of a democratic society.

5. But even giving this much weight to consensus may exaggerate the role which intellectual factors play in the attainment of democratic stability. The temptation to assign a controlling influence to the place of ideas in the operation of democracy is very great. Partly this results from our tendency to confuse the textbook model of democracy with the reality and to assume the high order of rationality in the system that the model presupposes (e.g., an alert citizenry aware of its rights and duties, cognizant of the basic rules, exercising consent, enjoying perfect information and choosing governors after carefully weighing their qualifications, deliberating over the issues, etc.). It is not my purpose to ridicule this model but to underscore the observation that it can easily mislead us into placing more weight than the facts warrant upon cognitive elements—upon ideas, values, rational choice, consensus, etc—as the cementing forces of a democratic society. An *ad hominem* consideration may also be relevant here: as intellectuals and students of politics, we are disposed both by training and sensibiilty to take political ideas seriously and to assign central importance to them in the operation of the state. We are therefore prone to forget that most people take them less seriously than we do, that they pay little attention to issues,

rarely worry about the consistency of their opinions, and spend little or no time thinking about the values, presuppositions, and implications which distinguish one political orientation from another. If the viability of a democracy were to depend upon the satisfaction of these intellectual activities, the prognosis would be very grim indeed.

Research from many different lines of inquiry confirms unequivocally that the role heretofore assigned to ideas and to intellectual processes in general has been greatly exaggerated and cannot adequately explain many political phenomena which, on *a priori* grounds, we have expected them to explain. Witness, for example, the research on the non-rational factors which govern the voting decision, on the effects—or rather the non-effects—of ideology on the loyalty and fighting effectiveness of German and American soldiers, on the differences between the views of party leaders and followers, on the influence of personality on political belief, and on group determinants of perception.[36] We now have evidence that patriotism and the strength of one's attachment to a political community need not depend upon one's approval of its intellectual, cultural, or political values. Indeed, our present research clearly confirms that men and women who express "patriotism" in extreme or chauvinistic form usually have the least knowledge and understanding of American democratic ideals, institutions, and practices.

Abundant anecdotal data from the observation of dictatorial and other nations further corroborates the conclusion

---

[35] Lipset, op. cit., p. 21-2.

[36] Cf., for example, Campbell, et al., op. cit.; Bernard R. Berelson, Paul F. Lazarsfeld, and William N. McPhee, *Voting* (Chicago, 1954), especially ch. 14; Edward A. Shils and Morris Janowitz, "Cohesion and Disintegration in the German Wehrmacht in World War II," *Public Opinion Quarterly*, Vol. 12 (1948), pp. 280-315; Herbert McClosky, "Conservaitsm and Personality," this *Review*, Vol. 52 (March, 1958), pp. 27-45; T. W. Adorno et al. *The Authoritarian Personality*, (New York, 1950), ch. XVII; Richard Crutchfield, "Conformity and Character," *American Psychologist*, Vol. 10 (1955), pp. 191-198.

that men may become attached to a party, a community, or a nation by forces that have nothing to do with ideology or consensus. Many of these forces are so commonplace that we often neglect them, for they include family, friends, home, employment, property, religion, ethnic attachments, a common language, and familiar surroundings and customs. These may lack the uplifting power of some political doctrines, but their ability to bind men to a society and its government may nevertheless be great. This observation, of course, is less likely to hold for the intelligentsia than for the inarticulates, but even the political behavior of intellectuals is never governed exclusively by appeals to the mind.

The effect of ideas on democratic viability may also be diminished by the obvious reluctance of most men to press their intellectual differences to the margin and to debate questions that may tear the community apart. So long as no urgent reason arises for bringing such differences to the surface, most men will be satisfied to have them remain dormant. Although there are men and women who are exceptions to this generalization, and who cannot bear to leave basic questions unresolved, they are likely to be few, for both the principles and practices of an "open society" strongly reinforce tolerance for variety, contingency and ambiguity in matters of belief and conscience. As our data on freedom of opinion suggest, few Americans expect everyone to value the same things or to hold identical views on public questions. The tendency to ignore, tolerate, or play down differences helps to create an illusion of consensus which for many purposes can be as serviceable as the reality.[37]

---

[37] Robert G. McCloskey, loc. cit., suggests that the American political tradition is marked by "ambivalence" toward certain of our fundamental values and that this may discourage the achievement of "consensus" in the usual sense. He believes, however, that "Americans have learned to live with, and even to ignore, inconsistencies in the values system, in keeping with our pragmatic spirit." Whether this ability is uniquely American or whether it is characteristic of all "open," democratic societies is a ques-

6. To conclude, as we have in effect, that ideological awareness and consensus are overvalued as determinants of democratic viability is not to imply that they are of no importance. While disagreements among Americans on fundamental values have tended to be passive and, owing to apathy and the relative placidity of our politics, easily tolerated; while they do not follow party lines and are rarely insinuated into the party struggle; and while no extremist movement has yet grown large enough to challenge effectively the governing principles of the American Constitution, this happy state of affairs is not permanently guaranteed. Fundamental differences could *become* activated by political and economic crises; party differences could *develop* around fundamental constitutional questions, as they have in France and other democracies; and powerful extremist movements are too familiar a phenomenon of modern political life to take for granted their eternal absence from the American scene.

Obviously a democratic nation also pays a price for an electorate that is weakly developed ideologically. Lacking the intellectual equipment to assess complex political events accurately, the unsophisticated may give support to causes that are contrary to their own or to the national interest. In the name of freedom, democracy, and the Constitution, they may favor a McCarthy, join the John Birch Society, or agitate for the impeachment of a Supreme Court Justice who has worked unstintingly to uphold their constitutional liberties. They may also have difficulty discriminating political integrity from demagoguery, maturity and balanced judgment from fanaticism, honest causes from counterfeits. Our findings on the attitudes shown by ordinary Americans toward "extreme" political beliefs (Left

tion well worth investigating. It could, conceivably, be a natural outgrowth of democratic ideology itself, no element of which can be conceived and enforced absolutely without infringing other elements. On this last point, see Sidney Hook, *The Paradoxes of Freedom* (Berkeley, 1962), pp. 14-62.

Wing beliefs, Right Wing beliefs, totalitarianism, isolationism, etc.) verify that the possibilities just cited are not merely hypothetical. Those who have the least understanding of American politics subscribe least enthusiastically to its principles, and are most frequently "misled" into attacking constitutional values while acting (as they see it) to defend them.

There is, however, reason to believe that ideological sophistication and the general acceptance of liberal democratic values are increasing rather than declining in the United States. Extreme ideological politics of the type associated with Marxism, fascism and other doctrinaire networks of opinion may be waning, as many sociologists believe,[38] but the same observation does not hold for the influence of democratic ideas. On the contrary, democratic ideology in the United States, linked as it is with the articulate classes, gives promise of growing as the articulate class grows. Many developments in recent American life point to an increase in "articulateness": the extraordinary spread of education, rapid social mobility, urbanization, the proliferation of mass media that disseminate public information, the expansion of the middle class, the decline in the size and number of isolated rural groups, the reduction in the proportion of people with sub-marginal living standards, the incorporation of foreign and minority groups into the culture and their increasing entrance into the professions, and so on. While these developments may on the one side have the effect of reducing the tensions and conflicts on which extreme ideologies feed, they are likely on the other side to beget a more articulate population and a more numerous class of political influentials, committed to liberal democracy and aware of the rights and obligations which attend that commitment.

---

[38] Cf. Daniel Bell, *The End of Ideology* (Glencoe, 1960), pp. 369-375; S. M. Lipset, op. cit., pp. 403-17; Edward Shils, loc. cit.

APPENDIX A. THE EFFECT OF ACQUIESCENCE OR "RESPONSE-SET"

Because response to scale items are subject to a response-set known as acquiescence, i.e., a tendency to agree (or disagree) with items regardless of what the items say, all procedures in the present study have routinely been run with acquiescence controlled. For this purpose we employed a specially constructed acquiescence scale, consisting of 19 pairs of contradictory or near-contradictory items. Each respondent received an acquiescence score of 0 to 38, depending upon the number of "agree" and "disagree" responses he registered on the scale. For convenience we have divided our sample into those who scored high, middle, or low on acquiescence, and have compared the influentials and electorate within each acquiescence level.

As the accompanying table shows (Table 8), variations in acquiescence have a powerful effect on the scale scores (and implicitly the item scores) of both the political elite and the public. It is equally plain, nevertheless, that the differences between the two samples of democratic and related ideological values remain large and statistically significant even when acquiescence is held constant; they cannot, therefore, be explained as mere artifacts of response-set. Then, too, although one cannot discern it from these tables, acquiescence functions in the case of some items to reduce rather than to enlarge the "actual" differences between the influentials and the electorate.

The question might also be raised whether we are doing the inquiry a disservice by conceiving acquiescence *entirely* as a response-set which artificially inflates or deflates the scores registered by respondents on certain items or scales. Our research has yielded a vast amount of data on acquiescence which suggests that the tendency to agree or disagree with items indiscriminately reflects personality and cognitive capacities that are strongly associated with the ability to sort out, understand, relate, and internalize norms.

TABLE 8. INFLUENTIALS VS. THE ELECTORATE: PERCENTAGES SCORING HIGH-LOW ON SELECTED SCALES WITH ACQUIESCENT RESPONSE-SET CONTROLLED

	%'s Down					
	Low Acq.		Mid Acq.		High Acq.	
	Infl.	Elect.	Infl.	Elect.	Infl.	Elect.
N =	1369	453	1159	520	492	471
Faith in procedural rights						
High	70	35	56	28	32	10
Low	6	21	13	27	28	45
Faith in democracy						
High	50	29	36	21	22	6
Low	8	19	16	28	28	42
Tolerance						
High	66	57	62	48	45	27
Low	13	21	15	29	29	48
Faith in freedom						
High	62	45	63	50	59	50
Low	17	32	15	27	20	26
Totalitarianism						
High	2	11	9	26	35	63
Low	80	52	54	30	21	5
F-authoritarianism						
High	4	9	14	24	46	67
Low	70	48	38	22	10	2
Political cynicism						
High	2	9	10	24	31	60
Low	74	51	47	25	20	6
Elitism						
High	12	21	27	35	45	60
Low	53	37	36	23	20	8

Conceivably, therefore, the electorate demonstrates a weaker grasp of democratic and constitutional principles not only because its members are more prone than the influentials to response-set (which means that they say yes to items that happen *in this case* to express undemocratic and "unconstitutional" sentiments), but also because they characteristically lack the habits, skills, or capacities for thinking about these matters in a coherent and sophisticated way. It appears, in short, that the correlation between acquiescence and the expression of certain poorly valued sentiments results not entirely from the influence of the former upon the latter, but also from the influence upon *both*—of a common, underlying, mental state.*

APPENDIX B. CHARACTERISTICS OF THE PAB GENERAL POPULATION SAMPLE

Because the self-administration and return of questionnaires left with respondents by interviewers represents a somewhat unorthodox sampling procedure, the

* The full presentation and explication of our findings on acquiescence cannot be accommodated within the limitations of the present paper, and I have put the matter aside for presentation in a separate paper.

accompanying table (Table 9) presents a description of the PAB general population sample utilized in this paper. For purposes of comparison, the table also includes the characteristics of two AIPO (Gallup) samples, interviewed in January-February, 1958; the September-November sample employed by the Survey Research Center, University of Michigan, in its study of the 1956 presidential election; and, where comparable, census and voting data.

As the figures make plain the PAB sample closely resembles in its social characteristics both the AIPO and Michigan SRC samples. Although some of the differences may be due to the differences in the time of polling as well as differences in the coding criteria employed.

In only one characteristic does the PAB sample deviate substantially from the other samples, namely, in the overrepresentation of the college-educated strata and the corresponding underrepresenta-

tion of the grade school educated. This, of course, was to be expected, in light of the length and complexity of the PAB questionnaire and the difficulty associated with its self-administration. It should, however, be kept in mind that oversampling the upper educated has tended to flatten rather than to accentuate the differences between the influentials and the electorate reported in this paper. Since the highly educated tend to embrace democratic values and the "rules of the game" more frequently than the less educated do, the item and scale scores we have reported for the general population of voters are doubtless slightly inflated. In other words, the differences in ideological outlook between the political stratum and the electorate are probably even a bit larger than we have reported. Hence, correcting for the educational bias in the sample would strengthen rather than weaken the conclusions of this paper.

TABLE 9. CHARACTERISTICS OF MCCLOSKY NATIONAL GENERAL POPULATION SAMPLE AND SELECTED OTHER SAMPLES

	AIPO Samples [a] (January, 1958)	Michigan SRC Sample [b] (1956 Presidential Election)	McClosky-PAB General population Sample (January, 1958)	Others
	(N-3024)	(N-1762)	(N-1484)	
	(%)	(%)	(%)	(%)
Sex				(1960 Census)
Men	48	44.7	51	48.4
Women	52	55.3	49	51.6
Age (1)				
21-29	16.5		17.3	
30-49	45.4		44.5	
50-	37.0		37.9	
Undesignated	1.0		.3	
Age (2)				
Under 35		30.2	28	
35-44		25.6	23.6	
45-54		19.1	20.6	
55-		25.0	27.7	

TABLE 9 Continued

	AIPO Samples [a] (January, 1958)	Michigan SRC Sample [b] (1956 Presidential Election)	McClosky-PAB General population Sample (January, 1958)	Others
	(N-3024)	(N-1762)	(N-1484)	
	(%)	(%)	(%)	(%)
Race				
White		91.3	93.1	
Negro		8.3	6.5	
Rural-Urban				(1960 Census)
Nrban (over 2500)		68	72.2	71.5
Rural (farm-nonfarm under 2500)		32	27.8	28.5
Region				PAB (Adjusted)
East	28	25.7	27.7	24.8 [e]
Midwest	32	34.4	35.7	35.7
South	25	26.7	19.7	22.8
West	15	13.3	16.9	16.9
Education				
College	15.5	18.7	27.2	
High school	51.5	50.6	51.2	
Grade school	33.0	30.7	21.6	
Religion				
Catholic		21.1	21.9	
Jew		3.2	2.5	
Prot, other, and NA		75.7	75.6	
Income				
Under 3000		24.3	20.4	
3000-5000		28.8	34.0	
5000-7500		25.6	26.6	
7500-10,000		10.8	9.4	
10,000-		7.6	5.7	
Refuse, NA, Dk		3.6	3.8	
				(Actual Congressional Vote, November, 1958 [d])
Party preference				
Democrat	56 [d]	57.1	56.9 [e]	56.6
Republican	44	42.9	43.1	43.4

[a] The figures for the AIPO sample are averages computed from two national surveys conducted by the Gallup Poll in January, 1958. The information on the characteristics of these samples was supplied by the AIPO in a letter to the author.
[b] In most cases, the figures from the Michigan SRC sample are computed from the information supplied in the codebook for Deck 6 of Study 417, September 1956. Urban rural figures are computed from a table in *The American Voter*, p. 454. Criteria for urban-rural are set out on p. 406.
[c] Michigan SRC included Md. and W. Va. in the South, while we had classified these states as Eastern. This column shows the PAB figures with Md. and W. Va. classified as Southern. SRC regional figures combine data from 1952 and 1956 (See *The American Voter*, p. 158.)
[d] Data on party preference for the AIPO and the national congressional elections of 1958 are taken from a Gallup news release, May 24, 1959.
[e] Two-party vote only. PAB sample contained 821 Democrats, 623 Republicans, and 40 Independents, Other, and DK's.

The Fear of Equality[*]

ROBERT E. LANE

We move in equalitarian directions; the distribution of income flattens out; the floor beneath the poorest paid and least secure is raised and made more substantial. Since the demise of Newport and Tuxedo Park, the very rich have shunned ostentatious display. The equality of opportunity, the chance to rise in the world is at least as great today as it was thirty years ago. The likelihood of declining status is less.[1] Where does the energy for this movement come from? Who is behind it?

Since 1848, it has been assumed that the drive for a more equalitarian society, its effective social force, would come from the stratum of society with the most to gain, the working classes. This was thought to be the revolutionary force in the world—the demand of workers for a classless society sparked by their hostility to the owning classes. It was to be the elite among the workers, not the *lumpenproletariat*, not the "scum," who were to advance this movement, Just as "liberty" was the central solgan of the bourgeois revolution, so "equality" was the central concept in the working class movement. Hence it was natural to assume that whatever gains have been made in equalizing the income and status of

* I wish here to acknowledge the financial assistance for this study received in the form of a Faculty Research Fellowship for the Social Science Research Council and a modest grant from the former Behavioral Sciences Division of the Ford Foundation. I also wish to thank James D. Barber and David Sears for their helpful comments on this paper. Much of the material in this paper was first presented at the American Sociological Society Annual Meeting, Seattle, August, 1958.

SOURCE. Reprinted from *The American Political Science Review*, Vol. 53, 1959, by permission of the author and publisher. Copyright 1959, The American Political Science Association.

[1] See Natalie Rogoff, *Recent Trends in Occupational Mobility* (Glencoe, Ill.: Free Press, 1958), pp. 61-63.

men in our society came about largely from working class pressure.

But on closer investigation the demands for greater liberty or "freedom" turn out to have been of an ambiguous nature. The middle classes sought freedom of speech and action in large part for the economic gains that this would give them, and moralized their action with the theology of freedom. But the freedom that they gained was frightening, for it deprived them of the solidary social relationships and the ideological certainty which often gave order and meaning to their lives. On occasion, then, they sought to "escape from freedom."[2] The older unfree order had a value which the earlier social commentators did not appreciate.

There is a parallel here with the movement toward a more equalitarian society. The upper working class, and the lower middle class, support specific measures embraced in the formula "welfare state," which have equalitarian consequences. But, so I shall argue, many members of the working classes do not want equality. They are afraid of it. In some ways they already seek to escape from it. Equality for the working classes, like freedom for the middle classes, is a worrisome, partially rejected, by-product of the demand for more specific measures. Inequality has values to them which have been overlooked. It is these attitudes on status and equality that I shall explore here.

I. EXTENDED INTERVIEWS WITH FIFTEEN MEN

This discussion is based upon extended interviews of from ten to fifteen hours each (in from four to seven sessions) with a sample of American urban male voters. The sample is a random selection from the white members on a list of 220 registered voters in a moderate income (not low income) housing development where income is permitted to range be-

[2] Erich Fromm, *Escape from Freedom* (New York: Rinehart, 1941).

tween $4,000 and $6,500, according to the number of dependents in the family. Out of fifteen asked to participate, fifteen agreed, for a modest cash consideration. The characteristics of the sample, then, are as follows:

They are all men, white, married, fathers, urban, Eastern seaboard.

Their incomes range from $2,400 to $6,300 (except for one who had just moved from the project. His income was $10,000 in 1957.)

Ten had working class (blue collar) occupations such as painter, plumber, oiler, railroad fireman, policeman, machine operator.

Five had white collar occupations such as a salesman, bookkeeper, supply clerk.

Their ages ranged from 25 to 54; most are in their thirties.

Twelve are Catholic, two are Protestants, one is Jewish.

All are native born; their nationality backgrounds are: six Italian, five Irish, one Polish, one Swedish, one Russian, one Yankee. Most are second or third generation Americans.

All were employed at the time of the interviews.

Their educational distribution was: three had only grammar school education; eight had some high school; two finished high school; one had some college; one completed graduate training.

The interviews with these men were taped, with the permission of the interviewees, and transcribed. They were conducted by means of a schedule of questions and topics followed by conversational improved probes to discover the underlying meanings of the answers given. The kinds of questions employed to uncover the material to be reported are illustrated by the following: "What do you think the phrase 'All men are created equal' means?" "How would you feel if everyone received the same income no matter what his job?" "Sometimes one hears the term 'social class'—as in working class or middle class. What do you think this term 'social class' means?" "What class do you belong to?" "How do you feel about it?" There were also a number of questions dealing with status, private utopias, feelings of privilege or lack of privilege, and other topics, throughout the interview schedule which sometimes elicited responses bearing on the question of social and economic equality.[3]

II. HOW TO ACCOUNT FOR ONE'S OWN STATUS?

It is my thesis that attitudes toward equality rest in the first instance upon one's attitude towards one's own status. Like a large number of social beliefs, attitudes towards equality take their direction from beliefs about the self, the status of the self, one's self-esteem or lack thereof. It is necessary, therefore, first to explore how people see themselves in American hierarchical society.

The American culture and the democratic dogma have given to the American public the notion that "all men are created equal." Even more insistently, the American culture tells its members: "achieve," "complete," "be better, smarter, quicker, richer than your fellow men"; in short,

---

[3] One way of finding out whether these working class men reported their "true feelings" —the ones which form the basis of their relevant behavior and thought—to the listening professor, is to find out how they talk to each other. Fortunately, we have some evidence on this in the transcribed protocols of discussions where two groups of three men each, selected from the fifteen reported on here, argued with each other, without an interviewer present, on the job performance of certain public officials. In these discussions the main themes reported on below are apparent. Illustrative of one of these themes is Costa's remark to Woodside and O'Hara: "If you're the business man and I'm the working man, I don't care if you make a hundred million dollars a year, as long as I make a living. In other words, you got your money invested. You're supposed to make money." And O'Hara then chimes in "That's right."

"be unequal." The men I interviewed had received these inequalitarian messages, some eagerly, some with foreboding. Having heard them, they must account for their status, higher than some, lower than others. They must ask themselves, for example, "Why didn't I rise out of the working class, or out of the 'housing project class,' or out of the underpaid office help class?" And, on the other hand, "Why am I better off than my parents? or than the fellows down the road in the low rental project? or the fellows on relief?" Men confronted with these questions adopt a variety of interesting answers.

IS IT UP TO ME?

The problem of accounting for status is personally important for these men only if they think that their decisions, effort, and energy make a difference in their position in life. Most of my subjects accepted the view that America opens up opportunity to all people; if not in equal proportions, then at least enough so that a person must assume responsibility for his own status. Thus O'Hara, a maintenance oiler in a factory, in a typical response, comments that the rich man's son, and the poor man's son "have equal opportunity to be President . . . if they've got the education and the know how." But, he goes on to say, "some of them have a little more help than others." This is the constant theme: "all men can better themselves," the circumstances of American life do not imprison men in their class or station—if there is such a prison, the iron bars are within each man.

There were a few, of course, who stressed the differences of opportunity at birth, the mockery of the phrase "all men are created equal." Here, as only rarely in the interviews, a head of steam builds up which might feed radical social movements—but this is true for only a few of the sample. Three or four angry young or middle aged men deny the Jeffersonian phrase. Rapuano, an auto parts supply man, says:

How could you say we were born equal when, for instance, when I was born, I was born in a family that were pretty poor. You get another baby born in a family that has millions.

And Kuchinsky, a house painter, says:

Are we created equal? I don't believe we are, because everybody's got much more than one another and it's not right, I think. Of course, ah, we have no choice. I mean we can't do nothing about it. So we're not as equal as the next party, that's for sure.

And Ferrera, a salesman, says:

All men created equal? Ah, very hypocritical, cause all men are not created equal—and—I don't know—you really pick some beauties don't you? . . . The birth of an individual in a (social) class sort of disputes this.

To these men, then, subordination and life position is attributable not so much to the efforts of the individual, something for which he must assume responsibility, as to the circumstances of birth, over which he has no control. Yet for each of those men, the channels of advancement were seen as only partly blocked. Rapuano, for example, says elsewhere that income is generally proportionate to ability. Like the theme of "moral equality," the theme of differential life chances from birth is easily available. What is surprising is not that it is used at all, but rather that it is used so infrequently.

III. REDUCING THE IMPORTANCE OF THE STRUGGLE

When something is painful to examine, people look away, or, if they look at it, they see only the parts they want to see. They deny that it is an important something. So is it often with a person's class status when the reference is upward, when people must account not for the strength of their position, but for its weakness. How do they do this?

In the first place they may *insulate*

themselves, limit their outlook and range of comparisons. Ferrera, an insurance salesman, who says, "It's pretty hard for me to think there is anyone in the upper class and I'm not in the upper class," slides into a prepared position of insulated defense:

I think a lot of people place a lot of stress on the importance of social classes (but) I feel that I have a job to do, I have my own little unit to take care of. It I can do it to the best ability that is instilled in me at birth or progress through the years, I feel that I rightly deserve the highest classification you can get. I don't particularly like the headings, "upper, middle, working, and lower."

It is a resentful narrowing of focus in this case: two years at an inferior college may have led to ambitions which life then failed to fulfill. Contrast this to Woodside, a policeman with a Middlewestern rural background, who accepts the "categories" of social class rather willingly. He says, after dealing with the moral and intangible aspects of equality:

("Are there any people whom you regard as not equal to you?") Well, that is a tough question. Well, in fairness, I'd say all people are equal to one another in his own category. When I say category, I mean you couldn't exactly expect a person that had very little knowledge to be, we'll say, should have a position where a person with a lot more education had it.

Equality must be treated within classes, not between them, to be meaningful—and in this way the problem of placing oneself becomes tolerable, or sometimes rather gratifying.

A second device for reducing the importance of class position is to *deny its importance.* This is not to deny the importance of getting ahead, but to limit this to the problem of job classification, or occupational choice—nothing so damaging to the self-esteem as an ordering of persons on a class scale. Rapuano, resisting the class concept, says:

I don't think it (social class) is important. I mean whenever I went and asked for a job, the boss never asked me what class I was in. They just wanted to know if I knew my business. Oh yes, and I don't think in politics it makes any difference.

Others maintain that for other countries social class is important, but not for Americans. There are rich and poor, perhaps, but not status, class, or deference levels to be accounted for.

A third device for reducing the significance of the struggle for status and "success" is *resignation,* a reluctant acceptance of one's fate. When some men assume this posture of resignation one senses a pose; their secret hopes and ambitions will not down. For others it rings true. When Dempsey, a factory operative, speaks of his situation at the age of 54, one believes him:

> It's hard, very hard. We seem to be struggling along now, as it is, right here, to try and get above our level, to get out of the rut, as you might say, that we're probably in right now . . . (But) After you get to a certain age, there, you stop—and you say, "Well, I can't go any further." I think I've gotten to that point now.

But when Sokolsky reports that he is contented with his station in life, it does not seem authentic:

> Being in the average group (He wouldn't assign himself a class status) doesn't bother me. I know I make a living—as long as I make a living, and I'm happy and I have what I want—try to give my family what they want. It doesn't bother me—no. I'm satisfied.

But then he adds: "I hope to God my children will do better than their father did."

Contrast these views with those of Johnson, a plumber, who says, "I feel someday I'll be better off. I feel that way because I believe I have it within me to do it", and with Flynn, a white collar worker, who answers:

> No, I'm nowhere near satisfied. It seems to me every time I start to move up a little bit, all the levels move up one step ahead of me. I can't ever get out of this area. I have a certain desire and willingness to do something extra.

IV. THE WORKING CLASS GETS ITS SHARE

When comparing their status with those lower on the scale, however each man may define it, it is easy to point with pride to achievement, material well-being, standing in the community. But satisfaction with one's self and one's friends depends on seeing some advantage in one's situation *vis-a-vis* those who live and work on a higher status level. At first, this seems to be a difficult task, but in many simple ways it can be easily done. Our sample, for example, found ways of ascribing greater happiness, power, and even income to the working class than would be found in the upper class.

The equality of happiness is a fruitful vein. Lower income and status is more tolerable when one can believe that the rich are not receiving a happiness income commensurate with their money income. "Are the rich happier than people who are just average?" O'Hara does not think so:

> I think lots of times they're never happy, because one thing is, the majority of them that are rich have got more worries. You see a lot more of them sick than you do, I think, the average. I think a lot of your mental strain is a lot greater in the higher class—in the rich class—than in the other.

And Johnson, a maintenance plumber says:

> Well, even though this rich man can go places and do things that others can't afford, there's only certain things in life that I think make people happy. For instance, having children, and having a place to live—no matter where it is, it's your home . . . the majority of these big men—I don't think they devote as much time and get a thrill out of the little things in life that the average guy gets, which I think is a lot of thrills.

Indeed, hardly a man thought the rich were happier. And yet, O'Hara says, on another occasion, "What is the most important thing that money can buy? Happiness, when you come down to it." Perhaps he means that money buys happiness for the average man, but not for the rich. But more likely he means ("I can take care of a gnawing and illegitimate envy by appropriating happiness for me and my kind.")[4]

Power, like happiness, is awarded to the working (or lower middle) class. The sheer fact of numbers gives a sense of strength and importance. Costa, a factory operative, says, for example, "People like you (the interviewer) are the minority and people like me are the majority, so we get taken care of in the long run." Whether a person sees himself as middle class or working class, he is likely to believe that most people belong to his class. This being true, his class, people like him, become the most important force in electoral decisions. O'Hara puts it this way:

> The biggest part of the people in this country are working class. And I think they've got the most to do with—they've got a big part to do with running this country—because the lower class, a lot of them don't vote, when you come down to it, they don't have the education to vote, and your upper class isn't that much —isn't as great as the other so really when you come down to it, it's your working class that's deciding one way or the other.

Not only do they "have the biggest part to do with running the country," they are crucial for the economy. This is not only as producers—indeed no one mentioned the theme which romantic writers on the laboring man and the immigrant have often employed—"they cleared the land and built the cities." Rather it is because of their power to shatter the economy and their power to survive in a depression that they are important. Kuchinsky explains this as follows:

> I think the lower class of people are the important people. I think so because of the business end of it. Without us, I don't think the businessman could survive. I mean if we don't work—of course, they have the money, but, ah, a lot of times during the crash which was an awful

thing, too, I think a lot of 'em lived so high that they couldn't stand it any more when they went broke, and they committed a lot of suicides there. But we were used to living that way, it didn't bother us.

Today, as perhaps never before, the working class man can see his status loss compared to white collar workers compensated by income advantages. Thus, De Angelo, a factory operative and shop steward, reports:

> You got people working in offices, they might consider themselves upper class, y'know, a little better than the working man. But nine times out of ten the working man is making more money than he is.

And in the same vein, Rapuano says:

> I certainly would hate like hell to be a white collar worker in the middle class and making the money that the white collar worker does. I would rather be a worker in the lower class, and making their money, see?

Of course, this assignment of income advantages to the working class hinges upon the narrowing of the range of competition—but this is the range that makes a difference for these men.

V. MORAL EQUALITY

Another device for dealing with subordination in a society where invidious comparison with others is constantly invited represents, in effect, a borrowing from an older classical or religious tradition—an emphasis upon the intangible and immeasurable (and therefore comfortingly vague) spiritual and moral qualities. The only clearly adequate expression of this religious view was given by McNamara, a gentle and compassionate bookkeeper, who said "All men are created equal? That's our belief as Catholics," implying some sort of religious equality, perhpas such an idea as is captured in the phrase "equality of the soul." Woodside, a Protestant policeman, takes, in a way, a secular 18th Century version

---

[4] Brackets are used here and below to distinguish inferred meanings or imputed statements from direct quotations.

of this view when he says that men are equal "not financially, not in influence, but equal to one another as to being a person," Being a person, then, is enough to qualify for equal claims of some undefined kind.

But it seems probably that when men assert their own equality in this vague sense, typically phrased in some like O'Hara's terms: "I think I'm just as good as anybody else. I don't think there's any of them that I would say are better," something other than moral or spiritual equality is at issue. These moral qualities are what the educated commentator reads into the statement, but O'Hara means, if I may put words in his mouth "don't put on airs around me," "I'm trying to preserve my self-respect in a world that challenges it; I therefore assert my equality with all." "Just because you're a professor and I'm an oiler, it doesn't mean you can patronize me."). And when Sokolsky, a machine operator and part-time janitor, says, in the interview, "The rich guy—because he's got money he's no better than I am. I mean that's the way I feel," he is not talking about moral or spiritual qualities. He is saying, in effect to his prosperous older brother and his snobbish wife, ("Don't look down on me,") and the world at large: ("I may be small, but I will protect my self-esteem.") These men are posting notices similar to the motto on the early American colonies' flags: "Don't tread on me."

Speaking of moral virtues, we must observe how easy it would have been to take the view that the morality of the middle levels of society was superior because the rich received their wealth illegitimately. None of my clients did this. Nor did they stress the immoral lives of the wealthy classes, as did Merton's sample[5] some thirteen years ago—a commentary, perhaps, upon changing attitudes toward the upper classes taking place over this period. The psychic defenses against subordination available in stress-

ing moral equality or superiority were used—but only rarely.

VI. PEOPLE DESERVE THEIR STATUS

If one accepts the view that this is a land of opportunity in which merit will find a way, one is encouraged to accept the status differences of society. But it is more than logic which impels our men to accept these differences. There are satisfactions of identification with the going social order; it is easier to accept differences which one calls "just" than those that appear "unjust"; there are the very substantial self-congratulatory satisfactions of comparison with those lower on the scale. Thus this theme of "just disserts" applies to one's own group, those higher, and those lower.

So Kuchinsky says: "If you're a professor, I think you're entitled to get what you deserve. I'm a painter and I shouldn't be getting what you're getting." Furthermore confidence in the general equity of the social order suggests that the rewards of one's own life are proportionate to ability, efforts, and the wisdom of previous decisions. On ability, Costa, a machine operator, says:

I believe anybody that has the potential to become a scientific man, or a profesor, or a lawyer, or a doctor, should have the opportunity to pursue it, but there's a lot of us that are made to run a machine in a factory. No matter what opportunities some of us might have had, we would never have reached the point where we could become people of that kind. I mean everybody isn't Joe DiMaggio.

And on the wisdom of earlier decisions, Johnson, a plumber, says:

I don't consider myself the lower class. In between someplace. But I could have been a lot better off but through my own foolishness, I'm not. (Here he refers back to an earlier account of his life.) What causes poverty? Foolishness. When I came out of the service, my wife had saved a few dollars and I had a few bucks. I wanted to have a good time.

---

[5] Robert K. Merton, *Mass Persuasion; the Social Psychology of a War Bond Drive* (New York: Harper, 1946).

I'm throwing money away like water. Believe me, had I used my head right, I could have had a house. I don't feel sorry for myself—what happened, happened, you know. Of course you pay for it.

But the most usual mistake or deficiency accounting for the relatively humble position is failure to continue one's education due to lack of family pressure ("they should have made me"), or youthful indiscretion, or the demands of the family for money, or the depression of the thirties.

The upper classes deserve to be upper. Just as they regard their own status as deserved, so also do they regard the status of the more eminently successful as appropriate to their talents. Rapuano, an auto parts supply man, reports:

> Your income—if you're smart, and your ability calls for a certain income, that's what you should earn. If your ability is so low, why hell, then you should earn the low income. ("Do you think income is proportionate to ability now?") I would say so. Yes.

But there is a suggestion in many of the interviews that even if the income is divorced from talent and effort, in some sense it is appropriate. Consider Sokolsky again, a machine operator and part-time janitor, discussing the tax situation:

> Personally, I think taxes are too hard. I mean a man makes, let's say $150,000. Well, my God, he has to give up half of that to the government—which I don't think it right. For instance if a man is fortunate enough to win the Irish Sweepstakes, he gets 150—I think he has about $45,000 left. I don't think that's right.

Even if life is a lottery, the winner should keep his winnings. And De Angelo, a machine operator, comes spontaneously to the same conclusion:

> I think everybody needs a little (tax) relief. I mean, I know one thing, if I made a million dollars and the government took nine-tenths of it—boy, I'd cry the blues. I can't see that. If a man is smart enough to make that much, damn it, he's got a right to holler. I'm with the guy all the way.

Because he is "smart enough" to make the money, it is rightfully his. Surely, beyond the grave, there is a spectre haunting Marx.

The concept of "education" is the key to much of the thinking on social class and personal status. In a sense, it is a "natural" because it fits so neatly into the American myth of opportunity and equality, and provides a rationale for success and failure which does minimum damage to the souls of those who did not go to college. Thus in justifying their own positions, sometimes with reference to the interview situation, my clients imply, "If I had gone to college (like you) I would be higher up in this world." Costa, a machine operator, speaks this theme:

> Now what would be the advantage of you going 20 years to school so you wind up making $10,000 a year, and me going 8 years to school, making $10,000. You would be teaching the young men of tomorrow, the leaders of tomorrow, and I would be running a machine. You would have a lot more responsibility to the country as a whole than I would have. Why shouldn't you be rewarded in proportion.

McNamara, a mild mannered bookkeeper who went to night school to get his training in accounting and bookkeeping, emphasizes education in response to the question: "Do you think it's easy or hard to get from one class to another?"

> Well, I think it's hard because . . . not because of the class itself, or what the influence they have on you, but you just seem to reach a certain point, and if you don't have it, you just don't—you don't make the grade. I've found that to be true. I always seem to be one step away from a good spot. And it's no one's fault—it's my fault. I just don't have the education—just don't—just don't have what it takes to take that step.

And Sokolsky, a machine operator and part-time janitor, says, in his justification of income differences:

> A man that gets out of eighth grade—I don't think he would have the ability to do the job as a man that got out of college.

But later, he says, of politicians and businessmen:

If a man with more education has been in politics, he should get the job, but if there's a man that, let's say, just got out of high school, and he's been around in politics all his life, I think he should have a chance too. It's how good he is. There's some big business people who just haven't got it. (But) there could be some men with a gift of gab—maybe just out of eighth grade—they could sell anything.

What is it about education that justifies differences in income? In the above interviews it is clear that education is thought to increase skills which should be suitably rewarded. Furthermore, it appears that the time necessary for educational preparation deserves some reward—a recurrent theme. With education goes responsibility—and responsibility should be rewarded. But there is also some suggestion in the interview material that the pain and hard (unpleasant) work associated with going to school deserves compensation. People who did not like school themselves may be paying homage to those who could stick it out. It is a question whether O'Hara, a maintenance oiler, implies this when he says:

> I think a person that is educated deserves more than somebody that isn't. Somebody who really works for his money really deserves it more than somebody that's lazy and just wants to hang around.

In this and other ways, education serves as a peg on which to hang status; and, like "blood," whether a person got the education or not is not his "fault," or at least it is only the fault of an irresponsible youth, not a grown man.[6]

THE LOWER CLASSES DESERVE NO BETTER THAN THEY GET

By and large those in the lower orders are those who are paid daily (not weekly) or are on relief; they live in slums or in public housing projects (but not middle

income projects); they do not live respectable lives; they have only grammar school education; they may have no regular jobs. Closer to home, those slightly lower in status are people like 'The lady next door who has a little less than I have," the man who can't afford to take care of his kids properly in the project, people who spend their money on liquor, the person with less skill in the same line of work.

The rationale for their lower status turns chiefly on two things: their lack of education and therefore failure to know what they want or failure to understand lifemanship, and their general indifference. It is particularly this "not caring" which seems so salient in the upper working class mind. This is consonant with the general view that success is a triumph of the will and a reflection of ability. Poverty is for lazy people, just as middle status is for struggling people. Thus Ruggiero, an office building maintenance man, accounts for poverty by saying: "There's laziness, you'll always have lazy people." De Angelo, a factory operative, sees it this way:

> A guy gets married and, you know, he's not educated too well, he doesn't have a good job and he gets a large family and he's in bad shape, y'know what I mean. It's tough; he's got to live in a lousy rent —he can't afford anything better.

But De Angelo takes away some of this sympathy the next moment when he goes on to say:

> But then you get a lot of people who don't want to work; you got welfare. People will go on living on that welfare—they're happier than hell. Why should they work if the city will support them?

In general, there is little sympathy given to those lower in the scale, little reference to the overpowering forces of circumstance, only rare mention of sickness, death of a breadwinner, senility, factories moving out of town, and so forth. The only major cause of poverty to which no moral blame attaches is depression or "unemployment"—but this is not considered a strikingly important cause in the minds of my clients. They are Chris-

[6] Contrast de Tocqueville: "I never met in America a citizen so poor as not to cast a glance of hope and envy on the enjoyments of the rich or whose imagination did not possess itself by anticipation of those good things that fate still obstinately withheld from him." *Democracy in America* (New York: Vintage ed.), Vol. II, p. 137.

tian in the sense that they believe "The poor ye have with you always," but there is no trace of a belief that the poor are in any way "blessed."

VII. WHAT IF THERE WERE GREATER EQUALITY OF OPPORTUNITY AND INCOME?

We have examined here the working (and lower middle) class defenses of the present order. They are well organized and solidly built. By and large these people believe that the field is open, merit will tell. They may then deprecate the importance of class, limit their perspectives, accept their situation reluctantly or with satisfaction. They may see the benefits of society flowing to their own class, however they define it. They tend to believe that each person's status is in some way deserved.

How would these lower middle and working class men feel about a change in the social order such that they and their friends might suddenly be equal to others now higher or lower in the social order? Most of them wouldn't like it. They would fear and resent this kind of equality.

ABANDONMENT OF A RATIONALE

Changing ideas is a strain not to be lightly incurred, particularly when these ideas are intimately related to one's self-esteem. The less education one has, the harder it is to change such ideas. Painfully these men have elaborated an explanation for their situation in life; it helps explain things to their wives who take their status from them; it permits their growing children to account for relative social status in school; it offers to each man the satisfactions of social identity and a measure of social worth. Their rationales are endowed with moral qualities; the distribution of values in the society is seen as just and natural. While it gives satisfactions of an obvious kind to those who contemplate those beneath

them, it also gives order and a kind of reassurance, oddly enough, to those who glance upwards towards "society" or "the four hundred." This reassurance is not unlike the reassurance provided by the belief in a Just God while injustices rain upon one's head. The feudal serf, the Polish peasant, the Mexican peon believed that theirs was a moral and a "natural order"—so also the American working man.

THE PROBLEM OF SOCIAL ADJUSTMENT

Equality would pose problems of social adjustments, of manners, of how to behave. Here is Sokolsky, unprepossessing, uneducated, and nervous, with a more prosperous brother in the same town. "I'm not going to go over there," he says, "because everytime I go there I feel uncomfortable." On the question of rising from one social class to another, his views reflect this personal situation:

> I think it's hard. Let's say—let's take me, for instance. Supposing I came into a lot of money, and I moved into a nice neighborhood—class—maybe I wouldn't know how to act then. I think it's very hard, because people know that you just—word gets around that you . . . never had it before you got it now. Well, maybe they wouldn't like you . . . maybe you don't know how to act.

The kind of equality with others which would mean a rapid rise in his own status is a matter of concern, mixed, of course, with pleasant anticipation at the thought of "telling off" his brother.

Consider the possibility of social equality including genuine fraternization, without economic equality. Sullivan, a railroad fireman, deals with this in graphic terms:

> What is the basis of social class? Well things that people have in common. . . . Money is one, for instance, like I wouldn't feel very comfortable going around with a millionaire, we'll say . . . He could do a lot and say a lot—mention places he'd been and so on—I mean I wouldn't be able to keep up with him . . . and he wouldn't have to watch his money, and I'd have to be pinching mine to see

if I had enough for another beer, or something.

And, along the lines of Sokolsky's comments, Sullivan believes that moving upwards in the social scale is easier if one moves to a new place where one has not been known in the old connection. Flynn holds that having the right interests and conversational topics for the new and higher social group will make it possible —but otherwise it could be painful. Kuchinsky, the house painter, says "I suppose it would feel funny to get into a higher class, but I don't believe I would change. I wouldn't just disregard my friends if I came into any money." Clinging to old friends would give some security in that dazzling new world.

De Angelo, a factory operative, also considers the question of whether the higher status people will accept the *arriviste,* but for himself, he dismisses it:

I wouldn't worry much about whether they would accept or they wouldn't accept. I would move into another class. I mean —I mean—I don't worry much about that stuff. If people don't want to bother with me, I don't bother with them, that's all.

These fears, while plausible and all too human on the face of it, emerged unexpectedly from the interview material designed to capture ideas and emotions on other aspects of class status. They highlight a resistance to equalitarian movements that might bring the working class and this rejecting superior class—whether it is imaginary or not—in close association. If these were revolutionaries, one might phrase their anexieties: "Will my victims accept me?" But they are not revolutionaries.

These are problems of rising in status to meet the upper classes face to face. But there is another risk in opening the gates so that those of moderate circumstances can rise to higher status. Equality of opportunity, it appears, is inherently dangerous in this respect: there is the risk that friends, neighbors, or subordinates will surpass one in status. O'Hara has this on his mind. Some of the people who rise in status are nice, but:

You get other ones, the minute they get a little, they get big-headed and they think they're better than the other ones—where they're still—to me they're worse than the middle class. I mean, they should get down, because they're just showing their illiteracy—that's all they're doing.

Sokolsky worries about this possibility, too, having been exposed to the slights of his brother's family. But the worry over being passed by is not important, not salient. It is only rarely mentioned.

DEPRIVATION OF A MERITORIOUS ELITE

It is comforting to have the "natural leaders" of a society well entrenched in their proper place. If there were equality there would no longer be such an elite to supervise and take care of people— especially "me." Thus Woodside, our policeman, reports:

I think anybody that has money—I think their interest is much wider than the regular working man . . . and therefore I think that the man with the money is a little bit more educated, for the simple reason he has the money, and he has a much wider view of life—because he's in the knowledge of it all the time.

Here and elsewhere in the interview, one senses that Woodside is glad to have such educated, broad-gauged men in eminent positions. He certainly opposes the notion of equality of income. Something similar creeps into Johnson's discussion of social classes. He feels that the upper classes, who seem to be very nice people," are "willing to lend a helping hand—to listen to you. I would say they'd help you out more than the middle class (man) would help you out even if he was in a position to help you out." Equality, then, would deprive society, and oneself, of a group of friendly, wise, and helpful people who occupy the social eminences.

THE LOSS OF THE GOALS OF LIFE

But most important of all, equality, at least equality of income, would deprive people of the goals of life. Every one of the fifteen clients with whom I spent my evenings for seven months believed that equality of income would deprive men of their incentive to work, achieve, and develop their skills. These answers ranged, in their sophistication and approach, across a broad field. The most highly educated man in the sample, Farrel, answers the question "How would you feel if everyone received the same income in our society?" by saying:

> I think it would be kind of silly . . . Society, by using income as a reward technique, can often insure that the individuals will put forth their best efforts.

He does not believe, for himself, that status or income are central to motivation—but for others, they are. Woodside, our policeman, whose main concern is not the vistas of wealth and opportunity of the American dream, but rather whether he can get a good pension if he should have to retire early, comes forward as follows;

> I'd say that (equal income)—that is something that's pretty—I think it would be a dull thing, because life would be accepted—or it would—rather we'd go stale. There would be no initiative to be a little different or go ahead.

Like Woodside, Flynn, a white collar worker, responds with a feeling of personal loss—the idea of such an equality of income would make him feel "very mad." Costa, whose ambitions in life are most modest, holds that equality of income "would eliminate the basic thing about the wonderful opportunity you have in this country." Then, for a moment the notion of his income equalling that of the professional man passes pleasantly through his mind: "don't misunderstand me—I like the idea"; then again, "I think it eliminates the main reason why people become engineers and professors and doctors."

Rapuano, whose worries have given him ulcers, projects himself into a situation where everyone receives the same income, in this case a high one:

> If everyone had the same income of a man that's earning $50,000 a year, and he went to, let's say 10 years of college to do that, why hell, I'd just as soon sit on

my ass as go to college and wait till I could earn $50,000 a year, too. Of course, what the hell am I going to do to earn $50,000 a year—now that's another question.

But however the question is answered, he is clear that guaranteed equal incomes would encourage people to sit around on their anatomy and wait for their pay checks. But he would like to see some levelling, particularly if doctors, whom he hates, were to have their fees and incomes substantially reduced.

THAT THESE SACRIFICES SHALL NOT HAVE BEEN IN VAIN

The man I talked to were not at the bottom of the scale; not at all. They were stable breadwinners, churchgoers, voters, family men. They achieved this position in life through hard work and somes bitter sacrifices. They are distinguished from the lower classes through their initiative, zeal and responsibility, their willingness and ability to postpone pleasures or to forego them entirely. In their control of impulse and desire they have absorbed the Protestant ethic. At least six of them have two jobs and almost no leisure. In answering questions on "the last time you remember having a specially good time" some of them must go back ten to fifteen years. Nor are their good times remarkable for their spontaneous fun and enjoyment of life. Many of them do not like their jobs, but stick to them because of their family responsibilities—and they do not know what else they would rather do. In short, they have sacrificed their hedonistic inclinations, given up good times, expended their energy and resources in order to achieve and maintain their present tenuous hold on respectability and middle status.

Now in such a situation to suggest that men be equalized and the lower orders raised and one's own hard-earned status given to them as a right and not a reward for effort, seems to them desperate wrong. In the words of my research assistant, David Sears, "Suppose the Marshall Plan had provided a block and tackle for

Sisyphus after all these years. How do you think he would have felt?" Sokolsky, Woodside, and Dempsey have rolled the stone to the top of the hill so long, they despise the suggestion that it might have been in vain. Or even worse, that their neighbors at the foot of the hill might have the use of a block and tackle.

THE WORLD WOULD COLLAPSE

As a corollary to the view that life would lose its vigor and its savor with equality of income, there is the image of an equalitarian society as a world running down, a chaotic and disorganized place to live. The professions would be decimated: "People pursue the higher educational levels for a reason—there's a lot of rewards, either financial or social," says Costa. Sullivan says, "Why should people take the headaches of responsible jobs if the pay didn't meet the responsibilities?" For the general society, Flynn, a white collar man, believes that "if there were no monetary incentive involved, I think there'd be a complete loss. It would stop all development—there's no doubt about it." McNamara, a bookkeeper, sees people then reduced to a dead level of worth: with equal income "the efforts would be equal and pretty soon we would be worth the same thing." In two contrasting views, both suggesting economic disorganization, Woodside believes "I think you'd find too many men digging ditches, and no doctors," while Rapuano believes men would fail to dig ditches or sewers "and where the hell would we be when we wanted to go to the toilet?"

Only a few took up the possible inference that this was an attractive, but impractical ideal—and almost none followed up the suggestion that some equalization of income, if not complete equality, would be desirable. The fact of the matter is that these men, by and large, prefer an inequalitarian society, and even prefer a society graced by some men of great wealth. As they look out upon the social scene, they feel that an equalitarian society would present them with too many problems of moral adjustment, inter-personal social adjustment, and motivational adjustment which they fear and dislike. But perhaps, most important, their life goals are structured around achievement and success in monetary terms. If these were taken away, life would be a desert. These men view the possibility of an equalitarian world as a paraphrased version of Swinburne's lines on Jesus Christ, "Thou has conquered, oh pale equalitarian, and the world has grown gray with thy breath."

VIII. SOME THEORETICAL IMPLICATIONS

Like any findings on the nature of men's social attitudes and beliefs, even in such a culture-bound inquiry as this one, the new information implies certain theoretical propositions which may be incorporated into the main body of political theory. Let us consider seven such propositions growing more or less directly out of our findings on the fear of equality:

(1) The greater the emphasis in a society upon the availability of "equal opportunity for all," the greater the need for members of that society to develop an acceptable rationalization for their own social status.

(2) The greater the strain on a person's self-esteem implied by a relatively low status in an open society. the greater the necessity to explain this status as "natural" and "proper" in the social order. Lower status people generally find it less punishing to think of themselves as correctly placed by a just society than to think of themselves as exploited, or victimized by an unjust society.

(3) The greater the emphasis in a society upon equality of opportunity, the greater the tendency for those of marginal status to denigrate those lower than themselves. This view seems to such people to have the factual or even moral justification that if the lower classes "cared" enough they could be better off. It has a psychological "justification" in that it draws attention to one's own relatively

better status and one's own relatively greater initiative and virtue.

(4) People tend to care less about *equality* of opportunity than about the availability of *some* opportunity. Men do not need the same life chances as everybody else, indeed they usually care very little about that. They need only chances (preferably with unknown odds) for a slightly better life than they now have. Thus: Popular satisfaction with one's own status is related less to equality of opportunity than to the breadth of distribution of some opportunity for all, however unequal this distribution may be. A man who can improve his position one rung does not resent the man who starts on a different ladder half way up.

These propositions are conservative in their implications. The psychological roots of this conservatism must be explored elsewhere, as must the many exceptions which may be observed when the fabric of a social order is so torn that the leaders, the rich and powerful, are seen as illegitimate—and hence "appropriately" interpreted as exploiters of the poor. I maintain, however, that these propositions hold generally for the American culture over most of its history—and also that the propositions hold for most of the world most of the time. This is so even though they fly in the face of much social theory —theory often generalized from more specialized studies of radicalism and revolution. Incidentally, one must observe that it is as important to explain why revolutions and radical social movements do *not* happen as it is to explain why they do.

The more I observed the psychological and physical drain placed upon my sample by the pressures to consume—and therefore to scratch in the corners of the economy for extra income—the more it appeared that competitive consumption was not a stimulus to class conflict, as might have ben expected, but was a substitute for or a sublimation of it. Thus we would say:

(5) The more emphasis a society places upon consumption—through advertising, development of new products, and easy installment buying—the more

will social dissatisfaction be channeled into intra-class consumption rivalry instead of inter-class resentment and conflict. The Great American Medicine Show creates consumer unrest, working wives, and dual-job-holding, not antagonism toward the "owning classes."

As a corollary of this view: (6) The more emphasis is society places upon consumption, the more will labor unions focus upon the "bread and butter" aspects of unionism, as contrasted to its ideological elements.

We come, finally, to a hypothesis which arises from this inquiry into the fear of equality but goes much beyond the focus of the present study. I mention it here in a speculative frame of mind, undogmatically, and even regretfully.

(7) The ideals of the French Revolution, liberty and equality, have been advanced because of the accidental correspondence between these ideals and needs of the bourgeoisie for freedom of economic action and the demands of the working class, very simply, for "more". Ideas have an autonomy of their own, however, in the sense that once moralized they persist even if the social forces which brought them to the fore decline in strength. They become "myths"—but myths erode without support from some major social stratum. Neither the commercial classes nor the working classes, the historical beneficiaries of these two moralized ideas (ideals or myths), have much affection for the ideals in their universal forms. On the other hand, the professional classes, particularly the lawyers, ministers, and teachers of a society, very often do have such an affection. It is they, in the democratic West, who serve as the "hard core" of democratic defenders, in so far as there is one. It is they, more frequently than others, who are supportive of the generalized application of the ideals of freedom and equality to all men. This is not virtue, but rather a different organization of interests and a different training. Whatever the reason, however, it is not to "The People," not to the business class, not to the

working class, that we must look for the consistent and relatively unqualified defense of freedom and equality. The professional class, at least in the American culture, serves as the staunchest defender of democracy's two greatest ideals.

CHAPTER 4

Mass-Elite Linkage

DEMOCRACY assumes a relationship between people and government such that the people exert influence if not control over the acts of government. The manner in which the people exert such influence is crucial to the nature and extent of their power: if there are no mechanisms through which their will may be translated into action, there can be no democracy. The classic device by which popular preferences are made known is an election, but many other expressions of demands such as demonstrations and riots also play a part in this process. The three selections in this chapter explore the mechanisms of linkage between masses and elites; two concentrate on the electoral link, and the third on other forms of making demands.

Professors Angus Campbell, Philip Converse, Warren Miller, and Donald Stokes were founding members of the Survey Research Center of the University of Michigan and have together produced a very important body of data concerning characteristics of American voting behavior. In this chapter from their celebrated book *The American Voter*, they examine the role of ideas and ideology in shaping electoral decisions. In the second selection, Professor Campbell both summarizes many of their other findings and applies these speculatively to interpretation of past elections.

Professor Michael Lipsky of the University of Wisconsin specializes in the politics of civil rights and social welfare policy. His article is an attempt to employ data from several demonstrations and protests to build a theory of political protest. His books include *The Politics of Protest: Rent Strikes in New York City* and a forthcoming study of the politics of riot commissions.

A selected bibliography follows Chapter 5.

The Formation of Issue Concepts and Partisan Change

ANGUS CAMPBELL, PHILIP E. CONVERSE, WARREN E. MILLER, AND
DONALD E. STOKES

The popularity of the conservative-liberal distinction has been particularly notable in analyses of partisan change from election to election. If a liberal party wins an unusually strong popular vote, we are frequently informed that the public mandate is for a shift toward the left in governmental policy; if the party of the right gains new support, the public has become "cautious" or conservative about further political change. When the parties are loose coalitions of conservative and liberal wings, the meaning of the election outcome may be pursued at the level of legislative seats. Which wing within each of the parties showed the higher mortality rate in the balloting?

Any election may elicit diverse explanations, for change can hinge upon several crucial terms in the equation. If the Democratic Party is buried under a landslide of Republican votes, it may be argued that the electorate has become more conservative, that the Democratic Party has pushed too far to the left, that the Republican Party has moved in to capture votes of the "center," or any combination of the three.

Despite their differences, all these accounts depend on similar assumptions concerning the frames of reference used by the electorate to assess political events. Such accounts presume that some significant portion of the electorate (1) is sensitive to its own policy mood in terms of a left-right continuum; and (2) is sensitive as well to the shifting policy positions of both parties on the same continuum. The notion of the continuum is as crucial as the content here. The assumption is not

simply that people consider one party to be "left" and the other "right" in a dichotomous sense. Instead, there is presumed to be some discriminated as greater or lesser at differing points in time. Often it is presumed as well that people also have a sense of the distance of either party from a neutral point, a "middle of the road."

In view of the data we have presented these assumptions strain our credulity; yet, we cannot reject them out of hand. We have found some evidence to suggest that for a fraction of the American population these assumptions my be realistic. And the changes in the partisan vote division that attract these ideological descriptions rarely exceed a magnitude of 10 per cent of the active electorate. Thus it is conceivable that a balance of power may be held by a small minority of ideologues who are sensitive to shifts of the parties along a left-right continuum. Whether this view is valid is critical to an understanding of the issue meaning of partisan change.

If the liberal-conservative notion is not common, as we have maintained, the question remains as to what frames of reference for ordering issue concerns *do* enjoy more widespread use. Certainly the process of political evaluation is carried on by most citizens, and this process leads to more or less predictable organization of behavior. If ideology in a sophisticated sense is not widespread in the population, there must be surrogates for ideology that bring large aggregates to act *as though* propelled by ideological concerns. It is important to understand the character of these surrogates not only to satisfy intellectual curiosity, but also because the fact that they are surrogates rather than full-blown ideology may from time to

SOURCE. Reprinted from *The American Voter* by permission of the publisher, John Wiley & Sons, Inc. Copyright 1960, 1964 by John Wiley & Sons, Inc.

time lead to crucial differences in behavior.

THE FORMATION OF POLITICAL CONCEPTS AT A MASS LEVEL

Smith, Bruner, and White, in their volume *Opinions and Personality*, report an intensive analysis of the political attitudes of ten relatively well-informed and intelligent subjects. Nine of the ten, on the basis of their performance in a standardized test, ranked within the top 10 per cent of the national population in intellectual capacity. Of the tenth, the authors write:

> Many of the verbal coins used in the exchange of opinions were unfamiliar to him, so that we had to learn his views without relying on such standard pieces as "Socialism," "Liberalism," "veto" and "isolationism." . . . At a concrete level he functioned effectively, showing good common sense and practical judgment. It was in the realm of abstraction that his limitations were most marked. . . . He never read books, rarely listened to the radio, and did little more than scan newspapers and magazines as came his way. Both his information and his opinions were arrived at almost wholly through channels of conversation.[1]

Now "Sam Hodder," as this anonymous subject is called, was not a person of meager intelligence. He was *well above the average* in a basic intellectual capacity, standing in the top 20 per cent of a cross-section population. But limited to a grade school education and subsequent life as a factory employee, events had not conspired to foster those habits of abstract concept formation taken for granted in intellectual strata of the society. Despite substantial innate capacity, then, even Sam Hodder did not in practice measure up to the expectations of political concept formation that often seem assumed for the bulk of the electorate.

We would imagine that if we asked

[1] M. Brewster Smith, Jerome S. Bruner, and Robert W. White, *Opinions and Personality* (New York: John Wiley and Sons, 1956), p. 196.

Sam Hodder what he liked and disliked about the major parties, his predominant opinion would be that he liked the Democratic Party because "it is the party of the working man." If his political world was largely undifferentiated, he might have few perceptions beyond this. If there were further differentiation, he would perhaps indicate that the Republican Party had shown him it was actively against labor or the worker, or actively for big business, management, or one of the "natural" antagonists of the working man. He might be able, also, to document his impressions by reference to specific events or policy debates: the role of the parties in the Depression, or the championing of legislation such as Taft-Hartley or social security. His view of partisan politics might be more or less differentiated, but his evaluations would revolve around the perception that one of the parties took special pains to look after the day-to-day interests of a significant grouping in the population with which he identified.

This is not ideology in a programmatic sense. There is little comprehension here of the basic problems that lead to the need for political protection; nor is there any interest in "long-range plans" that would aim at resolution of these problems. In fact, there is little that requires abstract thinking at all. He is concerned with politics to the degree that he feels that political change might rob him and others like him of their jobs or of concrete benefits involving wages, working conditions, and the like. He has no conception of the modes whereby political power secures or protects interests—these are the concerns of group leadership, whether that leadership be of union or of party. Having perceived some correlation between group success and the emergence of concrete benefits, he is willing to put his faith in any leadership that has shown enough interest in his group to figure out what must be done to maintain its welfare. His partakes of ideology by endorsing a leadership that has ideology. He engages, so to speak, in an "ideology by proxy."

The difference between ideology and

"ideology by proxy" is more than academic, for at points of political change the concepts employed by Sam Hodder in his evaluations make for critical differences in attitude and behavior. If the fact of change in goals should actually be brought to Sam's attention, he would lack any independent reference points from which to evaluate the matter. Leadership programs have helped him in the past. If leadership ideas have changed, it is probably for good reason; the people at the top are in a better position to know what must be done than he is. He will always be able to judge what are, for him, the "results." Hence under certain circumstances the total flavor of political events may come to depend on the level at which the many "followers" like Sam Hodder have been in the habit of conceptualizing their relevant experience.

Favorable or unfavorable reactions to the political parties or candidates often consist of beliefs that they are agents that will aid or ignore this or that grouping in the population. In some of our protocols these perceptions are connected tightly with other comments more clearly ideological in character. But often it is apparent under probing by the interviewer that the respondent does not fit those notions of group benefit into any broader or more abstract frame of reference.

However simple these conceptions of politics may appear, there are many people in the American electorate whose modes of conceptualizing the political world and its social or economic consequences are a good deal less complex still and who appear even more remote from the type of thinking presumed by "ideology." Some of these people are staunch adherents of one of the political parties, although they freely admit it is simply a matter of family tradition and they personally have no idea what the parties "stand for." Others ignore the parties despite direct questioning, and focus their political evaluations upon the personal characteristics of the current candidates themselves—their sincerity, their religious beliefs, their family life,

their "popularity." And there are those who lack the interest or background to differentiate successfully between either the candidates or the parties.

It seems important to estimate the incidence of these various modes of conceptualizing issue controversy in a cross section of the adult population. Unfortunately, there are no simple yardsticks to measure the sophistication of a person's conceptualization. We cannot quantify the character of a person's political conceptions, even in the loose manner with which we measure the intensity of attitudes. We are interested in the presence or absence of certain abstractions that have to do with ideology; but we are also interested in the degree to which the individual's political world is differentiated and, most important, in the nature of the degree of "connectedness" between the elements that are successfully discriminated. In short, we are interested in the structure of thought that the individual applies to politics; and this interest forces us to deal in typologies and qualitative differences.

Toward this end we attempted to assign our 1956 respondents to various "levels" of conceptualization on the basis of their discursive responses in evaluating the good and bad points of the two parties and the two candidates, as described in Chapter 3. Despite the inevitable crudities of the categories employed, these levels seemed to provide a clear ordering in terms of conceptual sophistication. The expected ordering turned out to receive striking confirmation in other characteristics of the occupants at successive levels. We shall focus most of our attention upon four major levels.

The first of these (to be denoted Level A) embraces all respondents whose evaluations of the candidates and the parties have any suggestion of the abstract conception one would associate with ideology. We did not wish to be bound to familiar content in assessing this level of issue conceptualization. However, it rapidly became apparent that virtually all high-order abstractions used were familiar from current political commentary. Persons placed here talked in terms of the liberal-conservative continuum, or one of the narrower domains of abstract content involved in current ideological controversy: trends in the relationship between federal power and local autonomy, the fate of individual incentive under government "dole", and the like.

The second grouping (Level B) was reserved for persons whose issue comment revolved around fairly concrete and short-term group interest, or what we have already described in some detail as "ideology by proxy." In the next category (Level C) were persons engrossed in simplistic associations between the "goodness" and "badness" of the times and the identity of the party in power, or who appeared to have exhausted their view of the situation with mention of some rather isolated and specific issue. The final level (Level D) thereby contains individuals who evaluated the political objects without recourse to issues that might fairly be related to debates over domestic public policy. Excluded as true issue content, for example, were observations concerning mudslinging, charges of graft, comments on the personal attributes of the candidates, or references to their age, health, or past experience.

We were eager to avoid a number of potential pitfalls in a classification procedure of this order. We did not wish the assignment to be influenced by the partisan implication of the concepts employed. To the degree that the two parties tend to stress different ideological vocabularies, we desired to give each party vocabulary equal recognition. Similarly, the respondent who dislikes a party because it caters to the interests of special groups is employing concepts at the same level as the person who expresses gratitude for this interest, and should therefore receive the same classification. In short, we were not interested in the partisan product of the evaluation process, but rather in the character of the concepts that were playing a role in that process.

Secondly, we did not wish to confuse enthusiasm for quality of conception. A person who felt very strongly about a particular evaluation was not to be rated more highly than a person who used the same concepts for an offhand evaluation. To be sure, we would expect the individual who is intensely interested in politics to have arrived at different organizing concepts than the person who pays little attention to political events. But we need not think that a sense of pleasure or displeasure about a candidate or party that is fuzzy in focus and vague in source is intrinsically weak in its motivational significance for the individual. Particularly if the person lacks the capacity to organize what might seem more "telling" evaluative structures, these vague premonitions can be emotionally consuming.

DIFFERENCES IN POLITICAL CONCEPT-FORMATION: ILLUSTRATIONS FROM A CROSS-SECTION SAMPLE

LEVEL A, IDEOLOGY AND NEAR-IDEOLOGY

We shall consider two categories of respondents distinguished within Level A. The first was reserved for persons whose comments imply the kinds of conception of politics assumed by ideological interpretations of political behavior and political change. We shall refer to these individuals as "ideologues."

Some people clearly perceived a fundamental liberal-conservative continuum on which various of the political objects might be located and along which these objects might shift relative positions over time. These ideologies are not, from a sophisticated point of view, exceptional observers. Their commentary is neither profound, stimulating, nor creative. But they have absorbed some of the ideological abstractions of our day, and are able to put them to use in their political evaluations. In brief, they are the persons who fulfill most clearly the assumptions about political perceptions discussed at the beginning of the chapter.

The first interview drawn from this

upper category within Level A is somewhat unusual in the degree of content
pertaining to state politics, but otherwise is quite representative of the responses that received this classification.
The respondent is a woman residing in
the suburbs of Chicago.

(I'D LIKE TO ASK YOU WHAT YOU THINK
ARE THE GOOD AND BAD POINTS ABOUT THE
TWO PARTIES. IS THERE ANYTHING IN PAR-
TICULAR THAT YOU LIKE ABOUT THE DEMO-
CRATIC PARTY?) No. (IS THERE ANYTHING
AT ALL YOU LIKE ABOUT THE DEMOCRATIC
PARTY?) No, nothing at all.

(IS THERE ANYTHING IN PARTICULAR THAT
YOU DON'T LIKE ABOUT THE DEMOCRATIC
PARTY?) From being raised in a notori-
ously Republican section—a small town
downstate—there were things I didn't like.
There was family influence that way.
(WHAT IN PARTICULAR WAS THERE YOU
DIDN'T LIKE ABOUT THE DEMOCRATIC
PARTY?) Well, the Democratic Party
tends to favor socialized medicine—and
I'm being influenced in that because I
came from a doctor's family.

(IS THERE ANYTHING IN PARTICULAR THAT
YOU LIKE ABOUT THE REPUBLICAN PARTY?)
Well, I think they're middle-of-the-road—
more conservative. (HOW DO YOU MEAN,
"CONSERVATIVE"?) They are not so subject to radical change. (IS THERE ANY-
THING ELSE IN PARTICULAR THAT YOU LIKE
ABOUT THE REPUBLICAN PARTY?) Oh, I
like their foreign policy—and the segregation business, that's a middle-of-the-
road policy. You can't push it too fast.
You can instigate things, but you have to
let them take their course slowly. (IS
THERE ANYTHING ELSE?) I don't like Mr.
Hodge. (IS THERE ANYTHING ELSE?) The
labor unions telling workers how to vote
—they know which side their bread is
buttered on so they have to vote the way
they are told to!

(IS THERE ANYTHING IN PARTICULAR THAT
YOU DON'T LIKE ABOUT THE REPUBLICAN
PARTY?) Mr. Hodge! (IS THERE ANY-
THING ELSE?) I can't think of anything.[2]

This respondent operates with a fairly
clear sense of the liberal-conservative distinction and uses it to locate both the
major parties and the more specific policy
positions espoused. The second interview
drawn to represent this category is somewhat weaker. The following remarks,
transcribed from a woman in a small
Ohio city, serve to illustrate the marginal
inclusions in this category:

(LIKE ABOUT DEMOCRATS?)[3] Well, that
depends on what you are thinking of—
historically or here lately. I think they
are supposed to be more interested in the
small businessman and low tariffs. (IS
THERE ANYTHING IN PARTICULAR THAT YOU
LIKE ABOUT THE DEMOCRATIC PARTY?)
Nothing except it being a more liberal
party, and I think of the Republicans as
being more conservative and interested in
big business.

(DISLIKE ABOUT DEMOCRATS?) I think
extravagance, primarily. (IS THERE ANY-
THING ELSE?) Nothing that occurs to me
offhand.

(LIKE ABOUT REPUBLICANS?) Well, I
never thought so. I have been a Republican the last several years because of the
personalties involved, I guess.

(DISLIKE ABOUT REPUBLICANS?) This
again is traditional—just that they give
too much support to big business and
monopoly concerns. (ANY OTHER THINGS
YOU DON'T LIKE ABOUT THE REPUBLICAN
PARTY?) No.

In this case the concept of the liberal-
conservative continuum appears to be relatively peripheral. The respondent feels
that evaluations based on concepts of this
order favor the Democratic Party, but by
her own account the "personalities" have
in recent years loomed larger in her voting
decisions. However, these concepts *are*
present, and although not impressively
developed, are used in a manner that implies that the respondent is sensitive to
changes over time in the location of

---

[2] In order to preserve space, we shall omit
reproduction of responses to the questions
regarding the candidates, save where such
responses add integrally to our understanding of the manner in which the respondent
evaluates politics.

[3] The initial questions having to do with the
parties and candidates are the same throughout. Once having quoted them in full, we
shall abbreviate them in this fashion, although further probing that was introduced
under each "root" question will continue to
be reproduced in full.

political objects on the underlying continuum.

It is striking, then, that responses of only 2½ per cent of our cross-section sample warranted inclusion in this top category. Since people placed here are much more likely to take a fuller role in politics than are persons lower on the scale, they bulk some-what larger in the active electorate. But these ideologies still represent no more than 3½ per cent of our actual voters in 1956. In view of the fact that the partisan division of the national vote for federal office often shifts by as much as 5 or 10 per cent within the biennial or quadrennial period, it is clear that this group alone could account for only a minor portion of such short-term change, either by switching party or by staying at home.

There is, however, a more substantial group of respondents who have some claim to ideological perception. We have segregated them from the upper layer of ideologues because we are somewhat less confident that they fulfill the assumptions that we are examining. These people displaying "near-ideology" consist of three general types.

The first type is most similar to the full "ideologue." Frequently these people employ the liberal-conservative distinction, but their use of these concepts has little of the dynamic or highly relativistic quality found in the ideologue. "Liberalism" or "conservatism" is a status attribute of a party: there is less sense here of a continuum embracing many shadings of position, with objects shifting inward toward the center or outward toward extremes over time. Others give no explicit recognition to the liberal-conservative distinction, but employ organizing concepts of a sufficiently high order of abstraction to cut some swath through areas of ideological controversy. An interview drawn to exemplify this type of "near-ideology" comes from a man in southern Ohio:

(LIKE ABOUT DEMOCRATS?) Yes, I like their platform. (WHAT IS THAT?) They're more inclined to help the working class of people, that is the majority in our country. And I like the idea of stopping the hydrogen bomb tests. It would make for more friendly feelings toward other countries, and they would be more friendly to us. I think the Democratic Party wants peace as much as the Republican Party.

(DISLIKE ABOUT DEMOCRATS?) Yeah, there's a lot of things. One thing is they're too much for federal control of utilities. (IS THERE ANYTHING ELSE YOU DON'T LIKE ABOUT THE DEMOCRATIC PARTY?) Well it seems they don't always run the best men there are for their offices. (FOR EXAMPLE?) There's several I could mention that don't have the best reputation in the world.

(LIKE ABOUT REPUBLICANS?) Well, they play up to individual rights, which is good. That's good—it makes a person feel independent.

(DISLIKE ABOUT REPUBLICANS?) They believe in big industry, utilities, etc. (ANYTHING ELSE YOU DON'T LIKE?) They've passed a lot of labor bills I don't approve of.

This respondent does not introduce the liberal-conservative distinction explicitly. This opening comment about Democratic interest in the working class is of the group-interest type that will form the broad criterion for Level B. But he also includes commentary about the problem of federal control over utilities and the value of individual rights. Both of these observations involve abstractions common to the ideological disputes of our era. The respondent's own position concerning the role of government toward utilities is left rather unclear: he resents tendencies of the Democrats toward federal control yet appears to dislike the Republican position as well. Here as elsewhere, however, we restrict our attention to the nature of the concepts employed rather than become involved in judgments of the coherence of ideological positions. Another 2 per cent of our sample was considered to be of this type. These people constituted about 2½ per cent of our 1956 voters. Up to this point, then, we have accounted for about 4½ per cent of the total sample, and for slightly less than 6 per cent of our voters.

A second type of interview considered "near-ideology" included persons who used one or another of the labels common to ideological discussion, but in a context rather bare of supporting perceptions, so that we must take it on faith that the term had the normal connotations for the user. Generally the flavor of the context is not one to cast great doubt on the appropriateness of the meaning, but the lack of supporting material usually indicates that other simpler concepts are equally or more prominent in the individual's thinking about politics. The respondent drawn to exemplify the second type is a man from Texas:

(LIKE ABOUT DEMOCRATS?) (After a long delay.) I think the Democrats are more concerned with all the people. (How DO YOU MEAN?) They put out more liberal legislation for all the people.

(DISLIKE ABOUT DEMOCRATS?) They have a sordid history over the past 20 years, though no worse than the Republican Administrations. (How DO YOU MEAN?) Oh, things like deep freezes and corruption in government.

(LIKE ABOUT REPUBLICANS?) NO!

(DISLIKE ABOUT REPUBLICANS?) Oh, they're more for a moneyed group.

Here the bulk of the content follows the lines of group benefit concepts that are generally classified at a lower level. Nevertheless, the term "liberal" is employed in a context of some reasonable meaning, and it is possible that fuller probing would have developed a more explicit indication of more abstract ideological conceptions. The second type of near-ideology adds another 3½ per cent of the sample to Level A, and another 5 per cent of our total of 1956 voters. Thus it is the largest group so far considered, although we have accounted for about 8 per cent of the sample up to this point.

The final type of interview classified as near-ideology within Level A was in one sense the inverse of the preceding type. Whereas respondents of the preceding type had absorbed labels but had difficulty bringing appropriate specific information to them, individuals here were laden with information but showed no tendency to distill such detail to a higher level of abstraction. We find among these people, as well as those of the preceding type, an increasing tendency to depend upon party and group concepts as organizing focuses for issue content, rather than ideological positions. Thus responses of these types are already merging with the concept usages in individuals in Level B.

The interview drawn to represent this final type of near-ideology was contributed by a man in southern California:

(LIKE ABOUT DEMOCRATS?) The Democratic Party is more for higher social security. They're more for old age pensions and better working conditions for the working man. They want a higher standard of living for all people, not just a few. The promises that are made by the Democrats are kept if at all possible. The facts are told to the American people.

(DISLIKE ABOUT DEMOCRATS?) It seems to me they could handle their campaign better. (How DO YOU MEAN?) Well, for instance, they could do a little better job of selling to the public. They should try and quiet Truman down so he will not pull a boner as in the Democratic convention. (DO YOU HAVE ANY OTHER DISLIKES FOR THE DEMOCRATIC PARTY?) No.

(LIKE ABOUT REPUBLICANS?) Not one thing! (IN GENERAL, IS THERE ANYTHING THAT YOU LIKE ABOUT THE REPUBLICAN PARTY?) No!

(DISLIKE ABOUT REPUBLICANS?) I dislike everything about the Republican Party. (COULD YOU EXPLAIN WHAT YOU MEAN?) I was growing up at the time of the Hoover Administration. What a time I had, too. There was barely enough to eat. I don't think the Republicans wanted that, but they did nothing to stop it. Not until Roosevelt came along and made things start to happen. Now the Republican Party still stands for big business, at the expense of the farmer and the working man. Promises made are not kept—ask the poor farmer, if no one else.

Over the course of these remarks there are points at which summary constructs familiar in ideological discussion would be highly appropriate. However, the recital of specific measures supported by the Democrats is not generalized to such a level of abstraction. Instead, the "standard of living" is used to sum up the direction of party policy, and this matter is treated as a benefit linked to a group, albeit a large group, within the population. Similarly, a perception of Republican passivity in the face of the Depression is vividly contrasted in the subject's mind with initiatives taken by Roosevelt. Yet this is not seen as a special case of a general posture toward change. Rather, it is left as a concrete vignette, developed once again into a proposition about group interest.

We did not feel that any of the types of response discussed here as "near-ideology" provided satisfactory support for assumptions concerning ideological perceptions. We include them as part of Level A, however, for it is possible that some among them would, in other settings, so amplify their observations as to merit "ideologue" classification.

If the reader has been struck by this generosity of assignment, he should hold this fact in mind as we measure our progress across the electorate. For despite our attempts at generous estimates, we find that with all of the ideologues and near-ideologues of Level A cumulated we have only covered about 12 per cent of all subjects interviewed, and 15 per cent of our 1956 voters. In other words, about 85 per cent of the 1956 electorate brought simpler conceptual tools to bear on their issue concerns.

LEVEL B. GROUP BENEFITS

In the last interviews to be cited from Level A, we noted an increasing tendency to evaluate the political objects in terms of their response to interests of visible groupings in the population. Such perceptions are the dominant themes characterizing Level B, and constitute what we have described earlier as "ideology by proxy."

Such relationships between political object and group can be appreciated at a simple and concrete level. A party or candidate is sympathetic with or hostile to the group. There is little comprehension of "long-range plans for social betterment," or of basic philosophies rooted in postures toward change or abstract conceptions of social and economic structure or causation. The party or candidate is simply endorsed as being "for" or "against" a group with which the subject is identified or as being above the selfish demands of groups within the population. Exactly *how* the candidate or party might see fit to implement or avoid group interests is a moot point, left unrelated to broader ideological concerns. But the party or candidate is "located" in some affective relationship toward a group or groups, and the individual metes out trust on this basis.

As was the case with Level A, several types might be distinguished within Level B. Some respondents tended to perceive politics in terms of a competition of these group interests, with the political parties arraying themselves in favor of one group and in opposition to another. However, many respondents did not develop the discussion of group benefit beyond the context of a single group, nor did they express a feeling that the party or candidate not seen as favorable was actively pursuing a threatening policy, either by ignoring or seeking to harm the group, or by supporting another group seen as a natural antagonist. In terms of numbers, Level B was fairly evenly split between these two types.

In addition to this content distinction, there was a considerable range in the quality of response within both types. For example, some of the people who paired the parties with opposing interest groups could bring little further content to the matter under probing. For analytic purposes, these rather shallow versions of the group benefit themes were separated from the normal run of responses of this sort.

People having relatively substantial perceptions of a competition of group interests make up the first category of any size that we have encountered. Fourteen per cent of our sample received this classification. Although the perception of group interest provides a tangible criterion for inclusion at this level, the reader is urged to compare the illustrative interviews drawn randomly from this group with those of the higher level in terms of the more general grasp of politics that is represented. These illustrative responses come from an Ohio farm woman:

(LIKE ABOUT DEMOCRATS?) I think they have always helped the farmers. To tell you the truth, I don't see how any farmer could vote for Mr. Eisenhower. (IS THERE ANYTHING ELSE YOU LIKE ABOUT THE DEMOCRATIC PARTY?) We have always had good times under their Administration. They are more for the working class of people. Any farmer would be a fool to vote for Eisenhower.

(DISLIKE ABOUT DEMOCRATS?) No, I can't say there is.

(LIKE ABOUT REPUBLICANS?) No.

(DISLIKE ABOUT REPUBLICANS?) About everything. (WHAT ARE YOU THINKING OF?) They promise so much but they don't do anything. (ANYTHING ELSE?) I think the Republicans favor the richer folks. I never did think much of the Republicans for putting into office a military man.

(NOW I'D LIKE TO ASK YOU ABOUT THE GOOD AND BAD POINTS OF THE TWO CANDIDATES FOR PRESIDENT. IS THERE ANYTHING IN PARTICULAR ABOUT STEVENSON THAT MIGHT MAKE YOU WANT TO VOTE FOR HIM?) I think he is a *very smart* man. (IS THERE ANYTHING ELSE?) I think he will do what he says, will help the farmer. We will have higher prices (ANYTHING ELSE?) No.

(IS THERE ANYTHING IN PARTICULAR ABOUT STEVENSON THAT MIGHT MAKE YOU WANT TO VOTE AGAINST HIM?) No. But I have this against Stevenson, but I wouldn't vote against him. In the Illinois National Guards he had Negroes and Whites together. They ate and slept together. I don't like that. I think Negroes should have their own place. I don't see why they would want to mix.

(IS THERE ANYTHING IN PARTICULAR ABOUT EISENHOWER THAT MIGHT MAKE YOU WANT TO VOTE FOR HIM?) No.

(IS THERE ANYTHING IN PARTICULAR ABOUT EISENHOWER THAT MIGHT MAKE YOU WANT TO VOTE AGAINST HIM?) Yes. He favors Wall Street. I don't think he is physically able, and he will step aside and that Richard Nixon will be President. (ANYTHING ELSE?) To tell the truth, I never thought he knew enough about politics to be a President. He is a military man. He takes too many vacations and I don't see how he can do the job.

One theme that appears here, the attention to specific "promises," deserves special comments. In the upper ranges, particularly among the full ideologues, references to promises made or broken are almost nonexistent. But as we depart from the upper level, references of this sort increase in frequency to the point at which they become almost the center of any attention paid to content with policy implication.[4] The political "promise," in the form retained by the respondent, has characteristics that contrast sharply with the sorts of concerns associated with ideology. Promises arise *de novo* with each campaign; they have minimal roots in either a party tradition or a long-range program. The tendency to focus upon these pledges as the issue core of politics seems to token narrow time perspectives, concrete modes of thought, and a tremendously oversimplified view of causality in social, economic, and political process.

With the interview involving perceptions of conflicting group interest added to those of Level A, we have now accounted for about one-quarter of our sample and slightly less than one-third of the voters. Another 17 per cent of the respondents talked of benefits accruing to a single group through the aid of a single party. The interview drawn to illustrate this type comes from a man in Texas:

(LIKE ABOUT DEMOCRATS?) Well, I don't know. I've just always before been a Democrat. My daddy before me always was. (CAN YOU NAME ANY GOOD THINGS

---

[4] This is not true within Level D, of course, for subjects were classified here only if there was no reference to the sort of issue material made concrete in the campaign promise.

THAT YOU LIKE ABOUT THE PARTY?) Well, no, I guess not.

(DISLIKE ABOUT DEMOCRATS?) I don't know of anything.

(LIKE ABOUT REPUBLICANS?) No.

(DISLIKE ABOUT REPUBLICANS?) Well, I just don't believe they are for the common people. (ANYTHING ELSE THAT YOU DON'T LIKE ABOUT THE REPUBLICAN PARTY?) No, I don't think so.

(LIKE ABOUT STEVENSON?) No, ma'am.

(DISLIKE ABOUT STEVENSON?) Well, I wouldn't know hardly how to put that. I just don't hardly think he's the man for President.

(LIKE ABOUT EISENHOWER?) Well, his past is all. (IS THERE ANYTHING ELSE THAT MIGHT MAKE YOU WANT TO VOTE FOR HIM?) No.

(DISLIKE ABOUT EISENHOWER?) Nothing but the right man in the Democratic Party.

These interviews, chosen randomly from among the more capable responses falling in Level B, serve to represent the conflict-of-interest and the single-group interest responses. As we have suggested, some interviews of rather low calibre with group-benefit mentions were separated to form a lower category within Level B. By and large, the quality of responses here is close to what we shall later encounter in Level C, despite the group references. These poorer interviews of Level B, making up another 11 per cent of the sample, include responses similar to that of a New York City woman:

(LIKE ABOUT DEMOCRATS?) Well, my father is a Democrat and I'm one by inheritance sort of. I know nothing about politics but I like the Democratic Party because I know they are more for the poorer people.

(DISLIKE ABOUT DEMOCRATS?) Nope.

(LIKE ABOUT REPUBLICANS?) No, there isn't.

(DISLIKE ABOUT REPUBLICANS?) Yes. They are out to help the rich people.

(LIKE ABOUT STEVENSON?) I heard him talk on TV, and he is a wonderful talker.

I believe what he says and I think he will make a good President. I think he is capable and honest and I like him.

(DISLIKE ABOUT STEVENSON?) No.

(LIKE ABOUT EISENHOWER?) He is a fine man. A good military man, through, not a good President.

(DISLIKE ABOUT EISENHOWER?) Yes, he was not a good President because he relied too much on his helpers. They led him. He didn't lead them.

As we complete our survey of the range of interviews included in Level B, it seems undeniable that we have moved to levels of conceptualization remote from those presumed by ideological interpretations of political behavior. Yet Levels A and B taken together account for little more than half of the total sample, and for only some 60 per cent of the 1956 respondents who voted.

LEVEL C, THE "GOODNESS" AND "BADNESS" OF THE TIMES

The third level coincides closely with the third quartile of our sample. In some ways interviews classified here are most effectively defined in negative terms. On the one hand, these responses do not include perceptions of group interest, and they lack as well any sense of a structure of concepts that might be conceived to border on ideology. On the other hand, these interviews escape classification in Level D by virtue of some reference, however nebulous or fragmentary, to a subject of controversy over public policy.

The issue content of this sort tends to be sparse within each interview and heterogeneous from interview to interview. Nonetheless, it is subject to some characterization. The most prevalent type of response provided the denotation for this level. Typically, there is a perception of the economic state of the immediate family, which is an index of the "goodness" or "badness" of the times. The possibility that what happens to some may not happen to others in the same way seems too differentiated a view of society or politics to have much role in the evaluation process. And, of course, once the nature of the times is assessed, the leap to party culpability is simple and direct.

A second prominent type of response assigned to Level C involved the concrete detail that had issue relevance but appeared to stand as an isolated structure, an island of cognition in a sea of darkness. A prototype is the elederly woman economically dependent on her social security checks, who associates this aid appreciatively with the Democratic Party. Beyond this single policy item, however, she professes to know nothing whatever about politics, and is unable under probing to supply further content. Thus while Level C includes vague generalities about the times, it includes as well these isolated and specific issue perceptions.

Several characteristics not used as criteria for assignment had great incidence in these Level C interviews. There is a vastly increased tendency for the respondent to plead great ignorance of anything political. Now and again there is some apparent element of modesty underlying this confession; in the great majority of the cases, however, it is easy to see what the individual means. Furthermore, there seems to be an increasingly moral cast to evaluations at this level. Irritation and concern over matters of graft and campaign "mudslinging" are given frequent vent. Such observations are not absent from responses at higher levels; but in Levels C and D they come to form the main thrust of the individual's perceptions with monotonous regularity. An impressive proportion of individuals at these lower levels roundly condemns both parties for "running each other down so." These people seem genuinely depressed by any cross-party criticism of policy and platform. When a person has just watched or listened to some of the campaign speeches, these reactions often remain much more salient than the content of the criticism itself.

Let us present some sample interviews from Level C. While we limit ourselves to two illustrations, these illustrations stand for about one-quarter of our interviews. Hence responses of this sort out-

number all those of Level A by more than 2 to 1, and they outnumber responses of the top ideological category by a ratio approaching 10 to 1. The first interview comes from a woman in New York City:

(LIKE ABOUT DEMOCRATS?) What was in all the papers last week? Stevenson will see to it that they stop testing the bomb and I'm in favor of that. I don't want them to explode any more of those bombs. (IS THERE ANYTHING THAT YOU LIKE ABOUT THE DEMOCRATIC PARTY?) I don't know anything about the party, really. I just want them to stop testing the bomb.

(DISLIKE ABOUT DEMOCRATS?) I don't know much about the parties. (IS THERE ANYTHING YOU DON'T LIKE ABOUT THE DEMOCRATIC PARTY?) No—I don't know much about the whole thing.

(LIKE ABOUT REPUBLICANS?) My husband's job is better. (Laughed) (HOW DO YOU MEAN?) Well, his investments in stocks are up. They go up when the Republicans are in. My husband is a furrier and when people get money they buy furs.

(DISLIKE ABOUT REPUBLICANS?) No. (IS THERE ANYTHING AT ALL YOU DON'T LIKE ABOUT THE REPUBLICAN PARTY?) No—I don't know that much about the parties.

(LIKE ABOUT STEVENSON?) As I mentioned before, he's saying stop testing the bomb because it can cause so much damage. My hsuband says that's such a minor point, but I don't think so.

(DISLIKE ABOUT STEVENSON?) Nothing, nothing at all.

(LIKE ABOUT EISENHOWER?) No, nothing in particular. (IS THERE ANYTHING AT ALL?) No.

(DISLIKE ABOUT EISENHOWER?) That he might die and Nixon would be President, and I don't care for Nixon. He might not have his four-year term. There's a lot said about the other sickness that he had—not the heart attack.

The second interview comes from a woman in Louisville:

(LIKE ABOUT DEMOCRATS?) Well, I really don't know enough about politics to speak. I never did have no dealings with it. I thought politics was more for men anyway. (WELL, IS THERE ANYTHING YOU

LIKE ABOUT THE DEMOCRATIC PARTY?) I like the good wages my husband makes. (IT IS THE REPUBLICANS WHO ARE IN NOW.) I know, and it's sort of begun to tighten up since the Republicans got in. (IS THERE ANYTHING ELSE YOU LIKE ABOUT THE DEMOCRATIC PARTY?) No.

(DISLIKE ABOUT DEMOCRATS?) No, I couldn't think of a thing.

(LIKE ABOUT REPUBLICANS?) Well, truthfully, the Republican Party just doesn't interest me at all. (THERE ISN'T ANYTHING YOU LIKE ABOUT IT?) No—I just am not particularly interested in either one.

(DISLIKE ABOUT REPUBLICANS?) I just don't know. It's immaterial to me about the Republican Party. I never thought enough about them to get interested in them.

(LIKE ABOUT STEVENSON?) Well, I'll tell you, I haven't read enough about either one of the candidates to know anything about them at all. (IS THERE ANYTHING ABOUT STEVENSON THAT MIGHT MAKE YOU WANT TO VOTE FOR HIM?) None other than that he's a Democrat.

(DISLIKE ABOUT STEVENSON?) No.

(LIKE ABOUT EISENHOWER?) No.

(DISLIKE ABOUT EISENHOWER?) Well, just that he's a Republican.

LEVEL D, ABSENCE OF ISSUE CONTENT

The remaining quarter of the sample failed to comment upon any issues of political debate in their responses to the unstructured questions. While vote turnout is relatively low within this group, these people still account for 17 per cent of our voters in 1956, and hence by themselves outnumber our ideologues in the active electorate by a 5-1 ration.

To the degree that occupants of Level D have perceptions of the parties at all, they are bound up in moralistic themes like mudslinging and chicanery. More often the parties are poorly discriminated, and comment is devoted almost entirely to the personal characteristics of the candidates—their popularity, their sincerity, their religious practice, or home life.

Initially our interest in the upper ranges

of response was such that we planned no differentiation of types within Level D. It became apparent in the classification process that three broad types were emerging clearly. The first group consisted of party-oriented people. These were persons whose only conscious connection to the political process seemed to lie in a potent sense of membership within a party. They tended by and large to pay little attention to the candidates, and their presence in Level D indicates that they were unable to suggest how their party differed in its stands from the opposing party. The second type stood in sharp contrast in its preoccupations. These people had little information about or patience with the parties. The prevailing theme was "parties don't make any difference. It's the man who counts." Once again, the fact of location in Level D signifies that there were no issue implications in the subsequent perceptions of the candidates. These perceptions had to do almost exclusively with comparisons of looks, sincerity, popularity, religious practice, and family life.

The third type comprises the individuals who were unable to say anything about politics at all, save to explain why they found it difficult to pay any attention to it. This set of respondents was not, however, completely inactive politically, as about one quarter of them, for one reason or another, managed to vote in 1956.

Since Level D comprised one quarter of the sample it was feasible to return to the interviews and subdivide respondents into these types. The distribution that emerged within Level D was as follows:

	Proportion of Level D
Simple party orinetation	1/5
Simple candidate orientation	2/5
No political perceptions	1/5
Unclassified (mixed types)	1/5

Let us turn to samples of these major types. A woman from California was drawn from the party-oriented individuals in Level D.

(LIKE ABOUT DEMOCRATS?) I'm a Democrat. (IS THERE ANYTHING YOU LIKE ABOUT THE DEMOCRATIC PARTY?) I don't know.

(DISLIKE ABOUT DEMOCRATS?) I'm a Democrat, that's all I know. My husband's dead now—he was a Democrat. (IS THERE ANYTHING YOU DON'T LIKE ABOUT THE PARTY?) I don't know.

(LIKE ABOUT REPUBLICANS?) I don't know.

(DISLIKE ABOUT REPUBLICANS?) I don't know.

(LIKE ABOUT STEVENSON?) Stevenson is a good Democrat. (IS THERE ANYTHING ELSE ABOUT HIM THAT MIGHT MAKE YOU WANT TO VOTE FOR HIM?) No, nothing.

(DISLIKE ABOUT STEVENSON?) I don't know. (IS THERE ANYTHING ABOUT HIM THAT MIGHT MAKE YOU WANT TO VOTE AGAINST HIM?) No.

(LIKE ABOUT EISENHOWER?) I don't know. (IS THERE ANYTHING ABOUT EISENHOWER THAT MIGHT MAKE YOU WANT TO VOTE FOR HIM?) I don't know.

(DISLIKE ABOUT EISENHOWER?) I don't know. (IS THERE ANYTHING ABOUT HIM THAT MIGHT MAKE YOU WANT TO VOTE AGAINST HIM?) No.

An illustration of the candidate type within Level D comes from a Massachusetts man.

(LIKE ABOUT DEMOCRATS?) I haven't heard too much. I don't get any great likes or dislikes.

(DISLIKE ABOUT DEMOCRATS?) I hate the darned backbiting.

(LIKE ABOUT REPUBLICANS?) No.

(DISLIKE ABOUT REPUBLICANS?) No.

(LIKE ABOUT STEVENSON?) No, I don't like him at all.

(DISLIKE ABOUT STEVENSON?) I have no use for Stevenson whatsoever. I had enough of him at the last election. I don't like the cut-throat business—condemn another man and then shake hands with him five minutes later.

(LIKE ABOUT EISENHOWER?) As a man I like Eisenhower better. Not particularly for the job of President, but he is not so apt to cut your throat.

(DISLIKE ABOUT EISENHOWER?) No.

The interviews that had virtually nothing to say may be rapidly disposed of. The illustration drawn came from a woman in Missouri:

(LIKE ABOUT DEMOCRATS?) No—I don't know as there is.

(DISLIKE ABOUT DEMOCRATS?) No.

(LIKE ABOUT REPUBLICANS?) No, it's the same way I am about the other party.

(DISLIKE ABOUT REPUBLICANS?) No. Parties are all about the same to me.

(LIKE ABOUT STEVENSON?) No, I don't think so.

(DISLIKE ABOUT STEVENSON?) No.

(LIKE ABOUT EISENHOWER?) I really don't care which man is best or otherwise. I don't know about either one of the men enough to give an opinion.

(DISLIKE ABOUT EISENHOWER?) No.

We have now accounted for our total sample. This profile of an electorate is not calculated to increase our confidence in interpretations of elections that presume widespread ideological concerns in the adult population. To be sure, we have been able to assess only those aspects of political conceptualization that are revealed in conscious verbal materials. It might be argued for example that in tranquil times when no need for innovative leadership is felt, the poorly educated might find such leadership disturbing without being able to say exactly why. Such ineffable sentiment might, for the inarticulate, come to focus on reactions to personal attributes of the candidate. This is a possibility, yet one which we are not inclined to credit highly. If there were strong links between elements of the "deeper self" and reactions to ideological position that do bypass conscious concept formation and evaluation, we might have expected a stronger association between our measurement of conservatism and partisan decisions. Many of the people who reacted with dismay to the possibility of change suggested by the scale items undoubtedly failed to think of themselves, at a conscious level, as "conservative," if for no other reason than the fact the concept is not part of their cognitive tool chest.

But the fact remains that both the structured approach and the analysis of free answers lead to precisely the same conclusions: The concepts important to ideological analysis are useful only for that small segment of the population that is equipped to approach decisions at a rarefied level (see Table 1).

TABLE 1. SUMMARY OF THE DISTRIBUTION OF THE TOTAL SAMPLE AND OF 1956 VOTERS IN LEVELS OF CONCEPTUALIZATION

	Proportion of Total Sample	Proportion of Voters
A. Ideology		
I. Ideology	2½%	3½%
II. Near-ideology	9	12
B. Group Benefits		
I. Perception of conflict	14	16
Single-group interest	17	18
II. Shallow group benefit responses	11	11
C. Nature of the times	24	22
D. No issue content		
I. Party orientation	4	3½
II. Candidate orientation	9	7
III. No content	5	3
IV. Unclassified	4½	4
	100%	100%

Voters and Elections: Past and Present*

ANGUS CAMPBELL

INTRODUCTION

To the mystification of most politicians and the agonized protest of many scholars, much research on the vote in recent years has devoted itself to a detailed examination of the behavior of the individual voter, in apparent disregard of the collective decisions of the electorate. Paul Lazarsfeld set the pace in 1940 when he

* Presented at the annual meeting of the Southern Historical Association, Asheville, North Carolina, November 7, 1963.

SOURCE. Reprinted from *The Journal of Politics,* Vol. 26, (1964) by permission of the publisher. Copyright 1964, The Southern Political Science Association.

undertook in his famous Erie County study to "follow the vagaries of the individual voter along the path to his vote."[1] For twenty years the major studies of the vote have followed in this general pattern, some of them placing the emphasis on sociological setting, others on perceptions, attitudes and other psychological variables, but mainly preoccupied, as Lazarsfeld was, with the motives, the conflicts and the decisions of the individual voter. Many interesting facts have come from these studies and much has been learned about voting but there has been recurrent criticism that in concentrating on the voter Lazarsfeld and his succesors have ignored "the vote," that they have not come to grips with the "important" problems in politics.[2]

It was perhaps inevitable that the entry of the behavorial scientist into the study of politics should have concentrated as it did on the individual member of the polity. This was the point closest to his own intellectual habits and most readily comprehended in terms of his previous research experience. It was a necessary point of departure from which progress toward a bridging of the conceptual gap between the voter and the vote could be made. It should now be recognized, however, that we are moving beyond this phase of our inquiries into the nature of voting. Within the last few years a number of attempts have been made to move "upward" from the study of micro-political units to an understanding of the flow of the total vote, to apply the insights gained from the study of the individual voter to the explantation of the behavior of the electorate. The results of these studies represent the beginning of a new phase in political analysis.

[1] Paul F. Lazarsfeld et al. *The People's Choice* (New York: Duell, Sloan and Pearce, 1944), v-178.
[2] For example, Avery Leiserson, although not unfriendly to the "behavioral approach," observed in 1958 that "the weakness of the behavioralists lies in an overemphasis upon methods of data collection and quantitative analysis of miniscular problems of questionable relevance to the sweeping institutional complexes of politics." See his *Parties and Politics* (New York: Knopf, 1958), p. 371.

ARGUMENT

Our intention in this paper is to present several attempts to apply information drawn from contemporary studies of voting to the illumination of certain regularities in the collective vote as recorded in the election statistics of the past hundred years. It will not be possible to describe in any detail the actual studies which underlie the analysis to be presented. As a minimum it may be said that since 1948 the Survey Research Center of The University of Michigan has conducted a series of detailed surveys of the perceptions and motives of the national electorate. These have been sample surveys but they do not bear a very close resemblance either in methods or intent to the newspaper polls. We are not primarily interested in predicting the vote, as the polls typically are. On the contrary, we have been trying to come to an understanding of the individual voting decision and, as we extend the number of elections studies, to an understanding of American elections as collective acts.[3]

Our program of study of the American voter has led us to a considerable number of descriptive facts about the present-day electorate. Many of these may seem quite commonplace; others depart rather dramatically from popular beliefs about American politics. The following short list of general statements drawn from our research findings will lead us to our subsequent discussion of the characteristics of elections.

1. Two underlying political attributes characterize the members of the electorate. One is their level of intrinsic interest in politics. People differ greatly in this trait, from the activist who is ready to respond to everything political to the disengaged person who lives in a wholly nonpolitical world. This intrinsic interest level, whether high or low, is relatively stable over time for each individual and

[3] See Angus Campbell, Philip E. Converse, Warren E. Miller and Donald E. Stokes, *The American Voter* (New York: John Wiley and Sons, 1960), v-573.

is one of the standing predispositions which underlie individual response to on-going political events.

2. The second basic political attribute is party identification. Most members of the electorate feel some degree of psychological attachment to one of the major parties. This partisan identification is remarkably resistant to passing political events and typically remains constant through the life of the individual. It exercises an important influence on perceptions, attitudes, and behavior.

3. These two political predispositions, intrinsic interest and party identification, are related. Generally speaking, the people most concerned and most responsive to political stimuli are also the most strongly party identified. Most people who call themselves independent or nonpartisan are relatively disinterested in politics.

4. These basic predispositions determine the standing position from which the individual moves as he responds to contemporary political conditions. National and international events, the personal characteristics of the major candidates, the current image of the major parties, and issues of national policy create short-term political forces. These short-term forces assume importance for the individual citizen as they occur and are perceived by him. His behavior at any particular point in time derives from the interaction of his political predispositions and the short-term forces generated by the current political situation.

5. Extent of information concerning political affairs varies greatly within the electorate. Most people are poorly informed on questions of national policy and show little evidence of organized ideology regarding governmental action.[4] They do not associate the two parties with

[4] The term "ideology" is used here in the sense it is commonly employed by political scientists and social theorists. Downs, for example, defines ideology as "a verbal image of the good society and of the chief means of constructing such society." See Anthony Downs. *An Economic Theory of Democracy* (New York: Harper and Bros., 1957), p. 96.

clear alternatives on national issues. Level of information is associated with both interest in politics and strength of party identification. Highly informed people tend to be interested in politics and identified with a party.

Now, transposing these characteristics of voters to the characteristics of the collective vote, we come to the following propositions regarding the elections themselves:

1. The size of the turnout in national elections depends on a combination of intrinsic political interest and the impact of short-term political forces. People with a high level of intrinsic interest vote in most or all national elections; people with little intrinsic interest vote only when additionally stimulated by impelling short-term forces. The weaker the total impact of the short-term forces, the smaller will be the total turnout.

2. The smaller the turnout in a national election, the greater the proportion of the vote which is contributed by people of established party loyalties and the more closely the partisan division of the vote will approach the basic underlying division of standing commitments to the two parties, what Lord Bryce referred to years ago as the "normal voting strength."

3. The larger the turnout, the greater the proportion of the vote which is made up of marginal voters, people who have relatively weak party identification, relatively little intrinsic political interest, and relatively little political information.

4. If the sum of the short-term forces is approximately balanced in its partisan impact, the total vote will not vary from the vote division to be expected from the underlying "normal party strength." If the sum of the short-term forces favors one candidate-party alternative over the other it will swing the vote division toward that alternative, with the greatest movement occurring among the marginal voters. The greater the total impact of the short-term forces, the greater will be the potential deflection from the "normal party strength."

If these assumptions regarding the nature of our national elections have validity they should obviously fit the facts of American electoral history. Of course we do not have interview survey data to draw on for more than the last few years but we do have reasonably accurate aggregative turnout and partisanship data for the presidential and congressional elections for at least the last one hundred years. These voting statistics have been the subject of much scholarly analysis and numerous regularities in the movement of the vote over the time have been pointed out. Let us now consider a selection of these recurring relationships or cycles in terms of the general understanding of the nature of the vote which we have briefly outlined.

1. When we look at the two-party division of the national vote over the past seventy years we find that the fluctuations in the two-party division of the vote in the presidential years are much greater than those in the off years. Donald Stokes and Warren Miller have recently pointed out that the variation in the proportion voting Republican in the presidential elections between 1892 and 1960 is over twice as great as the variation in the proportions voting Republican in the off-year elections during this period and that the variation of the Republican vote for Congressmen in the presidential years is almost half again as great as that of the vote in the off years.[5] The greater stability of the off-year votes over this seventy-year period must reflect some underlying difference in these two kinds of elections.

The most immediately apparent difference in the presidential and off-year elections is the greater turnout in the presidential years. In terms of our earlier language this is brought about by the presence of short-term forces in the presidential elections which are stronger than those in the mid-term elections. The electorate is under stronger pressure in the presidential years than it is in the off

years. This pressure brings to the polls in the presidential elections a large number of marginal voters who do not bother to vote in the less impressive off-year elections. These people are less party-identified and therefore more mobile than the regular core voters who have enough intrinsic interest in political matters to participate in all national elections. As the fortunes of politics vary from year to year these marginal people shift their votes from one party to the other and contribute a substantial part of the large variability in the vote in the presidential years which we have noted. In the off-year elections these people do not turn out; the decision is left largely to the core regulars whose greater degree of party loyalty makes them less mobile.

It is true, of course, that deflections from the basic "normal" vote do occur in off-year elections; the party balance in Congress obviously does not remain constant. It is also true that local circumstances sometimes create dramatic swings in individual congressional districts and that a swing in one direction in one district may be offset by an opposite swing in another district. But we know that in recent elections the total amount of party-crossing has been less in the off-year elections than in the elections of the President. The people who vote in off-year elections are difficult to move and the short-term forces that might move them are relatively weak. Party loyalty plays a more dominant role than it does in most presidential elections and party loyalty changes very little from one year to the next.[6]

---

[5] Donald E. Stokes and Warren E. Miller, "Party Government and the Saliency of Congress," *Public Opinion Quarterly*, **26**, 1962, 531-546.

[6] It is noteworthy that in the decades immediately following the Civil War the variations in the partisanship of both the presidential and congressional votes were much smaller than they have been since. Donald Stokes has suggested that this was a period of rigid partisanship when "partisan attachments were more tightly fixed . . . than they have ever again been. Perhaps a full generation's time was needed for the tremendous passions of war and reconstruction to loosen their grip on a electorate whose memories gradually faded and whose older members gave way to the new." See Donald E. Stokes and Gudmund R. Iversen, "On the Existence of Forces Restoring Party Competition," *Public Opinion Quarterly*, **2**, 1962, 159-171.

2. It is well-known to every politician that since the Civil War the party which wins the White House almost invariably loses seats in the House of Representatives in the following off-year election. "This normal off-year reaction against the party in power," as one widely-read historian calls it, is usually attributed to a natural disillusionment with the President's party as it fails to come up to the expectations created during the enthusiasm of the campaign. Since winning Presidents commonly poll a higher vote in their second campaign than they do in their first, however, this is not a fully satisfying explanation.

We would suggest that the familiar off-year loss does not depend on an inevitable cooling of the public ardor for the President's party, although this undoubtedly occurs in particular years. It depends rather on a pattern of circulation of votes which is characteristic of presidential and off-year elections. In the relatively stimulating circumstances of a presidential election the turnout is high. As we have just noted, the regular voters whose intrinsic political interest is high enough to take them to the polls even under less stimulating conditions are joined by marginal voters who are less concerned with politics but may be activated if the stakes seem high. Ordinarily one of the two candidates standing for the presidency will be benefited by the political circumstances of the moment more clearly than the other, either because of embarrassments of the party in power, the personal qualities of the candidates, domestic or international conditions, or for other reasons. The advantaged candidate will draw to him the votes of a majority of the marginal voters, who have relatively little party attachment and are responsive to such short-term influences. He will also profit from some defections by regular voters from the opposition party who are sufficiently tempted to break away from their usual party vote at least temporarily. In moving toward the advantaged candidate both the regular and the marginal voters, especially the latter, tend to support both the candidate

and his party ticket. In the off-year election which follows, two movements occur. The regular voters who moved across party lines to support a presidential candidate they preferred are likely to move back to their usual party vote when that candidate is no longer on the ticket. The marginal voters who had given the winning candidate a majority of their votes in the presidential election do not vote in the election which follows. Both of these movements hurt the party of the candidate who benefited from the votes of the two groups in the presidential election. The loss of congressional seats is the result.

The 1934 election, the only exception to the law of off-year loss, offers an interesting test of the explanation we are proposing. It would appear from such retrospective information as we can obtain in our surveys that the small gain the Democrats achieved in 1934 depended on the fact that the two types of movement we have described as characteristic of off-year elections were blunted by the massive realignment of partisan orientations which was taking place at that time.[7] Mr. Roosevelt and the New Deal brought many new adherents to the Democratic Party, some of whom had previously been Republican and many of whom had been politically inactive. This type of realignment, which in the 1930's displaced the Republican Party as the majority party in this country, has been an uncommon occurrence in the nation's political history, however.

3. Professor V. O. Key has pointed out in one of his books that since the election of 1892 whenever there has been a significant increase in the turnout in a presidential election the increment of votes has always gone very largely to one party; it is not divided between the two.[8] To quote his statement, "An unusually rapid rate of growth in the total number of voters from one election to the next is accom-

---

[7] Campbell Converse, Miller and Stokes, *The American Voter*, p. 153.

[8] V. O. Key, Jr. *Politics, Parties and Pressure Groups*, 4th edition (New York: Crowell, 1958), p. 638.

panied by an exceptionally high rate of increase in the number of supporters of one of the parties but not the other." He cites the elections of 1896, 1916, and 1952.

What are the characteristics of these high turnout swing elections? We have detailed information on only one such election, 1952, but it may provide a key to the understanding of the others as well. The most striking fact about the flow of the vote in the 1952 election was the universality with which the various segments of the electorate moved toward the Republican candidate. It was not a situation in which some groups became more Democratic than they had been in 1948 but were offset by other groups moving in the other direction. There was virtually no occupational, religious, regional or other subdivision of the electorate which did not vote more strongly Republican in 1952 than it had in 1948.

A second impressive fact about the 1952 election was the relative insignificance of policy issues in the minds of the voters. There were no great questions of policy which the public saw as dividing the two parties. Instead the voters were thinking about "the mess in Washington," the stalemate in Korea, and General Eisenhower's heroic image. It would appear that the flow of the vote from the Democratic majorities of the previous twenty years to the Republican victory in 1952 was a response to short-term forces which were largely unilateral. They favored the Republican alternative and they were not offset by balancing forces favoring the Democrats. Having little policy content they did not set interest group against interest group, class against class, region against region.

The third important characteristic of the 1952 election was the fact that, despite the decisiveness of the Eisenhower victory, the underlying Democratic advantage in the basic party attachments of the electorate was not disturbed. We know from our national surveys that the proportions of the electorate identifying themselves as Democrats or Republicans did not change throughout the eight years

of the Eisenhower administration. In 1960, when the candidacy of Mr. Eisenhower was no longer a consideration, the vote swung strongly back toward the "normal" Democratic majority, despite the severe handicap to the Democrats of a Catholic candidate at the head of their ticket.

What kinds of forces have the capacity to produce this surge phenomenon, with an upswing in turnout moving unidirectionally toward one party and a subsequent decline to a normal division of the vote?[9]

* * *

It is our belief that the more basic quality of these surge elections is the absence of great ideological issues. The fact that so many of them have been dominated by persons of military background dramatize this lack. If Mr. Eisenhower may be taken as an example, the public image of these gentlemen has little to do with great issues of public policy. With certain notable exceptions, the dramatic swings of turnout and partisanship during the last hundred years do not give the impression of an aroused electorate taking sides in a great debate on national policy.[10] On the contrary these swings in

---

[9] The concept of the surge election was developed as an outgrowth of the Survey Research Center's studies of the 1952 and 1956 elections. See Angus Campbell, "Surge and Decline," *Public Opinion Quarterly,* **24,** 1960, 397-418.

[10] It is important to distinguish between surge elections, in which the swing in the vote is only temporary and is followed by a return to the "normal" vote division, from those elections which we have called "realigning," in which the vote surge is associated with an underlying realignment of party loyalties. There have been three major periods of realignment in the last century, in 1856-1860 with the birth of the Republican Party, in 1896 with the ascendance of the Republican Party, and in 1932-1936 with the resurgence of the Democratic Party. Neither Lincoln, McKinley nor Roosevelt, it may be noted, was a military figure and none of them possessed any extraordinary personal appeal at the time he first took office. The quality which did distinguish these elections was the presence of a great national issue and the association of the two major parties with relatively clearly contrasting programs for its solution. In some

the vote appear to be more a reaction to circumstances and personalities than to issues in the usual sense. Public interest in these immediate events and persons is translated into political action, with a high turnout of voters and a general movement toward the party which happens to be in a position to profit from the situation. The movement is unidirectional because the circumstances which produce it are not seen as favorable by one section of the electorate and unfavorable by another. They tend rather to create a generally positive or negative attitude throughout the electorate, resulting in the almost universal type of shift which we observed in 1952.

4. This conclusion brings us to the consideration of a theory of American politics which enjoys a certain respectability, the belief that the major oscillations in the presidential vote over the last hundred years reflect a cyclical movement from a conservative to a liberal mood in the minds of the voters. This theory was orginally identified with Professor Arthur Schlesinger and has been implicit in much political commentary for many years.[11]

Professor Schlesinger contended in 1939 that electoral history since 1841 could be divided into epochs of some fifteen or sixteen years duration which alternated between conservative and liberal governmental policies, resulting from shifts in predominant public sentiment. "Apparently the electorate embarks on conservative policies until it is disillusioned or wearied or bored and then attaches itself to liberal policies until a similar course is run." By examining the legislation enacted over the previous hundred years he found it possible to identify succeeding periods in which these sentiments seemed to dominate.

Like many another student of society, Professor Schlesinger is led to explain the

cycles he observes in collective behavior (in this case the legislative acts of Congress) by speculations regarding the motives of the individual members of the collectivity. Social theorists commonly feel the need of an underlying psychology to support their explanations of the behavior of the total society. As long as no direct evidence from the individual level is available their psychological suppositions cannot be tested and some of them have passed into the domain of what Professor Galbreath calls the "conventional wisdom." For the past twenty years, however, it has been possible to assess the motives of the individual members of society directly. One need not be overly confident about the precision with which these assessments are carried out; measuring the human mind undoubtedly has its problems. But there is no doubt that we have learned enough to know that some of the speculations about why people behave as they do do not accurately describe people as they actually are.

In our view Professor Schlesinger's theory of electoral cycles is based on just such an erroneous assumption regarding the characteristics of the electorate. He apparently believes that the voters go to the polls with some relatively clear intention regarding the legislation they want their representaives to enact. For a period they want what he calls "liberal" legisaltion; then with an apparent sense of appropriate limits they choose a government which will take them back toward the conservative side of the scale. So by the use of the franchise the citizenry guides the ship of state on a zigzag course within the shoals of ideological extremity.

This description of the motivation of the vote, congenial as it is with the traditional theories of democratic government, bears very little resemblance to the facts of the case. Consider 1952 as an example. This was a year which many people interpreted as a swing to the right, a conservative reaction to two decades of

degree, national politics during these realigning periods did take on an ideological character. . . .

[11] A. M. Schlesinger. "Tides of American Politics," *Yale Review,* **29,** 1939, 217-230.

liberal government.[12] If fact it was a rare person indeed among the people we interviewed in 1952 who had a program of legislation he wanted the new government to undertake. They wanted to get the crooks out of the Internal Revenue Service and the troops out of Korea and they certainly admired General Eisenhower. But far from voting for a conservative program, only a small percentage had any apparent comprehension of what a conservative-liberal, or left-right dimension in politics implies.[13] And, as we have observed earlier, those voters who contribute the greatest part of the shift in surge elections like 1952 are even less well-informed about politics than the average.

If the flow of the vote in 1952 did not express a conservative mood in the electorate, how is it to be explained? It would be much more parsimonious and much more in keeping with the evidence at hand to say that it simply expressed a desire for a change in stewardship of the federal establishment. Accumulating grievances and dissatisfactions over the last years of Democratic government finally led to a vote for a new administration. The voters were not asking for any specific platform of legislation; they just wanted a new bunch of fellows to run things better.

We do not have the kind of information about earlier swings in the national vote that we have about 1952 and one cannot be sure how closely the 1952 pattern fits the earlier experience. We know there have been occasions when national crises have polarized the electorate around a major issue and brought about far-reaching realignments in party strength. Such occasions have been infrequent, however, and it seems highly probable that the election of 1952 was more representative of the American elections than the highly charged situations of 1856-60, 1896, and 1932-36 were. The electorate seems quite

[12] Professor Schlesinger had predicted that a conservative swing would come in 1948. He undoubtedly would feel that the 1952 vote was simply a slightly delayed version of the reaction he had expected.
[13] Campbell, Converse, Miller and Stokes, *The American Voter*, Chapter 9.

capable of expressing its intolerance of circumstances it finds exasperating and it sometimes responds strongly to the personal qualities of an attractive candidate but it is not well enough informed to follow a deliberate program of choice between conservative and liberal alternatives in governmental policies.

CONCLUSION

The attempts of sociologists and psychologists over the last twenty years to apply new methods of quantitative research to the study of political phenomena have not been very well received by some students of American politics in other academic disciplines. They have thought we have been asking the wrong questions and they have some doubts as to whether we can ever answer the right questions.

It would be foolish to deny that behavioral studies of the vote have their limitations. They are certainly lacking in time depth although this fault should become less serious as present programs of research are extended. They undoubtedly have greater applicability to some kinds of problems than to others and there are some kinds of questions to which they have nothing whatever to say. Granting these and other restrictions on his scope, what does the behavioral scientist have to offer the scholar who is primarily interested in the collective behavior of society? The burden of this paper has been the argument that he is uniquely equipped to provide a realistic statement of the nature of the individual acts which make up the collectivity. He need not accept on faith the hypothetical man invented by social and economic theorists. He has devised ways of finding and measuring men as they are and he often finds that in real life they do not closely resemble the man who has been deductively created.

The question is, of course, whether or not this specialized information can be fruitfully applied to the illumination of questions of collective behavior. Can it extend our understanding of the workings of our political system? The history of attempts to find the connection between aggregative events and the component individual acts is not reassuring. Arnold Toynbee has recently deplored our "ignorance of the relation between collective results and the underlying individual human acts" and asserts that it has characterized all scholarly effort since Aristotle.

Despite this authoritative observation it is possible to feel a cautious optimism for the future, at least within the narrow field of political behavior which we have been discussing. Tentative feelers are being put out from both sides of the gap.

The efforts of Sellers and other historians to find new insights in behavioral studies for the identification of patterns in presidential elections are most intriguing. From the other side, behavioral researchers are increasingly moving from their preoccupation with the individual voting decision to a concern for the characteristics of the total vote. It would be hazardous to predict where these converging interests will lead but the integration of historical evidence from the elections of the past with survey data from the elections of the present seems a natural intellectual enterprise and it is not totally unrealistic to hope that something worthwhile will come from it.

Protest as a Political Resource*

MICHAEL LIPSKY

The frequent resort to protest activity by relatively powerless groups in recent American politics suggests that protest represents an important aspect of minority group and low income politics.[1] At the same time that Negro civil rights strategists have recognized the problem of using protest as a meaningful political in-

* This article is an attempt to develop and explore the implications of a conceptual scheme for analyzing protest activity. It is based on my studies of protest organizations in New York City, Chicago, Washington, D.C., San Francisco, and Mississippi, as well as extensive examination of written accounts of protest among low-income and Negro civil rights groups. I am grateful to Kenneth Dolbeare, Murray Edelman, and Rodney Stiefbold for their insightful comments on an earlier draft. This paper was developed while the author was a staff Associate of the Institute for Research on Poverty at the University of Wisconsin. I appreciate the assistance obtained during various stages of my research from the Rabinowitz Foundation, the N.Y. State Legislative Internship Program, and the Brookings Institution.

SOURCE. Reprinted from *The American Political Science Review*, Vol. 62, 1968, by permission of the author and publisher. Copyright 1968, The American Political Science Association.

[1] "Relatively powerless groups" may be defined as those groups which, relatively speaking, are lacking in conventional political resources. For the purposes of community studies, Robert Dahl has compiled a useful comprehensive list. See Dahl, "The Analysis of Influence in Local Communities," *Social Science and Community Action*, Charles R. Adrian, ed. (East Lansing, Michigan, 1960), p. 32. The difficulty in studying such groups is that relative powerlessness only becomes apparent under certain conditions. Extremely powerless groups not only lack political resources, but are also characterized by a minimal sense of political efficacy, upon which in part successful political organization depends. For reviews of the literature linking orientations of political efficacy to socioeconomic status, see Robert Lane, *Po-*

strument,[2] groups associated with the "war on poverty" have increasingly received publicity for protest activity. Saul Alinsky's Industrial Areas Foundation, for example, continues to receive invitations to help organize low income communities because of its ability to mobilize poor people around the tactic of protest.[3] The riots which dominated urban affairs in the summer of 1967 appear not to have diminished the dependence of some groups on protest as a mode of political activity.

This article provides a theoretical perspective on protest activity as a political resource. The discussion is concentrated on the limitations inherent in protest which occur because of the need of protest leaders to appeal to four constituencies at the same time. As the concept of protest is developed here, it will be argued that protest leaders must nurture and sustain an organization comprised of people with whom they may or may not share common values. They must articulate goals and choose strategies so as to maximize their public exposure through communications media. They must maximize the impact of third parties in the political conflict. Finally, they must try to maxi-

mize chances of success among those capable of granting goals. The tensions inherent in manipulating these four constituencies at the same time form the basis of this discussion of protest as a political process. It is intended to place aspects of the civil rights movement in a framework which suggests links between protest organizations and the general political processes in which such organizations operate.

I. PROTEST CONCEPTUALIZED

Protest activity as it has been adopted by elements of the civil rights movement and others has not been studied extensively by social scientists. Some of the most suggestive writings have been done as case studies of protest movements in single southern cities.[4] These works generally lack a framework or theoretical focus which would encourage generalization from the cases. More systematic efforts have been attempted in approaching the dynamics of biracial committees in the South,[5] and comprehensively assessing the efficacy of Negro political involvement in Durham, N. C. and Philadelphia, Pa.[6] In their excellent assessment of Negro politics in the South, Matthews and

litical Life (New York, 1959), ch. 16; and Lester Milbrath, Political Participation (Chicago, 1965), ch. 5. Further, to the extent that group cohesion is recognized as a necessary requisite for organized political action, then extremely powerless groups, lacking cohesion, will not even appear for observation. Hence the necessity of selecting for intensive study a protest movement where there can be some confidence that observable processes and results can be analyzed. Thus, if one conceives of a continuum on which political groups are placed according to their relative command of resources, the focus of this essay is on those groups which are near, but not at, the pole of powerlessness.

[2] See, e.g., Bayard Rustin, "From Protest to Politics: The Future of the Civil Rights Movement," Commentary (February, 1965), pp. 25-31; and Stokely Carmichael, "Toward Black Liberation," The Massachusetts Review, Auutmn, 1966.

[3] On Alinsky's philosophy of community organization, see his Reveille for Radicals (Chicago, 1945); and Charles Silberman, Crisis in Black and White (New York, 1964), ch. 10.

[4] See, e.g., Jack L. Walker, "Protest and Negotiation: A Case Study of Negro Leadership in Atlanta, Georgia," Midwest Journal of Political Science (May, 1963), pp. 99-124; Jack L. Walker, Sit-Ins in Atlanta: A Study in the Negro Protest, Eagleton Institute Case Studies, No. 34 (New York, 1964); John Ehle, The Free Men (New York, 1965) [Chapel Hill]; Daniel C. Thompson, The Negro Leadership Class (Englewood Cliffs, N.J., 1963) [New Orleans]; M. Elaine Burgess, Negro Leadership in a Southern City (Chapel Hill, N.C., 1962) [Durham].

[5] Lewis Killian and Charles Grigg, Racial Crisis in America: Leadership in Conflict (Englewood Cliffs, N.J., 1964).

[6] William Keech, "The Negro Vote as a Political Resource: The Case of Durham," (unpublished Ph.D. Dissertation, University of Wisconsin, 1966); John H. Strange, "The Negro in Philadelphia Politics 1963-65," (unpublished Ph.D. Dissertation, Princeton University, 1966).

Prothro have presented a thorough profile of Southern Negro students and their participation in civil rights activities.[7] Protest is also discussed in passing in recent explorations of the social-psychological dimensions of Negro ghetto politics[8] and the still highly suggestive, although pre-1960's, work on Negro political leadership by James Q. Wilson.[9] These and other less systematic works on contemporary Negro politics,[10] for all of their intuitive insights and valuable documentation, offer no theoretical formulations which encourage conceptualization about the interaction between recent Negro political activity and the political process.

Heretofore the best attempt to place Negro protest activity in a framework which would generate additional insights has been that of James Q. Wilson.[11] Wilson has suggested that protest activity be conceived as a problem of bargaining in which the basic problem is that Negro groups lack political resources to exchange. Wilson called this "the problem of the powerless."[12]

While many of Wilson's insights remain valid, his approach is limited in applicability because it defines protest in terms of mass action or response and as utilizing exclusively negative inducements in the bargaining process. Negative inducements are defined as inducements which are not

absolutely preferred but are preferred over alternative possibilities.[13] Yet it might be argued that protest designed to appeal to groups which oppose suffering and exploitation, for example, might be offering positive inducements in bargaining. A few Negro students sitting at a lunch counter might be engaged in what would be called protest, and by their actions might be trying to appeal to other groups in the system with positive inducements. Additionally, Wilson's concentration on Negro civic action, and his exclusive interest in exploring the protest process to explain Negro civic action, tend to obscure comparison with protest activity which does not necessarily arise within the Negro community.

Assuming a somewhat different focus, protest activity is defined as a mode of political action oriented toward objection to one or more policies or conditions, characterized by showmanship or display of an unconventional nature, and undertaken to obtain rewards from political or economic systems while working within the systems. The "problem of the powerless" in protest activity is to activate "third parties" to enter the implicit or explicit bargaining arena in ways favorable to the protesters. This is one of the few ways in which they can "create" bargaining resources. It is intuitively unconvincing to suggest that fifteen people sitting uninvited in the Mayor's office have the power to move City Hall. A better formulation would suggest that the people sitting in may be able to appeal to a wider public to which the city administration is sensitive. Thus in successful protest activity the *reference publics* of protest *targets* may be conceived as explicitly or implicitly reacting to protest in such a way that target groups or individuals respond in ways favorable to the protesters.[14]

---

[7] Donald Matthews and James Prothro, *Negroes and the New Southern Politics* (New York, 1966). Considerable insight on these data is provided in John Orbell, "Protest Participation among Southern Negro College Students," this *Review*, **61** (June, 1967), pp. 446-56.
[8] Kenneth Clark, *Dark Ghetto* (New York, 1965).
[9] *Negro Politics* (New York, 1960).
[10] A complete list would be voluminous. See, e.g., Nat Hentoff, *The New Equality* (New York, 1964); Arthur Waskow, *From Race Riot to Sit-in* (New York, 1966).
[11] "The Strategy of Protest: Problems of Negro Civic Action," *Journal of Conflict Resolution*, V. 3 (September, 1961), pp. 291-303. The reader will recognize the author's debt to this highly suggestive article, not least Wilson's recognition of the utility of the bargaining framework for examining protest activity.
[12] *Ibid.*, p. 291.

[13] See *Ibid.*, pp. 291-292.
[14] See E. E. Schattschneider's discussion of expanding the scope of the conflict, The Semisovereign People (New York, 1960). Another way in which bargaining resources may be "created" is to increase the relative cohesion of groups, or to increase the perception of group solidarity as a precondition to greater cohesion. This appears to be the

It should be emphasized that the focus here is on protest by relatively powerless groups. Illustrations can be summoned, for example, of activity designated as "protest" involving high status pressure groups or hundreds of thousands of people. While such instances may share some of the characteristics of protest activity, they may not represent examples of developing political resources by relatively powerless groups because the protesting groups may already command political resources by virtue of status, numbers or cohesion.

It is appropriate also to distinguish between the relatively restricted use of the concept of protest adopted here and closely related political strategies which are often designated as "protest" in popular usage. Where groups already possess sufficient resources with which to bargain, as in the case of some economic boycotts and labor strikes, they may be said to engage in "direct confrontation."[15] Similarly, protest which represents efforts to "activate reference publics" should be distinguished from "alliance formation," where third parties are induced to join the conflict, but where the value orientations of third parties are sufficiently similar to those of the protesting group that concerted or coordinated action is possible. Alliance formation is particularly desirable for relatively powerless groups if they seek to join the decision-making process as participants.

The distinction between activating reference publics and alliance formation is made on the assumption that where goal orientations among protest groups and the reference publics of target groups are

similar, the political dynamics of petitioning target groups are different than when such goal orientations are relatively divergent. Clearly the more similar the goal orientations, the greater the likelihood of protest success, other things being equal. This discussion is intended to highlight, however, those instances where goal orientations of reference publics depart significantly, in direction or intensity, from the goals of protest groups.

Say that to protest some situation, A would like to enter a bargaining situation with B. But A has nothing B wants, and thus cannot bargain. A then attempts to create political resources by activating other groups to enter the conflict. A then organizes to take action against B with respect to certain goals. *Information concerning these goals must be conveyed through communications media* (C, D, and E) *to* F, G, *and* H, *which are B's reference publics.* In response to the reactions of F, G, and H, or in anticipation of their reactions, B responds, *in some way,* to the protesters' demands. This formulation requires the conceptualization of protest activity when undertaken to create bargaining resources as a political process which requires communication and is characterized by a multiplicity of constituencies for protest leadership.

A schematic representation of the process of protest as utilized by relatively powerless groups is presented in Figure 1. In contrast to a simplistic pressure group model which would posit a direct relationship between pressure group and pressured, the following discussion is guided by the assumption (derived from observation) that protest is a highly indirect process in which communications media and the reference publics of protest targets play critical roles. It is also a process characterized by reciprocal relations, in which protest leaders frame strategies according to their perception of the needs of (many) other actors.

In this view protest constituents limit the options of protest leaders at the same time that the protest leader influences their perception of the strategies and rhetoric which they will support. Protest

---

primary goal of political activity which is generally designated "community organization." Negro activists appear to recognize the utility of this strategy in their advocacy of "black power." In some instances protest activity may be designed in part to accomplish this goal in addition to activating reference publics.

[15] For an example of "direct confrontation," one might study the three-month Negro boycott of white merchants in Natchez, Miss., which resulted in capitulation to boycott demands by city government leaders. See *The New York Times*, December 4, 1965, p. 1.

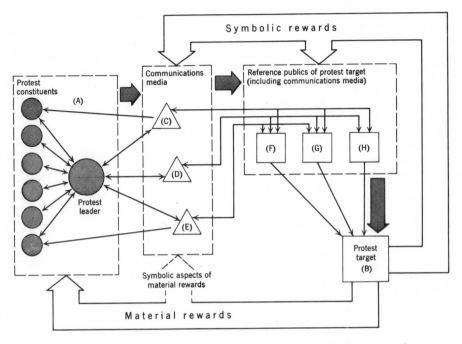

Figure 1. Schematic representation of the process of protest by relatively powerless groups.

activity is filtered through the communications media in influencing the perceptions of the reference publics of protest targets. To the extent that the influence of reference publics is supportive of protest goals, target groups will dispense symbolic or material rewards. Material rewards are communicated directly to protest constituents. Symbolic rewards are communicated in part to protest constituents, but primarily are communicated to the reference publics of target groups, who provide the major stimuli for public policy pronouncements.

The study of protest as adopted by relatively powerless groups should provide insights into the structure and behavior of groups involved in civil rights politics and associated with the "war on poverty." It should direct attention toward the ways in which administrative agencies respond to "crises." Additionally, the study of protest as a political resource should in-

fluence some general conceptualizations of American political pluralism. Robert Dahl, for example, describes the "normal American political process" as

> one in which there is a high probability that an active and legitimate group in the population can make itself heard effectively at some crucial stage in the process of decision.[16]

Although he agrees that control over decisions is unevenly divided in the population, Dahl writes:

> When I say that a group is heard "effectively" I mean more than the simple fact that it makes a noise; I mean that one or more officials are not only ready to listen to the noise, but expect to suffer in some significant way if they do not placate the group, its leaders, or its most vociferous members. To satisfy the group may require one or more of a great variety of

[16] *A Preface to Democratic Theory* (Chicago, 1956), pp. 145-146.

actions by the responsive leader: pressure for substantive policies, appointments, graft, respect, expression of the appropriate emotions, or the right combination of reciprocal noises.[17]

These statements, which in some ways resemble David Truman's discussion of the power of "potential groups,"[18] can be illuminated by the study of protest activity in three ways. First, what are the probabilities that relatively powerless groups can make themselves heard effectively? In what ways will such groups be heard or "steadily appeased"?[19] Concentration on the process of protest activity may reveal the extent to which, and the conditions under which, relatively powerless groups are likely to prove effective. Protest undertaken to obstruct policy decisions, for example, may enjoy greater success probabilities than protest undertaken in an effort to evoke constructive policy innovations.[20]

Second, does it make sense to suggest that all groups which make noises will receive responses from public officials? Perhaps the groups which make noises do not have to be satisfied at all, but it is other groups which receive assurances or recognition. Third, what are the probabilities that groups which make noises will receive tangible rewards, rather than symbolic assurances?[21] Dahl lumps these rewards together in the same paragraph, but dispensation of tangible rewards clearly has a different impact upon groups than the dispensation of symbolic rewards. Dahl is undoubtedly correct when he suggests that the relative fluidity

of American politics is a critical characteristic of the American political system.[22] But he is less precise and less convincing when it comes to analyzing the extent to which the system is indeed responsive to the relatively powerless groups of the "average citizen."[23]

The following sections are an attempt to demonstrate the utility of the conceptualization of the protest process presented above. This will be done by exploring the problems encountered and the strains generated by protest leaders in interacting with four constituencies. It will be useful to concentrate attention on the maintenance and enhancement needs not only of the large formal organizations which dominate city politics,[24] but also of the ad hoc protest groups which engage them in civic controversy. It will also prove rewarding to examine the role requirements of individuals in leadership positions as they perceive the problems of constituency manipulation. In concluding remarks some implications of the study of protest for the pluralist description of American politics will be suggested.[25]

---

[17] *Ibid.*

[18] *The Governmental Process* (New York, 1951), p. 104.

[19] See Dahl, *A Preface to Democratic Theory*, p. 146.

[20] Observations that all groups can influence public policy at some stage of the political process are frequently made about the role of "veto groups" in American politics. See *Ibid.*, pp. 104ff. See also David Reisman, *The Lonely Crowd* (New Haven, 1950), pp. 211ff., for an earlier discussion of veto-group politics. Yet protest should be evaluated when it is adopted to obtain assertive as well as defensive goals.

[21] See Murray Edelman, *The Symbolic Uses of Politics* (Urbana, Ill., 1964), ch. 2.

[22] See Dahl, *Who Governs?* (New Haven, 1961), pp. 305ff.

[23] In a recent formulation, Dahl reiterates the theme of wide dispersion of influence. "More than other systems, [democracies] ... try to disperse influence widely to their citizens by means of the suffrage, elections, freedom of speech, press, and assembly, the right of opponents to criticize the conduct of government, the right to organize political parties, and in other ways." *Pluralist Democracy in the United States* (Chicago, 1967), p. 373. Here, however, he concentrates more on the availability of options to all groups in the system, rather than on the relative probabilities that all groups in fact have access to the political process. See pp. 372ff.

[24] See Edward Banfield, *Political Influence* (New York, 1961), p. 263. The analysis of organizational incentive structure which heavily influences Banfield's formulation is Chester Barnard, *The Functions of the Executive* (Cambridge, Mass., 1938).

[25] In the following attempt to develop the implications of this conceptualization of protest activity, I have drawn upon extensive field observations and bibliographical research. Undoubtedly, however, individual assertions, while representing my best judgment concerning the available evidence, in the future may require modification as the result of further empirical research.

II. PROTEST LEADERSHIP AND ORGANIZATIONAL BASE

The organizational maintenance needs of relatively powerless, low income, ad hoc protest groups center around the tension generated by the need for leadership to offer symbolic and intangible inducements to protest participation when immediate, material rewards cannot be anticipated, and the need to provide at least the promise of material rewards for protest participation. Protest leaders must try to evoke responses from other actors in the political process, at the same time that they pay attention to participant organizational needs. Thus relatively deprived groups in the political system not only receive symbolic reassurance while material rewards from the system are withheld,[26] but protest leaders have a stake in perpetuating the notion that relatively powerless groups retain political efficacy despite what in many cases is obvious evidence to the contrary.

The tension embraced by protest leaders over the nature of inducements toward protest participation accounts in part for the style adopted and goals selected by protest leaders. Groups which seek psychological gratification from politics, but cannot or do not anticipate material political rewards, may be attracted to militant protest leaders. To these groups, angry rhetoric may prove a desirable quality in the short run. Where groups depend upon the political system for tangible benefits, or where participation in the system provides intangible benefits, moderate leadership is likely to prevail. Wilson has observed similar tendencies among Negro leaders of large, formal organizations.[27] It is no less true for leadership of protest groups. Groups whose members derive tangible satisfactions from political participation will not condone leaders who are stubborn in compromise or appear to question the foundations of the system. This coincides with Truman's observation:

Violation of the "rules of the game" normally will weaken a group's cohesion, reduce its status in the community, and expose it to the claims of other groups.[28]

On the other hand, the cohesion of relatively powerless groups may be strengthened by militant, ideological leadership which questions the rules of the game and challenges their legitimacy.

Cohesion is particularly important when protest leaders bargain directly with target groups. In that situation, leaders' ability to control protest constituents and guarantee their behavior represents a bargaining strength.[29] For this reason Wilson stressed the bargaining difficulties of Negro leaders who cannot guarantee constituent behavior, and pointed out the significance of the strategy of projecting the image of group solidarity when the reality of cohesion is a fiction.[30] Cohesion is less significant at other times. Divided leadership may prove productive by bargaining in tandem,[31] or by minimizing strain among groups in the protest process. Further, community divisions may prove less detrimental to protest aims when strong third parties have entered the dispute originally generated by protest organizations.

The intangible rewards of assuming certain postures toward the political system may not be sufficient to sustain an organizational base. It may be necessary to renew constantly the intangible rewards of participation. And to the extent that people participate in order to achieve tangible benefits, their interest in a protest organization may upon the organization's relative material success. Protest

---

[26] As Edelman suggests, cited previously.
[27] *Negro Politics*, p. 290.

[28] *The Governmental Process*, p. 513.
[29] But cf. Thomas Schelling's discussion of "binding oneself," *The Strategy of Conflict* (Cambridge, Mass., 1960), pp. 22ff.
[30] "The Strategy of Protest," p. 297.
[31] This is suggested by Wilson, "The Strategy of Protest," p. 298; St. Clair Drake and Horace Cayton, *Black Metropolis* (New York, 1962, rev. ed.), p. 731; Walker, "Protest and Negotiation," p. 122. Authors who argue that divided leadership is dysfunctional have been Clark, p. 156; and Tilman Cothran, "The Negro Protest Against Segregation in the South," *The Annals*, **357** (January, 1965), p. 72.

leaders may have to tailor their style to present participants with tangible successes, or with the apperance of success. Leaders may have to define the issues with concern for increasing their ability to sustain organizations. The potential for protest among protest group members may have to be manipulated by leadership if the group is to be sustained.[32]

The participants in protest organizations limit the flexibility of protest leadership. This obtains for two reasons. They restrict public actions by leaders who must continue to solicit active participant support, and they place restraints on the kinds of activities which can be considered appropriate for protest purposes. Poor participants cannot commonly be asked to engage in protest requiring air transportation. Participants may have anxieties related to their environment or historical situation which discourages engagement in some activities. They may be afraid of job losses, beatings by the police, or summary evictions. Negro protest in the Deep South has been inhibited by realistic expectations of retribution.[33] Protest over slum housing conditions are undermined by tenants who expect landlord retaliation for engaging in tenant

organizing activity.[34] Political or ethical mores may conflict with a proposed course of action, diminishing participation.[35]

On the other hand, to the extent that fears are real, or that the larger community perceives protest participants as subject to these fears, protest may actually be strengthened. Communications media and potential allies will consider more soberly the complaints of people who are understood to be placing themselves in jeopardy. When young children and their parents made the arduous bus trip from Mississippi to Washington, D.C. to protest the jeopardizing of Head Start funds, the courage and expense represented by their effort created a respect and visibility for their position which might not have been achieved by local protest efforts.[36]

Protest activity may be undertaken by organizations with established relationship patterns, behavior norms, and role expectations. These organizations are likely to have greater access to other groups in the political system, and a demonstrated capacity to maintain themselves. Other protest groups, however, may be ad hoc arrangements without demonstrated internal or external relationship patterns. These groups will have different organizational problems, in response to which it is necessary to engage in different kinds of protest activity.

The scarcity of organizational resources also places limits upon the ability

---

[32] This observation is confirmed by a student of the Southern civil rights movement:

Negroes demand of protest leaders constant progress. The combination of long-standing discontent and a newfound belief in the possibility of change produces a constant state of tension and aggressiveness in the Negro community. But this discontent is vague and diffuse, not specific; the masses do not define the issues around which action shall revolve. This the leader must do.

Lewis Killian, "Leadership in the Desegregation Crises: An Institutional Analysis," in Muzafer Sherif (ed.), Intergroup Relations and Leadership (New York, 1962), p. 159.

[33] Significantly, southern Negro students who actively participated in the early phases of the sit-in movement "tended to be unusually optimistic about race relations and tolerant of whites [when compared with inactive Negro students]. They not only were better off, objectively speaking, than other Negroes but felt better off." Matthews and Prothro, op. cit., p. 424.

[34] This is particularly the case in cities such as Washington, D.C., where landlord-tenant laws offer little protection against retaliatory eviction. See, e.g., Robert Schoshinski, "Remedies of the Indigent Tenant: Proposal for Change, Georgetown Law Journal, **54** (Winter, 1966), pp. 541ff.

[35] Wilson regarded this as a chief reason for lack of protest activity in 1961. He wrote: ". . . some of the goals now being sought by Negroes are least applicable to those groups of Negroes most suited to protest action. Protest action involving such tactics as mass meetings, picketing, boycotts, and strikes rarely find enthusiastic participants among upper-income and higher status individuals": "The Strategy of Protest," p. 296.

[36] See The New York Times, February 12, 1966, p. 56.

of relatively powerless groups to maintain the foundations upon which protest organizations develop. Relatively powerless groups, to engage in political activity of any kind, must command at least some resources. This is not tautological. Referring again to a continuum on which political groups are placed according to their relative command of resources, one may draw a line somewhere along the continuum representing a "threshold of civic group political participation." Clearly some groups along the continuum will possess some political resources (enough, say, to emerge for inspection) but not enough to exercise influence in civic affairs. Relatively powerless groups, to be influential, must cross the "threshold" to engage in politics. Although the availability of group resources is a critical consideration at all stagtes of the protest process, it is particularly important in explaining why some groups seem to "surface" with sufficient strength to command attention. The following discussion of some critical organizational resources should illuminate this point.

Skilled professionals frequently must be available to protest organizations. Lawyers, for example, play extremely important roles in enabling protest groups to utilize the judicial process and avail themselves of adequate preparation of court cases. Organizational reputation may depend upon a combination of ability to threaten the conventional political system and of exercising statutory rights in court. Availability of lawyers depends upon abiilty to pay fees and/or the attractiveness to lawyers of participation in protest group activity. Volunteer professional assistance may not prove adequate. One night a week volunteered by an aspiring politician in a housing clinic cannot satisfy the needs of a chaotic politicial movement.[37] The need for skilled professionals is not restricted to lawyers. For example, a group seeking to protest an urban renewal policy might require the services of architects and city planners in order to present a viable alternative to a city proposal.

Financial resources not only purchase legal assistance, but enable relatively powerless groups to conduct minimum programs of political activities. To the extent that constituents are unable or unwilling to pay even small membership dues, then financing the cost of mimeographing flyers, purchasing supplies, maintaining telephone service, paying rent, and meeting a modest payroll become major organizational problems. And to the extent that group finances are supplied by outside individual contributions or government or foundation grants, the long-term options of the group are sharply constrained by the necessity of orienting group goals and tactics to anticipate the potential objections of financial supporters.

Some dependence upon even minimal financial resources can be waived if organizations evoke passionate support from constituents. Secretarial help and block organizers will come forward to work without compensation if they support the cause of neighborhood organizations or gain intangible benefits based upon association with the group. Protest organizations may also depend upon skilled nonprofessionals, such as college students, whose access to people and political and economic institutions often assist protest groups in cutting across income lines seeing to seek support. Experience with ad hoc political groups, however, suggests that this assistance is sporadic and undependable. Transient assistance is particularly typical of skilled, educated, and employable volunteers whose abilities can be applied widely. The die-hards of ad hoc political groups are often those people who have no place else to go, nothing else to do.

[37] On housing clinic services provided by political clubs, see James Q. Wilson, *The Amateur Democrat: Club Politics in Three Cities* (Chicago, 1962), pp. 63-64, 176. On the need for lawyers among low income people, see e.g., *The Extension of Legal Services to the Poor*, Conference Proceedings (Washington, D.C., n.d.), exp. pp. 51-60; and "Neighborhood Law Offices: The New Wave in Legal Services for the Poor," *Harvard Law Review*, **80** (February, 1967), pp. 805-850.

Constituent support will be affected by the nature of the protest target and whether protest activity is directed toward defensive or assertive goals. Obstructing specific public policies may be easier than successfully recommending constructive policy changes. Orientations toward defensive goals may require less constituent energy, and less command over resources of money, expertise and status.[38]

III. PROTEST LEADERSHIP AND COMMUNICATIONS MEDIA

The communications media are extremely powerful in city politics. In granting or withholding publicity, in determining what information most people will have on most issues, and what alternatives they will consider in response to issues, the media truly, as Norton Long has put it, "set . . . the civic agenda."[39] To the extent that successful protest activity depends upon appealing to, and/or threatening, other groups in the community, the communications media set the limits of protest atcion. If protest tactics are not considered significant by the media, or if newspapers and television reporters or editors decide to overlook protest tactics, protest organizations will not succeed. Like the tree falling unheard in the forest, there is no protest unless protest is perceived and projected.

A number of writers have noticed that the success of protest activity seems directly related to the amount of publicity it receives outside the immediate arena in which protest takes place. This view has not been stated systematically, but hints can be found in many sources. In the literature on civil rights politics, the relevance of publicity represents one of the few hypotheses available concerning the dynamics of successful protest activity.[40]

When protest tactics do receive coverage in the communications media, the way in which they are presented will influence all other actors in the system, including the protesters themselves. Conformity to standards of newsworthiness in political style, and knowledge of the prejudices and desires of the individuals who determine media coverage of political skills, represent crucial determinants of leadership effectiveness.

The organizational behavior of newspapers can partly be understood by examining the maintenance and enhancement needs which direct them toward projects of civic betterment and impressions of accomplishment.[41] But insight may also be gained by analyzing the role requirements of reporters, editors, and others who determine newspaper policy. Reporters, for example, are frequently motivated by the desire to contribute to civic affairs by their "objective" reporting of significant events; by the premium they place on accuracy; and by the credit which they receive for sensationalism and "scoops."

These requirements may be difficult to accommodate at the same time. Reporters demand newsworthiness of their subjects in the short run, but also require reliability and verifiability in the longer run. Factual accuracy may dampen newsworthiness. Sensationalism, attractive to some newspaper editors, may be inconsistent with reliable, verifiable narration of events. Newspapers at first may be attracted to sensationalism, and later demand verifiabiilty in the interests of com-

---

[38] An illustration of low income group protest organization mobilized for veto purposes is provided by Dahl in "The Case of the Metal Houses." See *Who Governs?*, pp. 192ff.

[39] Norton Long, "The Local Community as an Ecology of Games," in Long, *The Polity*, Charles Press, ed. (Chicago, 1962), p. 153. See pp. 152-154. See also Roscoe C. Martin, Frank J. Munger, *et al.*, *Decisions in Syracuse: A Metropolitan Action Study* (Garden City, N.Y., 1965; originally published: 1961), pp. 326-327.

[40] See, e.g., Thompson, *op. cit.*, p. 134, and *passim;* Martin Oppenheimer, "The Southern Student Movement: Year I," *Journal of Negro Education*, **33** (Fall, 1964), p. 397; Cothran, *op. cit.*, p. 72; Pauli Murray, "Protest Against the Legal Status of the Negro," *The Annals*, **357** (January, 1965), p. 63; Allan P. Sindler, "Protest Against the Political Status of the Negroes," *The Annals*, **357** (January, 1965), p. 50.

[41] See Banfield, *op. cit.*, p. 275.

munity harmony (and adherence to professional journalistic standards).

Most big city newspapers have reporters whose assignments permit them to cover aspects of city politics with some regularity. These reporters, whose "beats" may consist of "civil rights" or "poverty," sometimes develop close relationships with their news subjects. These relationships may develop symbiotic overtones because of the mutuality of interest between the reporter and the news subject. Reporters require fresh information on protest developments, while protest leaders have a vital interest in obtaining as much press coverage as possible.

Inflated reports of protest success may be understood in part by examining this relationship between reporter and protest leader. Both have role oriented interests in projecting images of protest strength and threat. In circumstances of great excitement, when competition from other news media representatives is high, a reporter may find that he is less governed by the role requirement of verification and reliability than he is by his editor's demand for "scoops" and news with high audience appeal.[42]

On the other hand, the demands of the media may conflict with the needs of protest group maintenance. Consider the leader whose constituents are attracted solely by pragmatic statements not exceeding what they consider political "good taste." He is constrained from making militant demands which would isolate him from constituents. This constraint may cost him appeal in the press.[43] How-

ever, the leader whose organizing appeal requires militant rhetoric may obtain eager press coverage only to find that his inflamatory statments lead to alienation of potential allies and exclusion from the explicit bargaining process.[44]

News media do not report events in the same way. Television may select for broadcast only thirty seconds of a half-hour news conference. This coverage will probably focus on immediate events, without background or explanatory material. Newspapers may give more complete accounts of the same event. The most complete account may appear in the weekly edition of a neighborhood or ethnic newspaper. Differential coverage by news media, and differential new media habits in the general population,[45] are significant factors in permitting protest leaders to juggle conflicting demands of groups in the protest process.

Similar tensions exist in the leader's relationship with protest targets. Ideological postures may gain press coverage and constituency approval, but may alienate target groups with whom it would be desirable to bargain explicitly. Exclusion from the councils of decision-making may have important conse-

---

[42] For a case study of the interaction between protest leaders and newspaper reporters, see Michael Lipsky, "Rent Strikes in New York City: Protest Politics and the Power of the Poor," (unpublished Ph.D. dissertation, Princeton University, 1967), pp. 139-49. Bernard Cohen has analyzed the impact of the press on foreign policy from the perspective of reporters' role requirements: see his *The Press and Foreign Policy* (Princeton, N.J., 1963), esp. chs. 2-3.

[43] An example of a protest conducted by middle-class women engaged in pragmatic protest over salvaging park space is provided in John B. Keeley, *Moses on the Green*, Inter-University Case Program, No. 45 (University, Ala., 1959).

[44] This was the complaint of Floyd McKissick, National Director of the Congress of Racial Equality, when he charged that ". . . there are only two kinds of statements a black man can make and expect that the white press will report. . . . First . . . is an attack on another black man. . . . The second is a statement that sounds radical, violent, extreme—the verbal equivalent of a riot. . . . [T]he Negro is being rewarded by the public media only if he turns on another Negro and uses his tongue as a switchblade, or only if he sounds outlandish, extremist or psychotic." Statement at the Convention of the American Society of Newspaper Editors, April 20, 1967, Washington, D.C., as reported in *The New York Times*, April 21, 1967, p. 22. See also the remarks of journalist Ted Poston, *Ibid.*, April 26, 1965, p. 26.

[45] Matthews and Prothro found, for example, that in their south-wide Negro population sample, 38 percent read Negro-oriented magazines and 17 percent read newspapers written for Negroes. These media treat news of interest to Negroes more completely and sympathetically than do the general media. See pp. 248ff.

quences, since the results of target group deliberations may satisfy activated reference publics without responding to protest goals. If activated reference publics are required to increase the bargaining position of the protest group, protest efforts thereafter will have diminished chances of success.

IV. PROTEST LEADERSHIP AND "THIRD PARTIES"

I have argued that the essence of political protest consists of activating third parties to participate in controversy in ways favorable to protest goals. In previous sections I have attempted to analyze some of the tensions which result from protest leaders' attempts to activate reference publics of protest targets at the same time that they must retain the interest and support of protest organization participants. This phenomenon is in evidence when Negro leaders, recognized as such by public officials, find their support eroded in the Negro community because they have engaged in explicit bargaining situations with politicians. Negro leaders are thus faced with the dilemma that when they behave like other ethnic group representatives they are faced with loss of support from those whose intense activism has been aroused in the Negro community, yet whose support is vital if they are to remain credible as leaders to public officials.

The tensions resulting from conflicting maintenance needs of protest organizations and activated third parties present difficulties for protest leaders. One way in which these tensions can be minimized is by dividing leadership responsibilities. If more than one group is engaged in protest activity, protest leaders can, in effect, divide up public roles so as to reduce as much as possible the gap between the implicit demands of different groups for appropriate rhetoric, and what in fact is said. Thus divided leadership may perform the latent function of minimizing tensions among elements in the protest

process by permitting different groups to listen selectively to protest spokesmen.[46]

Another way in which strain among different groups can be minimized is through successful public relations. Minimization of strain may depend upon ambiguity of action or statement, deception, or upon effective inter-group communication. Failure to clarify meaning, or falsification, may increase protest effectiveness. Effective intra-group communication may increase the likelihood that protest constitutents will "understand" that ambiguous or false public statements have "special meaning" and need not be taken seriously. The Machiavellian circle is complete when we observe that although lying may be prudent, the appearance of integrity and forthrightness is desirable for public relations, since these values are widely shared.

It has been observed that "[t]he militant displays an unwillingness to perform those administrative tasks which are necessary to operate an organization. Probably the skills of the agitator and the skills of the administrator . . . are not incompatible, but few men can do both well."[47] These skills may or may not be incompatible as personality traits, but they indeed represent conflicting role demands on protest leadership. When a protest leader exhausts time and energy conducting frequent press conferences, arranging for politicians and celebrities to appear at rallies, delivering speeches to sympathetic local groups, college symposia and other forums, constantly picketing for publicity and generally making "contacts," he is unable to pursue the direction of office routine, clerical tasks, research and analysis, and other chores.

The difficulties of delegating routine tasks is probably directly related to the skill levels and previous administrative experiences of group members. In addition, to the extent that involvement in protest organizations is a function of rewards received or expected by individuals because of the excitement or entertainment value of participation, then the diffi-

---

[46] See footnote 31.
[47] Wilson, *Negro Politics,* p. 225.

culties of delegating routine, relatively uninteresting chores to group members will be increased. Yet attention to such details affects the perception of protest groups by organizations whose support or assistance may be desired in the future. These considerations add to the protest leader's problem of risking alienation of protest participants because of potentially unpopular cooperation with the "power structure."

In the protest paradigm developed here, "third parties" refers both to the reference publics of target groups and, more narrowly, to the interest groups whose regular interaction with protest targets tend to develop into patterns of influence.[48] We have already discussed some of the problems associated with activating the reference publics of target groups. In discussing the constraints placed upon protest, attention may be focused upon the likelihood that groups seeking to create political resources through protest will be included in the explicit bargaining process with other pressure groups. For protest groups, these constraints are those which occur because of class and political style, status, and organizational resources.

The established civic groups most likely to be concerned with the problems raised by relatively powerless groups are those devoted to service in the public welfare and those "liberally" oriented groups whose potential constituents are either drawn from the same class as the protest groups (such as some trade unions), or whose potential constituents are attracted to policies which appear to serve the interest of the lower class or minority groups (such as some reform political clubs).[49] These civic groups have frequently cultivated clientele relationships with city agencies over long periods. Their efforts have been reciprocated by agency

officials anxious to develop constituencies to support and defend agency administrative and budgetary policies. In addition, clientele groups are expected to endorse and legitimize agency aggrandizement. These relationships have been developed by agency officials and civic groups for mutual benefit, and cannot be destroyed, abridged or avoided without cost.

Protest groups may well be able to raise the saliency of issues on the civic agenda through utilization of communications media and successful appeals or threats to wider publics, but admission to policy-making councils is frequently barred because of the angry, militant rhetorical style adopted by protest leaders. People in power do not like to sit down with rogues. Protest leaders are likely to have phrased demands in ways unacceptable to lawyers and other civic activists whose cautious attitude toward public policy may reflect not only their good intentions but their concern for property rights, due process, pragmatic legislating or judicial precedent.

Relatively powerless groups lack participation of individuals with high status whose endorsement of specific proposals lend them increased legitimacy. Good causes may always attract the support of high status individuals. But such individuals' willingness to devote time to the promotion of specific proposals is less likely than the one-shot endorsements which these people distribute more readily.

Similarly, protest organizations often lack the resources on which entry into the policy-making process depends. These resources include maintenance of a staff with expertise and experience in the policy area. This expertise may be in the areas of the law, planning and architecture, proposal writing, accounting, educational policy, federal grantsmanship or publicity. Combining experience with expertise is one way to create status in issue areas. The dispensing of information by interest groups has been widely noted as a major source of influence. Over time the experts develop status in their areas of competence somewhat independent of the in-

---

[48] See Wallace Sayre and Herbert Kaufman, *Governing New York City* (New York, 1960), pp. 257ff. Also see Banfield, *op. cit.*, p. 267.

[49] See Wilson, *The Amateur Democrats*, previously cited. These groups are most likely to be characterized by broad scope of political interest and frequent intervention in politics. See Sayre and Kaufman, *op. cit.*, p. 79.

fluence which adheres to them as information-providers. Groups which cannot or do not engage lawyers to assist in proposing legislation, and do not engage in collecting reliable data, cannot participate in policy deliberations or consult in these matters. Protest oriented groups, whose primary talents are in dramatizing issues, cannot credibly attempt to present data considered "objective" or suggestions considered "responsible" by public officials. Few can be convincing as both advocate and arbiter at the same time.

V. PROTEST LEADERSHIP AND TARGET GROUPS.

The probability of protest success may be approached by examining the maintenance needs of organizations likely to be designated as target groups.[50] For the sake of clarity, and because protest activity increasingly is directed toward government, I shall refer in the following paragraphs exclusively to government agencies at the municpal level. The assumption is retained, however, that the following generalizations are applicable to other potential target groups.

Some of the constraints placed on protest leadership in influencing target groups have already been mentioned in preceding sections. The lack of status and resources that inhibit protest groups from participating in policy-amking conferences, for

example, also helps prevent explicit bargaining between protest leaders and city officials. The strain between rhetoric which appeals to protest participants and public statements to which communications media and "third parties" respond favorably also exists with reference to target groups.

Yet there is a distinguishing feature of the maintenance needs and strategies of city agencies which specifically constrain protest organizations. This is the agency director's need to protect "the jurisdiction and income of his organization [by] . . . [m] anipulation of the external environment."[51] In so doing he may satisfy his reference groups without responding to protest group demands. At least six tactics are available to protest targets who are motivated to respond in some way to protest activity but seek primarily to satisfy their reference publics. These tactics may be empolyed whether or not target groups are "sincere" in responding to protest demands.

1. Target groups may dispense symbolic satisfactions. Appearances of activity and commitment to problems substitute for, or supplement, resource allocation and policy innovations which would constitute tangible responses to protest activity. If symbolic responses supplement tangible pay-offs, they are frequently coincidental, rather than intimately linked, to projection of response by protest targets. Typical in city politics of the symbolic response is the ribbon cutting, street corner ceremony or the walking tour press conference. These occasions are utilized not only to build agency constituencies,[52] but to satisfy agency reference publics that attention is being directed to problems of civic concern. In this sense publicist tactics may be seen as defensive maneuvers. Symbolic aspects of the actions of public officials can also be recognized in the commissioning of expensive studies and the rhetorical flourishes with which "massive attacks," "comprehensive programs," and "co-

---

[50] Another approach, persuasively presented by Wilson, concentrates on protest success as a function of the relative unity and vulnerability of targets. See "The Strategy of Protest," pp. 293ff. This insight helps explain, for example, why protest against housing segregation commonly takes the form of action directed against government (a unified target) rather than against individual homeowners (who present a dispersed target). One problem with this approach is that it tends to obscure the possibility that targets, as collections of individuals, may be divided in evaluation of and sympathy for protest demands. Indeed, city agency administrators under some circumstances act as partisans in protest conflicts. As such, they frequently appear ambivalent toward protest goals: sympathetic to the ends while concerned that the means employed in protest reflect negatively on their agencies.

[51] Sayre and Kaufman, op. cit., p. 253.
[52] See Ibid., pp. 253ff.

ordinated planning" are frequently promoted.

City agencies establish distinct apparatus and procedures for dealing with crises which may be provoked by protest groups. Housing-related departments in New York City may be cited for illustration. It is usually the case in these agencies that the Commissioner or a chief deptuy, a press secretary and one or two other officials devote whatever time is necessary to collect information, determine policy and respond quickly to reports of "crises." This is functional for tenants, who, if they can generate enough concern, may be able to obtain shortcuts through lengthy agency procedures. It is also functional for officials who want to project images of action rather than merely receiving complaints. Concentrating attention on the maintenance needs of city politicians during protest crises suggests that pronouncements of public officials serve purposes independent of their dedication to alleviation of slum conditions.[53]

Independent of dispensation of tangible benefits to protest groups, public officials continue to respond primarily to their own reference publics. Murray Edelman has suggested that:

> Tangible resources and benefits are frequently not distributed to unorganized political group interests as promised in regulatory statutes and the propaganda attending their enactment.[54]

His analysis may be supplemented by suggesting that symbolic dispensations may not only serve to reassure unorganized political group interests, but may also contribute to reducing the anxiety level of organized interests and wider publics which are only tangentially involved in the issues.

2. Target groups may dispense token material satisfactions. When city agencies respond, with much publicity, to cases brought to their attention representing examples of the needs dramatized by protest organizations, they may appear to respond to protest demands while in fact only responding on a case basis, instead of a general basis. For the protesters served by agencies in this fashion it is of considerable advantage that agencies can be influenced by protest action. Yet it should not be ignored that in handling the "crisis" cases, public officials give the appearance of response to their reference publics, while mitigating demands for an expensive, complex *general* assault on problems represented by the cases to which responses are given. Token responses, whether or not accompanied by more general responses, are particularly attractive to reporters and television news directors, who are able to dramatize individual cases convincingly, but who may be unable to "capture" the essence of general deprivation or of general efforts to alleviate conditions of deprivation.

3. Target groups may organize and innovate internally in order to blunt the impetus of protest efforts. This tactic is closely related to No. 2 (above). If target groups can act constructively in the worst cases, they will then be able to preempt protest efforts by responding to the cases which best dramatize protest demands. Alternatively, they may designate all efforts which jeopardize agency reputations as "worst" cases, and devote extensive resources to these cases. In some ways extraordinary city efforts are precisely consistent with protest goals. At the same time extraordinary efforts in the most heavily dramatized cases or the most extreme cases effectively wear down the "cutting-edges" of protest efforts.

Many New York City agencies develop informal "crisis" arrangements not only to project publicity, as previously indicated, but to mobilize energies toward solving "crisis" cases. They may also develop policy innovations which allow them to respond more quickly to "crisis" situations. These innovations may be im-

---

[53] See Lipsky, *op. cit.*, chs. 5-6. The appearance of responsiveness may be given by city officials *in anticipation* of protest activity. This seems to have been the strategy of Mayor Richard Daley in his reaction to the announcement of Martin Luther King's plans to focus civil rights efforts on Chicago. See *The New York Times*, February 1, 1966, p. 11.

[54] Edelman, *op. cit.*, p. 23.

portant to some city residents, for whom the problems of dealing with city bureaucracies can prove insurmountable. It might be said, indeed, that the goals of protest are to influence city agencies to handle every case with the same resources that characterize their dispatch of "crisis" cases.[55]

But such policies would demand major revenue inputs. This kind of qualitative policy change is difficult to achieve. Meanwhile, internal reallocation of resources only means that routine services must be neglected so that the "crisis" programs can be enhanced. If all cases are expedited, as in a typical "crisis" response, then none can be. Thus for purposes of general solutions, "crisis" resolving can be self-defeating unless accompanied by significantly greater resource allocation. It is not self-defeating, however, to the extent that the organizational goals of city agencies are to serve a clientele while minimizing negative publicity concerning agency vigilance and responsiveness.

4. Target groups may appear to be constrained in their ability to grant protest goals.[56] This may be directed toward making the protesters appear to be unreasonable in their demands, or to be well-meaning individuals who "just don't understand how complex running a city really is." Target groups may extend sympathy but claim that they lack resources, a mandate from constituents, and/or authority to respond to protest demands. Target groups may also evade protest demands by arguing that "If-I-give-it-to-you-I-have-to-give-it-to-e v e r y-one."

The tactic of appearing constrained is particularly effective with established civic groups because there is an undeniable element of truth to it. Everyone knows that cities are financially undernourished. Established civic groups expend great energies lobbying for higher levels of funding for their pet city agencies. Thus they recognize the validity of this con-

straint when posed by city officials. But it is not inconsistent to point out that funds for specific, relatively inexpensive programs, or for the expansion of existing programs, can often be found if pressure is increased. While constraints on city government flexibility may be extensive, they are not absolute. Protest targets nonetheless attempt to diminish the impact of protest demands by claiming relative impotence.

5. Target groups may use their extensive resources to discredit protest leaders and organizations. Utilizing their excellent access to the press, public officials may state or imply that leaders are unreliable, ineffective as leaders ("they don't really have the people behind them"), guilty of criminal behavior, potentially guilty of such behavior, or are some shade of "left-wing." Any of these allegations may serve to diminish the appeal of protest groups to potentially sympathetic third parties. City officials, in their frequent social and informal business interaction with leaders of established civic groups, may also communicate derogatory information concerning protest groups. Discrediting of protest groups may be undertaken by some city officials while others appear (perhaps authentically) to remain sympathetic to protest demands. These tactics may be engaged in by public officials whether or not there is any validity to the allegations.

6. Target groups may postpone action. The effect of postponement, if accompanied by symbolic assurances, is to remove immediate pressure and delay specific commitments to a future date. This familiar tactic is particularly effective in dealing with protest groups because of their inherent instability. Protest groups are usually comprised of individuals whose intense political activity cannot be sustained except in rare circumstances. Further, to the extent that protest depends upon activating reference publics through strategies which have some "shock" value, it becomes increasingly difficult to activate these groups, Additionally, protest activity is inherently unstable because of the strains placed upon

---

[55] See Lipsky, *op. cit.*, pp. 156, 249ff.

[56] On the strategy of appearing constrained, see Schelling, *op. cit.*, pp. 22ff.

protest leaders who must attempt to manage four constituencies (as described herein).

The most frequent method of postponing action is to commit a subject to "study." For the many reasons elaborated in these paragraphs, it is not likely that ad hoc protest groups will be around to review the recommendations which emerge from study. The greater the expertise and the greater the status of the group making the study, the less will protest groups be able to influence whatever policy emerges. Protest groups lack the skills and resource personnel to challenge expert recommendations effectively.

Sometimes surveys and special research are undertaken in part to evade immediate pressures. Sometimes not. Research efforts are particularly necessary to secure the support of established civic groups, which place high priority on orderly procedure and policy emerging from independent analysis. Yet it must be recognized that postponing policy commitments has a distinct impact on the nature of the pressures focused on policy-makers.

VI. CONCLUSION

In this analysis I have agreed with James Q. Wilson that protest is correctly conceived as a startegy utilized by relatively powerless groups in order to increase their bargaining ability. As such, I have argued, it is successful to the extent that the reference publics of protest targets can be activated to enter the conflict in ways favorable to protest goals. I have suggested a model of the protest process which may assist in ordering data and indicating the salience for research of a number of aspects of protest. These include the critical role of communications media, the differential impact of material and symbolic rewards on "feedback" in protest activity, and the reciprocal relationships of actors in the protest process.

An estimation of the limits to protest efficacy, I have argued further, can be gained by recognizing the problems encountered by protest leaders who somehow must balance the conflicting maintenance needs of four groups in the protest process. This approach transcends a focus devoted primarily to characterization of group goals and targets, by suggesting that even in an environment which is relatively favorable to specific protest goals, the tensions which must be embraced by protest leadership may ultimately overwhelm protest activity.

At the outset of this essay, it was held that conceptualizing the American political system as "slack" or "fluid," in the manner of Robert Dahl, appears inadequate because of (1) a vagueness centering on the likelihood that any group can make itself heard; (2) a possible confusion as to which groups tend to receive satisfaction from the rewards dispensed by public officials; and (3) a lumping together as equally relevant rewards which are tangible and those which are symbolic. To the extent that protest is engaged in by relatively powerless groups which must create resources with which to bargain, the analysis here suggests a number of reservations concerning the pluralist conceptualization of the "fluidity" of the American political system.

Relatively powerless groups cannot use protest with a high probability of success. They lack organizational resources, by definition. But even to create bargaining resources through activating third parties, some resources are necessary to sustain organization. More importantly, relatively powerless protest groups are constrained by the unresolvable conflicts which are forced upon protest leaders who must appeal simultaneously to four constituencies which place upon them antithetical demands.

When public officials recognize the legitimacy of protest activity, they may not direct public policy toward protest groups at all. Rather, public officials are likely to aim responses at the reference publics from which they originally take their cues. Edelman has suggested that regulatory policy in practice often consists of reassuring mass publics while at the same time dispensing specific, tangible values to narrow interest groups. It is suggested here that symbolic reassurances are dispensed as much to wide, potentially concerned publics which are not directly affected by regulatory policy, as they are to wide publics comprised of the downtrodden and the deprived, in whose name policy is often written.

Complementing Edelman, it is proposed here that in the process of protest symbolic reassurances are dispensed in large measure because these are the public policy outcomes and actions desired by the constituencies to which public officials are most responsive. Satisfying these wider publics, city officials can avoid pressures toward other policies placed upon them by protest organizations.

Not only should there be some doubt as to which groups receive the symbolic recognitions which Dahl describes, but in failing to distinguish between the kinds of rewards dispensed to groups in the political system, Dahl avoids a fundamental question. It is literally fundamental because the kinds of rewards which can be obtained from politics, one might hypothesize, will have an impact upon the realistic appraisal of the efficacy of political activity. If among the groups least capable of organizing for political activity there is a history of organizing for protest, and if that activity, once engaged in, is rewarded primarily by the dispensation of symbolic gestures without perceptible changes in material conditions, then rational behavior might lead to expressions of apathy and lack of interest in politics or a rejection of conventional political channels as a meaningful arena of activity. In this sense this discussion of protest politics is consistent with Kenneth Clark's observations that the image of power, unaccompanied by material and observable rewards, leads to impressions of helplessness and reinforces political apathy in the ghetto.[57]

Recent commentary by political scientists and others regarding riots in American cities seem to focus in part on the extent to which relatively deprived groups may seek redress of legitimate grievances. Future research should continue assessment of the relationship between riots and the conditions under which access to the political system has been limited. In such research assessment of the ways in which access to public officials is obtained by relatively powerless groups through the protest process might be one important research focus.

The instability of protest activity outlined in this article also should inform contemporary political strategies. If the arguments presented here are persuasive, civil rights leaders who insist that protest activity is a shallow foundation on which to seek long-term, concrete gains may be judged essentially correct. But the arguments concerning the fickleness of the white liberal, or the ease of changing discriminatory laws relative to changing discriminatory institutions, only in part explain the instability of protest movements. An explanation which derives its strength from analysis of the political process suggests concentration on the problems of managing protest constituencies. Accordingly, Alinsky is probably on the soundest ground when he prescribes protest for the purpose of building organization. Ultimately, relatively powerless groups in most instances cannot depend upon activating other actors in the political process. Longrun success will depend upon the acquisition of stable political resources which do not rely for their use on third parties.

---

[57] Clark, *op. cit.,* pp. 154ff.

CHAPTER 5

Political Change Processes

THE study of political change is just beginning. Two related reasons may account for the delay: political scientists have been concerned in the last three decades with the problem of stability—perhaps understandably in the light of world events; and the United States has been a remarkably stable nation, so that research into American political processes was far more likely to lead to explanations of stability than to document instances of change. For these reasons, only two of the selections in this chapter deal with the nature of political change as such, and both do so speculatively. Herman Kahn and Anthony Wiener engage in frank speculation about the social, economic, and political changes that are likely to occur by the year 2000, and Robert Dahl extends his understanding of how change has occurred in the past to establish some principles as to how it may come about in the future. The other two articles suggest in different ways that the characteristics of American politics are such that change is very difficult to bring about. Kent Jennings and Richard Niemi show how fully political ideas are transmitted from one generation to another, and Murray Edelman argues that the myths and symbols of politics may be employed in such ways as to prevent popular attention from focusing on the tangible realities of what is being done in public affairs.

Herman Kahn and Anthony J. Wiener are social scientists at the Hudson Institute, a private research firm that undertakes studies of foreign and domestic policy problems for the United States government and other sponsors. They have published a joint book entitled *The Year 2000* (1967) and Herman Kahn has written *On Thermonuclear War* and other strategic studies.

Professor Robert A. Dahl is one of the major figures of contemporary political science. During his career at Yale University, he has published *Who Governs?* (1961), *Modern Political Analysis* (1961), and *Pluralist Democracy in the United States: Conflict and Consent* (1967).

Professors Kent Jennings and Richard Niemi are political scientists teaching at the Universities of Michigan and Rochester respectively. Jennings' books include *The Electoral Process* and *Community Influentials.*

Murray Edelman is a professor of political science at the University of Wisconsin. His major work in this area is *The Symbolic Uses of Politics* (1964).

The Next Thirty-Three Years:
A Framework for Speculation

HERMAN KAHN AND ANTHONY J. WIENER

The pace at which various technological, social, political, and economic changes are taking place has reduced the relevance of experience as a guide to public-policy judgments. Scientists, engineers, and managers who deal directly with modern technology and who are also interested in broad policy issues often overestimate the likely social consequences of technological development and go to extremes of optimism or pessimism, while those more oriented to the cultural heritage often bank too heavily on historical continuity and social inertia. The problem, of course, is to sort out what changes from what continues and to discern what is continuous in the changes themselves.

At the Hudson Institute we have used three interrelated devices to facilitate making systematic conjectures about the

future.[1] We first identify those long-term trends that seem likely to continue. These include, for example, the world-wide spread of a more or less secular humanism, the institutionalization of scientific and technological innovation, and continuous economic growth. We have, in this paper, identified a "multifold trend" consisting of thirteen interrelated elements.

We then cluster significant events by thirty-three-year intervals, starting with 1900, in order to see which combinations give rise to new clusters, to define the qualitative changes in the combination of trends, and to identify emergent properties, such as the increasing self-consciousness of time and history.

Finally, we have attempted to construct significant baselines, statistical where possible, to project key variables in soci-

[1] These and related issues are taken up in some detail in our volume for the Working Papers of the Commission, *The Next Thirty-Three Years: A Framework for Speculation,* to be published in October, 1967, by the Macmillan Company as *Toward the Year 2000: A Framework for Speculation.*

SOURCE. Reprinted from *DAEDALUS:* Journal of the American Academy of Arts and Sciences, Summer, 1967, by permission of the publisher. Copyright 1967, The American Academy of Arts and Sciences.

ety—population, literacy, Gross National Product, energy sources, military strength, and the like. These variables and their growth rates tend both to furnish and to constrain the possibilities for any society. By selecting extrapolations of current or emerging tendencies that grow continuously out of today's world and reflect the multifold trend and our current expectations, we create a "surprise-free" projection—one that seems less surprising than any other specific possibility. Consistent with this projection we describe a "standard world" and several "canonical variations" that form the likely worlds of the future.

In this paper we shall seek to illustrate these methods and to provide some brief examples of some of our conclusions.

I

THE BASIC MULTIFOLD TREND

The basic trends of Western society, most of which can be traced back hundreds of years, have a common set of sources in the rationalization and secularization of society. For analytic purposes, we shall separate these basic trends into thirteen rubrics, though obviously one might wish to group them into fewer and more abstract categories or to refine the analysis by identifying or distinguishing many more aspects. As basic trends, these elements seem very likely to continue at least for the next thirty-three years, though some may saturate or begin to recede beyond that point.

There is a basic, long-term, multifold trend toward:

1. Increasingly Senate (empirical, this-worldly, secular, humanistic, pragmatic, utilitarian, contractual, epicurean, or hedonistic) cultures
2. Bourgeois, bureaucratic, "meritocratic," democratic (and nationalistic?) elites
3. Accumulation of scientific and technological knowledge
4. Institutionalization of change, especially research, development, innovation, and diffusion

5. World-wide industrialization and modernization
6. Increasing affluence and (recently) leisure
7. Population growth
8. Decreasing importance of primary occupations
9. Urbanization and (soon) the growth of megalopolises
10. Literacy and education
11. Increased capability for mass destruction
12. Increasing tempo of change
13. Increasing universality of these trends.

Speculations about the future have ranged from the literary speculations of Jules Verne and Edward Bellamy to the humanistic and philosophical writing of Jacob Burckhardt, Arnold Toynbee, and Pitirim Sorokin. Although the observations and philosophical assumptions have differed greatly, some of the empirical observations or contentions have had much in common. Thus when Sorokin finds a circular pattern of Idealistic, Integrated, and Sensate cultures, his categories bear comparison to what Edward Gibbon noted of Rome on a more descriptive level. If both the more theoretical and the more empirical observations are treated merely as *heuristic metaphors,* regardless of their authors' divsrse intentions, they may suggest possible patterns for the future without confining one to too narrow or too rigid a view. Metaphoric and heuristic use of these concepts broadens the range of speculations; one can then pick and choose from these speculations as the evidence is developed. Nevertheless, in using concepts this way, there is an obvious risk not only of superficiality and oversimplification but also of excessive or premature commitment to some idiosyncratic view. In this paper we shall illustrate only a few elements of the multifold trend.

THE INCREASINGLY SENSATE CULTURE

The use of the term *Sensate,* derived from Pitirim Sorokin, is best explained in contrast with Sorokin's other concepts:

"Integrated" (or Idealistic), "Ideational," and "Late Sensate."[2] One can characterize Ideational art by such terms as transcendental, supersensory, religious, symbolic, allegoric, static, worshipful, anonymous, traditional, and immanent. Idealistic or Integrated art can usually be associated with such adjectives as heroic, noble, uplifting, sublime, patriotic, moralistic, beautiful, flattering, and educational, while Sensate art would be worldly, naturalistic, realistic, visual, illusionistic, everyday, amusing, interesting, erotic, satirical, novel, eclectic, syncretic, fashionable, technically superb, impressionistic, materialistic, commercial, and professional. Finally, there are tendencies toward what would be called Late Sensate, characterized as underworldly, expressing protest or revolt, over-ripe, extreme, sensation-seeking, titillating, depraved, faddish, violently novel, exhibitionistic, debased, vulgar, ugly, debunking, nihilistic, pornographic, sarcastic, or sadistic.

Sensate, of course, does not intend a connotation of sensual or sensational; a word such as *worldly, humanistic,* or *empirical* would have been equally useful for our purposes.

Within a culture there is a considerable congruence or convergence among the various parts. If, for example, a culture is Sensate in art or in systems of truth, it tends to be Sensate in systems of government and family as well. While a high culture may seem vividly defined to an outside observer and appear to be pervasive in a society, the situation may be much more complicated. For example, in Cromwellian England the majority of the people actually rejected Puritan values, although this rejection might have been almost invisible to the visitor. Values are often enforced as well as exhibited by an elite. The degree of unity and pervasiveness of any particular culture is, in fact, a crucial issue, as is the question of the importance of the visible elites as opposed to the less visible, but perhaps more influential ones. In the United States to-day, for example, there is clearly a strong split between a large grup of intellectuals and the government on many issues. Public-opinion polls seem to indicate that although these intellectuals hold a "progressive" consensus and dominate discussion in many serious journals, they are not representative of the country. In particular the high culture can be thought of as secular humanist, and the public as more religious and less humanist.

Western culture as a whole is clearly Sensate and possibly entering a Late Sensate stage. The Sensate trend goes back seven or eight centuries, but its progress has not been uninterrupted. The Reformation, the Counter-Reformation, the Puritan era in England, some aspects of the later Victorian era, and to some degree such phenomena as Stalinism, Hitlerism, and Fascism—all represented, at least at the time, currents counter to the basic trend of an increasingly Sensate culture. Nevertheless, the long-term, all-embracing Sensate trend expanded from the West and now covers virtually the entire world. Whether this will continue for the next thirty-three or sixty-six years is an open question. If the obvious implications of the description of Late Sensate culture are valid, the long-term tendencies toward Late Sensate must stabilize or even reverse if the system is not to be profoundly modified.

BOURGEOIS, BUREAUCRATIC, "MERITO-CRATIC," DEMOCRATIC (AND NATIONALISTIC?) ELITES

By *bourgeois* we mean holding economic values and ideologies of the kind that characterized the new middle classes that emerged from the breakup of feudal society—values of personal and family achievement, financial prudence, economic calculation, commercial foresight, and "business" and professional success as a moral imperative. (The emergence of "bourgeois" elites in this sense is vividly described in such works as Max Weber's *The Protestant Ethic* and R. H. Tawney's *Religion and the Rise of Capitalism.*) Though Karl Marx and Friedrich Engels

---

[2] Pitirim A. Sorokin, *Social and Cultural Dynamics,* Vol. 4 (New York, 1962), pp. 737 ff.

might have been surprised, it is now clear that these values can, and perhaps must, also be present in socialist or Communist economies, especially if they are industrialized and "revisionist." By *democratic* we mean having a popular political base; this can also be totalitarian or tyrannical in the classical sense, provided it is not merely imposed from above and that there is some economic mobility and relative equality in access to opportunity. Bureaucratic and meritocratic administrations also characterize modern industrial societies, whether capitalist or Communist.

Bourgeois democracy tends to rest on some form of "social contract" concept of the relationship between the people and their government. The people "hire" and "fire" their governments, and no group has theocratic (Ideational) or aristocratic (Integrated) claims on the government. Clearly, democratic government is also an expression of democratic ideologiy—it is sustained by the idea of the consent of the governed. The idea is contractual; and the factors of sacredness, occultness, or charisma are restricted.

Nationalistic values are also associated with the rise of the middle class. Kings used nationalism to gain allies among the middle class against the nobles, the church, the emperor, or enemy states. The nationalist idea later involved a recognition that the people (the nation) have the contractual right to government of (and by) their own kind and eventually to self-government—or that the right to govern has to be justified as representing the will of the people and serving the general welfare. Even the totalitarian nationalism of Mussolini, Hitler, Stalin, and the Japanese officer corps usually made its basic appeal to and found its greatest response in the middle class (or, in the case of the Japanese, the agrarian middle class).

One can argue that the long-term nationalist trend is on the decline today, at least in what might be thought of as the NATO area, though this remains in many ways an open issue. (The West European nations could conceivably become more nationalist in the future, and a European political community might emerge that would be nationalist in the sense that "Europe" becomes the "nation.") In any case, Late Sensate culture carries implications of cosmopolitanism and pacifism and lack of particularist ethics or loyalties, except on a shifting, contractual basis. Nevertheless, it is probably safe to argue that over the next thirty-three years nationalism will increase in most of the underdeveloped and developing worlds, at least in the minimal sense that modern systems of public education and mass communication will integrate even the most peripheral groups into the common language and culture.

SCIENCE AND TECHNOLOGY

In order to provide a quick impression of science and technology (with an emphasis on technology) in the last third of the twentieth century, we list one hundred areas in which technological innovation will almost certainly occur.

Each item is important enough to make, by itself, a significant change. The difference might lie mainly in being spectacular (for example, transoceanic rocket transportation in twenty or thirty minutes, rather than supersonic in two or three hours); in being ubiquitous (widespread use of paper clothes); in enabling a large number of different things to be done (super materials); in effecting a general and significant increase in productivity (cybernation); or simply in being important to specific individuals (convenient artificial kidney). It could be argued reasonably that each of these warrants the description technological innovation, revolution, or breakthrough. None is merely an obvious minor improvement on what currently exists.

We should note that the one hundred areas are not ordered randomly. Most people would consider the first twenty-five unambiguous examples of progress. A few would question even these, since lasers and masers, for example, might make possible a particularly effective ballistic missile defense and, thus, accelerate the Soviet-American arms race. Similarly, the expansion of tropical agriculture and forestry could mean a geographical shift in economic and military power, as well as a dislocation of competitive industries. Nevertheless, there probably would be a consensus among readers that the first twenty-five areas do represent progress—at least for those who are in favor of "progress."

The next twenty-five areas are clearly controversial; many would argue that government policy might better restrain or discourage innovation or diffusion here. These "controversial areas" raise issues of accelerated nuclear proliferation, loss of privacy, excessive governmental or private power over individuals, dangerously vulnerable, deceptive, and degradable overcentralization, inherently dangerous new capabilities, change too cataclysmic for smooth adjustment, or decisions that are inescapable, yet at the same time too complex and far-reaching to be safely trusted to anyone's indivdual or collective judgment.

The last fifty items are included because they are intrinsically interesting and to demonstrate that a list of one hundred items of "almost certain" and "very significant" innovation can be produced fairly easily.[3]

One-hundred technical innovations likely in the next thirty-three years:

1. Multiple applications of lasers and masers for sensing, measuring, communicating, cutting, heating, welding, power transmission, illumination, destructive (defensive), and other purposes
2. Extremely high-strentgh or high-temperature structural materials
3. New or improved super-performance fabrics (papers, fibers, and plastics)
4. New or improved materials for equipment and appliances (plastics, glasses, alloys, ceramics, intermetallics, and cermets)
5. New airborne vehicles (ground-effect machines, VTOL and STOL, super-

helicopters, giant supersonic jets)
6. Extensive commercial application of shaped charges
7. More reliable and longer-range weather forecasting
8. Intensive or extensive expansion of tropical agriculture and forestry
9. New sources of power for fixed installations (for example, magneto-hydrodynamic, thermionic, and thermoelectric, radioactive)
10. New sources of power for ground transportation (storage-battery, fuel-cell propulsion or support by electromagnetic fields, jet engine, turbine)
11. Extensive and intensive world-wide use of high-altitude cameras for mapping, prospecting, census, land use, and geological investigations
12. New methods of water transportation (large submarines, flexible and special-purpose "container ships," more extensive use of large automated single-purpose bulk cargo ships)
13. Major reduction in hereditary and congenital defects
14. Extensive use of cyborg techniques (mechanical aids or substitutes for human organs, sense, limbs)
15. New techniques for preserving or improving the environment
16. Relatively effective appetite and weight control
17. New techniques in adult education
18. New improved plants and animals
19. Human "hibernation" for short periods (hours or days) for medical purposes
20. Inexpensive "one of a kind" design and procurement through use of computerized analysis and automated production
21. Controlled super-effective relaxation and sleep
22. More sophisticated architectural engineering (geodesic domes, thin shells, pressurized skins, esoteric materials)
23. New or improved uses of the oceans (mining, extraction of minerals, controlled "farming," source of energy)
24. Three-dimensional photography, illustrations, movies, and television

---

[3] In compiling this list we have received useful suggestions from Jane Kahn, John Menke, Robert Prehoda, and G. Harry Stine.

25. Automated or more mechanized housekeeping and home maintenance

26. Widespread use of nuclear reactors for power

27. Use of nuclear explosives for excavation and mining, generation of power, creation of high-temperature/high-pressure environments, or for a source of neutrons or other radiation

28. General use of automation and cybernation in management and production

29. Extensive and intensive centralization (or automatic interconnection) of current and past personal and business information in high-speed data processors

30. Other new and possibly pervasive techniques for surveillance, monitoring, and control of indivduals and organizations

31. Some control of weather or climate

32. Other (permanent or temporary) changes or experiments with the over-all environment (for example, the "permanent" increase in C-14 and temporary creation of other radioactivity by nuclear explosions, the increasing generation of CO_2 in the atmosphere, projects Starfire, West Ford, Storm Fury, and so forth)

33. New and more reliable "education" and propaganda techniques for affecting human behavior—public and private

34. Practical use of direct electronic communication with and stimulation of the brain

35. Human hibernation for relatively extensive periods (months to years)

36. Cheap and widely available or excessively destructive central war weapons and weapons systems

37. New and relatively effective counterinsurgency techniques (and perhaps also insurgency techniques)

38. New kinds of very cheap, convenient, and reliable birth-control techniques

39. New, more varied, and more reliable drugs for control of fatigue, relaxation, alertness, mood, personality, perceptions, and fantasies

40. Capability to choose the sex of unborn children

41. Improved capability to "change" sex

42. Other genetic control or influence over the "basic constitution" of an individual

43. New techniques in the education of children

44. General and substantial increase in life expectancy, postponement of aging, and limited rejuvenation

45. Generally acceptable and competitive synthetic foods and beverages (carbohydrates, fats, proteins, enzymes, vitamins, coffee, tea, cocoa, liquor)

46. "High quality" medical care for underdeveloped areas (for example, use of referral hospitals, broad-spectrum antibiotics, artificial blood plasma)

47. Design and extensive use of responsive and super-controlled environments for private and public use (for pleasurable, educational, and vocational purposes)

48. "Nonharmful" methods of "overindulging"

49. Simple techniques for extensive and "permanent" cosmetological changes (features, "figures," perhaps complexion, skin color, even physique)

50. More extensive use of transplantation of human organs

51. Permanent manned satellite and lunar installations—interplanetary travel

52. Application of space life systems or similar techniques to terrestrial installations

53. Permanent inhabited undersea installations and perhaps even colonies

54. Automated grocery and department stores

55. Extensive use of robots and machines "slaved" to humans

56. New uses of underground tunnels for private and public transportation

57. Automated universal (real time) credit, audit, and banking systems

58. Chemical methods for improved memory and learning

59. Greater use of underground buildings

60. New and improved materials and

equipment for buildings and interiors (variable transmission glass, heating and cooling by thermoelectric effect, electro-luminescent and phosphorescent lighting)

61. Widespread use of cryogenics

62. Improved chemical control of some mental illness and some aspects of senility

63. Mechanical and chemical methods for improving human analytical ability more or less directly

64. Inexpensive and rapid techniques for making tunnels and underground cavities in earth or rock

65. Major improvements in earth moving and construction equipment generally

66. New techniques for keeping physically fit or acquiring physical skills

67. Commercial extraction of oil from shale

68. Recoverable boosters for economic space launching

69. Individual flying platforms

70. Simple inexpensive video recording and playing

71. Inexpensive high-capacity, worldwide, regional, and local (home and business) communication (using satellites, lasers, light pipes, and so forth)

72. Practical home and business use of "wired" video communication for both telephone and television (possibly including retrieval of taped material from libraries or other sources) and rapid transmission and reception of facsimiles (possibly including news, library material, commercial announcements, instantaneous mail delivery, other printouts)

73. Practical large-scale desalinization

74. Pervasive business use of computers for the storage, processing, and retrieval of information

75. Shared-time (public and interconnected) computers generally available to home and business on a metered basis

76. Other widespread use of computers for intellectual and professional assistance (translation, teaching, literary research, medical diagnosis, traffic control, crime detection, computation, design, analysis, and, to some degree, as a general intellectual collaborator)

77. General availability of inexpensive transuranic and other esoteric elements

78. Space defense systems

79. Inexpensive and reasonably effective ground-based ballistic missile defense

80. Very low-cost buildings for home and business use

81. Personal "pagers" (perhaps even two-way pocket phones) and other personal electronic equipment for communication, computing, and data-processing

82. Direct broadcasts from satellites to home receivers

83. Inexpensive (less than $20), long-lasting, very small, battery-operated television receivers

84. Home computers to "run" the household and communicate with outside world

85. Maintenance-free long-life electronic and other equipment

86. Home education via video and computerized and programmed learning

87. Programmed dreams

88. Inexpensive (less than 1 cent a page) rapid, high-quality black and white reproduction; followed by colored, highly detailed photography reproduction

89. Widespread use of improved fluid amplifiers

90. Conference television (both closed-circuit and public communication systems)

91. Flexible penology without necessarily using prisons (by use of modern methods of surveillance, monitoring, and control)

92. Common use of individual power source for lights, appliances, and machines

93. Inexpensive world-wide transportation of humans and cargo

94. Inexpensive road-free (and facility-free) transportation

95. New methods for teaching languages rapidly

96. Extensive genetic control for plants and animals

97. New biological and chemical methods to identify, trace, incapacitate, or annoy people for police and military uses

98. New and possibly very simple methods for lethal biological and chemical warfare

99. Artificial moons and other methods of lighting large areas at night

100. Extensive use of "biological processes" in the extraction and processing of minerals

WORLD-WIDE INDUSTRIALIZATION, AFFLUENCE, AND POPULATION GROWTH

Many people—Kenneth Boulding, Peter Drucker, and John Maynard Keynes, for example—have pointed out that until the last two or three centuries no large human society had ever produced more than the equivalent of $200 per capita annually. With industrialization, mankind broke out of this pattern. By the end of this century, we expect that the nations of the world might be divided into the following five classes:

1. Preindustrial $50 to $200 per capita
2. Partially indus- $200 to $600 per trialized or   capita transitional
3. Industrial $600 to perhaps $1,500 per capita
4. Mass-consump-   Perhaps $1,500 to tion or advanced   something more than industrial $5,000 per capita
5. Postindustrial   Something over $4,000 to $16,000 per capita

We shall consider partially industrialized societies as being in a transition stage, without assuming that they will necessarily continue to industrialize. Those countries we call industrialized are roughly in the condition of interwar America or postwar Europe.

Many preindustrial or partially industrialized societies may also, of course, have dual economies—for example, northern and southern Italy. This problem, now defined in terms of urban and rural differences, may, by the year 2000, be most critical in the six most populous, least developed countries: China, India, Pakistan, Indonesia, Brazil, and Nigeria. These now contain, and in the future will probably continue to contain, about half of the world's population; they are now preindustrial, but presumably will be partially industrialized by the end of the century.

Problems caused by great development in major cities and less in lesser cities and rural areas are already evident in these countries. Despite important differences in average development, one can argue that most great cities today have achieved startlingly similar conditions of modernization, and are at least "twentieth century." Rio de Janeiro, Bangkok, and Athens have many of the virtues and problems of the major cities of the United States: twentieth-century slums, computers, labor displaced by automation, great universities, skilled craftsmen, a trend toward tertiary and quaternary occupations, startlingly similar price structures for many commodities and activities.

The post-World War II period has seen the emergence of the mass-consumption society, first in the United States and then in Western Europe and Japan. Japan, although it has less than $1,000 per capita, is by every superficial appearance a mass-consumption society today, while the Soviet Union, with a per-capita income of around $1,500, seems far short of that condition. Similarly $4,000 per capita will probably be sufficient for transition to a postindustrial economy for the Scandinavian countries or Great Britain, while countries with more ambitious goals in terms of world power (the U.S.S.R.), stronger traditions of economic striving (West Germany), or higher expectations of productive affluence (the U.S.) will not become postindustrial until higher levels of affluence have been reached.

The chart below (Table 1) indicates a rather impressionistic, but not wholly unreasonable economic ranking for the nations of the world in the year 2000. The figures express national populations in millions, and the total world population is estimated at 6.4 billion. On the whole, the descriptions are optimistic, but we would not care to defend in detail the specific rank order we have suggested. The numbers of identifying each group

TABLE 1. ECONOMIC GROUPINGS IN THE STANDARD WORLD

(5) Visibly Postindustrial		(3) Mature Industrial	
U.S.	320	¼ of Latin America	150
Japan	120	⅓ of Arab World	100
Canada	40	½ of E. & S.E. Asia	200
Scandinavia & Switzerland	25	Miscellaneous	50
France, W. Germany, Benelux,			———
Great Britain	215		500
	———		
	720	(2) Large & Partially Industrialized	
(5) Early Postindustrial		Brazil	200
		Pakistan	230
Italy	60	China	1,300
Soviet Union	350	India	1,000
E. Germany, Poland,		Indonesia	220
Czechoslovakia	135	Nigeria	150
Israel	5		———
Australia, New Zealand	25		3,100
	———		
	575	(1&2) Preindustrial or Small &	
		Partially Industrialized	
(4) Mass-Consumption			
		Rest of Africa	350
Spain, Portugal, Austria, Yugo-		⅔ Arab World	200
slavia, Albania, Greece,		Rest of Asia	160
Bulgaria, Hungary, Ireland	125	Rest of Latin America	40
Turkey	75		———
Mexico, Argentina, Colombia,			750
Venezuela, Chile	300		
Taiwan, S. Korea, Hong Kong,			
Malaysia, etc.	120		
	———		
	620		

correspond roughly to the levels of income of the previous table.

If this scenario is realized, the year 2000 will find a rather large island of wealth surrounded by "misery"—at least relative to the developed world and to "rising expectations." But even the poor countries will, for the most part, enjoy great improvements over their traditional standards of living. The postindustrial and industrial societies will contain about 40 per cent of the world's population, and more than 90 per cent of the world's population will live in nations that have broken out of the historical $50-$200 per-capita range. Yet at the same time the absolute gap in living standards between countries or sectors of countries with developed economies and those at preindustrial levels will have widened abysmally.

URBANIZATION, LITERACY, AND EDUCATION

The United States in the year 2000 will probably see at least three gargantuan megalopolises. We have labeled these—only half-frivolously—"Boswash," "Chipitts," and "Sansan." Boswash identifies the megalopolis that will extend from Washington to Boston and contain almost one quarter of the American population (something under 80 million people). Chipitts, concentrated around the Great Lakes, may stretch from Chicago to

Pittsburgh and north to Canada—thereby including Detroit, Toledo, Cleveland, Akron, Buffalo, and Rochester. This megalopolis seems likely to contain more than one eighth of the U.S. population (perhaps 40 million people or more). Sansan, a Pacific megalopolis that will presumably stretch from Santa Barbara (or even San Francisco) to San Diego, should contain more than one sixteenth of the population (perhaps 20 million people or more). These megalopolises will all be maritime. Boswash is on an extremely narrow strip of the North Atlantic coast; Chipitts, on Lake Erie and the southern and western shores of Lake Michigan and Lake Ontario; Sansan, on an even more narrow strip on the West Coast.

While all three will be recognizably American in culture, they will most likely be quite distinguishable sub-cultures. Sansan will presumably provide an informal "Bar-B-Q" culture, which has sometimes been called "wholesome degeneracy," and will include large and self-conscious, alienated, New Left, "hip," and bohemian groups. Chipitts, recently the site of successful architectural and urban-renewal programs, will probably still have traces of both the "Bible belt" and Carl Sandburg's "raw and lusty vitality." Boswash will, of course, be "cosmopolitan"—the home of New York liberals, Boston bankers, tired or creative intellectuals in publishing, entertainment, and the arts, and political Washington.

The three megalopolises should contain roughly one half of the total United States population, including the overwhelming majority of the most technologically and scientifically advanced, and prosperous intellectual and creative elements. Even Sansan will have a larger total income than all but five or six nations. Study of the United States in the year 2000 may largely be of Boswash, Chipitts, and Sansan.

Such structures will be typical of other countries as well. Thus, most of southeastern England is likely to be one megalopolis, though in this case it may be called a conurbation. The Japanese will

no doubt coin or borrow a word for the Tokyo-Osaka strip. Nevertheless, although between 80 and 90 per cent of the developed world's population will be urbanized by the end of the century, most people will still live in more traditional urban areas. Suburbia, then as now, will be a special kind of low-density urban living, quite different from rural patterns.

DECREASING IMPORTANCE OF PRIMARY OCCUPATIONS

Closely related to current trends toward very large urban agglomerations are the declining importance of primary and secondary occupations, and the growing importance of what are normally called tertiary occupations, though we shall distinguish between tertiary and quaternary occupations. (The primary occupations are, of course, fishing, forestry, hunting, agriculture, and mining. Secondary occupations are concerned with processing the products of a primary occupation. A tertiary occupation is a service rendered mostly to primary and secondary occupations. Quaternary occupations render services mostly to tertiary occupations or to one another.) There will undoubtedly be a large shift to quaternary occupations. Since these occupations are heavily concentrated in the government, the professions, the nonprofit private groups, and the like, this implies—in conjunction with other things—a shift from the private business enterprise as the major source of innovation, attention, and prominence in society. The lessening emphasis on primary occupations will be accompanied by a lessened dependence on access to inexpensive or convenient raw materials (rather than a situation of desperate shortages of usable or available raw materials). This, in turn, will make many factors of geography and location less crucial for the nation as a whole.

SOME PERSPECTIVES ON CHANGE

A second way of looking at the future is to identify the relevant clusters of events that have marked off different time periods in man's history. One can thus seek to identify the constants of each time, the secular trend lines, and the "turning points" of an era. For our purpose we begin by considering what a "surprise-free" projection might have been like in 1900 or 1933.

The year 1900

One world (Western dominated), though with many unassimilated, traditional cultures

Industrial, colonial, or "protected" societies

Declining United Kingdom and Franco—rising Germany, United States, Russia, and Japan

Parliamentary government and Christianity

Basic feeling in almost all classes of the white race (and in many nonwhite) of optimism, security, progress, order; a belief in the physical and moral supremacy of Western culture, and in rational and moral domestic and foreign politics; and, perhaps most important of all, a relative absence of guilt feelings

Intellectual acceptance of the ideas of Adam Smith, Darwin, and the Enlightenment.

It is interesting to note that the only two non-Western countries that had successfully begun to industrialize by 1900, Japan and Russia, did so more to serve their national security than to increase their standard of living. Except possibly for Turkey, Iran, Thailand, Ethiopia, and some Latin American countries, every nation that had failed to industrialize by 1900 was either a colony, a protectorate, or a *de facto* dependency. Thus, successfully industrialization was widely perceived as a matter of national independence, if not of national survival. Today these incentives are greatly reduced.

In 1900 it was clear that the two established powers of Western Europe—Great Britain and France—were losing in power relative to Germany, the United States, Japan, and Russia. One can think of Britain and France as "core" powers of the West, Germany (or at least Prussianized Germany) as "semiperipheral," the United States as "fully peripheral,"

and Russia and Japan as either fully peripheral or new "mixtures."

The Parliamentary ideal was widely accepted, and Christianity was almost everywhere triumphant or on the rise in 1900. National self-satisfaction, optimism, and faith in the future of most Western or Westernized people are, to modern eyes, perhaps the most striking characteristics of the year 1900—and ones which were soon to disappear in the tragic futilities of World War I and its aftermath.

The period 1900-1933

The first third of the twentieth century brought some surprises:

Russo-Japanese War

La Belle Epoque (1901-1913)

World War I (Europe devastated)

Five major dynasties (Hohenzollern, Hapsburg, Manchu, Romanov, and Ottoman) dethroned

Emergence of the United States as leading world power

Loss of European (and democratic) morale and prestige

Rise of Communism and the Soviet Union

Great Depression

Rise of Fascist ideologies and various dictatorships

Impact of new intellectual concepts (those of Bohr, de Broglie, Einstein, Freud, and Schroedinger)

The period 1933-1966

The next third of a century experienced still more unexpected changes and disturbing events:

Continued growth of Fascism and Communism

World War II—Europe again devastated

Mass murders and forced population movements on extraordinary scale before, during, and after World War II

Intense, nationalistic competition in the development and application of radically new technologies for peace and war

Decolonization

The Cold War and neutralism in the Third World

Emergence of two super-powers (U.S. and Soviet Union); five large powers (Japan, West Germany, France, China, United Kingdom); three intermediate powers (India, Italy, Canada)

Rise and decline of Italy, Canada and India

Decline and re-emergence of Europe

Decline and re-emergence of Japan

Reunification and centralization of China

Post-Keynesian, post-Marxian, and perhaps postcommunal and sophisticated "development" economics

Emergence of mass-consumption societies

"Second" industrial revolution

Chinese achieve nuclear status.

In looking at this sixty-six-year kaleidoscope, an Indian national is quoted as saying:

> For us in Asia there have been two epochal events in this century. The first was Japan's defeat of Russia in 1905. The second was China's atom bomb. . . . Asia and India are learning the uses of power in the modern world. The first lesson was taught by Japan in 1905. It demonstrated that an Asian country could master the West's weapons and use them to defeat the West. The second lesson was taught by China. It demonstrated that Asia could equal the West even in advanced military technology.[4]

To Asia—or some Asians—the century began with a nonwhite nation's successfully beating a white nation on its own ground, thus proving that Europe's supremacy was not necessarily permanent, and the second third of the century ended with the acquisition of nuclear weapons by a nonwhite nation. Both of these events were thought at the time to be of crucial and world-wide significance. It is said that during the first decade of the century there were Africans who did not know what Russia and Japan were, and yet knew that a nonwhite people had defeated a white nation.

[4] As quoted by Harrison E. Salisbury in *The New York Times*, August 18, 1966.

Most of these items would probably not have been predicted by any individual or policy research group "speculating about the next thirty-three years" in either 1900 or 1933. Probably the great divide was World War I. Preceded by the thirteen years that are still known as *la belle epoque,* these years were, for almost all the civilized world, an unprecedented era of sustained growth. While some of the period's glory has been dimmed by the passing of time and comparison with the post-World War II era of growth, the years are still remembered nostalgically. Not only did World War I terminate *la belle epoque,* but it shattered the moral and political structure of Europe. The effective triumph of democracy over despotism (or at least unenlightened monarchy) might have created a situation of high morale, but the cost of the war had been too high— particularly the seeming senselessness of many of the tactics, the moral effect of various revisionist and antiwar writers, and the disillusionment with the postwar settlement. The loss of European morale and prestige following 1918 was both grave and world-wide. The pessimism that seized the West was reflected in the popularity of such an author as Spengler. Although many Europeans expected the Russians or Asians to succeed to the West's power, an aberrant of Western culture, Nazism, came perilously close to conquering all of Europe. While Fascism and Nazism are no doubt heretical to the Western tradition, they are products of Western culture and result from identifiable and historically continuous religious, ideological, cultural, and structural forces within Western societies—trends that were emphasized by the pessimism and frustration that resulted from World War I.

Despite the widespread belief that poverty creates instability and messianic totalitarian movements such as Communism and Fascism, the four nations closest to catching up with or passing the advanced industrial powers—Japan, Russia,[5] Germany, and Italy—provided the serious instability of the first half of this century. This may turn out to be the prototype of some possibilities in the next sixty-six years as well. While poverty and preindustrial economies are not themselves indicia of stability, neither is industrialization or Westernization.

In the first third of the century, many new theories were, at least intellectually, profoundly upsetting. The self-assured, rationalistic, moralistic, and mechanically-minded Victorians were told, in effect, that solid matter is mostly empty; that time is relative and that perfectly accurate clocks run at different speeds; that the world is governed by the probabilistic laws of wave mechanics, rather than by simple deterministic "cause and effect" as suggested by Newtonian Mechanics[6]; and, finally, that a good deal of what passes for rational behavior is actually motivated by unconscious impulses and feelings of a socially unacceptable or reprehensible character. What is most striking is that these radical shifts in *Weltanschauung* were managed with so little disruption.

Perhaps the most significant aspect of the middle third of the twentieth century has been the sustained economic growth achieved in the post-World War II era. This has raised the real possibility of world-wide industrialization and of the emergence in more advanced industrial nations of what has been called a post-industrial culture. Some of this economic growth clearly derives from a growing sophistication in governmental economic

policies. As even the "classical" economist Milton Friedman recently said, "We are all Keynesians today, and we are all post-Keynesians as well." If this were not true, and the postwar world had been marked by the same violent swings between prosperity and depression as the interwar world, we would not now take such a sanguine view of future economic prospects. Today it is widely believed that, except possibly for China, almost all the Communist and capitalist governments are coming to understand how to keep their economies reasonably stable and growing; both the capitalists and their Marxists are, in this sense, "revisionist."

While we reject the so-called convergence theory, in which it is argued that Communism and capitalism will come to resemble each other so closely that they will be practically indistinguishable, it is clear that they are borrowing from each other—with the Marxists, however, doing more of the explicit borrowing. The current governmental success in economics and planning is a major cause of the emergence of mass-consumption societies in Western Europe, the United States, Japan, and Australia, and is one reason why such societies can be expected to emerge rapidly in the Soviet Union and Eastern Europe.

It is still an open question, however, whether the same thing can be achieved in communal societies (such as China is striving to be) and in the less developed nations generally. But at least two groups of less developed nations are now doing so well economically that it is reasonable to think of them as undergoing a kind of "second" industrial revolution. Thus, those parts of Europe that were left behind by the industrial revolution, or which were "transplanted," are now beginning to catch up.

Even more impressive are the growth rates rates in the Sinic cultures of the world outside China (including Malaysia and perhaps the Philippines, but possibly not Thailand). These countries seem able to sustain growth rates of about 8 per cent, except for the Philippines with 5 per cent. Wherever the Chinese and their

---

[5] From 1890 to 1914 (except for the years of the Russo-Japanese War—1904 and 1905), Russia grew in GNP at an average rate of 8 per cent and was thus, in some ways, undergoing a very successful industrialization.

[6] Of course, many physicists now believe that the world is deterministic, but that there are unknowable "hidden variables." In the early days of quantum mechanics and the uncertainty principle, however, many philosophers seized upon the latter as allowing for, or being identical with, free will and thus providing a belated and unexpected answer to the mechanists and determinists of the eighteenth and nineteenth centuries.

culture have gone in the world, they have done well, except in China. Until about 1800, China was, except for periodic interregna, an eminent culture in the world. It may once again be coming out of an interregnum, but whether or not it will achieve its "normal" status must now be judged unlikely or at best an open question.

The second third of the twentieth century ended with two superpowers, five large powers, three intermediate powers, and about 120 small powers. This structure and hierarchy seems likely to characterize the next decade or two as well. In fact, listing Japan and West Germany as the two largest of the five "large" powers is even more appropriate for the mid-seventies than for today.

The last third of the Twentieth Century
Continuation of long-term multifold trend
Emergence of postindustrial society
World-wide capability for modern technology
Need for world-wide zoning ordinances and other restraints
High (1 to 10 per cent) growth rates in GNP per capita
Increasing emphasis on "meaning and purpose"
Much turmoil in the "new" and possibly in the industrializing nations
Some possibility for sustained "nativist," messianic, or other mass movements
Second rise of Japan
Some further rise of Europe and China
Emergence of new intermediate powers: Brazil, Mexico, Pakistan, Indonesia, East Germany, Egypt
Some decline (relative of U.S. and Soviet Union)
A possible absence of stark "life and death" political and economic issues in the "old nations."

Except for the possible emergence of what we call, following Daniel Bell, the postindustrial society,[7] the listing is "sur-

[7] For a discussion of some features of the postindustrial society as Daniel Bell has used the term, see his "Notes on the Post-Industrial Society," *The Public Interest*,

prise-free": It assumes the continuation of the multifold trend, but excludes precisely the kinds of dramatic or surprising events that dominated the first two thirds of the century. More specifically, the "surprise-free" projection rules out *major changes in the old nations* that might be caused by such possibilities as invasion and war; civil strife and revolution; famine and pestilence; despotism (persecution) and natural disaster; depression or economic stagnation; the development of "inexpensive" doomsday or near-doomsday machines and nuclear "six-gun" weapons technology; resurgence of Communism or a revival of Fascism along with a racial, North-South, rich-poor, East-West dichotomy; an economically dynamic China, with 10 per cent annual growth rate, and a politically dynamic U. S., Soviet Union, Japan, or Brazil; development of the U.S. or other world-wide organizations, and possible regional or other multinational organizations; new religious philosophies or other mass movements, and a psychologically upsetting impact of the new techniques, ideas, and philosophies.

If the basic long-term multifold trend continues or is accelerated during the next thirty-three years, and there are no surprising but not-impossible disruptions of the sort listed above, then a postindustrial society seems likely to develop in the affluent parts of the world.

In a postindustrial world, per-capita income is about fifty times that in a pre-industrial society. Most "economic" activities are tertiary and quaternary rather than primary or secondary; business firms are, consequently, no longer the major source of innovation. There is an effective floor on income and welfare, and efficiency is not a primary consideration. There is widespread cybernation, a typical "doubling time" for social change of three to thirty years, and a common technological foundation for a world society. Work-oriented, achievement-oriented, advancement-oriented values and

Numbers 6 and 7 (Winter and Spring, 1967).

"national interest" values erode, and Sensate, secular, humanistic, perhaps self-indulgent, criteria become central, as do the intellectual institutions. Continuing education is widespread, and there is rapid improvement in educational techniques.

III

THE STANDARD WORLD AND ITS CANONICAL VARIATIONS

So far, we have been dealing with trends or clusters of "traits." To make any significant assumptions, we would want to combine the most likely predictions into a more or less coherent whole and specify them in more detail. This we would call our least improbable "alternative future," or our "Standard World."

One problem of long-range speculation is that the curve of probabilities often seems very flat—that is, no particular course of events seems more likely than another. In order to avoid the dilemma of Buridan's ass, we must make almost arbitrary choices among equally interesting, important, and plausible possibilities. If we are to explore any predictions at all, we must to some extent "make them up." The most salient of the projections we can make is one that is "surprise-free"; nevertheless it would be very surprising if in any thirty-three-year period the real world did not produce many political and technological surprises.

For the skeptical reader this "surprise-free" projection may be useful chiefly as a norm for comparison and disagreement. Although the "surprise-free" projection is similar in spirit to the "naive projection" of the economist, which assumes a continuation of current tendencies, it is more complex because it includes the implications of whatever empirical and theoretical considerations affect current expectations. (For example, a "naive" projection of world population to 2000 would be about 7.2 billion, but our "surprise-free" projection would be 6.4 billion.)

Each of the major alternatives to the Standard World that we have constructed fits into one of three categories: more "integrated," more "inward-looking," or in greater "disarray." The models in these categories envisage, respectively:

1. A relatively peaceful, relatively prosperous world with a relatively high degree of consultation among nations, with arms control and political co-ordination or even integration among all, or almost all, the "major" or minor powers.

2. Almost as peaceful and prosperous a world but with little arms control or general co-ordination.

3. A relatively troubled and violent world, but one in which no large central wars have occurred.

The following are eight canonical variations:

I. More integrated
    A. Stability-oriented
    B. Development-oriented

II. More inward-looking
    A. With an eroded Communist movement
    B. With an eroded democratic morale and some Communist dynamism
    C. With a dynamic Europe or Japan

III. Greater disarray
    A. With an eroded Communist movement
    B. With a dynamic Communist movement and some erosion of democratic morale
    C. With a dynamic Europe or Japan

By focusing attention on each of the above possibilities in turn, we get a sense of comparative structures and of a range of possibilities, while remaining within or fairly close to the "surprise-free" projections. Yet it should be clear that only a Procrustean theory could attempt to define the next ten to fifteen years (much less the next thirty-three) in terms of such single themes. The reality undoubtedly will be one in which one theme alternates with another, or in which there is a dialectical contention among political trends or open conflict. But for our standardized and canonical contexts (and for some but not all of the scenarios that illustrate them) we assume that there is little fluctuation from simple secular trends.

In these projections we assume that the ten major powers (which we have divided into the categories "super," "large," and "intermediate") develop more or less according to the figure below. One might have wanted to assume that the "Integrated World" develops more rapidly and with smaller disparities in income than the "Inward-Looking World," and that this in turn develops more rapidly than the "Disarray World." While this is reasonable, it is not by any means inevitable.

Figure 1 shows how the ten largest nations compared in GNP and population

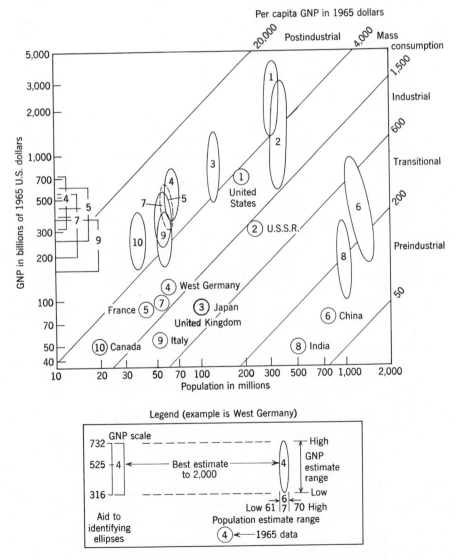

Figure 1. "Surprise-free" projections for the ten major countries.

in 1965 (numerals in circles), and the points they seem most likely to reach by the year 2000 (numerals in ellipses). The numerals identifying each country are in the order of our "best estimate" for 2000 GNP, although the differences among Canada, Italy, and India are not significant. The ellipses indicate a range of reasonable uncertainty for each year-2000 projection. In 1965, for example, the U.S. had a GNP of about $692 billion (by U.N. definition), a population of about 195 million, and a per-capita GNP of about $3,560. By the year 2000, its GNP could reach nearly $4,000 billion (almost the top of the chart) with more than $15,000 per-capita GNP; or, assuming a much lower growth rate, the GNP could be less than $1,500 billion and GNP per capita under $5,000. The range in population estimates is narrower. Our "best estimate" is for a GNP close to the top of the "reasonable range" and for a relatively moderate population growth. (Our report contains more detailed figures.) The ellipses for India and China slope backward because they are more likely to achieve relatively high GNP growth if they can limit population. We have labeled the GNP per-capita groups in terms of the classes discussed above.

Finally, we separate the 135 nations of the world into two classes—"old" (about 55) and "new" (about 80). "Old" nations are those that have had a relatively continuous existence at least since World War I; "new" nations are for the most part post-World War II creations or ancient countries recently emerged from colonial status. (Thus we consider West Germany to be an old nation; East Germany and China, newly integrated; Taiwan and India, newly independent; Egypt, new.) We assume—again in all worlds, and for the 1967-2000 period as a whole—the fulfillment of certain widespread current expectations of more or less sustained economic growth among all the major (and most minor) nations, and more or less sustained (but usually slackening) population growth. We also assume that except in periods of actual war or great crisis there will be freedom

of the seas, with foreign commerce moving freely without explicit reliance on national naval or other military power. We assume that there will be few and minor frontier changes, if any, in the old nations, chiefly because of general conditions of political stability or inertia rather than because of the balance—or lack of balance—of local military situations. We assume that most of the old nations will not be called on to use military power to advance their national interests—at least in any simple or direct way. Obviously nations may nonetheless experience benefits (or disutilities) from military power—for example, from their ability implicitly or explicitly to protect (or threaten) various other nations. Some small nations may obtain security benefits (or disutilities) from having sizable national military forces—for example, from being a more valuable ally or feeling freer to accept or reject offers of protection by larger nations. But by and large, for *most* of the old nations and many of the new, national security is assumed to be "free"—derived from the general condition of stability rather than from a nation's own efforts.

Of course, this stability, if it exists or is to continue, will be maintained in part by the willingness of various nations, especially the U.S. and the U.S.S.R., to intervene judiciously when situations arise that threaten the general equilibrium. Presumably the balance could be tipped by one of these nations trying either too hard or not hard enough—by intervening too readily in an attempt to control events or by failing to check forces tending to instability.

To go beyond the year 2000, we can speculate briefly on world society in the first third of the next century. We expect the rise of new great powers—perhaps Japan, China, a European complex, Brazil, Mexico, or India. There will be new political, perhaps even "philosophical", issues, and a leveling-off or diminishing of some aspects of the basic long-term multifold trend, such as urbanization. The postindustrial and industrial worlds will have been largely realized, as will population control, arms control, and some kind of moderately stable international security arrangement, though probably not a "world government." In the industrializing world, disorder, ideology, and irrational movements will probably continue to play disruptive, though geographically confined roles. In the U.S. and Western Europe, there will presumably be either a return to certain Hellenic or older European concepts of the good life, or an intensified alienation and search for identity, values, meaning, and purpose, a search made necessary and facilitated by the unprecedented affluence and permissiveness of the postindustrial economy.

Conflict and Conciliation

ROBERT DAHL

STABILITY AND CHANGE

Not so very long ago democracy was viewed almost everywhere as a radical, even revolutionary, system of government. A political system in which the national government is chosen by means of free elections in which most adult male citizens are entitled to vote and where political parties are actively competing for votes—this kind of system is a twentieth-century achievement. In most the constitutional democracies of the present day—Britain and Sweden, for examples—manhood suffrage was significantly restricted until the time of the First World War. (Women were excluded from voting in national elections in the United States, as nearly everywhere else, until 1919; in Switzerland, that paragon of stable democracy, women still have no right of suffrage under the federal constitution, though some cantons have granted it.) During most or all of the nineteenth century, many countries that are now constitutional democracies were

SOURCE. Reprinted from *Pluralist Democracy in the United States: Conflict and Consent,* by permission of the author and publisher, Rand McNally & Co. Copyright 1967, Rand McNally & Co.

oligarchies in which power was constitutionally lodged in the hands of a few—for example, Germany, Italy, Austria, and until the advent of the Third Republic in 1874, France.

In the period between the world wars, as the constitutional democracies were endangered by new revolutionary movements—Communism, Fascism, Nazism—the view that democracy is a radical or revolutionary system began to wane. While revolutionary dictatorship, not democracy, came to be widely looked upon—and in many democracies feared —as the wave of the future, advocates of democracy went over to the defensive. In the quarter century after the onset of the Great Depression in 1929-30, the very survival of the constitutional democracies was desperately challenged by the newer forms of revolutionary dictatorship in a series of contests where the outcome was highly uncertain. After the end of the Second World War, the contest extended to the developing parts of the world. There, where democratic political habits and traditions are lacking and human misery is greatest, revolutionary dictatorships frequently blend nationalism, Marxism, and opportunism with much of the rhetoric and some of the ultimate aims, but few of the practices, of constitutional democracy.

As the democracies assumed the posture of defense, their intellectuals frequently displayed a mood of pessimism and even a kind of desperate masochistic satisfaction in announcing the obsolescence of constitutional and pluralistic democratic systems. Perhaps because totalitarian change was so great a danger, political theorists, sociologists, and many other students of democratic life began to place heavier stress on the conditions necessary for a *stable* democracy. Perhaps because internal conflict had grown so menacing they also focused on *consensus*. Thus stability and consensus each became a sort of fetish, particularly among American political scientists and social theorists. By contrast, conflict and change were perceived not so much as offering the possibility of a better future (as democratic ideologues a century earlier would have said), but as menacing the foundations of existing democracy itself.

Quite possibly this intellectual mood reached a peak in the 1950s and has since been waning. However that may be, what is astonishing in retrospect is how much conflict many stable democracies have managed to absorb in the twentieth century, and how much change they have sponsored. In Britain, Sweden, Denmark, Belgium, and the Netherlands, to name a few cases, the extension of the suffrage and the democratization of political life were themselves profound yet ultimately peaceful changes. In almost every democracy, including the United States, twentieth-century leaders have carried through extensive—one might almost say revolutionary—programs of social reconstruction in order to mitigate the inequalities, the insecurities, and the injustices that industrialization and urbanization perpetuated, intensified, generated, or rendered more obviously unnecessary and capable of being eliminated. The heartening fact is that countries that already had achieved or were well advanced on the road to constitutional democracy before the First World War have nearly everywhere won and kept the loyalty of their people to democracy: for example, Switzerland, Britain, Norway, Sweden, Denmark, Iceland, Finland, Holland, Belgium, Canada, Australia, New Zealand —and, of course, the United States. In these countries, the working classes— once a source of internal danger because they were excluded from political life— have been integrated peacefully into the political system; in most of these countries, socialist and labor parties, drawing their strength mainly from skilled and unskilled workers, have participated extensively in government. Nor, in these countries, have the older elite groups, the aristocratic strata or the middle classes, been seriously alienated by democratization. In short, in these countries, extensive social and political changes have not prevented, but even have encouraged, conciliation among different social groups and the pacification of many ancient internal hostilities.

The United States, too, has undergone changes that half a century ago no one foresaw: the expansion of welfare measures and government intervention in the economy; the almost overnight assumption by the United States of its role as a major, *the* major, world power; and since the early 1950s huge steps toward the ultimate political, economic, and social liberation of Negroes.

To look upon constitutional pluralist democracies as incapable of significant change is, then, to misread the evidence of this century. In fact, perhaps only in the relatively small number of countries where democracy is quite firmly rooted can *extensive change* be reconciled with *extensive consent*. For there is a great deal of evidence to show that more profound changes can be made in the attitudes of people when they *participate* in changes (as they must if their consent is needed) than when they are *coerced*. Coercive change is more likely to produce speedy and outwardly dramatic yet superficial changes in attitudes. With participation, changes may seem to be taking place more slowly because consent is not won instantly, yet changes with consent are likely to be deeper and more longlasting.[1]

Nonetheless, it would be a false gloss on reality to say that change is easy in democracies, or to contend that change and stability pose no problems. For change almost always entails conflict between conservative social forces who gain or believe they gain from preserving the existing state of affairs or the direction in which things are moving, and their challengers whose aspirations require changes in the status quo or in the general direction of historical movement.

It is the set of problems involved in change and conflict, in stability and consensus that I now propose to explore. Before focusing explicitly on the American political system, however, it will help if we first try to sort out some of the key problems and possibilities.

CHANGE: INCREMENTAL, COMPREHENSIVE, REVOLUTIONARY

One of the commonest characteristics of literary utopias is that nothing ever changes. Yet it is a central fact of life that no living system is ever static. What is true of living organisms is also true of systems consisting of live human beings —economic systems, social systems, political systems.

Since change is ubiquitous, it is possible to examine it from a thousand different perspectives and to classify it in a thousand different ways. Let us focus our attention on *political* change and and the *sources* or causes of political change.

Political change may be distinguished as to location and magnitude. As to location, change may take place in:

1. The operting *structure* of government, as when a democratic republic replaces an oligarchy, a dictatorship replaces a democracy, a presidential system replaces a parliamentary system, or direct election of Senators replaces election by state legislatures.

2. The *policies* adopted and enforced by the government, as when Congress passed civil rights acts in 1964 and 1965, or Medicare in 1965.

3. The relative *influence* of different strata and groups on the policies and decisions of government, as after the election of 1800 when small farmers and southern planters clearly gained greater influence while New England commercial interests lost.

4. The social, ethnic, religious, phychological, or other significant *characteristics of political leaders*. (In what follows I propose to ignore this last kind of political change and concentrate on the others.)

Political change may be small or great with respect to each of these locations or dimensions. For the sake of simplicity, however, let me reduce change to three magnitudes.[2]

1. Incremental, or marginal, when
   a. The operating structure is unaltered, except perhaps in matters of detail.
   b. Changes in policies are gradual and incremental rather than sweeping innovations or reversals of established policies. And,
   c. These changes result from negotiating and bargaining among spokesmen for groups whose relative influence remains more or less stable or subject only to gradual changes.

2. Comprehensive, when
   a. The operating structure is unaltered, except in matters of detail.
   b. Sweeping innovations or decisive reversals of established policies occur. And,

---

[1] Sidney Verba, *Small Groups and Political Behavior* (Princeton, Princeton University Press, 1961), chs. 9, 10, "The Participation Hypothesis."

[2] The reader who enjoys playing with typologies—a somewhat barren enterprise to which social scientists are strongly addicted —may wish to construct for himself the eight possible combinations of "small" versus "large" changes in structures, politics, and group influence.

c. These policy changes result from significant shifts in the relative influence of different groups.

3. Revolutionary, when comprehensive change in policies and relative influence (2b and 2c) is also combined with profound alterations in the operating structure of government.

Incremental change is the normal pattern in American political life. Although incremental change often seems depressingly slow and is rejected by revolutionaries as inadequate, a few examples will show how much can be achieved by means of a series of small but steady changes. Anything that grows at the rate of 3 per cent a year will double in size about every twenty-three years; at 5 per cent a year it will double in fourteen years. The United States achieved its extraordinarily high gross national product by growing at a rate of about $3\frac{2}{3}$ per cent a year from the 1840s onwards. The population increased from seventeen million in 1840 to 184 million in 1960 by growing at an average rate of about 2 per cent a year. Gross national product per capita during this period grew at the rate of about $1\frac{2}{3}$ per cent a year; personal consumption at about $1\frac{3}{4}$ per cent a year. The world population explosion that has caused so much concern in recent years is produced by annual increments of only 2-4 per cent. The highest rate of growth in per capita gross national product in the 1950s in any industrial country, Communist or non-Communist, was less than 7 per cent. The average annual increase in the population of cities over twenty thousand in the United States from 1920-1950 was less than one-fifth of one per cent. Sixty-two per cent of the American population of voting age cast votes in the presidential election of 1964; if the percentage of the population voting were to grow by only 3 per cent a year, more than 95 per cent of the potential electorate would vote in the election of 1980. If output per man hour in the United States increases by 5 per cent annually, in fifty years each worker would produce eleven times as much as he does now.[3]

Incremental change, then, can be a powerful means for transforming a society—and has been so in the United States. However, comprehensive changes also occur at times; in fact, comprehensive changes are, as we shall see in later chapters, associated with some of the most dramatic events in American political history.

What of revolutionary political changes? The war between the American colonies and Britain is properly called a revolution, for it resulted in a profound change in the structure of government, in the relative influence of Americans and British officials, and in the policies pursued by the government. Making and adopting the Constitution might also be regarded as revolutionary in the sense employed here, even though that revolution, unlike the preceding one, was free of violence. For the Constitution clearly represented a decisive change in governmental structure; the policies of the new government, particularly Hamilton's economic policies, were sweeping innovations; and (the point is more debatable) the new government was associated, even if briefly, with a significant increase in the influence of men of commerce and finance. The Hartford Convention in 1814 and the South Carolina legislature in 1832 (of which more in the next chapter) might be said to have *sought* revolutionary change, unsuccessfully. The Civil War was one part revolution, one part the failure of a revolution. The Seces-

[3] The data on which the calculations in the paragraph are based were drawn from the following sources: Bruce M. Russett, ed., *World Handbook of Political and Social Indicators* (New Haven, Yale University Press, 1964), Tables 1, 7, 10, 45; Hearings Before the Joint Economic Committee, Congress of the United States, April 7-10, 1959, Part 2, Table 1, p. 271; Abram Bergson and Simon Kuznets, *Economic Trends in the Soviet Union* (Cambridge, Harvard University Press, 1963), Tables VIII.2, VIII.3, and VIII.4, pp. 337-340; *Congress and the Nation, op. cit.*, p. 1532. Louis J. Walinsky, "Keynes Isn't Enough," *The New Republic*, Vol. 154 (April 16, 1966), pp. 14-16.

sionists failed to revolutionize the structure of government by seceding and establishing an independent confederacy. Yet if the North defeated the South's revolution, Lincoln and the Republicans represented a decisive shift of influence away from southern planters to free farmers, commerce, industry, and northern labor; and the legislation and constitutional amendments enacted during and after the Civil War constituted sweeping, indeed revolutionary shifts in long-established policies. The challenge of the Confederacy was, however, the last large-scale appeal to a revolutionary change of regime that has been made in American politics; since that time, proposals for revolutionary change have been the exclusive monopoly of tiny political movements on the extreme fringes.

SOURCES OF POLITICAL CHANGE

Why do political changes come about? What generates the forces that lead to political changes?

To seek satisfactory answers to these questions would take us far beyond the confines of this book and into a domain where knowledge is rather speculative. Processes of change are obviously of critical importance to understanding the past, acting in the present, and shaping the future; they have been much studied, yet they are not at all well understood.

However, it is possible to distinguish some of the important factors that trigger political changes. One is changes in technique or technology. A new technique, instrument, or machine is introduced. Because it out-performs the old, practical men acting from practical motives replace the old with the new. As the new technique spreads, it alters opportunities, advantages, handicaps, relations among people, groups, regions. There are changes in access to resources of power, changes in perspectives, ideas, ideologies, changes in demands, changes in patterns of conflict and agreement. And so political change occurs.

The introduction of gunpowder into Europe ended the military superiority of the mailed and mounted knight; it heralded the day of the musket and foot-soldier. And so it helped to bring feudalism to an end. The mariner's compass vastly expanded the possibilities of navigation; it facilitated the discovery of the New World and the creation of overseas empires; its was to one of these that that Englishmen fled and created a new social, economic, and political order. Eli Whitney's invention of the cotton gin, as every American schoolchild is taught, made cotton a highly profitable crop; the profitability of cotton stimulated the spread of slavery and the domination of the South by a planter class. Thus, in the endless, complex, and little-understood chain of causes of which Whitney's invention is an early link, there is also the Civil War, the Ku Klux Klan, the "separate but equal" doctrine, the Supreme Court decision of 1954, and the Civil Rights Acts of 1964 and 1965.

Changes in social and economic institutions may also precipitate political changes. Institutional changes may of course be triggered by technological changes; the relationships are extraordinarily complex. The modern, privately owned, limited-liability business corporation was an institutional change that swept away most other forms of business in the nineteenth century. The competitive price system and the free market were institutional innovations of the late eighteenth and early nineteenth century. They responded to but they also generated technological changes; they created a new business class, a new middle class, a new urban proletariat, and a new set of problems, conflicts, and political changes that have not come to an end. In England, the same dense network of causes, one historian has argued, connects an innovation in 1795 by well-meaning justices of the peace trying to cope with rural unemployment and poverty to the triumph of the ideas of Adam Smith, the scrapping of all governmental controls over the price of labor, land, goods, and capital, and thence, in reaction and self-defense, to English socialism and the welfare state.[4] Why did the United States become a land of small free farmers in the nineteenth century, while Brazil did not? Both had a great supply of land. But the Englishmen who settled America did not bring feudal institutions here, whereas the Portuguese and Spanish in Latin America did.

There are, in the third place, ideas and beliefs. Simple mechanistic interpretations of history treat ideas in the minds of men as mere reflections of technology and institutions. Ideas are not, certainly, completely autonomous; but neither are technology and institutions. The relationships are too complex to try to sort out here. Yet ideas, beliefs, perspectives, and ideologies do change, and it is obvious that these changes often precipitate political changes. As Tocqueville pointed out in his introduction to *Democracy in America,* equality had long been spreading throughout Europe before the Americans founded their republic. Equality was spreading—ineluctably, so it seemed to him—as an idea and as a fact. If a growing equality in the actual conditions of life helps to sustain the idea of equality, may not the idea of equality help to sustain the fact of equality? Or, to take a more specific example, arguments over the virtues and vices of balanced budgets—an issue over which a number of Americans have displayed considerable passion—are above all a question of ideas and beliefs, indeed of abstract theories and models (even if often exceedingly primitive ones) of the relations between budgetary deficits and surpluses and such matters as full employment and foreign trade. Differences in ideas about these matters have steadily led to conflict between academic economists and conservative bankers.

Ideas, institutions, and techniques are intertwined in ways too complex to unravel. During Andrew Jackson's great conflicts over the Bank of the United States, why did none of the protagonists give serious consideration to a solution that would probably be one of the first to

[4] Polanyi, *The Great Transformation* (New York, Rinehart and Co., 1944).

occur to a presidential adviser or a member of Congress today: a government regulatory commission to keep the Bank in check? In large part, it seems, because the regulatory commission as an institution had really not yet been invented and its possibilities were not yet understood. The perceptions, ideas, ideology, if you will, that have developed with the growth of the regulatory state of the twentieth century were for all practical purposes not present in 1830. Jackson did not reject the idea of a regulatory commission in the sense that a critic of regulation might reject it today; nor could he have adopted the idea of a regulatory commission. For he simply did not perceive the idea as we do today, nor did anyone else in his time.

Thus perspectives change, social and economic institutions change, technology changes. And these changes trigger political changes. But government and politics are not necessarily mere by-products of changes. Government policy may trigger changes in ideas, in social and economic institutions, in technology. The policies and practice of the New Deal surely helped to change the perspectives of Americans about the proper role of government. It was government action that created a new institution in the Tennessee Valley Authority. It was government action that produced the institutions of modern social security (action in this country was long antedated by the innovation in Europe). And it was government action that led directly to the most awesome technological innovation in history, the unleashing of nuclear power.

THE DEPTH OF CHANGE AND CONFLICT

When one reads about some great revolution, one is inclined to suppose that sooner or later everyone in the society was, surely, drawn into the orbit of the revolution. Yet it might be far more realistic to assume—as some theorists have—that rapid historical changes and political conflicts of all kinds, even great revolutions, directly involve only the tiniest and most visible minorities, the activists and elites, in spheres political, social, economic, cultural, religious. Probably the truth usually lies somewhere between these extreme views. Unfortunately, it is impossible to specify precisely where the truth does lie, for our knowledge is severely limited.

The unhappy fact is that until the late 1930s, when systematic opinion surveys first began to be used, no means existed for measuring the spread of views and opinions in a population. As a result, we may never recapture the data needed for estimating in any except a very crude way how views were distributed in the past; we cannot therefore know much about detailed or rapid changes in views. We cannot go back to the eve of the Civil War and conduct a survey of the opinions of a properly selected sample of Americans and follow it up with one in 1865 to see what changes had occurred. Hence historical generalizations about the way opinions were distributed among Americans (or an yother population) before about 1936 must be treated with great caution. Yet we cannot hope to understand past changes and conflicts without making some assumptions as to attitudes in the general population— among voters, for example.

It is useful, I think, to take as a central hypothesis that certain general characteristics of political life which have been found to hold since the 1930s were also true of American citizens before the 1930s. There are, certainly, no plausible grounds for thinking otherwise, and there is a good deal of indirect evidence in support of the hypothesis.

What is striking from modern evidence is how many Americans there are to whom political life is totally foreign. A substantial proportion of American adults —probably not less than one out of four nor more than one out of two—are for all practical purposes a-political. Politics is so remote from their lives as to lack much meaning: They rarely vote or otherwise participate in politics, and their views on political matters are uninformed and shallow. These people constitute what might be called the a-political strata. They seem to constitute a significant pro-

portion of every citizen body in all historical periods. And there is not much doubt that in the United States the a-political strata have always constituted a sizeable group.

It is highly reasonable to suppose, then, that during all periods of American history the "burning issues of the day," the "great debates," the "fierce conflicts" of politics have scarcely engaged the attention of the a-political strata at all; perhaps a quarter to a half of the adults have always been so wholly involved in the events of their daily lives—worries over jobs, income, health, family, and friends —that they have barely followed what later generations regard as great historical events. Ordinary voters who do at least bother to vote are no doubt more engaged. But it is the minority of politically active citizens who are highly active politically —and most of all the tiny minority of leaders—who have always been most fully engaged in political conflicts. No matter how important historians might regard it today, to most Americans in 1854, the passage of the Kansas-Nebraska Act was doubtless very much less interesting and important than the marriage of a daughter, a son moving West, a death in the family, the baby's croupe, the bad harvest, the local scandal.

But of course when the leaders and the politically active citizens fail to resolve their differences, as they did in 1860, the cost in lives is levied on the whole people.

CONFLICT: MODERATE AND SEVERE

Utopias are not only marked by the absence of change. They are also unflawed by conflict. Most Utopias are pervaded by the deathly stillness of the graveyard. Yet in every political system there is perpetual and unceasing conflict.

In a republic, conflict is particularly visible because it is permitted; it is not all driven underground; it is protected, even institutionalized.

Now it is true that conflict can be dangerous to a political system. And citizens take a certain gamble when they opt for a republic. For the citizens of a republic may react to severe political conflict in ways that endanger or destroy the survival of their republic: by violence, suppressing one's opponents, civil war, secession, disloyalty, even by widespread demoralization, apathy, and indifference.

Yet to say that severe political conflict is undersirable is not to say that all political conflict is undesirable. So long as men have different views and the liberty to express their views, conflicts will exist. To condemn all political conflict as evil is to condemn diversity and liberty as evils. If you believe that some diversity is inevitable, and that liberty is desirable, then you must hold, logically, that political conflict is not only inevitable but desirable.

This is therefore the dilemma: In a democracy moderate political conflict is both inevitable and desirable. Yet severe political conflict is undesirable, for it endangers any political system, and not least a democracy. A democratic republic can escape from this dilemma only if conflict is somehow kept within bounds. But how is this possible? How can conflict, like atomic energy, be tamed and put to peaceful purposes?

It is not easy to say precisely what one means by the severity or intensity of a conflict, but the essential criterion appears to be this: Within a particular political system the more that the people on each side see the other side as enemies to be destroyed by whatever measures may be necessary, the more severe a conflict is. Evidence that a conflict is increasing in severity would therefore be an increasing harshness of language in which one's opponents were portrayed as implacable enemies to be annihilated; an increasing stress on or actual employment of violence against opponents; or an increasing use of means to victory that previously were regarded as impermissible, illegitimate, perhaps even illegal or unconstitutional.

What circumstances, then, are likely to lend moderation to a dispute or, conversely, to inflame it into a conflict of great severity?

To begin with the most obvious point, how severe a conflict is depends on how much is at stake. The more at stake, the harder a question is to settle.

But how severe a conflict is also depends on whether the people engaged in the dispute can discover mutually beneficial solutions. The ideal outcome, naturally, would be one in which all the contestants were not only better off than before but better off than under any alternative solution. To be sure, if solutions of this kind were common, conflict would rarely occur. Nonetheless, there is a clear difference between a dispute in which no contestants can come out ahead except by making others worse off ("If you win, I lose," or what mathematicians call a "zero-sum game"); and a dispute in which there is a solution under which no one will be worse off than before, and some may even be better off. If two people are faced with a deal in which every dollar A gains will make B worse off than he is now, neither of them has much incentive to negotiate. If the best solution for both is identical—if each stands to gain most by one solution— then negotiation is hardly necessary. If, on the other hand, A's best solution is different from B's, but there appear to be compromise solutions under which one or both might be better off than they are now, and neither worse off, both have every reason to negotiate in order to arrive at mutually acceptable decision.

The worst possible conflict, then, is one involving very high stakes and no solutions other than the mutually incompatible kind, "If you win, I lose." Consequently, conflicts involving two mutually incompatible ways of life among different citizens are bound to place an exceedingly serious strain on a republic. Here the term "way of life" means the rights, privileges, and human relationships a group most highly prizes—their families and friends, economic position, social standing, respect, religious beliefs, and political powers. Any group that sees its way of life at stake in a dispute will, obviously, be reluctant to compromise. If the whole society is divided and if no compromise is possible—if the conflict is over two completely incompatible ways of life—then a democracy is likely to break down. There are no cases, I think, in which a democratic republic has managed to settle conflicts of this kind peacefully.

So far we have been concerned with the characteristics of the conflict itself. But the severity of a conflict also depends on the people who are engaged in it, particularly their numbers and their location in the political system.

In a republic, elections mean that sheer numbers are often important. Hence how severe a conflict is depends in part on how many citizens hold similar or moderate views and how many hold extreme views. The greater the relative number of citizens who hold extreme (and opposing) views, the greater the danger that a conflict will be disruptive. Conversely, the greater the proportion of citizens who hold views that differ only slightly—that is, moderate views—the less the danger. In a stable republic, the great bulk of citizens will, presumably, more or less agree on many questions. In some cases, the agreement would pile up so heavily on one side of an issue that the matter would cease to produce much controversy. A graph of such a distribution would assume the shape that statisticians call, for obvious reasons, a

J-curve[5] (Figure 1). A vast number of questions that might be of abstract interest to philosophers, moralists, theologians, or others who specialize in posing difficult and troublesome questions are, in any stable political system, irrelevant to politics because practically everyone is agreed and no one can stir up much of a controversy. If a controversy does arise because of the persistence of a tiny dissenting minority, in a republic the chances are overwhelming that it will soon be settled in a way that corresponds with the view of the preponderant majority.

Sometimes people may disagree more markedly and yet hold moderate opinions. A distribution of this kind, which is sometimes called a bell-shaped or a double J-curve, is illustrated in Figure 2.

---

[5] For theory and data bearing on the discussion in this section, see particularly V. O. Key, Jr., *Public Opinion and American Democracy* (New York, A. A. Knopf, 1961), Ch. 2 and passim; and Robert A. Dahl, ed., *Political Oppositions in Western Democracies* (New Haven, Yale University Press, 1966). Discussions of relationships between the behavior of political parties and various distributions of political opinions may be found in Anthony Downs, *An Economic Interpretation of Democracy* (New York, Harper and Bros., 1957); and Gerald Garvey "The Theory of Party Equilibrium," *American Political Science Review*, Vol. 60 (March, 1966) pp. 29-38. A useful critique of some of the assumptions involved will be found in Donald E. Stokes, "Spatial Models of Party Competition," in Angus Campbell, Philip E. Converse, Warren E. Miller, and Donald E. Stokes, *Elections and the Political Order* (New York, John Wiley and Sons, 1966), ch. 9.

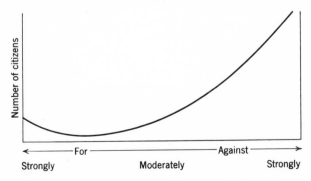

Figure 1. Agreement piles up heavily on one side: the J-curve.

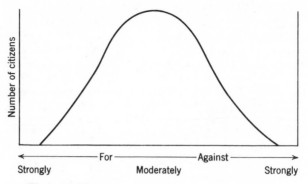

Figure 2. Disagreement is moderate: the bell curve.

When a conflict of views takes this shape, the chances are that it will be solved rather easily. Democratic systems with two major parties manage conflicts of this kind with special ease, because both parties tend to converge toward the center. Since an overwhelming number of voters are clustered at the center, and only a few at the extremes, the two major parties not only *may* ignore the extremes, they *must* do so if they want to win elections. The costs of making an appeal to voters with extreme attitudes is to lose the much more numerous support of moderates near the center.

In cases of the first two kinds, where opinion is strongly one-sided or over-whelmingly moderate, the conflict is not likely to be severe. If the extremes pre-dominate, however, conflicts of great severity are likely (Figure 3). Whenever extreme opinions gro wat the expense of moderate opinions or one-sided agree-ment, obviously conflict becomes much more dangerous, for it is much harder to find a basis for mutually profitable com-promises. Moreover, in these circum-stances the political parties find it prof-itable to adapt their appeals to the views of citizens at the extremes. While extreme

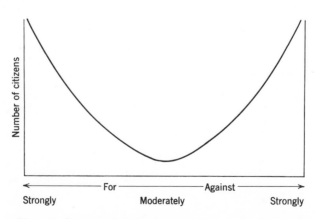

Figure 3. Disagreement is severe and extreme: the U-curve.

parties flourish, center parties grow weak. Sooner or later, one of the extreme parties or coalitions is likely to begin considering ways by which it may suppress or destroy the other, and violence is on the way.

The severity of a conflict depends, however, not only on the sheer numbers of people who hold divergent views, but also on their positions in the political system. Officials and other political leaders may be more moderate or more extreme in their views than ordinary citizens. Thus leaders may exaggerate or minimize the cleavages of opinion among the general population. The more they minimize cleavages, the less severe the political conflict; the more they emphasize and exaggerate differences of opinion, the more severe the conflict is likely to be. In Figure 4, leadership opinion is moderate, while rank-and-file opinion is sharply divided. In Figure 5, the situation is reversed; ordinary citizens are not as badly split as leaders. We would expect a situation like that suggested by Figure 5, to produce more severe political conflict and greater danger to a republic than the situation represented by Figure 4.

In a republic, what could produce differences between the attitudes of ordinary citizens and the attitudes of political leaders? If political leaders were chosen at random from the general population, then significant differences would be most unlikely. But the selection of political leaders is, as we know, very far from a random process. Even in a republic, some kinds of people are more likely to gain public office and power than others.

Citizens who are the most interested and active in politics are more likely to rise to the top than citizens who find politics uninteresting or otherwise unattractive. People who are interested and active in politics often differ in important respects from people who are less interested, less active, less effective, in short less influential. In the United States, for example, citizens who are most interested and active in politics and most confident that they can be effective tend also to have more education, higher incomes, and jobs of higher status. Because these conclusions are drawn from surveys made only since the 1930s, one cannot be certain that the differences of the last several decades existed earlier. But since much the same differences show up in other democratic countries, there is good reason to think that the socio-psychological factors so evident now were also present in earlier years in the United

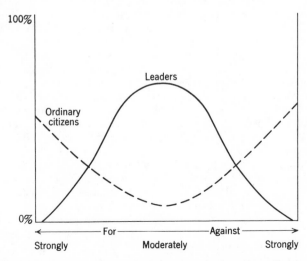

Figure 4. Moderation among leaders, extremism among ordinary citizens.

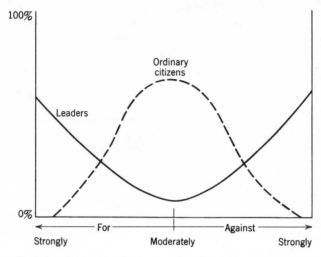

Figure 5. Extremism among leaders, moderation among ordinary citizens.

States. In any case, if the more active, interested, and influential strata of citizens tend to differ from the rest of the population in education, income, and occupations, is it not likely that they will also differ in political views? Hence instead of mirroring the political views of the rest of the population, leaders might be either more moderate or more antagonistic, and this may increase or decrease the severity of the conflict.

The way in which attitudes are distributed geographically is also relevant, particularly in countries where legislators are not chosen under some system of proportional representation. If a country is divided into election districts or states in which the office goes to the candidate with the most votes, and all other candidates with fewer votes are defeated, the intensity of a political conflict may depend on where different views are located in the country. An opposition minority that is concentrated in a particular region will find it easier to gain representation in the legislature than one that is dispersed more or less evenly throughout the nation. Moreover, even without extra representation because of the election system, a regional minority is in a relatively strong position to keep its views alive, to command conformity to its views within the region, to punish dissenters, and to portray their opponents as outsiders, aliens, foreigners.

The special effects of regionalism on conflict call attention to a broader observation—namely, that the severity of a conflict depends on the way in which one conflict is related to another. A society offers a number of different lines along which cleavages in a conflict can take place; differences in geography, ethnic identification, religion, and economic position, for example, all present potential lines of cleavages in conflicts. If all the cleavages occur along the same lines, if the same people hold opposing positions in one dispute after another, then the severity of conflicts is likely to increase. The man on the other side is not just an opponent; he soon becomes an enemy. But if (as Madison foresaw) the cleavages occur along different lines, if the same persons are sometimes opponents and sometimes allies, then conflicts are likely to be less severe. If you know that some of your present opponents were allies in the past and may be needed as allies again in the future, you have some reason to search for a solution to the dispute at hand that will satisfy both sides. The people on the other side may be your opponents today; but they are not your enemies, and tomorrow they may be your allies.

There is still one more factor to consider. Political institutions themselves may exacerbate conflicts, or make it easier to settle them. It is striking how in the hands of the English, the eighteenth-century Parliament became an institution for settling disputes that up until then—and in most other countries afterward—threatened the regime itself.[6] This development within Parliament does not wholly explain, of course, why Britain has not had a civil war since the seventeenth century; a fuller answer would require, among other things, an explanation of the path of parliamentary development itself. Nonetheless, the presence in Britain since the end of the seventeenth century of an institution that elaborated a set of conventions, devices, practices, and mechanisms for settling disputes has surely helped Britain to make changes and to negotiate internal conflicts peacefully for the past three hundred years.

It would take no great imagination to conceive of political institutions that would have the opposite effect, that would intensify rather than reduce conflict. Suppose, for example, that the American Constitution automatically awarded the Presidency and a majority on the Supreme Court to the party with the most numerous votes in an election, and awarded Congress to the party with the next largest number of votes. Conflict would then be built squarely into the constitutional system. (The attentive reader, remembering at this point that the Founding Fathers deliberately sought to build conflict into the constitutional structure, may wonder about the effects of their design on political conflicts in the United States. We shall come to that problem in due time.)

Although the extent to which political institutions intensify or soften conflicts is a highly complex matter, one might hope to distinguish political mechanisms according to whether they facilitate gaining *consent* through negotiation, or facilitate making *decisions* with or without much

consent, or facilitate both *consent* and *decisions*.

A system that required extensive consent but made it difficult to reach a decision—for example, a system in which all decisions had to be made by unanimous vote—would so greatly prolong negotiations and impede decisions that the prospect of mounting a revolution in order to get something done might become increasingly attractive. On the other hand, in a system where it was easy for leaders to make decisions without seeking the consent of others, minor questions could be settled with dispatch. But when ordinary citizens seriously disagreed with one another or with their leaders in such a system, decisions could be imposed without their consent; to secure obedience many citizens would have to be coerced by the government. By embittering and alienating citizens who were coerced, a system like this might ripen disputes into resistance and revolution. Thus a system that could somehow facilitate both negotiation of consent and arriving at decisions might serve best to keep conflicts from becoming so severe as to generate a revolution.

CONFLICT: A PARADIGM

Let me now draw together the threads of this discussion on conflict into a paradigm or model that will be helpful in understanding the next four chapters.

The intensity or severity of a political conflict in a republic is indicated by the extent to which people on each side see the other as an enemy to be destroyed; evidence that political disagreements are becoming severe is an increase in threats or actual use of violence, suppression of opponents, civil war, secession, disloyalty, or a marked increase in demoralization, apathy, indifference, or alienation.

The intensity or severity of a political conflict depends on at least four sets of factors:

1. The way in which politically relevant attitudes are distributed among the citizens and leaders.

[6] Archibald S. Foord. *His Majesty's Opposition 1714-1830* (London, Oxford University Press, 1964).

a. The greater the number of citizens who hold extreme (and opposing) views the more severe a conflict is likely to be. Conversely, the greater the number who hold moderate views, the less severe a conflict is likely to be.

b. The more extreme the views of political leaders and activists in comparison with the views of ordinary citizens, the more severe the conflict; conversely, the more moderate the views of leaders and activists in comparison with other citizens, the less severe the conflict is likely to be.

2. The patterns of cleavage.

The more conflicts accumulate along the same lines of cleavage, the more severe they are likely to be; conversely, the more conflicts intersect along different lines of cleavage, the less severe they are.

3. How much is at stake.

a. The more at stake, the more severe a conflict is likely to be.

b. A conflict in which no contestant can possibly make himself better off except by making other contestants worse off is likely to be more severe than a conflict in which there is a possibility that no contestant need be worse off than before, and some may be better off.

c. Conflicts involving incompatible "ways of life" are bound to be particularly severe.

4. The political institutions.

a. Political institutions and processes are likely to intensify conflicts if they require the groups involved to negotiate but do not provide any acceptable way by which leaders can terminate negotiations and arrive at a decision.

b. Political institutions and processes are likely to intensify conflicts if they make it possible for leaders to make decisions without engaging in negotiations to obtain the consent of the persons, groups, or parties involved.

c. Political institutions and processes are most likely to reduce the intensity of conflicts if they embody widespread agreement on procedures, *both* for negotiating in order to gain consent and for terminating the negotiations and arriving at a decision.

These propositions are summarized in Table 1.

TABLE 1. A PARADIGM: SOME FACTORS THAT MODERATE OR INTENSIFY POLITICAL CONFLICTS

	Conflict Is More Likely to Be	
	Moderate If:	Severe If:
1. The distribution of attitudes is	Convergent	Divergent
a. Attitudes of citizens are	Convergent	Divergent
b. Attitudes of political leaders and activists are	Convergent	Divergent
2. Lines of cleavage are	Overlapping (cross-cutting)	Non-overlapping (cumulative)
3. Threats to ways of life are	Absent	Present
a. Privileged groups feel	Secure	Seriously threatened
b. Aspiring groups feel	Successful	Frustrated
4. Political institutions provide		
a. Negotiations for consent but not decisions	No	Yes
b. Decisions without consent	No	Yes
c. Agreed processes for negotiating consent and arriving at decisions	Yes	No

Symbols and Political Quiescence

New forms of explanation of political phenomena are more common than the assertion that the success of some group was facilitated by the "apathy" of other groups with opposing interests. If apathy is not an observable phenomenon in a political context because it connotes an individual's mental state, quiescence is observable. It is the purpose of this paper to specify some conditions associated with political quiescence in the formation of business regulation policies. Although the same general conditions are apparently applicable to the formation of public policies in any area, the argument and the examples used here focus upon the field of government regulation of business in order to make the paper manageable and to permit more intensive treatment.

Political quiescence toward a policy area can be assumed to be a function either of lack of interest—whether it is simple indifference or stems rather from a sense of futility about the practical prospects of securing obviously desirable changes—or of the satisfaction of whatever interest the quiescent group may have in the policy in question. Our concern here is with the forms of satisfaction. In analyzing the various means by which it can come to pass, the following discussion distinguishes between interests in resources (whether goods or freedoms to act) and interests in symbols connoting the suppression of threats to the group in question. Few political scientists would doubt, on the basis of common sense evidence, that public policies have value to interested groups both as symbols and as instruments for the allocation of more tangible values. The political process has been much less thoroughly studied as a purveyor of symbols, however; and there

is a good deal of evidence, to be presented below, that symbols are a more central component of the process than is commonly recognized in political scientists' explicit or implicit models.[1]

Three related hypotheses will be considered:

(1) The interests of organized groups in tangible resources or in substantive power are less easily satiable than are interests in symbolic reassurance.

(2) Necessary conditions associated with the occurrence of the latter type of interest are:

   (a) the existence of economic conditions in some measure threatening the security of a large group;

   (b) the absence of organization for the purpose of furthering the common interest of that group;

   (c) widespread political responses suggesting the prevalence of inaccurate, oversimplified, and distorted perceptions of the issue.

(3) The pattern of political activity represented by lack of organization, distorted perception, interests in symbolic reassurance, and quiescence is a key element in the ability of organized groups to use political agencies in order to make good their claims on tangible resources and power, thus continuing the threat to the unorganized.

Available evidence bearing on these hypotheses will be marshalled as follows. First, some widely accepted propositions regarding group claims, quiescence, and techniques for satisfying group interests in governmental regulation of business will be summarized. Next, some pertinent experimental and empirical findings of other disciplines will be considered. Finally the paper will explore the possibility of integrating the various findings and ap-

SOURCE. Reprinted from *The American Political Science Review*, Vol. 54, 1960, with the permission of the author and publisher. Copyright 1960, The American Political Science Association.

[1] Harold Lasswell is a major exception, and some of his contributions will be noted.

plying them to the propositions listed above.

I

If the regulatory process is examined in terms of a divergence between political and legal promises on the one hand and resource allocations and group reactions on the other hand, the largely symbolic character of the entire process becomes apparent. What do the studies of government regulation of business tell us of the role and functions of that amorphous group who have an interest in these policies in the sense that they are affected by them, but who are not rationally organized to pursue their interest? The following generalizations would probably be accepted by most students, perhaps with occasional changes of emphasis:

(1) Tangible resources and benefits are frequently not distributed to unorganized political group interests as promised in regulatory statutes and the propaganda attending their enactment.

This is not true of legal fictions, but rather of the values held out to (or demanded by) groups which regard themselves as disadvantaged and which presumably anticipate benefits from a regulatory policy. There is virtually unanimous agreement among students of the antitrust laws, the Clayton and Federal Trade Commission acts, the Interstate Commerce acts, the public utility statutes and the right-to-work laws, for example, that through much of the history of their administration these statutes have been ineffective in the sense that many of the values they promised have not in fact been realized. The story has not been uniform, of course; but the general point hardly needs detailed documentation at this late date. Herring,[2] Leiserson,[3] Tru-

man,[4] and Bernstein[5] all conclude that few regulatory policies have been pursued unless they proved acceptable to the regulated groups or served the interests of these groups. Within the past decade Redford,[6] Bernstein[7] and others have offered a "life cycle" theory of regulatory history, showing a more or less regular pattern of loss of vigor by regulatory agencies. For purposes of the present argument it need not be assumed that this always happens but only that it frequently happens in important cases.[8]

(2) When it does happen, the deprived groups often display little tendency to protest or to assert their awareness of the deprivation.

The fervent display of public wrath, or enthusiasm, in the course of the initial legislative attack on forces seen as threatening "the little man" is a common American spectacle. It is about as predictable as the subsequent lapse of the same fervor. Again, it does not always occur, but it happens often enough to call for thorough explanation. The leading students of regulatory processes have all remarked upon it; but most of these scholars, who ordinarily display a close regard for rigor and full exploration, dismiss this highly significant political behavior rather casually. Thus, Redford

---

[2] E. Pendleton Herring, *Public Administration and the Public Interest* (New York, 1936), p. 213.

[3] Avery Leiserson, *Administrative Regulation: A Study in Representation of Interests* (Chicago: The University of Chicago Press, 1942), p. 14.

[4] David Truman, *The Governmental Process* (New York, 1951), ch. 5.

[5] Marver Bernstein, *Regulating Business by Independent Commissions* (New York: Princeton University Press, 1955), ch. 3.

[6] Emmette S. Redford, *Administration of National Economic Control* (New York, 1952). pp. 385-386.

[7] *Op. cit.,* note 5 above.

[8] In addition to the statements in these analytical treatments of the administrative process, evidence for the proposition that regulatory statutes often fail to have their promised consequences in terms of resource allocation are found in general studies of government regulation of business and in empirical research on particular statutes. As an example of the former see Clair Wilcox, *Public Policies Toward Business* (Chicago, 1955). As examples of the latter see Frederic Meyers, *"Right to Work" in Practice* (New York: Fund for the Republic, 1959); Walton Hamilton and Irene Till, *Antitrust in Action,* TNEC Monograph 16 (Washington: GPO, 1940).

declares that, "In the course of time the administrator finds that the initial public drive and congressional sentiment behind his directive has wilted and that political support for change from the existing pattern is lacking."[9]

Although the presumed beneficiaries of regulatory legislation often show little or no concern with its failure to protect them, they are nevertheless assumed to constitute a potential base of political support for the retention of these statutes in the law books. The professional politician is probably quite correct when he acts on the assumption that his advocacy of this regulatory legislation, in principle, is a widely popular move, even though actual resource allocations inconsistent with the promise of the statutes are met with quiescence. These responses (support of the statute; apathy toward failure to allocate resources as the statute promises) define the meanings of the law so far as the presumed beneficiaries are concerned.[10] It is the frequent inconsistency between the two types of response that is puzzling.

(3) The most intensive dissemination of symbols commonly attends the enact-

[9] Redford, *op. cit.,* p. 383. Similar explanations appear in Herring, *op. cit.,* p. 227, and Bernstein, *op. cit.,* pp. 82-83. Some writers have briefly suggested more rigorous explanations, consistent with the hypotheses discussed in this paper, though they do not consider the possible role of interests in symbolic reassurance. Thus Truman calls attention to organizational factors, emphasizing the ineffectiveness of interest groups "whose interactions on the basis of the interest are not sufficiently frequent or stabilized to produce an intervening organization and whose multiple memberships, on the same account, are a constant threat to the strength of the claim." Truman, *op. cit.,* p. 441. Multiple group memberships are, of course, characteristic of individuals in all organizations, stable and unstable; and "infrequent interactions" is a phenomenon that itself calls for explanation if a common interest is recognized. Bernstein, *loc. cit.,* refers to the "undramatic nature" of administration and to the assumption that the administrative agency will protect the public.
[10] *Cf.* the discussion of meaning in George Herbert Mead, *Mind, Self and Society* (Chicago: University of Chicago Press, 1934), pp. 78-79.

ment of legislation which is most meaningless in its effects upon resource allocation. In the legislative history of particular regulatory statutes the provisions least significant for resource allocation are most widely publicized and the most significant provisions are least widely publicized.

The statutes listed under Proposition 1 as having promised something substantially different from what was delivered are also the ones which have been most intensively publicized as symbolizing protection of widely shared interests. Trust-busting, "Labor's Magna Carta" (the Clayton Act), protection against price discrimination and deceptive trade practices, protection against excessive public utility charges, tight control of union bureaucracies (or, by other groups, the "slave labor law"), federal income taxation according to "ability to pay," are the terms and symbols widely disseminated to the public as descriptive of much of the leading federal and state regulation of the last seven decades; and they are precisely the descriptions shown by careful students to be most misleading. Nor is it any less misleading if one quotes the exact language of the most widely publicized specific provisions of these laws: Section 1 of the Sherman Act, Sections 6 and 20 of the Clayton Act, or the closed shop, secondary boycott, or emergency strike provisions of Taft-Hartley, for example. In none of these instances would a reading of either the text of the statutory provision or the attendant claims and publicity enable an observer to predict even the direction of future regulatory policy, let alone its precise objectives.

Other features of these statutes also stand as the symbols of threats stalemated, if not checkmated, by the forces of right and justice. Typically, a preamble (which does not pretend to be more than symbolic, even in legal theory) includes strong assurances that the public or the public interest will be protected. And the most widely publicized regulatory provisions always include other nonoperational standards connoting fairness, balance, or equity.

If one asks, on the other hand, for examples of changes in resource allocations that have been influenced substantially and directly by public policy, it quickly appears that the outstanding examples have been publicized relatively little. One thinks of such legislation as the silver purchase provisions; the court definitions of the word "lawful" in the Clayton Act's labor sections; the procedural provisions of Taft-Hartley and the Railway Labor Act; the severe postwar cuts in Grazing Service appropriations; and changes in the parity formula requiring that such items as interest, taxes, freight rates and wages be included as components of the index of prices paid by farmers.

Illuminating descriptions of the operational meaning of statutory mandates are found in Truman's study and in Earl Latham's *The Group Basis of Politics*.[11] Both emphasize the importance of contending groups and organizations in day-to-day decision-making as the dynamic element in policy formation; and both distinguish this element from statutory language as such.[12]

We are only beginning to get some serious studies of the familiarity of voters with current public issues and of the intensity of their feelings about issues; but successful political professionals have evidently long acted on the assumption that there is in fact relatively little familiarity, that expressions of deep concern are rare, that quiescence is common, and that, in general, the congressman can count upon stereotyped reactions rather than persistent, organized pursuit of material interests on the part of most constituents.[13]

(4) Policies severely denying resources to large numbers of people can be pursued indefinitely without serious controversy.

The silver purchase policy, the farm policy, and a great many other subsidies are obvious examples. The anti-trust laws, utility regulations, and other statutes ostensibly intended to protect the small operator or the consumer are less obvious examples; though there is ample evidence, some of it cited below, that these usually support the proposition as well.

The federal income tax law offers a rather neat example of the divergence between a widely publicized symbol and actual resource allocation patterns. The historic constitutional struggle leading up to the Sixteenth Amendment, the warm defenses of the principle of ability to pay, and the frequent attacks upon the principle through such widely discussed proposals as that for a 25 per cent limit on rates have made the federal tax law a major symbol of justice. While the fervent rhetoric from both sides turns upon the symbol of a progressive tax and bolsters the assumption that the system is highly progressive, the bite of the law into people's resources depends upon quite other provisions and activities that are little publicized and that often seriously qualify its progressive character. Special tax treatments arise from such devices as family partnerships, gifts *inter vivos*, income-splitting, multiple trusts, percentage depletion, and deferred compensation.

Tax evasion alone goes far toward making the symbol of "ability to pay" hollow semantically though potent symbolically. While 95 per cent of income from wages and salaries is taxed as provided by law, taxes are actually collected on only 67 per cent of taxable income from interest, dividends, and fiduciary investments, and on only about 36 per cent of taxable farm income.[14] By and large, the recipients of larger incomes can most easily benefit

[11] Truman, *op. cit.*, pp. 439-446; Earl Latham, *The Group Basis of Politics* (Ithaca: Cornell University Press, 1952), ch. 1.

[12] The writer has explored this effect in labor legislation in "Interest Representation and Labor Law Administration," *Labor Law Journal*, Vol. 9 (1958), pp. 218-226.

[13] Evidence for these propositions is contained in the writer's study of congressional representation, still not completed or published. See also Lewis A. Dexter, "Candidates Must Make the Issues and Give Them Meaning," *Public Opinion Quarterly*, Vol. 10 (1955-56), pp. 408-414.

[14] Randolph E. Paul, "Erosion of the Tax Base and Rate Structure," in Joint Committee on the Economic Report, *Federal Tax Policy for Economic Growth and Stability*, 84th Cong., 1st sess., 1955, pp. 123-138.

from exemptions, avoidances and evasions. This may be desirable public policy, but it certainly marks a disparity between symbol and effect upon resources.

II

These phenomena are significant for the study of the political process for two reasons. First, there is a substantial degree of consistency in the group interest patterns associated with policies on highly diverse subject matters. Second, they suggest that nonrational reaction to symbols among people sharing a common governmental interest is a key element in the process. The disciplines of sociology, social psychology, and semantics have produced some pertinent data on the second point; and to some of this material we turn next.

Harold Lasswell wrote three decades ago that "[P]olitics is the process by which the irrational bases of society are brought out into the open." He marshalled some support in case studies for several propositions that have since been confirmed with richer and more direct experimental evidence. "The rational and dialectical phases of politics," he said, "are subsidiary to the process of redefining an emotional consensus." He argued that "widespread and disturbing changes in the life-situation of many members of society" produce adjustment problems which are resolved largely through symbolization; and he suggested that "[P]olitical demands probably bear but a limited relevance to social needs."[15]

The frame of reference suggested by these statements is sometimes accepted by political scientists today when they study voting behavior and when they analyze the legislative process. Its bearing on policy formation in the administrative process is not so widely recognized. It is true that cognition and rationality are central to administrative procedures to a degree not true of legislation or voting.

But this is not at all the same thing as saying that administrative policies or administrative politics are necessarily insulated from the "process of redefining an emotional consensus."

Let us consider now some experimental findings and conclusions specifying conditions under which groups or personality types are prone to respond strongly to symbolic appeals and to distort or ignore reality in a fashion that can be politically significant.

(1) People read their own meanings into situations that are unclear or provocative of emotion. As phrased by Fensterheim, "The less well defined the stimulus situation, or the more emotionally laden, the greater will be the contribution of the perceiver."[16] This proposition is no longer doubted by psychologists. It is the justification for so-called projective techniques and is supported by a great deal of experimental evidence.

Now it is precisely in emotionally laden and poorly defined situations that the most widely and loudly publicized public regulatory policies are launched and administered. If, as we have every reason to suppose, there is little cognitive familiarity with issues, the "interest" of most of the public is likely to be a function of other socio-psychological factors. What these other factors are is suggested by certain additional findings.

(2) It is characteristic of large num-

---

[15] *Psychopathology and Politics* (Chicago: University of Chicago Press, 1930), pp. 184, 185.

[16] Herbert Fensterheim, "The Influence of Value Systems on the Perception of People," *Journal of Abnormal and Social Psychology,* Vol. 48 (1953), p. 93. Fensterheim cites the following studies in support of the proposition: D. Krech and R. S. Crutchfield, *Theory and Problems of Social Psychology* (New York, 1948); A. S. Luchins, "An Evaluation of Some Current Criticisms of Gestalt Psychological Work on Perception," *Psychological Review,* Vol. 58 (1951), pp. 69-95; J. S. Bruner, "One Kind of Perception: A Reply to Professor Luchins," *Psychological Review,* Vol. 58 (1951), pp. 306-312; and the chapters by Bruner, Frenkel-Brunswik, and Klein in R. R. Blake and G. V. Ramsey, *Perception: An Approach to Personality* (New York, 1951). See also Charles Osgood, Percy Tannenbaum and George Suci, *The Measurement of Meaning* (Urbana: University of Illinois Press, 1957).

bers of people in our society that they see and think in terms of stereotypes, personalization, and over-simplifications; that they cannot recognize or tolerate ambiguous and complex situations; and that they accordingly respond chiefly to symbols that over-simplify and distort. This form of behavior (together with other characteristics less relevant to the political process) is especially likely to occur where there is insecurity occasioned by failure to adjust to real or perceived problems.[17] Frenkel-Brunswik has noted that "such objective factors as economic conditions" may contribute to the appearance of the syndrome, and hence to its importance as a widespread group phenomenon attending the formulation of public policy.[18] Such behavior is sufficiently persistent and widespread to be politically significant only when there is social reinforcement of faith in the symbol. When insecurity is individual, without communication and reinforcement from others, there is little correlation with ethnocentricity or its characteristics.[19]

A different kind of study suggests the extent to which reality can become irrelevant for persons very strongly committed to an emotion-satisfying symbol. Festinger and his associates, as participant-observers, studied a group of fifteen persons who were persuaded that the world would come to an end on a particular day in 1956 and that they as believers would be carried away in a flying saucer. With few exceptions the participants refused to give up their belief even after the appointed day had passed. The Festinger study concludes that commitment to a belief is likely to be strengthened and reaffirmed in the face of clear disproof of its validity where there is a strong prior commitment (many of the individuals involved had actually given away their worldly goods) and where there is continuing social support of the commitment by others (two members who lost faith lived in environments in which they had no further contact with fellow-members of the group; those who retained their faith had continued to see each other). What we know of previous messianic movements of this sort supports this hypothesis.[20]

(3) Emotional commitment to a symbol is associated with contentment and quiescence regarding problems that would otherwise arouse concern.

It is a striking fact that this effect has been noticed and stressed by careful observers in a number of disparate fields, using quite different data and methods. Adorno reports it as an important finding of the *Authoritarian Personality* study:

> Since political and economic events make themselves felt apparently down to the most private and intimate realms of the individual, there is reliance upon stereotype and similar avoidances of reality to alleviate psychologically the feeling of anxiety and uncertainty and provide the individual with the illusion of some kind of intellectual security.[21]

In addition to the support it gets from psychological experiment, the phenomenon has been remarked by scholars in the fields of semantics, organizational theory, and political science. Albert Salomon points out that "Manipulation of social images makes it possible for

---

[17] Among the leading general and experimental studies dealing with the phenomenon are: M. Rokeach, "Generalized Mental Rigidity as a Factor in Ethnocentrism," *Journal of Abnormal and Social Psychology*, Vol. 43 (1948), pp. 259-277; R. R. Canning and J. M. Baker, "Effect of the Group on Authoritarian and Non-authoritarian Persons," *American Journal of Sociology*, Vol. 64 (1959), pp. 579-581; A. H. Maslow, "The Authoritarian Character Structure," *Journal of Social Psychology*, Vol. 18 (1943), p. 403; T. W. Adorno and others, *The Authoritarian Personality* (New York, 1950); Gerhart Saenger, *The Psychology of Prejudice* (New York, 1953), pp. 123-138; Erich Fromm, *Escape from Freedom* (New York, 1941); R. K. Merton, *Mass Persuasion* (New York, 1950).

[18] Else Frenkel-Brunswik. "Interaction of Psychological and Sociological Factors in Political Behavior," this *Review*, Vol. 46 (1952), pp. 44-65.

[19] Adorno, *op. cit.*

[20] Leon Festinger, Henry Riecken, and Stanley Shachter, *When Prophecy Fails* (Minneapolis: University of Minnesota Press, 1956).

[21] Adorno, *op. cit.*, p. 665.

members of society to believe that they live not in a jungle, but in a well organized and good society."[22] Harold Lasswell put it as follows:

It should not be hastily assumed that because a particular set of controversies passes out of the public mind that the implied problems were solved in any fundamental sense. Quite often a solution is a magical solution which changes nothing in the conditions affecting the tension level of the community, and which merely permits the community to distract its attention to another set of equally irrelevant symbols. The number of statutes which pass the legislature or the number of decrees which are handed down by the executive, but which change nothing in the permanent practices of society, is a rough index of the role of magic in politics. . . . Political symbolization has its catharsis function. . . .[23]

Chester Barnard, an uncommonly astute analyst of his own long experience as an executive, concluded that:

Neither authority nor cooperative disposition . . . will stand much overt division on formal issues in the present stage of human development. Most laws, executive orders, decisions, etc., are in effect formal notice that all is well—there is agreement, authority is not questioned.[24]

Charles Morris, a leading logician and student of semantics, has analyzed the role of language in shaping social behavior and inculcating satisfaction with existing power relationships. He points to the possibility that exploited groups will "actively resist changes in the very sign structure by which they are exploited." Defining such behavior as "socially pathic," he makes the following comment:

The signs in question may relieve certain anxieties in the members of society with

respect to the social behavior in which they are engaged, and so be cherished for this satisfaction even though the signs hinder or even make impossible the actual realization of the goals of such social behavior itself.[25]

Kenneth Burke makes much the same point. Designating political rhetoric as "secular prayer," he declares that its function is "to sharpen up the pointless and blunt the too sharply pointed."[26] Elsewhere, he points out that laws themselves serve this function, alleging that positive law is *itself* "the test of a judgment's judiciousness."[27]

(4) An active demand for increased economic resources or fewer political restrictions on action is not always operative. It is, rather, a function of comparison and contrast with reference groups, usually those not far removed in socioeconomic status.

This is, of course, one of the most firmly established propositions about social dynamics; one that has been supported by macro-sociological analysis,[28] by psychological experiment,[29] and by observation of the political process, particularly through contrast between politically quiescent and protest or revolutionary activity.[30]

The proposition helps explain failure to demand additional resources where such behavior is socially sanctioned and supported. It also helps explain the insatiability of the demand by some organized groups for additional resources (i.e., the absence of quiescence) where

---

[22] Albert Salomon, "Symbols and Images in the Constitution of Society," in L. Bryson, L. Finkelstein, H. Hoagland and R. M. MacIver (eds.), *Symbols and Society* (New York, 1955), p. 110.
[23] Lasswell, *op cit.*, p. 195.
[24] Chester I. Barnard, *The Functions of the Executive* (Cambridge: Harvard University Press, 1938), p. 226.
[25] Charles Morris, *Signs, Language and Behavior* (New York, 1946), pp. 210-211.
[26] Kenneth Burke, *A Grammar of Motives* (New York, 1945), p. 393.
[27] *Ibid.*, p. 362.
[28] Mead, *op. cit.;* Ernst Cassirer, *An Essay on Man* (New Haven: Yale University Press, 1944).
[29] See James G. March and Gerbert A. Simon, *Organizations* (New York, 1958), pp. 65-81, and studies cited there.
[30] See, *e.g.,* Murray Edelman, "Causes of Fluctuations in Popular Support for the Italian Communist Party since 1946," *Journal of Politics,* Vol. 20 (1958), pp. 547-550; Arthur M. Ross, *Trade Union Wage Policy* (Berkeley and Los Angeles: University of California Press, 1948).

there is competition for such resources among rival organizations and where it is acquisitiveness that is socially supported.

(5) The phenomena discussed above (the supplying of meaning in vague situations, stereotypes, oversimplification, political quiescence) are in large measure associated with social, economic, or cultural factors affecting large segments of the population. They acquire political meaning as group phenomena.

Even among the psychologists, some of whom have at times been notably insensitive to socialization and environment as explanations and phases of the individual "traits" they claim to "identify" or "isolate," there are impressive experimental findings to support the proposition. In analyzing the interview material of his *Authoritarian Personality* study, Adorno concluded that "our general cultural climate" is basic in political ideology and in streotyped political thinking; and he catalogued some standardizing aspects of that climate.[31] His finding, quoted above, regarding the relation of symbols to quiescence is also phrased to emphasize its social character. Lindesmith and Strauss make a similar point, emphasizing the association between symbols and the reference groups to which people adhere.[32]

Another type of research has demonstrated that because interests are typically bound up with people's social situation, attitudes are not typically changed by *ex parte* appeals. The function of propaganda is rather to activate socially rooted interests. One empirical study which arrives at this conclusion sums up the thesis as follows:

Political writers have the task of providing "rational" men with good and acceptable reasons to dress up the choice which is more effectively determined by underlying social affiliations.[33]

George Herbert Mead makes the fundamental point that symbolization itself has no meaning apart from social activity: "Symbolization constitutes objects . . . which would not exist except for the context of social relationships wherein symbolization occurs."[34]

III

These studies offer a basis for understanding more clearly what it is that different types of groups expect from government and under what circumstances they are likely to be satisfied or restive about what is forthcoming. Two broad patterns of group interest activity *vis-a-vis* public regulatory policy are evidently identifiable on the basis of these various modes of observing the social scene. The two patterns may be summarized in the following shorthand fashion:

(1) Pattern A: a relatively high degree of organization—rational, cognitive procedures—precise information—an effective interest in specifically identified, tangible resources—a favorably perceived strategic position with respect to reference groups—relatively small numbers.

(2) Pattern B: shared interest in improvement of status through protest activity—an unfavorably perceived strategic position with respect to reference groups—distorted, stereotyped, inexact information and perception—response to symbols connoting suppression of threats—relative ineffectiveness in securing tangible resources through political activity—little organization for purposeful action—quiescence—relatively large numbers.

[31] Adorno, *op. cit.*, p. 655.

[32] Alfred R. Lindesmith and Anselm L. Strauss, *Social Psychology* (New York, 1956), pp. 253-255. For a report of another psychological experiment demonstrating that attitudes are a function of group norms, see I. Sarnoff, D. Katz, and C. McClintock, "Attitude-Change Procedures and Motivating Patterns," in Daniel Katz and others (eds.), *Public Opinion and Propaganda* (New York, 1954), pp. 308-9; also Festinger *et al.*, *op. cit.*

[33] Paul F. Lazarsfeld, Bernard Berelson and Hazel Gaudet, *The People's Choice* (New York, 1944), p. 83. For an account of an experiment reaching the same conclusion see S. M. Lipset, "Opinion Formation in a Crisis Situation," *Public Opinion Quarterly*, Vol. 17 (1953), pp. 20-46.

[34] Mead, *op. cit.*, p. 78.

It is very likely misleading to assume that some of these observations can be regarded as causes or consequences of others. That they often occur together is both a more accurate observation and more significant. It is also evident that each of the patterns is realized in different degrees at different times.

While political scientists and students of organizational theory have gone far toward a sophisticated description and analysis of Pattern A, there is far less agreement and precision in describing and analyzing Pattern B and in explaining how it intermeshes with Pattern A.

The most common explanation of the relative inability of large numbers of people to realize their economic aspirations in public policy is in terms of invisibility. The explanation is usually implicit rather than explicit, but it evidently assumes that public regulatory policy facilitating the exploitation of resources by knowledgeable organized groups (usually the "regulated") at the expense of taxpayers, consumers, or other unorganized groups is possible only because the latter do not know it is happening. What is invisible to them does not arouse interest or political sanctions.

On a superficial level of explanation this assumption is no doubt valid. But it is an example of the danger to the social scientist of failure to inquire transactionally: of assuming, in this instance (1) that an answer to a questioner, or a questionnaire, about what an individual "knows" of a regulatory policy at any point in time is in any sense equivalent to specification of a group political interest; and (2) that the sum of many individual knowings (or not-knowings) as reported to a questioner is a *cause* of effective (or ineffective) organization, rather than a consequence of it, or simply a concomitant phase of the same environment. If one is interested in policy formation, what count are the assumptions of legislators and administrators about the determinants of future political disaffection and political sanctions. Observable political behavior, as well as psychological findings, reveals something of these assumptions.

There is, in fact, persuasive evidence of the reality of a political interest, defined in this way, in continuing assurances of protection against economic forces understood as powerful and threatening. The most relevant evidence lies in the continuing utility of old political issues in campaigns. Monopoly and economic concentration, anti-trust policy, public utility regulation, banking controls, and curbs on management and labor are themes that party professionals regard as good for votes in one campaign after another, and doubtless with good reason. They know that these are areas in which concern is easily stirred. In evaluating allegations that the public has lost "interest" in these policies the politician has only to ask himself how much apathy would remain if an effort were made formally to repeal the anti-trust, public utility, banking, or labor laws. The answers and the point become clear at once.

The laws may be repealed in effect by administrative policy, budgetary starvation, or other little publicized means; but the laws as symbols must stand because they satisfy interests that are very strong indeed: interests that politicians fear will be expressed actively if a large number of voters are led to believe that their shield against a threat has been removed.

More than that, it is only as symbols of this sort that these statutes have utility to most of the voters. If they function as reassurances that threats in the economic environment are under control, their indirect effect is to permit greater exploitation of tangible resources by the organized groups concerned than would be possible if the legal symbols were absent. Those who are deprived become defenders of the very system of law which permits the exploiters of resources to act effectively.

To say this is not to assume that everyone objectively affected by a policy is simply quiescent rather than apathetic or even completely unaware of the issue. It is to say that those who are potentially able and willing to apply political sanctions constitute the politically significant group. It is to suggest as well that incumbent or aspiring congressmen are less concerned with individual constituents' familiarity or unfamiliarity with an issue as of any given moment than with the possibility that the interest of a substantial number of them *could* be aroused and organized if he should cast a potentially unpopular vote on a bill or if a change in their economic situations should occur. The shrewder and more effective politicians probably appreciate intuitively the validity of the psychological finding noted earlier: that where public understanding is vague and information rare, interests in reassurance will be all the more potent and all the more susceptible to manipulation by political symbols.

The groups that succeed in using official agencies as instrumentalities to gain the resources they want are invariably organized so as to procure and analyze pertinent information and then act rationally. Most voters affected by the regulatory policy are certain on the other hand to secure distorted information, inadequate for intelligent planning of tactics or strategy.

We have already noted that it is one of the demonstrable functions of symbolization that it induces a feeling of well-being; the resolution of tension. Not only is this a major function of widely publicized regulatory statutes, but it is also a major function of their administration. Some of the most widely publicized administrative atcivities can most confidently be expected to convey a misleading sense of well-being to the onlooker because they suggest vigorous activity while in fact signifying inactivity or protection of the "regulated."

One form this phenomenon takes is noisy attacks on trivia. The Federal Trade Commission, for example, has long been noted for its hit-and-miss attacks on many relatively small firms involved in deceptive advertising or unfair trade practices while it continues to overlook much of the really significant activity it is ostensibly established to regulate: monopoly, interlocking directorates, and so on.[35]

Another form it takes is prolonged, repeated, well-publicized attention to a significant problem which is never solved. An excellent example is the approach of the FCC to surveillance of program content in general and to discussions of public issues on the air in particular. In the postwar period we have had the Blue Book, the Mayflower Policy, the abolition of the Mayflower Policy, and the announcement of a substitute policy; but the radio or television licensee is in practice perfectly free, as he has been all along, to editoralize, with or without opportunity for opposing views to be heard, or to eschew serious discussion of public affairs entirely.

The most obvious kinds of dissemination of symbolic satisfactions are to be found in administrative dicta accompanying decisions and orders, in press releases, and in annual reports. It is as common here as in labor arbitration to "give the rhetoric to one side and the decision to the other." Nowhere does the FCC wax so emphatic in emphasizing public service responsibility, for example, as in decisions permitting greater concentration of control in an area, condoning license transfers at inflated prices, refusing to impose sanctions for flagrantly sacrificing program quality to profits, and so on.[36]

The integral connection is apparent between symbolic satisfaction of the disorganized, on the one hand, and the success of the organized, on the other, in using governmental instrumentalities as aids in securing the tangible resources they claim.

Public policy may usefully be understood as the resultant of the interplay among groups.[37] But the political and socio-psychological processes discussed

---

[35] *Cf.* Wilcox, *op. cit.*, pp. 281, 252-255.

[36] Many examples may be found in the writer's study entitled *The Licensing of Radio Services in the United States, 1927 to 1947* (Urbana: University of Illinois Press, 1950).
[37] For discussions of the utility of this view to social scientists, see Arthur F. Bentley, *The Process of Government* (New York: The Principia Press, 1908, reprint 1949); Truman, *op. cit.* But *cf.* Stanley Rothman, "Systematic Political Theory," this *Review*, Vol. 54, pp. 15-33 (March, 1960).

here mean that groups which would otherwise present claims upon resources may be rendered quiescent instead by their success in securing nontangible values. Far from representing an obstacle to organized producers and sellers, they become defenders of the very system of law which permits the organized to pursue their interests effectively, at the expense of the disorganized or unorganized.

Thurman Arnold has pointed out how the anti-trust laws perform precisely this function:

> The actual result of the antitrust laws was to promote the growth of great industrial organizations by deflecting the attack on them into purely moral and ceremonial channels . . . every scheme for direct control broke to pieces on the great protective rock of the antitrust laws . . .
>
> The antitrust laws remained as a most important symbol. Whenever anyone demanded practical regulation, they formed an effective moral obstacle, since all the liberals would answer with a demand that the antitrust laws be enforced. Men like Senator Borah founded political careers on the continuance of such crusades, which were entirely futile but enormously picturesque, and which paid big dividends in terms of personal prestige.[88]

Arnold's subsequent career as Chief of the Anti-trust Division of the Department of Justice did as much to prove his point as his writings. For a five-year period he instilled unprecedented vigor into the Division, and his efforts were widely publicized. He thereby unquestionably made the laws a more important symbol of the protection of the public; but despite his impressive intentions and talents, monopoly, concentration of capital, and restraint of trade were not seriously threatened or affected.

This is not to suggest that signs or symbols in themselves have any magical force as narcotics. They are, rather, the only means by which groups not in a position to analyze a complex situation rationally may adjust themselves to it, through stereotypization, oversimplification, and reassurance.

There have, of course, been many instances of effective administration and enforcement of regulatory statutes. In each such instance it will be found that organized groups have had an informed interest in effective administration. Sometimes the existence of these groups is explicable as a holdover from the campaign for legislative enactment of the basic statute; and often the initial administrative appointees are informed, dedicated adherents of these interests. They are thus in a position to secure pertinent data and to act strategically, helping furnish "organization" to the groups they represent. Sometimes the resources involved are such that there is organization on both sides; or the more effective organization may be on the "reform" side. The securities exchange legislation is an illuminating example, for after Richard Whitney's conviction for embezzlement key officials of the New York Stock Exchange recognized their own interest in supporting controls over less scrupulous elements. This interest configuration doubtless explains the relative popularity of the SEC both with regulated groups and with organized liberal groups.

IV

The evidence considered here suggests that we can make an encouraging start toward defining the conditions in which myth and symbolic reassurance become key elements in the governmental process. The conditions[39] are present in substantial degree in many policy areas other than business regulations. They may well be maximal in the foreign policy area, and a similar approach to the study of foreign policy formation would doubtless be revealing.

Because the requisite conditions are always present in some degree, every instance of policy formulation involves a "mix" of symbolic effect and rational reflection of interests in resources, though

---

[88] *The Folklore of Capitalism* (New Haven: Yale University Press, 1937), pp. 212, 215, 216.

[39] They are listed above under "Pattern B."

one or the other phenomenon may be dominant in any particular case. One type of mix is exemplified by such governmental programs outside the business regulation field as public education and social security. There can be no doubt that these programs do confer important tangible benefits upon a very wide public, very much as they promise to do. They do so for the reasons suggested earlier. Business organizations, labor organizations, teachers' organizations, and other organized groups benefit from these programs and have historically served to focus public attention upon the resources to be gained or lost. Their task has been all the easier because the techniques for achieving the benefits are fairly readily recognizable.

But the financing of these same programs involves public policies of a different order. Here the symbol of "free" education and other benefits, the complexity of the revenue and administrative structure, and the absence of organization have facilitated the emergence of highly regressive payroll, property, and head taxes as the major sources of revenue. Thus, business organizations, which by and large support the public schools that provide their trained personnel and the social security programs that minimize the costs of industrial pensions, pay relatively little for these services; while the direct beneficiaries of the "free" programs pay a relatively high proportion of the costs. Careful analysis of the "mix" in particular programs should prove illuminating.

If the conditions facilitating symbolic reassurance are correctly specified, there is reason to question some common assumptions about strategic variables in policy formulation and reason also to devise some more imaginative models in designing research in this area. The theory discussed here suggests, for example, a tie between the emergence of conditions promoting interests in symbolic reassurance and widened freedom of policy maneuver for those attempting to assert leadership over the affected group. It implies that the number of adherents of a political interest may have more to do with whether the political benefit offered is tangible or symbolic than with the quantity or quality of tangible resources allocated. It suggests that the factors that explain voting behavior can be quite different from the factors that explain resource allocations through government. The fact that large numbers of people are objectively affected by a governmental program may actually serve in some contexts to weaken their capacity to exert a political claim upon tangible values.

A number of recent writers, to take another example, have suggested that it is the "independence" of the independent regulatory commissions which chiefly accounts for their tendency to become tools of the groups they regulate. The hypotheses suggested here apply to regulatory programs admiinstered in cabinet departments as well; and their operation is discernible in some of these programs when the specified conditions are present. The Grazing Service and the Anti-trust Division are examples.

In terms of research design, the implications of the analysis probably lie chiefly in the direction of emphasizing an integral tie of political behavior to underlying and extensive social interaction. Analysts of political dynamics must have a theory of relevance; but the directly relevant may run farther afield than has sometimes been assumed. Political activities of all kinds require the most exhaustive scrutiny to ascertain whether their chief function is symbolic or substantive. The "what" of Lasswell's famous definition of politics is a complex universe in itself.

The Transmission of Political Values
from Parent to Child *

M. KENT JENNINGS AND RICHARD G. NIEMI

In understanding the political development of the pre-adult one of the central questions hinges on the relative and differentiated contributions of various socializing agents. The question undoubtedly proves more difficult as one traverses a range of polities from those where life and learning are almost completely wrapped up in the immediate and extended family to those which are highly complex social organisms and in which the socialization agents are extremely varied. To gain some purchase on the role of one socializing agent in our own complex society, this paper will take up the specific question of the transmission of certain values from parent to child as observed in late adolescence. After noting parent-child relationships for a variety of political values, attention will be turned to some aspects of family structure which conceivably affect the transmission flows.

I. ASSESSING THE FAMILY'S IMPACT

"Foremost among agencies of socialization into politics is the family." So begins Herbert Hyman's discussion of the sources of political learning.[1] Hyman

explicitly recognized the importance of other agents, but he was neither the first nor the last observer to stress the preeminent position of the family. This viewpoint relies heavily on both the direct and indirect role of the family in shaping the basic orientations of offspring. Whether the child is conscious or unaware of the impact, whether the process is role-modeling or overt transmission, whether the values are political and directly usable or "nonpolitical" but transferable, and whether what is passed on lies in the cognitive or affective realm, it has been argued that the family is of paramount importance. In part this view draws heavily from psychoanalytic theory, but it is also influenced by anthropological and national character studies, and by the great emphasis on role theory in sociological studies of socialization. In part the view stems also from findings in the area of partisan commitment and electoral behavior indicating high intergenerational agreement. Unfortunately for the general thesis, such marked correlations have been only occasionally observed in other domains of political life. Indeed, other domains of political life have been rarely explored systematically with respect to the central question of articulation in parent-child political values.[2] Inferences, backward and forward extrapolations, and retrospective and projective data have carried the brunt of the argument.

A recent major report about political socialization during the elementary years seriously questions the family's overriding

SOURCE. Reprinted from *The American Political Science Review*, Vol. 62, 1968, by permission of the author and publisher. Copyright 1968, The American Political Science Association.
* Revised version of a paper delivered at the annual meeting of the American Political Science Association, New York, September, 1966. Financial support for the study reported here comes from The Danforth Foundation and the National Science Foundation. We wish to acknowledge the assistance of Michael Traugott in the preparation of this paper.

[1] Herbert Hyman, *Political Socialization* (New York: Free Press of Glencoe, 1959), p. 69.

[2] Most of these few studies, cited by Hyman, *op. cit.*, pp. 70-71, are based on extremely limited samples and nearly all took place between 1930-1950.

importance. In contrast to the previously-held views that the family was perhaps preeminent or at least co-equal to other socializing agents stands the conclusion by Robert Hess and Judith Torney that "the public school is the most important and effective instrument of political socialization in the United States," and that "the family transmits its own particular values in relatively few areas of political socialization and that, for the most part, the impact of the family is felt only as one of several socializing agents and institutions."[3] Hess and Torney see the primary influence of the family as the agent which promotes early attachment to country and government, and which thus "insures the stability of basic institutions."[4] Hence, "the family's primary effect is to support consensually-held attitudes rather than to inculcate idosyncratic attitudes."[5] The major exception to these conclusions occurs in the area of partisanship and related matters where the family's impact is predictably high.

The Hess and Torney argument thus represents a major departure from the more traditional view. They see the family's influence as age-specific and restricted in its scope. In effect, the restriction of the family's role removes its impact from much of the dynamic qualities of the political system and from individual differences in political behavior. The consensual qualities imparted or reinforced by the family, while vital for comprehending the maintenance of the system, are less useful in explaining adjustments in the system, the conflicts and accommodations made, the varied reactions to political stimuli, and the playing of diverse political roles. In short, if the family's influence is restricted to inculcating a few consensual attributes (plus partisan attachment), it means that much of the

socialization which results in indivdual differentiation in everyday politics and which effects changes in the functioning of the political system lies outside the causal nexus of the parent-child relationship.

The first and primary objective of the present article will be to assay the flow of certain political values from parent to child. Our attention will be directed toward examining the variation in the distributions of the offsprings' values as a function of the distribution of these same values among their parents. This is not to say that other attitudinal and behavioral attributes of the parents are unimportant in shaping the child's political orientations. For example, children may develop authoritarian or politically distrustful attitudes not because their parents are authoritarian or distrustful but because of other variables such as disciplinary and protection practices.[6] Such transformations, while perhaps quite significant, will not be treated here. Rather, we will observe the degree to which the shape of value distributions in the child corresponds to that of his parent. Most of the values explored do not reflect the basic feelings of attachment to the political system which supposedly originate in the early years,[7] but much more of the secondary and tertiary values which tend to distinguish the political behavior of individuals and which contribute to the dynamics of the system.

STUDY DESIGN

The data to be employed come from a study conducted by the Survey Research Center of the University of Michigan in

---

[3] Robert D. Hess and Judith V. Torney, *The Development of Basic Attitudes and Values Toward Government and Citizenship During the Elementary School Years*, Part I (Cooperative Research Project No. 1078, U. S. Office of Education, 1965), pp. 193, 200.

[4] *Ibid.*, p. 191.

[5] *Ibid.*, p. 192.

[6] Illustrative of this argument is Frank A. Pinner's careful rendering in "Parental Overprotection and Political Distrust," *The Annals*, **361** (September, 1965), 58-70. See, in the same issue, Fred I. Greenstein, "Personality and Political Socialization: The Theories of Authoritarian and Democratic Character," pp. 81-95.

[7] In addition to the Hess and Torney report, evidence for this is supplied by, *inter alios*, Fred I. Greenstein, *Children and Politics* (New Haven: Yale University Press, 1965); and David Easton and Jack Dennis, "The Child's Image of Government," *The Annals*, **361** (September, 1965), 40-57.

the spring of 1965. Interviews were held with a national probability sample of 1669 seniors distributed among 97 secondary schools, public and nonpublic.[8] The response rate for students was 99 percent. For a random third of the students the father was designated for interviewing, for another random third the mother was designated, and for the other third both parents were assigned. In the permanent absence of the designated parent, the other parent or parent surrogate was interviewed. Interviews were actually completed with at least one parent of 94 percent of the students, and with both parents of 26 percent of the students, or 1992 parents altogether. Among parents the response rate was 93 percent.[9] Two features of the student and parent samples should be underscored. First, since the sample of students was drawn from a universe of 12th graders, school drop-outs in that age cohort, estimated at around 26 percent for this time period, were automatically eliminated. Second, due mainly to the fact that more mothers than fathers constitute the head of household in single-parent families, the sample of parents is composed of 56 percent mothers.[10]

Our basic procedure will be to match the parent and student samples so that parent-student pairs are formed. Although the actual number of students for whom we have at least one parent respondent in 1562, the base number of pairs used in the analysis is 1992. In order to make maximum usage of the interviews gathered, the paired cases in which both the mother and father were interviewed (430) are each given half of their full value.[11] A further adjustment in weighting, due to unavoidably imprecise estimates at the time the sampling frame was constructed, results in a weighted total of 1927 parent-student pairs.[12]

Using 12th graders for exploring the parental transmission of political values carries some distinct characteristics. In the first place, most of these pre-adults are approaching the point at which they will leave the immediate family. Further political training from the parents will be minimal. A second feature is that the formal civic education efforts of society, as carried out in the elementary and secondary schools, are virtually completed. For whatever effect they may have on shaping the cognitive and cathectic maps of individuals, these various formal and informal modes of citizenship preparation will generally terminate, although other forms of educational preparation may lie ahead, especially for the college bound. A final consideration is that while the family and the educational system have come to some terminal point as socializing agents, the pre-adult has yet to be much affected by actual political practice. Neither have other potentially important experiences, such as the establishment of his own nuclear family and an occupational role, had an opportunity to

---

[8] Of the original ninety-eight schools, drawn with a probability proportionate to their size, eighty-five (87%) agreed to participate; matched substitutes for the refusals resulted in a final total of ninety-seven out of 111 contacted altogether (87%).

[9] Additional interviews were conducted with 317 of the students' most relevant social studies teachers and with the school principals. Some 21,000 paper-pencil questionnaires were administered to all members of the senior class in 85 percent of the sample schools.

[10] In any event, initial controls on parent (as well as student) sex suggest that parent-student agreement rates on the values examined here differ little among parent-student sex combinations. This will be discussed in more detail below.

[11] The alternative to half-weighting these pairs is to subselect among those cases where both mother and father were interviewed. Half weighting tends to reduce the sampling variability because it utilizes more data cases.

[12] It proved impossible to obtain accurate, recent figures on 12th grade enrollment throughout the country. Working with the data available and extrapolating as necessary, a sampling frame was constructed so that schools would be drawn with a probability proportionate to the size of the senior class. After entry was obtained into the sample schools and precise figures on enrollments gathered, differential weights were applied to correct for the inequalities in selection probabilities occasioned by the original imprecise information. The average weight equals 1.2.

exert their effects. Thus the 12th grader is at a significant juncture in his political life cycle and it will be instructive to see the symmetry of parental and student values at this juncture.

ADOLESCENT REBELLION

It should be emphasized that we are not necessarily searching for patterns of political rebellion from parental values. Researchers have been hard-pressed to uncover any significant evidence of adolescent rebellion in the realm of political affairs.[13] Pre-adults may differ politically from their parents—particularly during the college years—but there is scant evidence that the rebellion pattern accounts for much of this deviance. Data from our own study lend little support to the rebellion hypotheses at the level of student recognition. For example, even of the 38 percent of the student sample reporting important disagreements with their parents less than 15 percent placed these disagreements in a broadly-defined arena of political and social phenomena. And these disagreements do not necessarily lie in the province of rebellion, as one ordinarily construes the term.

There is, furthermore, some question as to whether adolescent rebellion as such occurs with anything approaching the frequency or magnitude encountered in sociological writings and the popular literature. As two scholars concluded after a major survey of the literature dealing with "normal" populations:

> In the large scale studies of normal populations, we do not find adolescents clamor-

ing for freedom or for release from unjust constraint. We do not find rebellious resistance to authority as a dominant theme. For the most part, the evidence bespeaks a modal pattern considerably more peaceful than much theory and most social comment would lead us to expect. "Rebellious youth" and "the conflict between generations" are phrases that ring; but, so far as we can tell, it is not the ring of truth they carry so much as the beguiling but misleading tone of drama.[14]

To say that rebellion directed toward the political orientations of the parents is relatively rare is not to say, however, that parent and student values are consonant. Discrepancies can occur for a variety of reasons, including the following:

1. Students may consciously opt for values, adopted from other agents, in conflict with those of their parents without falling into the rebellion syndrome.

2. Much more probable are discrepancies which are recognized neither by the parent nor the off-spring.[15] The lack of cue-giving and object saliency on the part of parents sets up ambiguous or empty psychological spaces which may be filled by other agents in the student's environment.

3. Where values are unstable and have low centrality in a belief system, essentially random and time-specific responses to stimuli may result in apparent low transmission rates.

4. Another source of dissonant relationships, and potentially the most confounding one, is that life cycle effects are operative. When the pre-adult reaches the current age of his parents, his political behavior might well be similar to that of his parents even though his youthful attitudes would not suggest such congru-

[13] Hyman, *op. cit.*, p. 72, and n. 6, p. 89. See also Robert E. Lane, "Fathers and Sons: Foundations of Political Belief," *American Sociological Review,* 24 (August, 1959), 502-511; Eleanor E. Maccoby, Richard E. Matthews, and Anton S. Morton, "Youth and Political Change," *Public Opinion Quarterly,* 18 (Spring, 1954), 23-39; Russell Middleton and Snell Putney, "Political Expression of Adolescent Rebellion," *American Journal of Sociology,* 68 (March, 1963), 527-535; and Robert H. Somers, "The Mainsprings of the Rebellion: A Survey of Berkeley Students in November, 1964," in Seymour Martin Lipset and Sheldon S. Wolin (eds.), *The Berkeley Student Revolt* (Garden City, N. Y.: Doubleday, 1965), p. 547.

[14] Elizabeth Douvan and Martin Gold, "Modal Patterns in American Adolescence," in Lois and Martin Hoffman (eds.), *Review of Child Development Research* (New York: Russell Sage Foundation, 1966), Vol. II, p. 485.

[15] For an analysis of students' and parents' knowledge of each other's political attitudes and behavior, see Richard G. Niemi, "A Methodological Study of Political Socialization in the Family" (unpublished Ph.D. thesis, University of Michigan, 1967).

ency. This is an especially thorny empirical question and nests in the larger quandry concerning the later life effects of early socialization.

II. PATTERNS OF PARENT-CHILD CORRESPONDENCES

Confronted with a number of political values at hand we have struck for variety rather than any necessary hierarchy of importance. We hypothesized a range of correlations dependent in part on the play of factors assumed to alter the parent-student associations (noted above). We have purposely deleted values dealing with participative orientations and, as noted previously, those delving into sentiments of basic attachment and loyalty to the regime. The values selected include party identification, attitudinal positions on four specific issues, evaluations of socio-political groupings, and political cynicism. For comparative purposes we shall glance briefly at parent-student congruences in the religious sphere.

To measure agreement between parents and students we rely primarily on correlations, either of the product-moment or rank-order variety. While the obvious alternative of percentage agreement may have an intuitive appeal, it has several drawbacks. Percentage agreement is not based on the total configuration of a square matrix but only on the "main diagonal." Thus two tables which are similar in percentage agreement may represent widely differing amounts of agreement if deviations from perfect agreement are considered. Moreover, percentage agreement depends heavily on the number of categories used, so that the degree of parent-student similarity might vary for totally artificial reasons. Correlations are more resistant to changes in the definition of categories. Finally, correlations are based on relative rankings (and intervals in the case of product-moment correlations) rather than on absolute agreement as percentage agreement usually is. That is, if student scores tend to be higher (or lower) than parent scores on a particular variable, but the students are ranked similarly to their parents, a high correlation may be obtained with very little perfect agreement.

PARTY IDENTIFICATION

Previous research has established party identification as a value dimension of considerable importance in the study of political behavior as well as a political value readily transmitted from parents to children. Studies of parent-youth samples as well as adult populations indicate that throughout the life cycle there is a relatively high degree of correspondence between respondents' party loyalties and their parents'. Our findings are generally consistent with those of these earlier studies.

The substantial agreement between parent and student party affiliations is indicated by a tau-b (also called tau-beta) correlation of .47, a statistic nearly unaffected by the use of three, five, or all seven categories of the party identification spectrum generated by the question sequence.[16] The magnitude of this statistic reflects the twin facts of the presence of a large amount of exact agreement and the absence of many wide differences between students and parents. When the full 7×7 matrix of parent-student party loyalties is arrayed (Table 1), the cells in which parents and students are in unison account for a third of the cases. The cells representing maximum disagreement are very nearly empty. Despite our earlier contention, collapsing categories and considering percentage agreement in the resulting table does make good substantive sense with regard to party identification. In this instance the collapsed categories have a meaning beyond just broader segments of a continuum, and

---

[16] This figure is based on parent-student pairs in which both respondents have a party identification; eliminated are the 2 percent of the pairs in which one or both respondents are apolitical or undecided. The product-moment correlation for these data is .59. The standard SRC party identification questions were used: see Angus Campbell, Philip E. Converse, Warren E. Miller, and Donald E. Stokes, *The American Voter* (New York: Wiley, 1960), ch. 6.

TABLE 1. STUDENT-PARENT PARTY IDENTIFICATION

Parents	Strong Dem.	Weak Dem.	Ind. Dem.	Ind.	Ind. Rep.	Weak Rep.	Strong Rep.	Total
				Students				
Party identification								
Strong Dem.	9.7%	8.0	3.4	1.8	.5	.9	.5	24.7%
Weak Dem.	5.8	9.0	4.2	2.6	.7	1.6	.7	24.7
	(32.6)ᵃ			(13.2)		(3.6)		(49.4)
Ind. Dem.	1.6	2.1	2.1	1.7	.8	.7	.2	9.3
Ind.	1.1	1.6	1.6	2.7	1.2	.9	.5	9.7
Ind. Rep.	.1	.5	.8	.9	.9	1.3	.5	4.9
	(7.0)			(12.7)		(4.1)		(23.9)
Weak Rep.	.3	2.1	1.6	2.3	1.9	5.0	1.9	15.0
Strong Rep.	.2	.9	.8	.8	2.4	3.3	3.5	11.7
	(3.4)			(9.7)		(13.6)		(26.7)
Total	18.8%	24.2	14.5	12.8	8.4	13.6	7.7	100.0%
	(43.0)			(35.7)		(21.3)		

tau-b = .47 $N = 1852$

ᵃ The full 7 × 7 table is provided because of the considerable interest in party identification. For some purposes, reading ease among them, the 3 × 3 table is useful. It is given by the figures in parentheses; these figures are (within rounding error) the sum of the numbers just above them.

are associated with a general orientation toward one party or the other or toward a neutral position between them. Thus arrayed, 59 percent of the students fall into the same broad category as their parents, and only seven percent cross the sharp divide between Republicans and Democrats.

The observed similarity between parents and students suggests that transmission of party preferences from one generation to the next is carried out rather successfully in the American context. However, there are also indications that other factors (temporarily at least) have weakened the party affiliations of the younger generation. This is most obvious if we compare the marginal totals for parents and students (Table 1). The student sample contains almost 12 percent more Independents than the parent sample, drawing almost equally on the Republican and Democratic proportions of the sample. Similarly, among party identifiers a somewhat larger segment of

the students is but weakly inclined toward the chosen party. Nor are these configurations simply an artifact of the restricted nature of the parent sample, since the distribution of party identification among the parents resembles closely that of the entire adult electorate as observed in November, 1964 (SRC 1964 election study).

A number of factors might account for the lesser partisanship of the students, and we have only begun to explore some of them. On the one hand, the students simply lack their parents' long experience in the active electorate, and as a consequence have failed as yet to develop a similar depth of feeling about the parties.[17] On the other hand, there are no

[17] This is suggested by an analysis of different age groups among the active electorate: see *Ibid.*, pp. 161ff. For evidence that the depth of adult attachment to party is not necessarily uniform across electoral systems see M. Kent Jennings and Richard G. Niemi, "Party Identification at Multiple Levels of Government," *American Journal of Sociology,* **72** (July, 1966), 86-101.

doubt specific forces pushing students toward Independence. The experience of an ever-widening environment and the gradual withdrawal of parental power may encourage some students to adopt an Independent outlook. The efforts of schools and of teachers in particular are probably weighted in the same direction. If these forces are at work, high school students may be gradually withdrawing from an earlier position of more overt partisanship. But, whatever the exact nature of the causes, they clearly draw off from the partisan camp a small but significant portion of the population as it approaches full citizenship.

OPINIONS ON SPECIFIC ISSUES

One way in which political values are expressed is through opinions on specific issues. However, as Converse has shown, many opinions or idea elements not only tend to be bounded by systems of low constraint but are also quite unstable over relatively short periods of time among mass publics.[18] Hence in comparing student responses with parent responses the problem of measurement may be compounded by attitude instability among both samples. Rather than being a handicap instabilities actually sharpen the test of whether significant parent-to-child flows occur. One would not expect unstable sentiments to be the object of any considerable political learning in the family. It seems unlikely that many cues would be given off over matters about which the parents were unsure or held a fluctuating opinion. Even in the event of numerous cues in unstable situations, the ambivalent or ambiguous nature of such cues would presumably yield instability in

the child. In either case the articulation between parent and child beliefs would be tempered.

We have selected four specific issues for examination. Two involve public schools; given the populations being studied, schools are particularly relevant attitude objects. Furthermore these two issues envelope topics of dramatic interest to much of the public—integration in the schools and the use of prayers in schools. After an initial screening question weeded out those without any interest at all on the issues, the respondents were asked if they thought the government in Washington should "see to it that white and Negro children go to the same schools" or if the government should "stay out of this area as it is none of its business." On the prayers in school question the respondents were asked if they believed "schools should be allowed to start each day with a prayer" or that "religion does not belong in the schools."[19] Taken in the aggregate the high school seniors proved less likely to sanction prayers in school than did the parents (although a majority of both answered in the affirmative) and more willing to see the federal government enforce segregation than were the adults (with both yielding majorities in favor). These differences are moderate; no more than 14 percentage points separate like-paired marginals on the prayer issue and no more than 10 points on the integration issue. The cross-tabulation of parent and student responses produces moderately strong coefficients, as shown in the first two entries of Table 2.

Combining as they do some very visible population groupings along with topics of more than usual prominence in the mass media and local communities, it

[18] Philip E. Converse, "The Nature of Belief Systems in Mass Publics," in David E. Apter (ed.), *Ideology and Discontent* (New York: Free Press of Glencoe, 1964), pp. 206-261. The following section borrows from Converse's discussion. Robert E. Agger takes a somewhat different view of instabilities in "Panel Studies of Comparative Community Political Decision-Making," in M. Kent Jennings and L. Harmon Zeigler (eds.), *The Electoral Process* (Englewood Cliffs, N.J.: Prentice-Hall, 1966), pp. 265-289.

[19] Sizeable proportions of both parents and students elected to state a middle or "depends" response, particularly on the first question. Such responses occupy a middle position in our calculation of the rank order correlations. On the first issue 10 percent of the pairs were dropped because either the parent or child opted out on the initial screen; the corresponding figure for the second issue is 19 percent.

TABLE 2. CORRELATIONS BETWEEN PARENT-STUDENT ATTITUDES ON FOUR ISSUES

Federal government's role in integrating the schools	.34[a]
Whether schools should be allowed to use prayers	.29
Legally elected Communist should be allowed to take office	.13
Speakers against churches and religion should be allowed	.05

[a] Each of the correlations (tau-b) in this table is based on at least 1560 cases.

would be surprising if there were not at least a moderate amount of parent-student overlap. The wonder is not that correlations are this high, but rather that they are not higher. If correlations no higher than this are produced on issues which touch both generations in a manner which many issues assuredly do not, then one would speculate that more remote and abstract issues would generate even less powerful associations.

This hypothesizing is borne out by the introduction of two other issues. Both parents and students were asked to agree or disagree with these two statements: "If a Communist were legally elected to some public office around here, the people should allow him to take office"; and "If a person wanted to make a speech in this community against churches and religion, he should be allowed to speak." In general, the pre-adults took a slightly more libertarian stance on the two issues than did the parents, but the differences in any of the like-paired marginals do not exceed 14 percent. These similarities mask extremely tenuous positive correlations, however, as the second pair of items in Table 2 reveals.

These two issues carry neither the immediacy nor the concreteness which may be said to characterize the two issues dealing with integration and prayers in the schools. Indeed, one might question whether the two statements represent issues at all, as the public normally conceives of issues. At any rate it is improbable that the students are reflecting

much in the way of cues emitted from their parents, simply because these topics or related ones are hardly prime candidates for dinner-table conversation or inadvertent cue-giving. Nor do they tap some rather basic sentiments and attitude objects which permeate the integration and prayers issues. Such sentiments are more likely to be embedded in the expressive value structure of the parents than are those having to do with some of the more abstract "fundamental" tenets of democracy as exemplified in the free speech and right to take office issues. That adults themselves have low levels of constraint involving propositions about such fundamental tenets has been demonstrated by McClosky, and Prothro and Grigg.[20] Given this environment, the lower correlation for the two more abstract propositions is predictable.

Although the issues we have examined by no means exhaust the variety of policy questions one might pose, they probably exemplify the range of parent-student correspondences to be found in the populace. On all but consensual topics—which would perforce assume similar distributions among virtually all population strata anyway—the parent-student correlations obtained for the integration and prayer issues probably approach the apex. In part this may be due to unstable opinions and in part to the effects of agents other than the family. It is also possible that the children will exhibit greater correspondences to their parents later in the life cycle. But for this particular point in time, the articulation of political opinions is only moderately strong on salient, concrete issues and virtually nil on more abstract issues.

EVALUATIONS OF SOCIO-POLITICAL GROUPINGS

Collectivities of people which are distinguished by certain physical, locational,

[20] Herbert McClosky, "Consensus and Ideology in American Politics," this *Review*, **58** (June, 1964), 361-382; and James W. Prothro and Charles W. Grigg, "Fundamental Principles of Democracy: Bases of Agreement and Disagreement," *Journal of Politics*, **22** (May, 1960), 276-294.

social, religious, and membership characteristics (the list is obviously not exhaustive) often come to serve as significant political reference groups for individuals. While distinguishable groups may carry affective neutrality, it seems to be in the nature of mass behavior that these groups most often come to be viewed with greater or lesser esteem. The intersection of group evaluations and the political process comes when claims or demands are made by or upon significant portions of such groupings. The civil rights movement of the past decade is perhaps the most striking contemporary example. As Converse has suggested, social groupings are likely to have greater centrality for mass publics than abstract idea elements per se.[21] Thus when particular issues and public policies become imbued with group-related properties, the issues acquire considerably more structure and concreteness for the mass public than would be the normal case.

To what extent is the family crucial in shaping the evaluations of social groupings and thus—at a further remove—the interpretation of questions of public policy? Some insight into this may be gained by comparing the ratings applied by the parents and students to eight sociopolitical groupings. While the groups all carry rather easily recognized labels, they do differ in terms of their relative visibility and their inclusive-exclusive properties. They include Protestants, Catholics, Jews, Negroes, Whites, Labor Unions, Big Business, and Southerners.

To measure the attitudes toward these groups, an instrument dubbed the "feeling thermometer" was used. The technique was designed to register respondents' feelings toward a group on a scale ranging from a cold 0 to a warm 100. In the analysis we will treat this scale as interval level measurement. We have also examined the data using contingency tables and ordinal statistics; our conclusions are the same regardless of the method used.

Turning first to the mean ratings, given

[21] Converse, *op. cit.*

TABLE 3. CORRELATIONS BETWEEN PARENT-STUDENT GROUP EVALUATIONS

Group Evaluated	Parent-Student Correlations	Mean Ratings	
		Parent	Student
Catholics	.36 [a]	72	70
Southerners	.30	66	62
Labor unions	.28	60	60
Negroes	.26	67	69
Jews	.22	67	63
Whites	.19	84	83
Protestants	.15	84	79
Big business	.12	64	63

[a] Each of the product-moment correlations in this table is based on at least 1880 cases. The corresponding tau-b's are (top to bottom) .28, .22, .22, .20, .18, .19, .13, .08.

in Table 3, we find a striking similarity in student and parent aggregate scores. The largest difference is five points and the average difference is only 2.2 points. Additionally, the standard deviations for the two samples (not shown) are extremely similar across all groupings. Nor were there significant tendencies for one sample to employ more than the other the option of "unawareness" or "no feelings" (a reading of 50 on the thermometer) about the groupings. Moreover, the aggregate differences which do occur are not immediately explicable. For example, students rate Southerners slightly lower than parents, as we expected, but the difference in ratings of Negroes is negligible, which was unanticipated. Students rate Whites and Protestants somewhat lower than parents. This is not matched, however, by higher evaluations of the minority groups—Jews, for example.

Given these extraordinarily congruent patterns it is rather startling to see that they are patently not due to uniform scores of parent-child pairs. As shown in Table 3, the highest correlation between the parent and student ratings is .36 and the coefficients range as low as .12. Even the highest correlation is well below that found for party identification (where the product-moment coefficient was .59 for the seven-fold classification), and for several groupings the relationships between parent and student scores are very feeble. If the child's view of socio-political groupings grows out of cue-giving in the home, the magnitude of the associations should exceed those observed here.

It is beyond the task of this paper to unravel thoroughly these findings. The range of correlations does provide a clue as to the conditions under which parent-student correspondences will be heightened. In the first place the three categories producing the lowest correlations appear to have little socio-political relevancy in the group sense. Whites and Protestants are extremely inclusive categories and, among large sectors of the public, may simply not be cognized or treated in everyday life as groupings highly differentiated from society in general. They are, in a sense, too enveloping to be taken as differentiated attitude objects. If they do not serve as significant attitude objects, the likelihood of parent to child transmission would be dampened. In the third case—Big Business—it seems likely that its visibility is too low to be cognized as a group qua group.

As the parent-student correlations increase we notice that the groupings come to have not only highly distinguishable properties but that they also have high visibility in contemporary American society. Adding to the socio-political saliency thereby induced is the fact that group membership may act to increase the parent-student correlations. One would hypothesize that parent-student pairs falling into a distinguishable, visible grouping would exhibit higher correlations in rating that same grouping than would nonmembers. Taking the four groupings for whom the highest correlations were obtained, we divided the pairs into those where both the parent and the child— except in the case of labor unions—were enveloped by the groupings versus those outside the groupings. Although none of the hypothesized relationships was contravened, only the coefficients for evaluations of Southerners provided a distinct demarcation between members and non-

members (tau-b = .25 for Southern pairs, .14 for non-Southerners). It is quite possible that measures capturing membership identification and intensities would improve upon these relationships.

As with opinions on specific issues, intrapair correlations on group evaluations are at best moderately positive, and they vary appreciably as a result of socio-political visibility and, to a small degree, group membership characteristics. What we begin to discern, then, is a pattern of congruences which peak only over relatively concrete, salient values susceptible to repeated reinforcement in the family (and elsewhere, perhaps), as in party identification and in certain issues and group evaluations. It is conceivable that these results will not prevail if we advance from fairly narrow measures like the ones previously employed to more global value structures. We now turn to an illustrative example. It so happens that it also provides an instance of marked aggregate differences between the two generations.

POLITICAL CYNICISM

Political cynicism and its mirror image, trust, offer an interesting contrast to other variables we are considering. Rather than referring to specific political issues or actors, cynicism is a basic orientation toward political actors and activity. Found empirically to be negatively related to political participation, political cynicism has also been found to be positively correlated with measures of a generally distrustful outlook (personal cynicism).[22] Political cynicism appears to be a manifestation of a deep-seated suspicion of others' motives and actions. Thus this attitude comes closer than the rest of our values to tapping a basic psycho-political predisposition.

Previous research with young children suggests that sweeping judgments, such as

[22] Robert E. Agger, Marshall N. Goldstein, and Stanley A. Pearl, "Political Cynicism: Measurement and Meaning," *Journal of Politics*, 23 (August, 1961), p. 490; and Edgar Litt, "Political Cynicism and Political Futility," *Journal of Politics*, 25 (May, 1963), 312-323.

the essential goodness of human nature, are formed early in life, often before cognitive development and information acquisition make the evaluated objects intelligible. Greenstein, and Hess and Easton, have reported this phenomenon with regard to feelings about authority figures; Hess and Torney suggest similar conclusions about loyalty and attachment to government and country.[23] Evaluative judgments and affective ties have been found among the youngest samples for which question and answer techniques are feasible. This leads to the conclusions that the school, mass media, and peer groups have had little time to influence these attitudes.

It seems to follow that the family is the repository from which these feelings are initially drawn. Either directly by their words and deeds or indirectly through unconscious means, parents transmit to their children basic postures toward life which the children carry with them at least until the development of their own critical faculties. Although our 12th graders have been exposed to a number of influences which could mitigate the initial implanting, one should expect, according to the model, a rather strong correspondence between parent and student degrees of political cynicism.

To assess the cynicism of parents and students, a Guttman scale was constructed from five questions asked of both samples. All questions dealt with the conduct of the national government.[24] In each

sample the items formed a scale, with coefficients of reproducibility of .93 and .92 for parents and students, respectively. The aggregate scores reflect a remarkably lesser amount of cynicism among students than among parents. This is apparent in the marginal distributions in Table 4, which show the weight of the parent distribution falling much more on the cynical end of the scale. Similarly, while a fifth of the students were more cynical than their parents, three times this number of parents were more cynical than their children. The students may be retreating from an even more trusting attitude held earlier, but compared to their parents they still see little to be cynical about in national political activity.

Here is a case where the impact of other socialization agents—notably the school—looms large. The thrust of school experience is undoubtedly on the side of developing trust in the political system in general. Civic training in school abounds in rituals of system support in the formal curriculum. These rituals and curricula are not matched by a critical examination of the nation's shortcomings or the possible virtues of other political forms. Coupled with a moralistic, legalistic, prescriptive orientation to the study of government is the avoidance of conflict dimensions and controversial issues.[25] A

[23] Greenstein, *op. cit.,* Ch. 3; Robert D. Hess and David Easton, "The Child's Changing Image of the President," *Public Opinion Quarterly,* **24** (Winter, 1960), 632-644; and Hess and Torney, *op. cit.,* pp. 73ff.

[24] The items are as follows:

(1) Do you think that quite a few of the people running the government are a little crooked, not very many are, or do you think hardly any of them are?

(2) Do you think that people in the government waste a lot of the money we pay in taxes, waste some of it, or don't waste very much of it?

(3) How much of the time do you think you can trust the government in Washington to do what is right—just

about always, most of the time, or only some of the time?

(4) Do you feel that almost all of the people running the government are smart people who usually know what they are doing, or do you think that quite a few of them don't seem to know what they are doing?

(5) Would you say that the government is pretty much run by a few big interests looking out for themselves or that it is run for the benefit of all the people?

[25] These are old charges but apparently still true. After a survey of the literature on the subject and on the basis of a subjective analysis of leading government textbooks in high schools, Byron G. Massialas reaches similar conclusions: see his "American Government: 'We are the Greatest'," in C. Benjamin Cox and Byron G. Massialas (eds.), *Social Studies in the United States: A Critical Appraisal* (New York: Harcourt, Brace, & World, Inc., 1967), pp. 167-195.

direct encounter with the realities of political life is thus averted or at least postponed. It would not be surprising, then, to find a rather sharp rise in the level of cynicism as high school seniors move ahead in a few years into the adult world.

Students on the whole are less cynical than parents; relative to other students, though, those with distrustful, hostile parents should themslves be more suspicious of the government, while those with trusting parents should find less ground for cynicism. Against the backdrop of our discussion, it is remarkable how low the correspondence is among parent-student pairs. Aside from faint markings at the extremities, students' scores are very nearly independent of their parents' attitudes (Table 4). The cynicism of distrustful parents is infrequently implanted in their children, while a smaller group of students develops a cynical outlook despite their parents' views. Political cynicism as measured here is not a value often passed from parent to child. Regardless of parental feelings, children develop a moderately to highly positive view of the trustworthiness of the national government and its officials.

These findings do not mean that parents fail to express negative evaluations in family interaction nor that children fail to adopt some of the less favorable attitudes of their parents. What is apparently not transmitted is a *generalized* cynicism about politics. Thus while warmth or hostility toward specific political objects with high visibility may be motivated by parental attitudes, a more pervasive type of belief system labelled cynicism is apparently subject to heavy, undercutting influences outside the family nexus. These influences are still operative as the adolescent approaches adult status.

Working with another encompassing set of values we encountered much the same patterns as with cynicism. After obtaining their rank orderings of interest in international, national, state, and local political matters the respondents were allocated along a 7-point scale of cosmopolitanism-localism through an adaptation of Coombs' unfolding technique.[26] On the whole the students are considerably more cosmopolitan than the parents, and the paired correlation is a modest .17.

[26] A description of this operation and some results are given in M. Kent Jennings, "Pre-Adult Orientations to Multiple Systems of Government," *Midwest Journal of Political Science,* **XI** (August, 1967), 291-317. The underlying theory and technique are found in Clyde Coombs, *A Theory of Data* (New York: Wiley, 1964), esp. Ch. 5.

TABLE 4. RELATIONSHIP BETWEEN PARENT-STUDENT SCORES OF THE CYNICISM SCALE

| | Students | | | | | | | |
| | Least Cynical | | | Most Cynical | | | Row | Marginal |
Parents	1	2	3	4	5	6	Totals	Totals [a]
Least Cynical—1	25%	27	33	13	1	2	101%	8%
2	19	28	38	9	1	5	100	12
3	18	28	37	10	3	4	100	33
4	16	23	41	13	3	4	100	17
5	15	19	35	19	3	9	100	9
Most Cynical—6	12	22	36	18	4	8	100	21
Marginal totals [a]	17%	25	37	13	3	5		100%
	tau-b = .12				$N = 1869$			

[a] Marginal totals show the aggregate scaler patterns for each sample.

Both life cycle and generational effects are undoubtedly at work here,[27] but the central point is that the students' orientations only mildly echo those of their parents.

What results from juxtaposing parents and their children on these two measures of cynicism and cosmopolitanism-localism is the suspicion that more global orientations to political life do not yield parent-student correspondences of greater magnitude than on more specific matters. If anything, the opposite is true—at least with respect to certain specifics. It may be that the child acquires a minimal set of basic commitments to the system and a way of handling authority situations as a result of early experiences in the family circle. But it appears also that this is a foundation from which arise widely diverse value structures, and that parental values are in extceremely variable and often feeble guide as to what the pre-adult's values will be.

RELIGIOUS BELIEFS

Up to this point we have traversed a range of political and quasi-political values, and have witnessed varying, but generally modest degrees of parent-student correspondences. To what extent does this pattern also characterize other domains of social values? For comparative purposes we can inject a consideration of religious beliefs. Like party preference, church affiliation among pre-adults is believed to be largely the same as parental affiliation. Such proves to be the case among our respondents. Of all parent-student pairs 74 percent expressed the same denominational preference. That this percentage is higher than the agreement on the three-fold classification of party identification (Democrat, Republican, Independent) by some 15 percent suggests that by the time the pre-adult is preparing to leave the family circle he has internalized the church preference of his parents to a moderately greater extent than their party preference.

There are some prefectly valid reasons

---

[27] This is discussed in more detail in Jennings, *op. cit.*

for this margin. To a much greater extent than party preference, church preference is likely to be reinforced in a number of ways. Assuming attendance, the child will usually go to the same church throughout childhood; the behavior is repeated at frequent intervals; it is a practice engaged in by greater or lesser portions of the entire family and thus carries multiple role-models; formal membership is often involved; conflicting claims from other sources in the environment for a change of preference are minimal except, perhaps, as a result of dating patterns. Religious affiliation is also often imbued with a fervid commitment.

In contrast, party preference is something which the child himself cannot transform into behavior except in rather superficial ways; reinforcement tends to be episodic and varies according to the election calendar; while the party preference of parents may vary only marginally over the pre-adult years, voting behavior fluctuates more and thus sets up ambiguous signals for the child; other sources in the environment—most noticeably the mass media—may make direct and indirect appeals for the child's loyalty which conflict with the parental attachments. Given the factors facilitating intrafamilial similarities in church preference, and the absence of at least some of these factors in the party dimension, it is perhaps remarkable that congruity of party identification approaches the zone of church-preference conguruity.

We found that when we skipped from party identification to other sorts of political values the parent-student correlations decreased perceptibly. May we expect to encounter similar behavior in the realm of religious values? One piece of evidence indicates that this is indeed the case. Respondents were confronted with a series of four statements having to do with the literal and divine nature of the Bible, ranging from a description of the Bible as "God's word and all it says is true" to a statement denying the contemporary utility of the book.

Both students and parents tended to

view the Bible with awe, the parents slightly more so than the students. But the correlation (tau-beta) among parent-student pairs is only a moderately strong .30. As with political values, once the subject matter moves out from central basic identification patterns the transmission of parental values fades.[28] And, as with political values, this may be a function of instability—although this seems less likely for the rendering of the Bible—the impingement of other agents —particularly likely in this case—or the relative absence of cue-giving on the part of the parents. The more generalizable proposition emerging from a comparison of political and religious orientations is that the correlations obtained diminish when the less concrete value orientations are studied.

III. FAMILY CHARACTERISTICS AND TRANSMISSION PATTERNS

We have found that the transmission of political values from parent to child varies remarkably according to the nature of the value. Although the central tendencies lie on the low side, we may encounter systematic variations in the degree to which values are successfully transmitted according to certain properties of family structure. That is, whether the transmittal be conscious and deliberate or unpurposive and indirect, are there some characteristics of the family unit which abet or inhibit the child's acquisition of parental values? We shall restrict ourselves to a limited set of variables having theoretical interest.

In order to dissect the parent-student relationships by controlling for a variety of independent variables, we shall retain the full parent-student matrices and then observe correlations within categories of

the control variables.[29] The political values to be examined include party identification, political cynicism, political cosmopolitanism, four specific political issues, and the ratings assigned to three minority population groupings—Catholics, Negroes, and Jews. This makes ten variables altogether, but for some purposes the issues and the group ratings are combined into composite figures.

PARENT AND STUDENT SEX COMBINATIONS

Various studies of adolescents have illustrated the discriminations which controls for sex of parent and sex of child may produce in studying the family unit.[30] Typically these studies have dealt with self-development, adjustment problems, motivational patterns, and the like. The question remains whether these discriminations are also found in the transmission of political values.

Part of the common lore of American political behavior is that the male is more dominant in political matters than the female, in his role both of husband and of father. And among pre-adults, males are usually found to be more politicized than females. While our findings do not necessarily challenge these statements, they do indicate the meager utility of sex roles in explaining parent-student agreement. The correlations be-

---

[28] To compare directly the amount of correspondence on interpretation of the Bible with church membership information, which is nominal-level data, we used the contingency coefficient. Grouping parent and student church affiliations into nine general categories, the coefficient is .88, compared to .34 for the Bible question.

[29] A more parsimonious method is to develop agreement indexes and to relate the control variables to these indexes. This results in a single statistic and contingency table for each control variable rather than one for each category of the control variable. Experience with both methods indicates that similar conclusions emerge, but retaining the full matrices preserves somewhat better the effects of each category of the control variable.

[30] See, e.g., Charles E. Bowerman and Glen H. Elder, "Adolescent Perception of Family Power Structure," *American Sociological Review*, 29 (August, 1964), 551-567; E. C. Devereux, Urie Bronfenbrenner, and G. J. Suci, "Patterns of Parent Behavior in the United States of America and the Federal Republic of Germany: A Cross-National Comparison," *International Social Science Journal*, 14 (UNESCO, 1963), 1-20; and Morris Rosenberg, *Society and the Adolescent Self-Image* (Princeton: Princeton University Press, 1965), Ch. 3.

tween parent-student values show some variation among the four combinations of parent and student sex, but the differences are usually small and inconsistent across the several values. Of the sixty possible comparisons for the ten political variables (i.e., $\binom{4}{2} = 6$ pairs of correlations for each variable), only eight produce differences in the correlations greater than .10, and thirty-three fall within a difference of less than .05. The average parent-student correlations for these variables are Mother-Son, .22; Mother-Daughter, .24; Father-Son, .20; Father-Daughter, .22. Thus the values of the father are not more likely to be internalized than those of the mother; nor do sons register consistently different rates of agreement than daughters. Finally, the particular sex mix of parent and child makes little difference. We also found that the use of sex combinations as controls on other bivariate relationships usually resulted in minor and fluctuating differences. Whatever family characteristics affect differential rates of value transmission, they are only marginally represented by sex roles in the family.

AFFECTIVITY AND CONTROL RELATIONSHIP

Another set of family characteristics employed with considerable success in studies of the family and child development has to do with the dimension of power or control on the one hand, and the dimension of attachment or affectivity on the other.[31] One salient conclusion has been that children are more apt to use

their parents as role models where the authority structure is neither extremely permissive nor extremely autocratic and where strong (but not overprotective) supportive functions and positive affects are present.

Although these dimensions have been employed in various ways in assessing the socialization of the child, they have rarely been utilized in looking at value transmission per se. In the nearest approach to this in political socialization studies, college students' reports suggested that perceived ideological differences between parent and child were higher when there was emotional estrangement, when the parental discipline was perceived as either too high or too low, and when the parent was believed to be interested in politics.[32] Somewhat related findings support the idea that affective and power relationships between parent and child may affect the transferral of political orientations.[33]

Affectivity and control relationships between pre-adults and their parents were operationalized in a number of ways, too numerous to give in detail. Suffice it to say that both parent and offspring were queried as to how close they felt to each other, whether and over what they disagreed, the path of compatibilities over the past few years, punishment agents, perceived level of parental control, parent and student satisfaction with controls, the nature and frequency of grievance processing, and rule-making procedures.

In accordance with the drift of previous research we hypothesized that the closer the student felt to his parent the more susceptible he would be to adopting, either through formal or informal learning, the political values of the parent. This turned out to be untrue. The closeness of parents and children, taking either the parent's report or the child's report, accounts for little variation in the parent-student correlations. This is true whether closeness to mother or father is considered and regardless of the student's sex. Similarly, other measures of affective relationships give little evidence that this dimension

---

[31] A discussion of these dimensions is found in Murray Straus, "Power and Support Structure of the Family in Relation to Socialization," *Journal of Marriage and the Family,* **26** (August, 1964) 318-326. See also Wesley C. Becker, "Consequences of Different Kinds of Parental Discipline," in Martin and Lois Hoffman (eds.), *Review of Child Development* (New York: Russell Sage Foundation, 1964), Vol. 1, pp. 169-208; William H. Sewell, "Some Recent Developments in Socialization Theory and Research," *The Annals,* **349** (September, 1963), 163-181; Glen H. Elder, Jr., "Parental Power Legitimation and Its Effects on the Adolescent," *Sociometry,* **26** (March, 1963), 50-65; and Douvan and Gold, *op. cit.*

[32] Middleton and Putney, *op. cit.*
[33] Lane, *op. cit.;* and Maccoby *et al., op. cit.*

prompted much variation in the correlations among pairs.

Turning to the power relationships between parent and child we hypothesized two types of relationships: (1) the more "democratic" and permissive these relationships were the greater congruency there would be; and (2) the more satisfied the child was with the power relationships the greater would be the congruency. Where patterning appears it tends to support the first hypothesis. For example, those students avowing they have an "average" amount of autonomy agree slightly more often with their parents than do those left primarily to their own resources and those heavily monitored by their parents. More generally, however, the power configuration—either in terms of its structure or its appraised satisfactoriness—generated few significant and consistent differences. This proved true whether we relied on the parent's account or the student's.

As with sex roles, the affective and control dimensions possess weak explanatory power when laid against parent-to-student transmission patterns. In neither case does this mean that these characteristics are unimportant for the political socialization of the young. It does mean that they are of little help in trying to account for the differential patterns of parent-student congruences.

LEVELS OF POLITICIZATION

Another set of family characteristics concerns the saliency and cue-giving structure of political matters within the family. One would expect parents for whom politics is more salient to emit more cues, both direct and indirect. Other things being equal, the transmission of political values would vary with the saliency and overt manifestations of political matters. Cue-giving would structure the political orientations of the child and, in the absence of rebellion, bolster parent-student correspondences. The absence of cue-giving would probably inject considerable instability and ambiguity in the child's value structure. At the same time this absence would invite the injection of

other socializing agents whose content and direction might vary with parental values. In either event parental-offspring value correspondences should be reduced in the case of lower political saliency and cue-giving.

Turning to the data, it is evident that while the hypothesis receives some support for party identification and political cynicism, it does not hold generally. Illustratively, Table 5 provides the parent-student correlations for party identification, cynicism, cosmopolitanism, averaged group evaluations, and two pairs of issues. The two politicization measures capture different elements of family politicization —the extent of husband-wife conversations about politics (reported by parents) and the frequency of student-parent conversations related to political affairs (reported by students). The correspondence between parent and student cynicism is mildly related to both of these measures, while party identification is clearly affected by parental conversations, but not by student-parent political discussions. The other opinions and values show no consistent relationships with either measure of politicization. Similar results were obtained when politicization was measured by the general political interest among parents and students, parent-student disagreements regarding political and social matters, and parents' participation in political campaigns.

That the level of family politicization affects somewhat the flow of party identification and cynicism but is unrelated to the transmission of other variables should not be ignored. The extremely salient character of party loyalties, which results in the higher overall parent-student correlation, and the summary nature of the cynicism variable suggest characteristics that may determine the relevancy of family politicization for the transmission of political values. The essential point, though, is that the level of politicization does not uniformly affect the degree of parent-student correspondence. Students with highly politicized backgrounds do not necessarily resemble their parents more closely than students from unpoli-

TABLE 5. FAMILY POLITICIZATION AND PARENT-STUDENT AGREEMENT OF A RANGE OF POLITICAL VALUES[a]

Frequency of:	Party Identifi-cation	Political Cynicism	Cosmo-politan-ism-Lo-calism	Group Ratings [b]	Prayer and Inte-gration Issues [c]	Free-dom Issues [c]
Husband-Wife Political Conversations						
Very often	.54	.19	.22	.20	.36	.13
Pretty often	.49	.15	.11	.20	.30	.10
Not very often	.45	.11	.14	.24	.28	.06
Don't talk	.32	.08	.22	.23	.32	.08
Student-Parent Political Conversations						
Several times/week	.49	.16	.17	.22	.32	.08
Few times/month	.45	.12	.16	.21	.35	.14
Few times/year	.41	.10	.18	.30	.18	—.05
Don't talk	.47	.02	.12	.20	.26	.06

[a] Each tau-b correlation in this table is based on at least 82 cases.
[b] Average ratings of Negroes, Catholics, and Jews on the "feeling thermometer."
[c] See p. 230 for a description of these issues.

ticized families. Whether it is measured in terms of student or parent responses, taps spectator fascination with or active engagement in politics, or denotes in-dividual-level or family-level properties, varying amounts of politicization do not uniformly or heavily alter the level of correspondence between parent and off-spring values.[34]

Since our findings are mostly on the null side, it is important to consider the possibility that interaction effects con-found the relationship between family characteristics and transmission patterns. Previous work suggests that affectivity and power relations in the family will be re-lated to parent-child transmission pri-marily among highly politicized families. Only if politics is important to the parents will acceptance or rejection of parental values be affected by the parent-child re-lationship. In order to test this hypothesis, student-parent agreement was observed, controlling for family politicization and affectivity or power relations simultane-

ously. No strong interaction effects emerge from this analysis. The affectivity and power dimensions sometimes affect only the highly politicized, sometimes the most unpoliticized, and at other times their effect is not at all dependent on the level of politicization.[35] The lack of im-pressive bivariate relationships between family characteristics and the transmission rate of political values is not due to the confounding influence of multiple effects within the family.

With hindsight, reasons for the failure of the hypothesized relationships bearing on family structure can be suggested. But to give a clear and thorough explanation and test alternative hypotheses will be difficult and time-consuming. One ex-ploratory avenue, for example, brings in student perceptions of parental attitudes as an intervening variable. Another is con-cerned with the relative homogeneity of the environment for children of highly

[34] Nor was the intensity of parental feelings related in any consistent fashion to the amount of parent-student correspondence.

[35] There is a moderate tendency for those children feeling most detached from their parents to exhibit greater fluctuation in agreement with their parents—at various levels of politicization—than is true of those feeling most attached to their parents.

politicized backgrounds versus youngsters from unpoliticized families. A third possibility is the existence of differential patterns of political learning and, in particular, a differential impact of the various socializing agents on children from politically rich versus those from politically barren backgrounds.[36] It is also possible that knowledge about later political development of the students would help explicate these perplexing configurations.

IV. A CONCLUDING NOTE

In our opening remarks we noted the conflicting views regarding the importance of the family as an agent of political learning for the child. This paper has been primarily concerned with a fairly narrow aspect of this question. We sought evidence indicating that a variety of political values held by pre-adults were induced by the values of their parents. Thus our test has been rather stringent. It has not examined the relative impact of the family vis-a-vis other socializing agents, the interaction effects of the family and other agents, nor the other ways in which the family may shape political orientations.

Having said this, it is nevertheless clear that any model of socialization which rests on assumptions of pervasive currents of parent-to-child value transmissions of the types examined here is in serious need of modification. Attitude objects in the concrete, salient, reinforced terrain of party identification lend support to the model. But this is a prime exception. The data suggest that with respect to a range of other attitude objects the correspondences vary from, at most, moderate support to virtually no support. We have suggested that life cycle effects, the role of other socializing agents, and attitude instabilities help account for the very

[36] At another level, the explanation may be in the lack of validity of students' and parents' reports of family structure. See Niemi, *op. cit.* Ch. II and pp. 184-185.

noticeable departures from the model positing high transmission. Building these forces into a model of political learning will further expose the family's role in the devolpment of political values.

A derivative implication of our findings is that there is considerable slack in the value-acquisition process. If the eighteen-year old is no simple carbon copy of his parents—as the results clearly indicate—then it seems most likely that other socializing agents have ample opportunity to exert their impact. This happens, we believe, both during and after childhood. These opportunities are enhanced by the rapid sociotechnical changes occurring in modern societies. Not the least of these are the transformations in the content and form of the mass media and communication channels, phenomena over which family and the school have relatively little control. It is perhaps the intrusion of other and different stimuli lying outside the nexus of the family and school which has led to the seemingly different *Weltanschauung* of the post-World-War-II generation compared with its immediate predecessor.

The place of change factors or agents thus becomes crucial in understanding the dynamics at work within the political system. Such factors may be largely exogenous and unplanned in nature, as in the case of civil disturbances and unanticipated consequences of technical innovations. Or they may be much more premeditated, as with radical changes in school organization and curriculum and in enforced social and racial interaction. Or, finally, they may be exceedingly diffuse factors which result in numerous individual student-parent differences with no shift in the overall outlook of the two generations. Our point is that the absence of impressive parent-to-child transmission of political values heightens the likelihood that change factors can work their will on the rising generation. Shifting demands on the political system and shifting types of system support are natural outgrowths of these processes.

SELECTED BIBLIOGRAPHY OF MAJOR EMPIRICAL WORKS

The following list includes books that have contributed in important ways to the body of empirical knowledge about politics in the United States. Readers are encouraged to examine such journals at *The American Political Science Review, The American Sociological Review,* and *Public Opinion Quarterly* for articles that present current findings. No effort has been made here to include items from that very large body of literature.

Agger, Robert, Daniel M. Goldrich, and Bert A. Swanson. *The Rulers and the Ruled.* (New York: John Wiley & Sons, Inc., 1964.) A comparative study of community decision making in four cities.

Alford, Robert A. *Party and Society.* (Chicago: Rand McNally, 1963.) The relationship of social class to political behavior in the United States, Britain, Australia, and Canada.

Almond, Gabriel and Sidney Verba. *The Civic Culture: Political Attitudes and Democracy in Five Nations.* (Princeton: Princeton University Press, 1963.) Survey evidence concerning political orientations in the United States, Britain, Germany, Italy, and Mexico.

Berelson, Bernard, Paul Lazarsfeld, and William McPhee. *Voting.* (Chicago: University of Chicago Press, 1954.) A panel study of the process of voting decision in one community.

Burdick, Eugene and A. J. Brodbeck (eds.). *American Voting Behavior.* (Glencoe, Ill.: The Free Press, 1959.) Contains several good articles synthesizing and commenting upon voting research to that date.

Campbell, Angus, Philip E. Converse, Warren E. Miller, and Donald E. Stokes. *The American Voter.* (New York: John Wiley & Sons, Inc., 1960.) The leading source on the psychological processes leading to the voting decision. Based on national survey data.

————. *Elections and the Political Order.* (New York: John Wiley & Sons, Inc., 1965.) A collection of articles by the same authors, updating and expanding the findings with later research.

Dahl, Robert A. *Who Governs? Democracy and Power in an American City.* (New Haven: Yale University Press, 1961.) Classic study, from the "pluralist" perspective, of decision making in a city.

Domhoff, G. William. *Who Rules America?* (Englewood Cliffs, N.J.: Prentice-Hall, 1967.) A study of national elites which concludes that a governing class shapes all important decisions in the United States.

Easton, David and Jack Dennis. *Children in the Political System.* (New York: McGraw-Hill Book Company, 1969.) How children acquire their political attitudes.

Greenstein, Fred. *Children in Politics.* (New Haven: Yale University Press, 1963.) Images of politics and government on the part of schoolchildren in one city.

Hunter, Floyd. *Community Power Structure: A Study of Decision Makers.* (Chapel Hill: The University of North Carolina Press, 1953.) Classic study of community power, concluding that elite control exists.

Hyman, Herbert. *Political Socialization.* (Glencoe, Ill.: The Free Press, 1959.) Inventories studies of socialization processes up to that date.

Key, V. O. Jr. *The Responsible Electorate.* (Cambridge: Harvard University Press, 1966.) Reanalysis of voting studies, concluding that the general public shows considerable purposeful rationality in voting decisions.

Kornhauser, William. *The Politics of Mass Society.* (Glencoe, Ill.: The Free Press, 1959.) Inventories studies of elite and mass attitudes and behavior from the perspective of concern for stability in modern societies.

Lane, Robert. *Political Ideology: Why The American Common Man Believes What He Does.* (Glencoe, Ill.: The Free Press, 1962.) Depth interviews of working men, seeking to understand the relationship between work situations and political attitudes.

————. *Political Life: Why People Get Involved in Politics.* (Glencoe, Ill.: The Free Press, 1959.) Useful inventory of studies of political participation to that date.

Lipset, Seymour Martin. *Political Man: The Social Bases of Politics.* (Garden City, N.Y.: Doubleday & Co., 1960.) A political sociologist's analysis of the sociology of political attitudes and behavior.

Matthews, Donald. *The Social Background of Political Decision-Makers.* (New York: Random House, 1955.) A collection of background data on political officeholders through time.

Matthews, Donald and James Prothro. *Negroes and the New Southern Politics.* (New York: Harcourt, Brace and World, 1966.) A thorough survey study of Negro political attitudes in the South.

Milbrath, Lester. *Political Participation.* (Chicago: Rand McNally, 1965.) An inventory of findings about participation.

Mills, C. Wright. *The Power Elite.* (New York: Oxford University Press, 1956.) Classic argument to the effect that a "power elite" controls the United States.

Stouffer, Samuel. *Communism, Conformity, and Civil Liberties.* (Garden City, N.Y.: Doubleday & Co., 1955.) Study conducted in the height of the "McCarthy era" of the 1950's, concluding that elites are more responsive to civil liberties principles than masses.

Vidich, Arthur J. and Joseph Bensman. *Small Town in Mass Society.* (Garden City, N.Y.: Doubleday & Co., 1958.) Perceptive study of social control mechanisms in a small town.

Wilson, James Q. *Negro Politics.* (New York: The Free Press of Glencoe, 1960.) The failure of leaders to remain representative of their communities after they gain influence.

CHAPTER 6

Power and Process in the Contemporary United States

WHAT have we learned? What are the implications of the findings and interpretations just examined for analysis and evaluation of political prescriptions? Clearly,
we have some synthesizing and some sifting to do before we can emerge with even
the bare outline of understanding of the "is" or the manner in which it evolves.
But we should be able to extract enough from these illustrative articles to see how
judicious use of empirical research may permit us to approach contemporary
prescriptions with more searching judgmental criteria. In this chapter, I shall
draw selectively upon various articles to suggest features of the present distribution and usage of power in the United States. The next chapter will consider
the nature of political change processes, as well as some approaches to evaluation
and some final problems in the use of empirical research in political theory.

   The findings of empirical studies such as those just sampled purport to describe
key characteristics of the American political system today. Selective mining of
these data (even though we have before us but a few articles in each of only four
areas) ought to provide some benchmarks that we could use as measuring
standards. I shall try to pull together some highlights of these findings around
two central foci: elite and mass values and ideology, and elite and mass behavior
and interaction.

ELITES AND MASSES: VALUES AND IDEOLOGY

   The findings from the Michigan Survey Research Center studies of the voting
behavior of the general electorate provide an adequate starting point. For many,

these findings may come as a surprise: the general electorate is very marginally attuned to politics, and it seems evident that most people have little or no sense of the "liberal" or "conservative" implications of particular issues or candidates. Only about 12% of the electorate even has the capacity to conceptualize politics in issue-based terms, with the rest relying on the cues given them by various reference groups, by the general conditions of the times, or by personal characteristics of the candidates such as their appearance or their families. Political party loyalties are a powerful structuring element, with occasional intrusions of ethnic or religious identifications. The researchers use these findings to document their case for the nonideological and nonissue-based character of mass orientations toward politics. Indeed, the data would seem to suggest that clarity of issue-based appeals to the mass public would be irrelevant and that the prospects of drawing mass support for specific policy goals would be slight. Thus there is no support in these findings for the thought that cogent and persuasive appeals to the mass public could result in substantial changes in political orientations in this country. Of course, elites rarely make such specific appeals, and that might be a leading cause of such apparent incapacity.

By contrast, McClosky's studies show that elites are much better able to recognize policy issues and to relate them to party or ideological positions. Elites are not only much more aware, but also much more partisan, in their orientation toward politics. They appear to be the definers and formulators of issues and the principal proponents of various positions in regard to public problems, for which the relatively inert masses have little interest or concern. Furthermore, in ideological capacity and in the actual substance of attitudes toward public policy questions, elites are demonstrably *not* the same as the general public. This does not foreclose the possibility that elites actually act in ways that the mass public finds acceptable, of course, nor that the public actually chooses between competing elite positions along lines that assure that government action follows popular preferences. But it does raise very serious questions about such possibilities: there is no indication that there is any clear popular preference, either for purposes of guiding elites while in office or for use as a basis for choice between competing elites at an election. (There may be latent preferences, or preferences that go unheard or unheeded, but the result is the same.) In such a context, elites might be free to do what they wished, and elections might be chiefly rituals where legitimacy is secured for an elite to proceed with its program. Of course, there remains the possibility that internal divisions within elites operate as self-containing forces, or that individual members of elites hold self-limiting commitments to tradition or public benefit standards of action.

Elites also differ from the general public in the level of their commitments to norms of "tolerance" and other forms of procedural regularity and fairness that are often associated with democracy. Indeed, on every specific measure of free speech and fair play that was employed in the McClosky and Prothro and Griggs studies, elites scored higher than did masses—and the gaps between them were occasionally wide. Masses showed quite low levels of willingness to permit certain speakers to be heard, and their tolerance for dissent generally appears considerably lower than that of elites. These are not isolated findings, as the ample footnote citations in both articles testify. What explains them, and what implications flow from such conclusions?

For one thing, there may be methodological or interpretive reservations to be entered. All of these findings rest on survey evidence obtained in a brief interview, or (in the case of the McClosky elite sample) by questionnaire. It might be that elites are just better educated, more intelligent, or more ideologized—so that they recognize the application of the general principle of "free speech" in the specific situation better than do masses. Perhaps masses too would endorse such applications if given time to realize the issues involved, or if alerted to the inconsistency between endorsement of the general principle and denial of its specific application; interviewing experience suggests that this phenomenon occurs in some cases. It is possible also that elites are quicker to recognize some standard principles and to respond with the expected democratic rhetoric—but that such differences between elites and masses are all that the evidence necessarily indicates. The survey method does not tap more than attitudes, and we have no way of knowing how either elites or masses would actually act in any given situation. Elites might articulate democratic rhetoric while shutting off dissent, or masses might take on role requirements in office and honor free speech.

These considerations suggest that we need not romanticize elites as the "carriers of the creed" as do Prothro and Griggs, at least until some further evidence is obtained. But surely we must acknowledge the implication that elites are disproportionately responsive to the norms and policy questions which arise within the system, and their possession of such initiative must be recognized as a factor in determining how government action is brought about. Masses appear unable to be the initiators of new policies or of expansions in what we recognize as democratic qualities in politics, although they may be the real source of impetus toward such ends.

It may be that the norms and expectations to which elites apparently are more responsive are simply those which their class origins and subsequent adoption of role orientations would lead them to—and which middle class political scientists happen to look for as evidence of "democratic" tendencies. Because it is a system constructed in their image, and one that serves their preferences, it may be quite natural for elites to score higher in support of the assumptions and procedures that support it. Working classes, emerging from a different environment and with different expectations about the utility of the norms of the established political system, as well as different political goals and priorities, might well develop distinctive values. Surveys that sought to measure possession of such values might develop findings that workers do hold "democratic" attitudes. We might also recognize that any semipermanent underclass might quite reasonably be less receptive to (indeed, even cynical of) the norms of a system whose rules operated to foreclose them from some of the rewards to which they aspire.

Consistent with the foregoing implication of a class-differentiated attachment to "traditional" (middle-class?) democratic attitudes is a suggestion in the data that researchers may have been looking for the wrong things. They may have taken the capacity to articulate some of their favorite phrases, or to respond affirmatively to questionnaire items reflecting partisan political matters with which only some respondents had reason to be familiar, as indicative of the full range of political values. Actually, such responses may be no more than what we have previously called "the political applications" of some core values of liberal ideology. The critical question then would be whether elites and masses held similar *basic* political values. If they do, differing only in the alacrity of responses and to some extent in the substance of their views on certain relatively superficial political applications, then we might speculate that elites and masses are essentially united on the goals and purposes of political order, and that elite action is probably faithfully representative of inchoate popular preference on all important questions. (This does not preclude the possibility, of course, that elites manage to instill those basic values in the general public as a means of self-perpetuation; this is a vital empirical question, but one as yet neither asked nor answered.) If, on the other hand, elites and masses hold fundamentally differing basic values, then we may speculate that there must be a variety of ways in which elites operate to reduce, contain, repress, and deflect lower class thrusts toward their ends. The implications for the prospect of change are absolutely critical: in the latter situation, the task is to remove the blinders and/or the constraints from the masses, whose basic values, it may be assumed, stand ready to support change to a very different form of political system. But if the former situation is the case, both elites and masses are possessed of the same basic goals and commitments (varying only slightly in their political applications), and he who would seek change cannot find a ready source of support in the masses. He must instead seek to convert, to change the basic values of elements of both elites and masses far enough to be adequate to the task of bringing about change. In such circumstances, of course, it is difficult to generate sufficient numerical or other support to accomplish substantial change, and most likely there will be some undermining minimal changes occurring in the desired direction before it is possible to develop a large enough constituency to accomplish fundamental change.

If I may be permitted to indulge in a private speculation, I wonder if this is not one of the keys to the remarkable stability of the American system. Although elites and masses differ somewhat in their perceptions of democratic norms and in the partisanship which they exhibit regarding specific issues (for many of the reasons outlined in this section), they appear to fully share certain basic political values. Indeed, perhaps elites have them merely somewhat more completely internalized than do masses. The values, of course, are those of the liberal inheritance—individualism, property rights paramount among the natural rights, limited government, legalism, materialism, equality so far as is consistent with the preceding, and religion. I suggested at the outset of the last paragraph that researchers may have overestimated the differences between elites and masses in part because they were looking for the wrong things: if they had been looking at respondents' attitudes on such fundamental values as those just itemized, they might have found much higher degrees of consensus. In McClosky's study, for example, the least difference between elites and masses occurs at the single point where his queries touched upon some of the fundamental values, in this case property and race (Table 5.) The propositions that some people (races) are better than others and that inferior races spoil nice neighborhoods draw nearly the same levels of agreement from both elites and masses, and the image of the "tolerant" or "democratic" elite likewise fades. My point is that Louis Hartz may have been right: perhaps almost all of us *do* subscribe to the ideology of liberalism, and it is therefore vastly more difficult to find support for significant change in this country than in others. The depth to which these values are shared has not been researched, and we are only beginning to see evidence about the insistence with which they are transmitted by a wide variety of socializing agents.

A further factor leading in the same direction, but one for which there is much greater evidence and more widely shared support, is the finding that support for the characteristics and institutions of this political system is substantially higher than in other countries. Both masses and elites express the conviction that this system is adequate to their needs and deserving of their support. Along with broad-based support for the existing order, new members of the society are inculcated not only with the elements of the liberal tradition but the very partisan alignments that sustain it. Jennings and Niemi show, for example, that parental political positions survive in the rising generation and through them into the future, and the public schools complete the task of handing on both political values and partisan attitudes. Under such circumstances, the perpetuation of the basic values *and* the established class-based variants of specific political and partisan applications seem indicated.

ELITES AND MASSES: BEHAVIOR AND INTERACTION

Once again, we may begin with the most visible act by which mass influence is made known within the political process—elections. In one sense, this may be misleading: although they are the most visible occasions for the expression of mass preferences, they are by no means the only way in which demands are asserted or effective pressures brought to bear. We know too much about pressure groups and Washington lobbyists and riots and even the effects of great books to take elections as the exclusive or even the chief channel through which desires are made known to decision-makers. But elections *are* the occasion when the greatest number of people do take part in some formal way in their governmental processes, and if there is to be broad popular impact on government or policy at some point, it should be evident surrounding elections.

However, the voting studies suggest that, as instruments of popular control over policy and/or officeholders, elections are meaningful if at all only under special circumstances or in very general terms. We have already seen that the general public is very low in knowledge and capacity to respond to issues, reacting instead to party, ethnic, religious, or candidate attachments. Party identification is one of the constants of American politics, varying only slightly over generations. Very few voters, relatively speaking, know enough, care enough, or are mentally and socially capable of making the kind of independent electoral choice that democratic mythology would impose on them. For the most part, voters support their parties, and occasionally (when conditions are perceived as being very bad) they punish the incumbent party by voting the other one into office. Three interpretations sum up these findings:

1. Elections are chiefly means of obtaining ratification of the acts of incumbents—occasions for the electorate to indicate its acquiescence in whatever the government has been doing for the last four years.

2. This is because each party enjoys the support of broad and permanent social groupings, the Republicans drawing principally on upper class, rural, Protestant, and business interests, and the Democrats on lower class, urban, minority group, and labor support. These great social coalitions, once formed, appear to remain stable through time, until events and problems converge and cut so deeply as to split the larger of them.

3. The kind of event sufficient to split one of these social coalitions and to restructure party alignments verges on the cataclysmic: only the Civil War and the Great Depression of 1930 have accomplished such major realignments in the past century. After the Civil War, the Republicans were dominant for nearly seventy years, with only the two Democratic intrusions (Cleveland and Wilson) and with the reinforcing assistance of the election of 1896. After the Depression, the Democrats took over and have remained in office, with the single exception of the Eisenhower years until the election of Nixon in 1968. Despite all the

political dynamism inspired by war and domestic violence in 1968, polls continued to show the Democratic party as the majority party by comfortable margins.

These findings cause the leading electoral analysts to categorize the significance of American elections into only three classifications. The first and most frequent type of election is the maintaining election, by which is meant an election that does no more than return the party with the larger coalition to office. Second is the realigning election or realigning era of successive elections, by which is meant a period when cataclysmic events have succeeded in rending the majority coalition and installed a new coalition in office behind the other party. Third is the dual category of deviating and then reinstating elections, the series of elections taking place when for some reason the minority party wins a particular election without affecting the underlying structure of social coalitions, and subsequently the dominant party returns to office. The Wilson and Eisenhower elections are cited as the kinds of aberrations that constitute deviating years, and the elections of Harding and Kennedy represent the return of the same dominant social coalition, which then endures into the future until another cataclysmic event restructures the parties again. This interpretation suggests that popular preferences are not often transmitted in very clear or specific fashion, and that for the most part policymakers can count on support for almost any kind of policy actions that they deem necessary or desirable. I do not mean that elites are subject to *no* restraints, but simply that elections are rarely devices for applying restraint. There are many potential sources of such restraints, as we have already noted several times, and it remains a matter of critical importance to seek empirical evidence as to which (if any) are indeed operable. And elections *can* be the source of restraint, if elites perceive them as such; indeed, even the prospect of elections can affect policy actions on the part of elites under certain special conditions, as was shown by the retirement of President Johnson in 1968. The point is simply that, for the most part, elites are free of popular control by means of elections. The instrument that is most often referred to as containing the democratic promise is ill-suited in the late twentieth century to serve that purpose. This is a critical assessment of a process of interaction between masses and elites, not exclusively an indictment of the American electorate. It is possible that issues would play a much larger role in voting choices if leaders took clear stands and/or party positions were distinct and substantively further apart. If the general public were habituated to the assumption of such responsibilities by elites, they might in turn develop the interests and capacities that would convert political discourse into a more obviously purposeful and rational activity. It seems clear that a widely dispersed and numerous electorate needs clear articulation of distinctive positions from visible leaders before broad popular opinion can form; when elites emphasize symbolic appeals or ethnic and religious loyalties, it is not unnatural for masses to respond in those terms—and it is difficult to be certain whether the cause lies in the behavior of elites or of masses, or in the joint process (or ritual) in which the two are engaged. In either event, I would speculate that only different bases of action on the part of elites, or by some existing (or would-be) members of elite groupings, can break the cycle. Some elites may not find it in their interest to do so, of course, because there would probably be significant (and, in many peoples' eyes, quite possibly undesirable) consequences from greater public involvement in issue-based campaigns and elections.

Even if elites sought to engage the general electorate more fully in issues of public policy, there would still remain several obstacles to realization of such ends. For one thing, the United States is in fact as well as in rhetoric a nation of great diversity. Segments of the general public differ from each other in economic interest, immediate social aspirations, life styles, and so on. Such differences are bound to be reflected in distinctive priorities of political goals and in varying levels of intensity with which shared goals are sought. In this context, the concept of a "majority will" or a "public opinion" on an issue is elusive if not illusory. How much does what segment of the population want a particular policy, and in what form and at what price in the way of self-denial of other goals? The implication is that there will be many perhaps widely variant views on most major issues, and elites, needing support for whatever government ultimately does, may not be able to find the type and level of government action that will satisfy enough of these different preferences. A second factor is the prospect of conflict among various viewpoints, with some people seeking assiduously to preserve the status quo and others just as avidly to establish new public policies. Conflict is probable in regard to any important issue area where the economic interests of different people or corporations collide. At any given moment, of course, there are several such conflict situations among segments of the electorate. Individual members of the general public may be animated by several different interests or concerns at the same time, and with distinctive priorities among them. Or a single person may want lower taxes *and* better housing for the urban slum dweller, and so be in conflict with himself. It would be difficult for the most willing elite to find and act upon "majority will" in this context. Finally, we may note that some viewpoints are better able to defend themselves than others by virtue of their status or political location or access to centers of decision-making power. Just as the general public is far from an undifferentiated mass of likeminded men on most issues, so are elites; the interests of relevant sectors of elites may conflict on any particular policy question, and the group with superior access or power may prevail despite efforts on the part of others who may be more numerous.

All three of these potential obstacles to fuller and more effective involvement of the mass public in policymaking may be illustrated through a single familiar episode. Ever since the mid-1930's polls showed substantial majorities of the general public in favor of medical care for the aged, but action was accomplished by the national government only in 1965. Does this indicate that elites were unresponsive to mass demands, or that the system somehow operated to prefer the negativism of the American Medical Association to the wishes of the people? Perhaps, but a great deal more would have to be known to sustain such an interpretation. How intensely felt were these preferences—did they hold priority over all or most other policy preferences, or were they merely acquiescence in an abstract "good idea" put forward by a pleasant female interviewer? Would most or any of the affirmative respondents have agreed to institute medical care instead of other programs? Which other programs? What type of medical care: doctor bills, hospital costs, both? How persuasive in changing popular preferences was the American Medical Association? How much should Presidents and other officials have been willing to sacrifice to compel a reluctant Chairman of the House Ways and Means Committee to produce such legislation for Congressional action? The point is that analysis and evaluation of the nature of public involvement in policymaking, and of mass-elite interactions generally, must take place in a total context of many wants and needs, differently felt by varying-sized segments of the population at one and the same time. These are only some of the realities of the contemporary political context, but we must take them into account en route to judgment.

Up to this point, we have been exploring the mass side of the mass-elite symbiosis, realizing that the electoral process and indeed the very nature of today's political context itself place bounds upon the role of the mass public. The obverse of this situation, of course, is that elites are particularly determinative of the products and qualities of the political system. Let us now formalize some implications about the elite side of mass-elite linkage.

I have already suggested that definitive acts by elites, particularly by men in government, are prerequisites to forming public opinion. Ratification normally follows, perhaps unconsciously, at the next election, and the new policy is incorporated into the established bundle of government activities, thereby gaining the support necessary to effective implementation and expansion. These considerations imply a sort of top-down process of initiating change, in which elites take the first steps, receive acquiescence, and then proceed further with their programs. No doubt those members of elites who are inclined to initiate such a program may search for indications of support among nonelites, and be encouraged to take bolder action by the urgings of small but alert segments of the general public. But the general implication seems to be that broad preferences cannot be generated and applied except by means of elite articulation of a specific proposal, followed by public discussion, position-taking, and (usually) ratification. Because of the visibility of government actions, and also because of the strong support extended to the established system and its actions particularly by the more educated and upper classes, elites in public office have a heavy advantage in gaining acquiescence for their programs. Several prospects follow: they may if so inclined shift the direction of government policy in bold new directions for which popular support would not otherwise have been forthcoming; they may carry on outdated or objectively irrelevant policies long after the public would have accepted substantial change; and in both cases they may be tempted to manipulate popular understanding and preferences to accord more completely with what they deem it necessary or desirable to do.

In short, governmental elites are relatively free agents. They have a wide range of alternatives from which to select, in confidence that popular preferences are not so sharply formed, nor so readily implemented, that their selection will be vetoed. Because of the popular propensity to acquiesce in the doings of their government, ratification can generally be anticipated for most of the actions which recommend themselves to governing elites. Where acquiescence is not clearly forthcoming, the apparatus of political salesmanship can always be brought to bear and the new program interpreted into the accepted general consensus. In this endeavor, nongovernmental elites may be willing participants. Monopolies of information, legitimacy, and power, and the size of the risks associated with the continuing success of the system itself, gain for government the benefit of the doubt in most cases, on the part of communications media, investors, institutions, businesses, and the people as well. Even if a particular action appears objectively wrong or ill-advised, it may be preferable to go along with it if only to avoid the impression that many other actions might also be unwise, or to deflect challenges to many proper things that government is doing. Despite some telling criticism of the Warren Commission Report, for example, there was no sentiment anywhere in government for a reexamination of the circumstances surrounding the assassination of President Kennedy.

The cooperation of other elites may be forthcoming also because of some sense of shared responsibility for the continued viability of the political and economic systems. Men who are in positions of power and status, whether in government or not, owe their perquisites to the system through which they gained them, and it is natural that they should be defensive of it. Quite without deliberate coordination, they may act to preserve the institutions and processes with which they are familiar—thereby creating a kind of "establishmentarianism." Although they may be divided over questions of immediate economic profitability, or over particular distributions of the rewards of the economy or polity, there are very broad areas in which their risks are shared, and on such matters they may act coherently as one—defending each other's mistakes, and avoiding at all costs the dangers that might flow from widespread popular disaffection from the basic features of the political system. Indeed, empiricists have suggested that agreements among elites are sometimes achieved upon a showing that otherwise the issue will be thrown open for public resolution. Because no one can be sure what will happen if the public becomes engaged, there is substantial pressure generated to reach some kind of resolution among themselves.

This finding leads to another possible implication: perhaps the most significant stage of elite-mass interaction occurs at the point where a public policy question verges on entry into broad public recognition as an issue. What determines whether something will or will not become an issue for public consideration and action? Some sought for years to make poverty a public issue, but in vain; public support for reform of the Selective Service System was sought for some time and with cogent arguments, but little broad awareness was accomplished. In order for a matter to enter broad political discourse, there apparently must be some visible members of established elites willing to carry it in specific form into public prominence; there must be an available and willing forum, either in the sense of extended previous discussion coupled with new and awakening events or a conveniently timed election campaign where attention has been focused by events; and the subject itself must be something that can be linked with one or more of the deeply held values or ideological elements of the American tradition. The first condition requires that elites be internally divided—so divided that one component is willing to risk the uncertainties of public participation rather than acquiesce in the alternative preferred by the dominant portion. The second requires a special concatenation of previous activities and new events that will operate to prepare the ground and create a forum. And the last establishes boundaries within which the issue must be framed. Together, these conditions may explain why it often makes better sense for established elites to abide by determinations made within their own circles, as well as why nonelites experience difficulty in projecting issues into public discourse.

These speculations are closely related to the power elite-pluralism controversy, and perhaps it would be well to address that question comprehensively. We have before us several illustrations of the broad differences that separate these two approaches. In addition, we now have good reason to see the critical significance of the question of what kinds of people hold office and what they do with their power. I believe it will quickly become apparent, if it is not already, that the really vital evidence has not yet been gathered. We simply do not know precisely what types of people make up determinative elites, how they acquired their power, or on what bases they act. Although the "who rules" question may never be fully answered, it surely would be possible to come closer to the answers through more sophisticated empirical research. In many cases, the right questions have simply not been asked. This is partly because of the relative infancy of the empirical-behavioral movement, and partly because of some of the problems in approach that are evidenced in this review of the power elite-pluralism controversy. Let us examine some of the salient problems in each orientation, assess their relative strengths and weaknesses, and then summarize the implications that emerge. In the course of this analysis, we shall see how far empirical studies *have come,* and *might aspire,* to answering the questions that are most critical for our purposes.

The Power Elite Argument

The chief advocates of the power elite position among empiricists were C. Wright Mills and Floyd Hunter,[1] until 1967, when a somewhat more data-based national analysis was published by G. William Domhoff under the title of *Who Rules America?*[2] Because the latter is national, more recent and more fully self-sustaining, I shall use it as the prototype of this argument. Domhoff's thesis includes three component elements:

1. There is a national "governing class" in the United States, identifiable from such independent sources as the Social Register in various key cities, a select list of private schools attended, and a relatively small number of exclusive gentlemens' club. Mere wealth is not enough, although in time it would probably be felt through movement into the circles represented by the foregoing indicia.

2. This governing class provides a very substantial portion (more than half) of the manpower that staffs the policymaking positions within the executive branch of the national government. In addition, members of the governing class hold predominant power in the major corporations, foundations, media, and universities. The governing class does not control the Congress, but on most issues this is not critical because the primacy of the executive branch enables it to secure the acquiescence of the Congress or to circumvent opposition in some way.

3. From these positions, the governing class acts coherently to commit the national government to particular policies that it deems essential or appropriate, and to structure public understanding of the issue in such a way as to draw forth support for such policies. In addition, the governing class consciously reaches out to co-opt new members from among the ranks of rising business executives and professional men. In this process, the governing class is aided by the willingness of talented men with leadership aspirations to conform their behavior and career lines to the perceived expectations of the governing class. There is thus a constant source of new members of the governing class, and those who might become (if frustrated in their aspirations) the leaders of a significant opposition are instead lined up with the governors in a continuing (and joint) process of cooptation.

On its face, the power elite thesis appears to be a complete interpretation of *who* the dispositive elites are, *where* they are located within the structure of gov-

---

[1] Floyd Hunter, *Community Power Structure* (Chapel Hill: University of North Carolina Press, 1963).
[2] G. William Domhoff, *Who Rules America?* (Englewood Cliffs, N.J.: Prentice Hall, 1967).

ernment, and *how* they operate to gain their ends. From the identification of the key officials and the assertion of common interests and background among them, together with the ascendancy of the executive branch over an admittedly decentralized Congress, the argument proceeds to allege particular uses of power. The implication is usually clear that the purposes for which these elites use their power are not the same as those which majorities of the general public would choose. Whether this is good or bad depends upon the particular power elitist in question; some are majoritarian democrats and some apparently would merely prefer a better or different elite in the governing role.

But this facile interpretation is vulnerable in several respects. Domhoff's identification of the "governing class" rests on a form of social background analysis which is at best uncertain and at worst circular and self-fulfilling: men are members of the "governing class" if they are found to be listed in the Social Register—but the Social Register is a publication that lists prominent people in many fields of endeavor, including politics, so that a man could be listed simply because he held a public office. What is more, the Social Register is published by independent entrepreneurs in various cities, and criteria for inclusion are as varied as the proclivities of the businessmen who seek to profit by publishing such a "register." Thus, the fact that a large proportion of the officeholders in the executive branch and the key corporate managerial positions are listed in the Social Register does not necessarily indicate that they are members of a cohesive and self conscious elite. Men in government are far from a cross-section of the population in terms of occupation, income, education, family status, and so forth, but that is the only necessary conclusion these facts support: they do not by themselves indicate cohesiveness or unity among such persons. This reservation could be entered against the other indicia by which Domhoff identifies the "governing class," but this example may serve to indicate the nature of the problem.

Assuming that the evidence does clearly establish the fact that men in government and in key positions in corporate and media management share certain "elite" social background characteristics, we move to an even more serious problem in the power elitist argument: can we fairly infer, from the fact of distinctiveness of social background, that these elites hold attitudes on public questions that are (1) homogeneous, and (2) different from those of the general public? If there is a mixture of opinion and differing levels of knowledge and intensity on an issue in the general public, might there not be the same or an analogous mixture of opinion and intensity among members of elites? The power elitist argument requires the assumption or the inference that the possession of similar (and atypical) social background characteristics leads to possession of *homogenous* attitudes that are *different* from those held by nonelites. It then requires the further inference that the *behavior* of elites accords with such distinctive and shared attitudes, and that popular acquiescence is manipulated out of an opinion structure that would otherwise have preferred another policy. But no inquiry has sought to measure elite attitudes with these questions in mind. Men in government differ on many issues (as any daily newspaper readily reveals), but perhaps not the fundamental ones. Men in government differ as a group from the general public, but apparently in more or less marginal ways, depending upon the issues at stake. There is little evidence available that would help to lay these questions to rest, and the argument cannot be either sustained or refuted until such evidence is on hand. The problem of relating attitudes to behavior is a further obstacle to acceptance of the required inferences: studies show that personal preferences are frequently modified, sometimes reluctantly, by decision-makers who act with a sense of obligations of office, role, or particular perceived expectations of others. V. O. Key's argument that elites act with a sense of noblesse oblige and in the public interest deserves empirical testing before the inference can be made that shared distinctive backgrounds among elites necessarily leads to behavior contrary to the interests or preferences of nonelites.

In a sense, the power elitist argument suffers from limitations of method and approach. These unsupported (though not implausible) inferences *have* to be made, because the only data gathered pertain to the social and economic characteristics of men in key places in business and government. Such data are more readily available than attitudinal materials, but it is hardly satisfactory to be controlled in one's conclusions by the happenstance of availability of data, and scientific judgment might well be suspended until obvious alternative hypotheses have been tested.

An alternative method, and one which is insisted upon by the pluralists (here represented by Robert Dahl's analytic approach), would focus upon the actual behavior of elites. Dahl would demand evidence that elites actually employed their apparent power in ways that were contrary to the preferences of nonelites, and he would maintain that such evidence could only be forthcoming from the study of actual decisions on recognized public issues. This is at least a very high standard of proof, and perhaps (as I shall indicate in the subsequent analysis of pluralism) one that involves some serious biases in itself. To satisfy this requirement, the power elitists would have to provide data on both attitudes and behavior of elites and contrast them with the preferences of nonelites—a tremendous task under real-life circumstances of governmental action. But it is certainly clear that some effort should be made to show the payoffs of elite analysis: unless the distinctiveness of elites (in social and economic terms) has meaning for their behavior, it is a relatively harmless aberration of democratic self-government.

A final problem with the power elite argument arises from its somewhat blithe assumption that the executive branch is, in all important matters, supreme over the Congress. There is no doubt that the executive has acquired increased leverage over the Congress in the twentieth century, but it may be too soon to dismiss the latter as insignificant. Too many Presidents have foundered on the configuration of power and the idiosyncratic workings of the seniority and committee systems in the Congress to permit such a conclusion. On some issues, perhaps, or under some circumstances such as an emergency in foreign affairs, the President and the executive branch can work their will. And they clearly do have a preponderance of information-gathering capacity and of expertise with which to influence the more parochial Congress. But new statutes may be required, or appropriations of money, and there comes a day of reckoning for most Presidents. The question really comes down to definitions of which issues are most critical, and at what level of generality the allegation of Congressional insignificance is made. These are component issues in the power elitist position, but they are not questions which proponents have been willing to face; most power elite analyses simply dismiss the Congress—in part, one suspects, because of their commitment to social background analyses as a sufficient tool for reaching judgments.

The Pluralist Argument

Most contemporary empiricists, at least in political science, employ one or another form of pluralist analysis. Perhaps the most careful and comprehensive statement of this approach is that contained in the several writings of Robert Dahl, and I shall use his work (particularly *Who Governs?*,[3] a study of decision making in New Haven, Connecticut) in illustration here. Essentially, the pluralists have remedied the failures of the power elitists to look at actual uses of power, but at what may be a high cost in breadth of frame of reference or perspective for the understanding of political interaction. Let me first reconstruct their approach, as applied to the national government.

Pluralists begin with a focus on actual decisions within the formal institutions of government and the way in which they are made. Proceeding out from the act of deciding, they identify the relevant persons or groups who played some part in the shaping of the decision. (Just as the social background approach is congenial to the sociologist, so is the institutional focus of pluralism specially congenial to the political scientist.) Because of their assumption that a decision is "made" when it has been officially taken by an authoritative branch of government, the pluralists tend to concentrate on those persons and groups that are visible at this stage. They center around the politics of influencing agency or Congressional action, and they emphasize interest groups' and lobbyists' activities. Because there is indeed a great deal of such activity, it is perhaps natural that pluralists

---

[3] Robert A. Dahl, *Who Governs?* (New Haven: Yale University Press, 1961).

should conclude that this constitutes the essence of political interaction, or at least all that is really meaningful.

Immensely illuminating insights have emerged from the analyses of the behavior of men in government and the pressures on them that have been conducted under these assumptions in the last thirty years; the discipline of political science has advanced immeasurably because of the understanding gained thereby. But if (or when) an approach which effectively portrays the dynamics of decision making in institutions is taken as a full characterization of an overall politicosocial process, it encounters several serious problems. Two should already be obvious: emphasis on actual decisions leads to an exclusiveness of focus on the institutions of government and possibly on overestimation of the significance of interplay within them, and a simultaneous overestimation of the differences between men in government concerning the issues that arise. If one concentrates exclusively on what happens within institutions, and on the factors that immediately influence behavior within them, he runs the risk of overlooking outside forces that shape the range of the matters to be considered, and of taking the particular issues that were raised as being the full and complete total of matters that are of public importance. In short, there is an acute risk of tunnel vision.

Perhaps less immediately obvious is the accompanying assumption that the interest groups that are admittedly active near the act of decision making represent a comprehensive compilation of the viewpoints and preferences of the entire population. In order to raise the pluralist analysis to the level of a general interpretation of the entire political process, one must assume that interest groups are highly inclusive—that practically all major interests and positions are represented by one or another of the organized associations that make themselves felt in American political decision making. This is an empirical question, at least in part, but it has not been asked or answered in this form. We know that not all persons belong to such groups, and it seems unlikely, then, that all interests are represented. Until it is, there is no more satisfactory basis for assuming that they *are* than that they *are not*—which is the position taken by some of the pluralists' critics. Nor is there any basis except simpleminded determinism for assuming that the whole range of issues is presented by interest groups or other political actors who happen to be operating within or near the institutions of government.

The latter point raises a further implication about pluralism: it rests on a relatively narrow (government- and conflict-oriented) definition of politics, which in turn sets limits on the frame of reference with which the analysis can proceed. Are we to assume that all matters of public importance are equally capable of being presented as political issues? Or are there practical limits to what kinds of questions can enter the realm of open political discourse? Because pluralism defines as politically relevant only those matters that actually *are* presented in the recognized political arena, it runs the risk of excluding matters that might be important to some persons or interests or objective definition of public necessity, but which never rise to the level of controversy. This leads to status quo implications: all that is important has been raised and dealt with, and all are represented and responded to by the system, so there can be no basis for argument that all is not well. If we question whether all persons or interests are represented in groups, or whether all possible issues have actually been raised, we are really questioning the validity of the assumptions that underlie the pluralist approach.

These two approaches, because of their distinct focal points, definitions, and methods, emerge with contrasting conclusions about the state of Amerian politics. The power elitists find a unified power elite shaping policy and controlling the government to the detriment of the masses. The pluralists find significant differences between segments of elites, representing the range of differences within the general public; they see government policy emerging from the compromising and bargaining among those elites, and they define the product as being in the general interest. The power elitists' broader frame of reference toward what is politically relevant, and their freedom from the benevolent or status quo assumptions of pluralism, are vitiated by the need to make unsupported inferences about uses of power. The pluralists' concentration on actual uses of power, however, runs the risk of ignoring extra-institutional forces that shape the range of matters considered and the nature of the interests that are reflected in the process of decision making. Questions central to the issue of the current nature of American politics are as yet unanswered: Do elites disagree among themselves about important matters? To what extent do their views reflect the preferences of the general public? On what bases do elites *act?* Do they then manipulate consent from the necessary segment of the public, or is that consent forthcoming for other reasons? As long as such questions go unasked, we shall not find satisfactory conclusions in the work of either set of empiricists.

In part, we are confronted with a problem arising out of different definitions of politics and different choices (and exclusive commitments) as to empirical research methods. If that were all there were, we might await some rapprochement between methodologies, or some well-funded honest broker between the warring camps. But I think that there is more: in many respects, *both* methods and approaches are deficient, and in similar ways. At a higher level of generality, they are much alike. Both concentrate on *how* decisions are made, as if that were the only question to be asked in order to characterize a political system. Neither asks about the substance of what government has done, or how it affects the people who live within the system. I do not mean that it is unimportant whether men who seek to take part in their political system are able to do so or not, but only that *a,* if not *the,* major payoff is whether or not they get what they were seeking in the way of tangible product, and in what ways the quality of their lives is affected by what their government does to or for them. The much-valued act of "taking part," and the whole process of elections itself, could be mere sham or ritual—depending on what actually comes out of government; but neither of these approaches would necessarily shed light on this critical question.

Nor does either approach encompass the full range of politically relevant factors bearing upon the outcome of government or the reactions of people to their government. Both operate at relatively instrumental levels, in contrast to potentially more revealing fundamental levels. The power elitists and the pluralists are both looking at the actions of men in government in isolation, abstracted from their context, and their conclusions are not even so very different—despite the spirited argument that rages between them. The power elitists, for example, acknowledge that it is not precisely the same elite individuals who run each particular subject area, but that there is a kind of effective division of labor among the general "governing class" so that a relatively small group controls most decisions in each, with occasional participation by larger segments of the governing class on major issues. What else is pluralism? With the limited perspective of the pluralists, the divisions among elites loom larger, and elites seem more inclusive. But it is clear that the groups of which they speak are far from inclusive of the public as a whole, and their linkage of identifiable elites to segments of the public may be just the illusions of earnest democrats. Neither approach seeks to investigate the role of more fundamental values and ideology. For all we know, Domhoff might be right but for practical purposes trivial: if we are indeed all captives of the same liberal ideology, rule by the governing class might produce results in the way of government action that would be precisely in accord with general popular preferences. The point is that both groups of researchers have assumed that there are great differences in fundamental values (as distinguished from political applications or economic interests) between elites and nonelites, or between classes—and have evaluated their findings accordingly. The power elitists consider it undesirable to have dominance by today's elite, because of what they fear from elite manipulation of masses. The pluralists consider their version of elitism to be desirable, because of what they fear from masses' pressures on elites. Perhaps both should worry instead about the *lack* of differences and healthy questioning of basic values, purposes, and policies in a time of great technological change and unprecedented internal and external circumstances.

CHAPTER 7

Political Change in the United States

No social process is more celebrated in rhetoric, nor more loosely conceptualized and empirically ignored, than social change and its sometime corollary, political change. Images of change abound, but the political system endures essentially as is. These apparent contradictions suggest the poverty of empirical evidence concerning the process of political change in advanced industrialized nations such as the United States. And yet, without a clear view of how change has come about in the American past, or of the conditions and processes requisite to change in the present, it will be extremely difficult to assess the relative prospects of attaining the kinds of change proposed by today's political prescriptions. The prescriptive political theorist must respond to present distributions of power and existing values, but he must also get from the unsatisfactory present to the preferable future—in short, he must consider what conditions, strategy, and tactics are appropriate to achieve movement toward the better world that he advocates. There is at present little descriptive evidence available for the guidance of either the theorist or one who would evaluate the relative merits of various prescriptions. In this section, we shall try to build a conceptual approach to the analysis of political change, and then fill it in as best we can from the empirical studies included in this book.

THE PROBLEM OF DEFINITION

The beginnings of rigor lie in precision of definition. Robert Dahl's chapter is one of the few attempts by political scientists to conceptualize the process of political change in the United States, and we may use that as a starting point. As I shall suggest in a moment, I think there are some important improvements to be made in Dahl's approach, but his definitions have the great merit of cutting through much of the vagueness surrounding the concept of "change." He distinguishes change as to *location* (the structure of government, the policies it produces, and the relative influence of various strata and groups over the actions of government) and as to *magnitude* (incremental, comprehensive, and revolutionary.) Incremental change implies unaltered structure of government and gradual modification of policies in a context of relatively stable patterns of influence. Comprehensive change occurs when the structure remains stable but sweeping changes in policies occur as a result of shifts in relative influence among groups. Revolutionary change, on the other hand, includes not only shifts in policies and relative influence but also profound alteration in the structure of government.

Some troublesome, though probably not insurmountable, problems inhere in these distinctions. Assuming that a change can be shown to have occurred in a specific period of time, there is still the partially value-preference question of whether the change has been slow or fast. Somewhat the same is true as to whether the change has been "marginal" or "fundamental." In all probability, such labeling problems would be different for each subject area, because the scope and speed of change—and the extent of change judged by the observer to be possible—would be distinctive; common to all such analyses, however, would be the prospect of disagreement among reasonable men as to what constituted timely or meaningful change, and thus whether incremental or comprehensive change had occurred. When empirical research under Dahl's definitions is contemplated, further difficulties may be envisioned in identifying changes in patterns of influence or in demonstrating the effects of new or revised policies. And, as Murray Edelman's analysis emphasizes, it would be extremely important to distinguish between policy change in the tangible sense of consequences for people, and mere symbolic or rhetorical change. Dahl's use of the Civil Rights Acts of 1964 and 1965 as illustrations of policy change permits the interpretation that the mere passage of legislation could qualify as change, and it is clear that significance should be attached only to those instances where the effects of the new policies were actually felt in substantial ways by members of the society. The empirical identification of such changes in the form of impact upon people or the economy, and the attribution of causal responsibility (for such changes) to the new government policy, would also present difficult problems in research and analysis.

Two other problems with Dahl's approach seem to me to be much more serious. The first is the perhaps characteristic and by now familiar pluralist narrowness in definition of politics. The only "political" issues for Dahl (and consequently the only thrusts toward change that fall within the range of his analysis) are those which in one way or another manage to intrude themselves into the recognized political arena. This begs the whole critical question of how and when matters can become political issues in this system, and it misses all the avid structuring of the form of the issue that precedes its entry into the recognized political arena. And, as is evident from Dahl's analysis, it places disproportionate emphasis upon the act of voting as the means of resolving issues. Perhaps this overemphasis on elections is a natural product of benevolent images of American democracy, but it has the effect of leading empirical analysis away from other arenas of potential decision-making authority such as elite consensus on preventing a question from becoming a public issue. Particularly in regard to the process of political change, definitions of what to look at in the attempt to understand politics should be as inclusive as possible—and surely there are serious costs to a definition that excludes much potential employment of power. Under the definition used, it is small wonder that Dahl finds the characteristic American process to be one of incremental change in response to many diverse thrusts from several quarters: he has looked only at those kinds of thrusts that have framed themselves so that they could come into the political arena and be dealt with by the conservatizing channels of American institutions; he has by definition excluded any unassimilable and deflected or excluded efforts, together with those that would have called for some other and more drastic form of change. Thus he may have saved the system from appearing unresponsive or excessively stable. (He might argue that he has taken into account all those pressures actually raised in recent American experience. If the self-limiting implications of that position are not clear from these paragraphs, the reader may wish to refer to the discussion of "defining from the is" in the next section.)

If we would understand change, we must employ the most sensitive antenna. We must establish the widest possible frame of reference, so that we see and trace every possible pressure and thrust within and without the political system. To do less is to load the dice in favor of self-congratulatory conclusions about responsiveness and steady incrementalism, or possibly, to build in applause for the status quo. The problem is simply this: established institutions and processes permit only certain relatively congenial pressures to be aired, and they repress or label illegitimate all that they cannot absorb. By the time an issue reaches the stage of public consideration within the bounds established by these institutions and processes, it has already been hammered into a form that can be accommodated without serious difficulty. But how many demands have been deflected or prevented from being aired? Perhaps the critical acts accomplished by the present structure of authority within the American political system occur outside of the range of Dahl's analysis, and the violence, tensions and alienation now evident may be the symptoms of unvented but high-pressure demands for change.

I do not argue that such is necessarily the case, but simply that, to inspire confidence, analysis must employ an all-encompassing frame of reference. I believe such scope is available through the definition offered in Chapter 1, where I urged that we look at the full range of uses of those resources that make for power. When power has been employed, even if only because some have conformed their behavior to what they perceive to be the expectations of others, we have entered the bounds of the definition. Particularly, we should be alert to the uses of power to prevent matters from becoming recognized political issues, or to shape public understanding of them if they do become issues. If we then find that the system admits only certain kinds of issues into real consideration, then we shall have a better basis for estimating its real responsiveness—and we shall be better able to estimate the prospects for realization of prescriptions, as well as for evaluating the utility of various suggested means of accomplishing change.

The second problem lies in Dahl's emphasis upon conflict as the prerequisite of change. This leads again to overemphasis upon those few matters that have succeeded in becoming political issues with broad public recognition, and to a focus on elections. It again ignores possible clandestine decision making of great significance, or deliberate prevention of issues from coming into political cognizance. More damaging, it operates to exclude a substantial proportion of major policy changes, in *both* tangible and symbolic senses, which occur through government action taken in total absence of conflict. Was there not a highly significant policy change in the years immediately after the end of the Second World War, when policymakers felt it necessary to invoke the policy of containment of the Soviet Union in place of the cooperation of the war years? No conflict preceded this policy change, nor was there even broad public consideration. I do not argue that the general public would have preferred another policy, but only that many major policy changes take place without any conflict, or an election, or even general discussion. Just as politics is conflict (but not *only* conflict), so is change a likely product of conflict (but not *only* of conflict.)

These two problems seem to me to indicate recurring flaws in the pluralist approach. Researchers who operate with such definitions and parameters are perhaps unconsciously led to nonneutral and self-congratulatory conclusions about the efficacy and benevolence of the American political system, and they tend to overvalue stability, perhaps out of a special concern for the dangers inherent in conflict. There surely *are* dangers in conflict, as the history of the world teaches us, but it is not unmitigated danger, and there is at least the theoretical possibility that at any time conflict may be functional. Conflict may be necessary to raise questions of change and adaptation to new environmental circumstances, because established forces are unlikely to willingly alter the status quo that has served them well; given their preference, they might well opt for stability even at the risk of alienating other segments of the population and endangering long-range support for the system. Thus conflict may be functional for the very continuity of the established system. Somewhat more tentatively, I would argue that conflict might be highly desirable even where it did not contribute to the continuity of the established system. At least theoretically, conflict could lead to a new or restructured political system in which the balance between deprivations suffered and satisfactions achieved would be more favorable to the majority of individuals within it. And there is always, of course, the problem of the point of view from which the evaluation is made: those who have are ever concerned about conflict, for it may result in the loss of the good things they prize, while those who do not have under the present structure may well see much to be gained through conflict and relatively little to be lost.

Most pluralists, particularly including Robert Dahl, would probably not disagree with these abstract reflections. It may be simply that the historical period in which they mapped out their empirical research designs was one in which the democratic qualities of the American political system were unquestioned and in which world upheavals focused special concern upon the fact of conflict. If so, perhaps we have now reached a level of self-awareness and sensitivity to the developmental stages of *all* polities (not just the "underdeveloped" nations) where it would be possible to purge concepts, definitions, and empirical approaches of all those time-specific and culture-bound elements of which we are aware. For our purposes as political theorists and analysts of the process of change, we should do so.

But let us not throw out the many valuable insights generated by the pluralists in the process of refining or discarding selected aspects of their approach. On the point that concerns us here, for example, Dahl is surely right when he stresses the problem of gaining consent for change within any political system. Ratification and acquiescence on the part of the various segments of the community must be gained somehow if the polity is to survive even in radically restructured form. Under most circumstances, of course, change will not be so drastic as to raise the issue of survival of the polity, and most occasions will necessitate only acceptance of new or revised economic levels or status positions; even such forms of ratification-seeking pose difficult problems, however. Conflict is not at all unlikely, and instability is indeed a threat. Theories of change must encompass the ways in which conflict is generated and channeled and absorbed within a system, and the effects that these processes have upon government actions and citizen reactions, without imposing a value-based negative onus upon the fact of conflict itself. In the case of the American system, such a theory would no doubt remark upon the extensive institutional and ideological insulation from really dangerous conflict which the system enjoys—and I think the evidence would sustain a characterization of the American system as one in which heavy emphasis upon stability has perhaps inadvertently tipped the scales against ready responsiveness to thrusts toward change.

BUILDING AND APPLYING A THEORY OF CHANGE IN THE UNITED STATES

As Dahl notes, evidence concerning political change, and the conditions that permit, promote, and impede change, is conspicuously lacking. We have only begun the task of clarifying the relative utility of various conceptual approaches to the study of political change. On the other hand, in the first section of this chapter we reviewed several implications from the empirical literature that have already marked out some tentative guideposts. We know that American political ideology and attitudes are highly stable, with powerful socializing agents transmitting them effectively from generation to generation. We also know that these values are highly supportive of present institutions and processes; although elites emerge from distinctive social milieu and hold distinctive attitudes on at least some matters, we have speculated that there are broad areas of shared values on fundamentals of the liberal tradition. Mass behavior at elections demonstrated heavy reliance on elites and traditional loyalties and interests. We speculated that change would require first events that were of a deep-cutting or fundamental nature as a means of focusing attention and generating willingness to consider action; previous discussion or argument that would have prepared a forum, and an occasion such as an election to give prominence to the issue; decisive action by elites or some of them who hold at least the semblance of legitimacy; and ultimately ratification in some form from the electorate. Many refinements need to be made in such a catalogue: in all probability, some form of threat to the continuation of the status quo must be perceived (first by elites and then by a substantial segment of nonelites) either from events or the mobilization of power by some segment of the society, before action will be forthcoming. Thus, we might hypothesize that some form of "creative tension" would be prerequisite to change. No doubt we could speculate further, but we would shortly run out of evidence to test our hypotheses. Perhaps the most useful approach at this stage of the development of empirical knowledge is to suggest some ways of looking at the process of change that would offer opportunities to make use of the available evidence. I shall suggest three possible ways of analyzing change, and indicate how some of the foregoing empirical studies relate to them.

1. The Occasions of Change in the Past

One obvious approach to the understanding of change in the United States would be to examine the occasions of change in the past and seek to determine what forces and conditions made them possible. In keeping with the emphasis in this book on the distinctiveness of each time period in a nation's development, of course, it would be essential to ascertain what gave particular weight to dispositive forces in any particular time period; we could not assume, because a particular factor occurred in the 1930's and led to change, that the same event or action would have the same effect today. Nor, on a larger scale, could we assume that economic forces and political ideology had the same relationship to each other today that they may have had at some earlier stage of American development. But we *would* anticipate that ideas, processes, and institutions of the present were only temporary, and that their forms were evolving from some past character through the present and continuing on into the future. (This is what I mean by the term "development," not necessarily any implication of progress or improvement.)

In order to understand the characteristic conditions of change in the past (which may well bear some resemblance to what might make for change in the present) we must first identify the occasions when change has indeed occurred. This is not an easy task, even with regard to the recent past. How can one measure relative changes in influence among political actors, except by some deterministic indicia? ("The Income Tax Amendment was passed, and this proves that the common man had gained ascendancy over the rich.") It would be possible to conduct social background analyses of public officeholders over time, but this would not assure that we had identified the actual holders of power (some nonofficeholders might have been calling the tune in all time periods), nor would it assure that we had assessed the actual uses of power even by the officeholders themselves. The best entry point would appear to be through examination of the consequences of public policies: we might seek to define what had happened to the society and the economy, and to individuals within them, as a result of various modifications in public policies. This route is not free from difficulty either, because of the fact that many forces are at work at any one time, and it will be difficult to demonstrate that any particular effects were actually caused by the policies in question. And, following Murray Edelman's argument, we would have to be careful to document tangible effects, rather than merely symbolic ones; but we would still encounter problems from the fact that for some people it is the symbolic rewards and satisfactions that are the really significant ones.

The difficulties inherent in empirical analysis of past instances of change may suggest why there is little solid evidence on this phenomenon. Indeed, the process itself is complex and slippery to deal with in either empirical or conceptual terms. Although this approach offers potential payoff, the enormity of investment of research time and energy necessary to establish a convincing case for particular interpretations has so far precluded its use; the only employment of this approach has been on highly generalized and necessarily uncertain bases, such as the trial undertaken by Robert Dahl in the later stages of his *Pluralist Democracy in the United States*. It is no discredit to Dahl's efforts to note that his analysis is not very helpful: with very generous definitions, he finds severe conflict to have occurred in the American polity about every twenty years, but he does not even attempt to link such situations to actual changes in policies in any precise manner.

2. Critical Points Where Change Must Occur

Another perhaps more promising approach would be to identify several vital points within the established political system where power is now wielded effectively, and to look carefully at the forces surrounding these critical junctures to see whether any change in their structure or operating patterns is underway. This approach would draw upon the knowledge of the operating characteristics of the current system that has been developed by the joint efforts of thousands of researchers; when distilled into several indicia in this manner, it might be possible to efficiently analyze movement of any kind in these characteristics. For example, one might focus upon the social basis of political parties, seeking to identify any movements or trends in the coalition supporting the incumbent majority party. If no change is noted in the makeup of this coalition, it would be one item of evidence indicative of continuation of the status quo rather than change. If these critical junctures have been well selected, so that most of the basic supports for the status quo are included, comprehensive analysis of movements and trends (if any) in all of them ought to yield defensible characterization of the presence, absence, and prospect of change. It seems safe to say that major change cannot occur in the United States without movement of some kind in the attitudes of elites, the kinds of men who make up elites, the injection of new issues or ideas into public discussion, and so forth; such realization could be put to work in a systematic way to assess the extent and speed of change at any given period. This approach would have the further advantage of incorporating in an operationalized manner all the possible political change consequences of technological innovations, economic or social change, events, or external pressures. If such changes are to have impact on the political system, it would have to show up at these junctures.

Of course the act of selecting the critical points for detailed analysis is determinative of the quality of the interpretation that can emerge. One obvious (but only rarely undertaken) approach is to explore long-term changes in public attitudes. Using both long-term projections and age-focused inquiry, it would be possible to build a picture of the probable consequences of extending the right to vote to eighteen year old citizens. But other linkages involving other forms of mobilizing power resources should also be explored. For example, it seems likely that the achievements of the black minority in the United States will always be dependent on the flexibility of white elites and the range of acquiescence on the part of the white majority, so long as race is the uniting and mobilizing factor for blacks. But suppose blacks began to frame their demands in class, rather than race, terms? The chances for a successful alliance with white working class people still seem very slim, but worth investigation. Similarly, the development of a class analysis (and a focus on the economic system as the source of societal ills) on the part of the student left should be examined. To what extent have students been able to ally with blacks or with workers? On what issues? To what extent do such alliances seem capable of generating power for change?

3. The Forces Seeking Change

Possibly the most familiar approach would be to identify some of the major forces (people, groups, corporations, and other power holders) which consciously seek to make significant changes either in policies or in the structure of influence within the political system, and then to follow the success or failure of their efforts. By cataloging their actions, it might be possible to build an inventory of when, how, and why some power holders bring change about and others do not. One would never be fully confident that he had identified all the possible movers and shakers, but it would probably be possible to identify enough so that interpretations of some of the reasons for success and failure of political movements and actors could be made. In effect, what would result would be a series of case studies. This might be the best way to begin in an unexplored area, but it would suffer all the drawbacks of case studies, such as a very limited capacity to generalize or to explain the process of change in any comprehensive manner.

For the moment, these general reflections and ways of looking at the process of change are about all that can be offered. Perhaps we have done more than appears, however: we have isolated a good many implications from these empirical studies as to the requisites and prospects of change in some identified critical juncture points of the American system; we have adapted a conceptual definition of change for our use; and we have set up the rudiments of a theory and some alternative approaches to analysis of political change. We ought, at least, to be better able to make demands upon the prescriptive theorists for rigorous application to the problem of specifying how (and how much) change can be accomplished in furtherance of their prescriptions.

"DEMOCRACY" AND OTHER EVALUATIVE APPROACHES

What—if any—contribution have the empirical studies presented here made to our capacity to evaluate, as opposed to merely describe, American political processes? So far, we have looked at the implications of these empirical works for our descriptive knowledge of the present distribution of power in the United States, and for understanding of the process of political change in the United States. But in many cases the empirical researchers themselves were not unwilling to draw conclusions, particularly about the state of "democracy" that they had found, and it may be that some insights are to be extracted from their application of evaluative standards and criteria to the data they developed in their studies.

There is ample evidence in the foregoing empirical studies to show that American empiricists are apparently unable to avoid using their data to make judgments about the state of "democracy" in the United States. Over and over again, researchers ask what implications emerge from their data for the health of the political process. Not all are so blunt about their views as Prothro and Grigg ("Our research design was based upon the major assumption that the United States is a democracy. Taking this point for granted, we prepared an interview schedule around the presumably basic principles of democracy. . . .") But most use some form of a definition of democracy as a measuring standard, apply it to their data, and emerge with a conclusion about the state of democracy in the United States. We must ask whether there is anything to be learned, either about "democracy" or about the proclivities of empirical researchers, from this act on their part, and then whether we wish to accept their conclusions about "democracy" while we are making use of other selected aspects of their findings.

Critical to all of these issues is the way in which the individual empiricist defines "democracy." Let us imagine a continuum ranging from a definition that is completely tailored to fit the existing characteristics of politics in the United States to a definition that is a wholly idealized version of the New England Town Meeting style of mass democracy, in which government policy fully matched knowledgeable public preference. In all cases, minimum standards of the familiar civil liberties and voting rights would be required. At the one pole, researchers would be wandering about with a flag labeled "democracy," and happily pinning it on to whatever their data led them to define as the "is" of American politics. At the other pole, historians and idealists would contemptuously reject all use of the term with reference to real governments, having in mind a fixed standard that could never be met by a political system encompassing 200 million people and operating under a high level of specialization and technology. The first definition has no evaluative content to it at all, for it is merely a deliberately constructed description of a possibly misunderstood "is"; the second has no descriptive component, for no system could ever meet its requirements. As an unattainable ideal, it would be interesting for speculation but hardly serviceable as a means of judging actual systems. Somewhere between the two is a balance of descriptive and prescriptive (evaluative) components, such that judgments can be made about the system's nearness to an attainable standard and governments can be compared as to more or less fulfilling an ascertainable criterion. Each researcher, of course, makes an accommodation between the "is" and the "ought" when he frames his definition, and the act is clearly one of value-based judgment. As such, it is likely to tell us much more about the researcher than about "democracy." If his standards are clearly articulated and operational, however, we can use his characterization not to determine the "democraticness" of a system but as a means of positioning it in relation to other systems about which we have similar information.

Each of us performs the act of defining "democracy" in much the same way—coming in with a personalized accommodation between is and ought, and using it as a measuring standard. The more we choose to emphasize mass policy making, the further we get from the "is," though we still may not approach very close to the New England Town Meeting model. Because they pay almost no attention to the nexus of popular preference and government policy output, and because they tend to define as democratic what they find to exist in the United States, I would suggest that the pluralists are fairly close to the "is" end of the continuum. A distinguishable step away is a definition such as that of Joseph Schumpeter, who contends that democracy should be understood as provisions whereby nonelites are able to choose their leaders, though not to control them in policy determinations.[1] This appears to be somewhat distinct from the "is" as described by most empiricists, and so distinguishable. A further step toward policy involvement is provided by E. E. Schattschneider's definition of democracy as involving choice by nonelites between two competing groups of elites, each of whom offered distinctive policy packages.[2] In this manner, nonelites approach closer to choice or control over policy (and further away from the "is").

These illustrations are not intended to be exhaustive, but merely to exemplify the various types of accommodations made in the process of creating an evaluative standard. Because the accommodation involved in defining "democracy" is a value-based one, we cannot accept a researcher's definition *or* his conclusion as binding upon us unless we agree with or are prepared to adopt his definitions and values. His definition is useful only for what it reveals about him. But this is true only of standards that involve value choices, such as "democracy," and it might be that other evaluative standards would be more generally useful. We have already seen, however, that the choice of standards is frequently one that necessarily involves value preference components. There is nothing wrong in this per se, of course, provided that readers are clear about the fact that acceptance of the standards of another means submission to his values, which they may perhaps not fully perceive in all dimensions. It may also be that other evaluative

---

[1] Joseph Schumpeter, *Capitalism, Socialism, and Democracy* (New York: Harper & Row, 1942).
[2] E. E. Schattschneider, *The Semi-Sovereign People* (New York: Holt, Rinehart & Winston, 1960).

standards emphasize particular values that readers find congenial. For example, an evaluative standard with a considerable empirical proportion could be created using policy output as a focus and comparing output to popular preferences as ascertained by opinion surveys; another similar route might compare policy produced with objective definitions of the nature of public problems. In both cases, the actions of government could be contrasted against a reasonably ascertainable standard of preference or necessity, and judgments made about the utility or responsiveness of the system accordingly. Or, if one sought to emphasize responsiveness and change, evaluation could be built around the stability-change equation and seek to measure the adaptability of the system. The value preference component is somewhat larger in this case, of course, because there is no way to specify how much or what kind of adaptability is requisite when several forms suffice to preserve the system's existence. In an even franker application of value-based criteria, but still potentially useful for some purposes, one might simply posit certain values such as equality or justice, with some effort to operationalize them for the purpose, and seek to measure the extent to which they were or were not attained in various areas of life.

The suggestion of this section is that the choice of evaluative standards necessarily involves value choices of one kind or another. In some cases, the proportion of value component in a standard is relatively slight, in others it is large. The choice of standard again depends on the purpose for which the standard is to be used; unless there is some compelling purpose, however, it would seem preferable that the standard be one which could be applied to all political systems—for the various political systems of the world differ less in kind than in matters of degree. If we are talking about important and universal characteristics of politics, rather than culture-specific aspects of a single system, our judgmental capacity will probably be enhanced by comparison with several ways of responding to those pressures. For this reason, the last few examples seem to offer better ways of reaching revealing evaluative dimensions than continued use of personalized and stereotype-laden definitions such as "democracy."

SUMMARY: THE USES OF EMPIRICAL FINDINGS

In examining the empiricists' findings about the present distribution of power and the manner of its use in the United States, speculating about what they mean for the process and prospects of political change, and exploring the evaluative standards employed by the empiricists, we have covered a wide field with sometimes ruthless selectivity and oversimplification. My purpose has been to suggest and exemplify what uses contemporary empirical research may have for students of American political thought, rather than to attempt the even more staggering task of building a comprehensive characterization of all possible implications from the massive body of empirical data now available in the social science disciplines. Needless to say at this point, I am convinced that the general intellectual activity of political theorizing and each specific act of evaluation and judgment about political matters is immensely improved by virtue of awareness and sophisticated use of properly selected findings drawn from empirical studies. If my efforts to communicate this conviction have been at all successful, the material in this book should give rise to at least some reflections in each of the following areas:

1. *The role of descriptive accuracy.* I see no way to think effectively about politics without seeking as much accurate knowledge as can be obtained about how things now work and why. At some point, of course, we must stop collecting information and act, because the world will not wait for us to become perfectly informed. In all cases, we must be alert to the possibility that we are not getting pure descriptive factual information. "Pure facts" may themselves be an unattainable ideal, because every act and event is understood through the eyes of the beholder, but careful attention on our part to the characteristic propensities toward misinterpretation on the part of fact-collectors can at least move us closer to gaining a relatively unbiased view of the political world. I am arguing simply that some evidence is better than none, and that the odds of avoiding mistakes are greater when we understand more about political behavior and environmental circumstances. The empirical findings that we have reviewed (and, let us hope, cleansed of some biases and misinterpretations) ought to provide us with some landmarks as to the nature of the "is" of American politics. Such landmarks should be serviceable for our own understanding, and for testing that of the prescriptive theorists who urge us to accept their proposals for a better world.

2. *Understanding of politics and the political.* From the earliest stages of this book, I have suggested that a major goal of intellectual inquiry in this field should be the searching out of the essence of our subject: the nature of politics, and the political activity of man. I think that our analysis of the work of the empirical researchers included here should have advanced us in this direction, *not* necessarily because of the particular findings that they have come up with as a result of their investigations, but because of the implications that we have drawn from them by continually trying to direct their findings at a background of asking the right questions. I have been speculating in this chapter, and I trust that readers have also, about the implications of their findings; we have also analyzed, compared, and synthesized the findings of several researchers who studied the same or related problems and relationships. In the course of this inquiry on our part, we have been led to consider the symbiotic linkage of elites and nonelites, the difficulties that are experienced by mass publics in participating in the policy-making of their government, and the complexities of understanding the process

of change, among other issues. Each of these areas of reflection has led us to some insights about the eternal and universal problems of political organization and operation, and hence to deeper understanding of politics. How much deeper and how much more useful an understanding depends on the extent to which we have individually reflected upon these problems: books and teachers may facilitate or impede the acquisition of understanding, but they can neither accomplish nor prevent it.

3. *Skills of analysis and evaluation.* We have not employed these empirical studies only for descriptive accuracy or for understanding of the nature of our subject; we have also sought to refine and perfect tools of analysis and evaluation for our own future use. We have seen, for example, the limited extent to which empiricists have been able to detach themselves from their cultural heritage. They are not value-free, as some have alleged, but moderately prescriptive theorists sincerely but sometimes unsuccessfully trying to detach themselves for the purpose of better describing the "is" of American politics. Sometimes they do not ask what we might consider to be the right questions, on which occasions we gain insight into their assumptions and purposes as well as an opportunity to reexamine the validity of our own definitions of what the right questions are. The intellectual experience of challenging these researchers, and testing the propriety of their versions of "the right questions," should sharpen our own skills and force us to reach at least temporary convictions as to what sorts of inquiry into what political problems are the most important for the purpose of reaching satisfactory judgments and taking action in the world.

4. *Criteria for challenging the prescriptive theorists.* Finally, the net result of this effort should be to establish a set of criteria with which to take on contemporary proposals for our political betterment. We know something of the "is" of American politics; we have an idea of the essential nature of politics and its eternal and critical problems; we have speculated about some of the parameters within which change can and may occur in the American system; and we have invested some time in self-consciously sharpening our skills of intellectual analysis and critical evaluation. From this platform of knowledge and capacity, we should be able to evaluate political prescriptions as autonomous individuals—testing, rejecting, selecting, and accepting when and where we see justification.